THE
NIBELUNGENLIED

with The Klage

THE
NIBELUNGENLIED

with The Klage

Edited and Translated, with an Introduction, by
William Whobrey

Hackett Publishing Company, Inc.
Indianapolis/Cambridge

21 20 19 18   1 2 3 4 5 6 7

For further information, please address
    Hackett Publishing Company, Inc.
    P.O. Box 44937
    Indianapolis, Indiana 46244-0937

    www.hackettpublishing.com

Cover design by Elizabeth L. Wilson and Rick Todhunter
Interior design by Elizabeth L. Wilson
Composition by Aptara, Inc.

Library of Congress Cataloging-in-Publication Data

Names: Whobrey, William T., 1956– editor and translator.
Title: The Nibelungenlied : with related texts/edited and translated, with an
    introduction, by William T. Whobrey.
Other titles: Nibelungenlied. English.
Description: Indianapolis : Hackett Publishing Company, 2018. |
    Includes bibliographical references.
Identifiers: LCCN 2017033264| ISBN 9781624666759 (pbk.) |
    ISBN 9781624666766 (cloth)
Subjects: LCSH: Epic poetry, German—Translations into English.
Classification: LCC PT1579.A3 W56 2018 | DDC 831/.21—dc23
LC record available at https://lccn.loc.gov/2017033264

The paper used in this publication meets the minimum requirements of American
National Standard for Information Sciences—Permanence of Paper for Printed
Library Materials, ANSI Z39.48–1984.

∞

CONTENTS

Introduction

The *Nibelungenlied* has not been lacking for editions or translations since the major manuscripts of the work were rediscovered in the middle of the eighteenth century. Karl Lachmann produced the first scholarly edition of the *Nibelungenlied* in 1826, and Karl Simrock (1802–76) very soon thereafter provided what became the most read and influential of early German translations in 1827. Simrock studied in Berlin under Friedrich von der Hagen and Karl Lachmann and was well acquainted with Jacob and Wilhelm Grimm and their work that was helping to define the new field of German philology. He played an important role in translating and thereby popularizing many medieval German texts, bringing them into a public consciousness that was just discovering its own so-called national literature. The twentieth century saw extensive work on the text, and a number of editions appeared as the epic remained popular with the public and educational institutions even after 1945. German scholarship has recently produced two excellent dual-language editions that lead the way in *Nibelungenlied* studies. One is the edition and translation of the C manuscript by Ursula Schulze from 2005, and the second is the superb result of a lifetime of work with the epic, namely Joachim Heinzle's edition and translation of the *Nibelungenlied* and the *Klage* from 2013.[1]

The first complete English translation was that of Jonathan Birch, based on Lachmann's edition and no doubt influenced by Simrock's success, published under the title *The Nibelungen Lied; or Lay of the Last Nibelungers* in Berlin in 1848. This was soon followed in 1850 by what could be considered the first widely read English translation of the nineteenth century by William Lettsom, which was subsequently revised and reprinted several times in London and New York up until 1909 and enjoyed broad recognition as the first accurate verse rendering of the original into English. Added to this are about a dozen English translations from the nineteenth and twentieth centuries, about equally divided between verse and prose versions. A number of translations appeared in the 1960s, including what is still among the best translations in English, though now out of print but still available as a Dover Thrift edition, the little-known prose rendition by D. G. Mowatt. It was published in Everyman's Library in 1962, where it replaced the earlier

---

1. The original Middle High German (MHG) text for this translation is taken from Joachim Heinzle's edition, which follows the B manuscript, and the C manuscript redactions are taken from Heinzle's notes. I have used the 2015 edition.

version by Margaret Armour. A. T. Hatto's excellent but now somewhat dated translation of 1965 is still in print and much used in teaching the text to English-speaking students. Two new translations have appeared in the past dozen years or so, one in 2006 in verse by Burton Raffel and the other in 2010 in prose by Cyril Edwards. Details for each can be found in the bibliography at the back of this book.

Any new translation of an eminent text such as the *Nibelungenlied* should be justified and guided by goals that distinguish it from previous translations. This translation has set itself three such goals. First, it endeavors to provide a readable, prose translation of a medieval epic that does not rely on anachronistic language to create a kind of faux medieval texture. Instead, it hopes to convey meaning through contemporary language that, while remaining accurate, also allows itself the flexibility to express complex concepts in a way that is interpretive while at the same time maintaining an engaging narrative flow. The balance is tricky at times, and it is hoped that readability has not been achieved by sacrificing accuracy, but also that accuracy can be defined in terms of interpretive stability rather than an overreliance on word-for-word translation that ends up being unnatural, and ultimately inaccurate in itself.

Second, this translation endeavors to be informed by the latest scholarship, and furthermore to present a translated text that provides the reader with a sense of the historical transmission of such a medieval work, which in the case of the *Nibelungenlied* is far more complex than previous translations would lead one to believe. The *Nibelungenlied* is not a single text, and probably never was. It existed in multiple versions, from the earliest oral transmissions to the extant manuscripts of the thirteenth century and later, and there were several versions of this story in circulation concurrently. These important redactions and interpretations are necessarily missing in previous translations that rely on a single manuscript, thereby creating the illusion that this medieval text was published in something like an approved and final "edition." While it may not be feasible to translate multiple texts at the same time, this book does include many of the important additions and redactions of the C manuscript, allowing the reader to see the parallel versions and often conflicting interpretations of key aspects of the narrative.

Finally, this translation presents the *Nibelungenlied* as a three-part epic. The epic in its thirty-nine chapters consists of two distinct parts, originally separate stories first about the hero Siegfried, his wife Kriemhild, and his death, and second about the destruction of the Burgundians. Chapter 19 ends the first part with Kriemhild's thirteen-year-long period of grieving for Siegfried. Chapter 20 begins with far-away matters at King Etzel's court, namely the death of Queen Helche and the king's quest for a new wife, and ends with the death of virtually everyone. This translation includes with the

Nibelungenlied for the first time in English its companion text, a kind of epilogue that formed the third part of the story, a work most commonly known by its original title, the *Klage*, or "Lament." As will be discussed in greater detail below, this companion text is especially important because it is nearly contemporary with the versions of the *Nibelungenlied* that have come down to us, and so provides critical insight into the reception and interpretation of our principal work already in the early thirteenth century. The *Klage* followed the *Nibelungenlied* in all of the complete manuscripts, and we have no complete manuscripts that contain only the *Klage*. The integration of this sequel with the main epic was in fact so flawless that the manuscript page layout remained the same, even though the two works have completely different verse forms. It is safe to say that a medieval readership would have expected to read the *Klage* alongside the *Nibelungenlied*, and so it is presented here.

There are several good introductions to the text and the many aspects of its interpretation. The introduction to Hatto's translation ("An Introduction to a Second Reading"), as well as Andersson's *A Preface to the Nibelungenlied* and McConnell's *A Companion to the Nibelungenlied* can be recommended as excellent first resources for the English reader. More references are listed in the bibliography. What follows, then, is meant simply to be an initial guide for the newer students of the text, going into more detail in some areas while only briefly sketching others. Much additional material has been included in the comprehensive notes that accompany the main text.

History and Story

Something should first be said about the origins of the story and its tenuous connections to actual historical events. Although the medieval concept of history was very different from our own, there is little doubt that certain historical events and characters formed the nucleus of several epic cycles that were written and rewritten in the twelfth and thirteenth centuries. Heroic figures and actions were popular and shaped much of the entertainment value of the "new" literature that the German nobility was enjoying in the late twelfth century. Characters such as Siegfried of Netherland, Dietrich of Verona, Master Hildebrand, and others must have been admired, perhaps even emulated, by the warrior classes of Emperor Friedrich Barbarossa's German-speaking lands. Some of these characters had historical antecedents while some did not; that is to say, some were fairly well grounded in historical reality, while others were clearly imaginary projections onto heroic archetypes. We can fairly quickly summarize what we know to be true historically and how that might be related to our story.

The Burgundians were an East Germanic tribe, like the Goths, located in modern-day Poland's Vistula River basin by the first century CE. Although not well known by earlier Roman writers such as Tacitus or Pliny, the Burgundians' movements to the southeast in the second century soon put them, along with other Germanic tribes such as the Marcomanni, on the Danube River and the front lines of the Roman Empire during the so-called Marcomannic Wars (166–80 CE). After their defeat, little was heard from the Burgundians until the end of the third century, when they suddenly threatened the western part of the Roman Empire from the banks of the Rhine River. The cause of their dislocation is not known, although it is possible that they were pushed farther westward by their East Germanic cousins, the Goths. By the end of the fourth century they had become clients of Rome, settling in *Germania Secunda* along the Middle Rhine, and were enlisted as troops to fight other Germanic peoples, notably the Alemanni. The Burgundian chieftain, or king, in the early fifth century was named Gundahar (modern Gunther), and he led his warriors on numerous raids into Roman Gaul from their settlements in Worms and Speyer. The Roman general Flavius Aetius put an end to this in 436–37 with an army consisting largely of mercenary troops, including Huns and other Burgundians who had previously remained in the east. The (western) Burgundians were decisively defeated and their king, Gundahar, killed. What little remained of the tribe was subsequently relocated to the area of Savoy, with its first capital in present-day Geneva, later in Lyons. The rise and catastrophic downfall of the historical Burgundians found its way into later stories and eventually into the *Nibelungenlied*, where Burgundy's capital is Worms and its king's name is Gunther. These cannot be coincidences, but beyond some obvious correlations very little else can be claimed with certainty.

The historical figure of Attila and the peoples called Huns loom large in the second part of our story. What we know about Attila, or Etzel in its Germanic post–second sound shift form, has little to do with what we read of him in the *Nibelungenlied*. Historical sources tell us that Attila ruled for almost twenty years from 434 to his death in 453. His territory was one of the most extensive to rival the Roman Empire, stretching from the shores of the Black Sea and the Dnieper west to the upper Danube, and later in parts all the way to what is now France. The Huns were a Eurasian nomadic group that expanded beyond the Volga River in the late fourth century CE. As their mounted archers pushed farther to the west, they dislocated those Germanic tribes that stood between them and the Roman Empire, causing great upheaval throughout central Europe. After Attila inherited the kingdom from his father Mundzuk, he soon began a number of military campaigns both east and west, against the Persians, into the Balkans all the way to Constantinople, and finally to the west of the Rhine, where he was decisively defeated in 451 by the same Flavius Aetius, now with Visigothic and Burgundian allies, in the Battle of the Catalaunian Plains near Troyes. Attila still managed to invade northern Italy the following year, but he soon retired back to the Danube and died early in 453. None of these events correspond to Etzel's role in the *Nibelungenlied*, with the exception of his reputation as a fabulously wealthy and powerful ruler. Attila's own encounter with the Burgundian mercenaries in 451 could have been conflated with that tribe's earlier defeat by Aetius, with the help of Hunnish troops, in 437.

The third historically based character encountered in the *Nibelungenlied* is Dietrich of Bern, or Verona (not Bern, Switzerland). Dietrich, probably the most popular Germanic hero in medieval literature, is loosely based on Theoderic the Great, a king of the Ostrogoths. Born in 454, he lived at a time when both Attila and Gunther of the Burgundians were already dead. Theoderic was raised in Constantinople, where he was held as a hostage by the emperor but also afforded a nobleman's education in Greek and Latin. He returned home to his tribal lands at the age of eighteen. After a victorious military campaign against Odoacer, who at the time held the title of King of Italy, Theoderic founded a kingdom in northern Italy centered around Ravenna. Upon his death in 526, Theoderic was interred in a mausoleum in Ravenna, his capital, that is to this day a remarkable memorial to his greatness. The prominence of Verona in the Dietrich legend is perhaps linked to the Lombardic kingdom that succeeded Gothic rule in northern Italy in the sixth century, with its capital in Verona. Although he left a considerable mark in the historical record, Theoderic's legendary alter ego, Dietrich of Bern, appears on the literary stage fairly late. With the exception of brief mention in three Old English poems (*Waldere, Deor,* and *Widsith* [late tenth, early eleventh centuries]), almost all that we know of the hero Dietrich comes to us from stories written in the thirteenth century, including a long Norwegian narrative poem, based on German sources, called the *Thidrekssaga* from around 1250. His fictional master-at-arms, Hildebrand, is immortalized in a short, fragmentary Old High German poem dated to a manuscript from the ninth century. There, Odoacer is mentioned as a common enemy, but already Dietrich and Hildebrand appear not as conquerors of Italy, but instead as exiles in the East, a role reversal that could be a result of the conflation of the vengeful killing of Odoacer by Theoderic in 493 and the earlier alliance between Gothic tribes and Attila.

The information about these historical figures and events is ample in Latin sources dating back to the sixth century, but parallel to these we must assume that a system of oral transmission existed in Germanic cultures that kept the legends of these heroic characters alive. It must also be assumed that such a long chain of oral transmission, while retaining some sense of ancient authority, shaped a heroic literature that was anything but static and that merged multiple sources with fertile artistic imagination. Northern sources, especially in Old Norse, are rich in heroic tradition and provide us with much of what we can know about these legendary heroes and their exploits. Some of the earliest evidence of the literary memory and commemoration of figures such as Siegfried, Attila, and Gunther can be found in a collection of heroic poems now commonly referred to as the *Poetic Edda*. The *Codex Regius* that contains these poems was not written until around 1270, but some of the poems it contains can be dated back to the tenth and eleventh centuries, with some evidence to support an even earlier date for the poem titled *Atlakviða*, perhaps late ninth century. The story as told in this early Old Norse poem contains plot lines that we would easily recognize from the second half of the *Nibelungenlied*. Gunnar, the king of the Burgundians, is in possession of the vast treasure of the *Niflungs*, which he and his brother Hogni (Hagen) have sunk in the Rhine River. Atli, king of the Huns, invites them both to visit him and his wife, Gudrun, their sister (Kriemhild in the *Nibelungenlied*) in the hopes of gaining possession of the treasure. Hogni is killed first, then Gunnar is placed into a pit of snakes and dies. This episode with Gunnar in the snake pit may be the basis for an image pictured on a relief stone (Ardre VIII) on the island of Gotland, dated to the early ninth century. Gudrun takes revenge first by killing her two sons, heirs to the Hunnish lands, and then her husband Atli. While the poem contains many of the same characters, they are assigned different roles than those in the *Nibelungenlied*, and it is clear that the motivation for deceit, treachery, and vengeance changes as a result, mainly because Siegfried plays no part in Gudrun's/Kriemhild's earlier life in the story.

The tales of Siegfried are legendary, and we have no convincing link between the hero and a historical person. There is evidence that the legends surrounding Siegfried, or Sigurd, such as the killing of the dragon Fafnir, were well known in eleventh-century Scandinavia, as demonstrated by the images on the stone of Ramsundsberg, west of Stockholm. The *Poetic Edda* also contains several poems about Sigurd that can be dated to around the same time, and the various scenes depicted on the stone correspond to those in the Eddic poem *The Lay of Fafnir*: Sigurd kills the dragon from below, roasts its heart on a spit and then burns and licks his thumb, and carries the treasure away on his horse Grani. The Sigurd/Siegfried of the *Nibelungen* legend is recognizable in other Old Norse analogs as well, including the *Volsunga saga*: Sigurd is first betrothed to Brynhild, then marries Gudrun, woos Brynhild for his brother-in-law Gunnar, and is finally killed at Brynhild's and Gunnar's behest. The blending of the legends around Attila and Gunther with the Siegfried stories created a new constellation of allies and enemies, in which Siegfried dies at the hands of Hagen, Kriemhild avenges not her brothers but rather her husband, and the Huns and the Burgundians alike are slaughtered to near extinction as a result.

This short outline of history and story is meant to make only two points. First, the stories and legends that coalesced into the text of the *Nibelungenlied* incorporate a limited historical core that dates back to the Germanic migration period of the fifth and sixth centuries. Second, the amalgamation of various heroic figures and the narratives associated with them produced complex rearrangements of roles and motivations. Given this convoluted mixture of history and legend over centuries, we can nonetheless make the assertion that the *Nibelungenlied* stands on its own as a singular artistic achievement of its time. Part of the reason for that achievement is the way in which the text claims ancient, oral authority, but still positions itself as contemporary within late twelfth-century society. It represents a reconfiguration of heroic legend alongside a new literary fashion, the courtly romance. The anachronistic language and terminology is purposeful, but not consistent, and the layer upon layer of late twelfth-century culture superimposed on the actions of Germanic tribal kings and their followers has formed its own "contemporary" feel, allowing it to compete favorably with the fashionable Arthurian romances and courtly love poetry so *en vogue* among French and German courts around 1200.

Form

This translation seeks to provide readers and students of the *Nibelungenlied* an accurate, modern, and above all readable English text. The means to that end is prose, but it is important to remember that the original text was written in verse, as was almost all German literature of the twelfth and thirteenth centuries. The numbering of each strophe in this translation, following the Heinzle edition, has been indicated rather prominently in square brackets, both to ease comparison across various editions and to remind the reader by way of a somewhat intrusive apparatus that a very distinct verse form lies behind the English. It is also important to consider, however briefly, the characteristics of this verse form and how it was uniquely suited to the task of adapting the archaic material found in the *Nibelungenlied* to book form. The basic unit of composition for our main text was the four-line strophe and not the rhymed couplet so much in fashion around 1200 in courtly romances. The strophic form itself was at the time of composition already an artefact, but it could be purposefully applied to the literary expression of heroic material. Its close relationship to the lyric form employed a generation earlier by the *Minnesänger* von Kürenberg around 1160 or 1170 would have served the *Nibelungenlied's* poet well as an anachronistic structure. The strophe has been and is still most often referred to in German simply as the *Nibelungen-strophe*. It consists of four long-lines (*Langzeile* or *Langvers*), each divided into two parts, or half-lines. This division, or caesura, represents a hard metrical boundary, within which each half-line has a basic arrangement of stressed and unstressed syllables. Half-lines have three stressed syllables, while the very last half-line has an additional, fourth foot. A typical long-line can be represented as follows:

$$(x) \mid x' \; x \mid x' \; x \mid x' \; x` \; \| \; x' \; x \mid x' \; x \mid x' \; - \mid$$

or with a final half-line, that is, the fourth long-line in the strophe:

$$(x) \mid x' \; x \mid x' \; x \mid x' \; x` \; \| \; x' \; x \mid x' \; x \mid x' \; x \mid x' \; - \mid$$

The third, final stressed syllable in the first half-line (*Anvers*) is usually a feminine ending (an unstressed syllable, but capable of carrying secondary stress), while the second half-line (*Abvers*) ending is masculine (a single stressed syllable). Pairs of long-lines form rhymed couplets. This is what a typical strophe in the original Middle High German looks like (str. 8):

x | x′ x | x′ x x | x′ x` || x | x′   x | x′x | x′ | a
Die drie künege wâren,   als ich gesaget hân
The three kings were,   as I have said,

x′ x | x′ x | x′ x` || x | x′   x | x′ x | x′ | a
von vil hôhem ellen,   in wâren undertân
of very great courage.   To them were beholden

x′   x | x′ x | x′ x` || x | x′   x | x′   x | x′ | b
ouch die besten recken,   von den man hât gesagt,
also the best warriors   of whom people have spoken,

x′ - | x′   x | x′x x` || x | x′   x | x′   x | x′   x | x′ | b
starc und vil küene,   in scharfen strîten unverzagt.
strong and very bold,   in hard battles unfearful.

This example shows that the meter within each half-line can vary considerably. For example, the use of an unstressed initial syllable, or anacrusis, in any given half-line is not consistent by any means. The translation of the opening strophe (of manuscripts A and C) in the main text conforms in English to this metrical pattern, so that readers might gain a realistic sense of this particular stanzaic form, along with the rather unique variations of this particular strophe, including internal rhyme.

The four-line strophe establishes a self-contained unit by lengthening and thereby emphasizing the final half-line. The very rare use of enjambment between strophes confirms this. The strophic form is well suited to the ears, since its boundaries are marked acoustically. The listener can easily hear the beginning and end of each strophe, and the form has often been compared to its musical cousins. The weight of the additional syllable serves not only as an acoustic cue but also as a way to create both tension and flow. As Hatto puts it, this device "invites reflection, and sometimes dark and gnomic utterance" (Hatto, 1965, 349). A few examples might help to illustrate some of the ways that this form, and especially the last line, can be used for effect. Most often, the strophe and its last line help to create boundaries of direct speech, although the poet is by no means confined to keeping individual speech within individual strophes. Often, the last line restates or summarizes what has been developed in the strophe to that point, acting as an emphatic coda. Sometimes the last line serves to project the present suddenly into the distant future, as in "They were later to accomplish great feats of courage in Etzel's lands" (str. 5), or "But later she would happily become the wife of a valiant warrior" (str. 18). This is a kind of foreshadowing that already assumes the reader's knowledge of the entire story, acknowledging both that certain events were destined to take place, while some others turned out quite differently than a character might have thought early on. The poet also uses this device to insert his own commentary, often with a good dose of irony, as in "They didn't know that death was very near" (str. 2169), or "Many of the brave knights removed their helmets and sat down on the corpses that had been laid low in the blood by their own hands. The guests had been poorly cared for" (str. 2082), and finally "The host was in great distress, as he should be, since his dear friends were being taken from him before his very own eyes. He had to fear for his life among his enemies. He was horrified. What good did it do him that he was a king?" (str. 1982). These few examples only scratch the surface in showing how the distinctive *Nibelungen* strophe was employed not only to create the illusion of an ancient verse form, but also to construct the narrative with cleverly interconnected building blocks. The reader is invited to discover how this form and function enhance one another.

Manuscripts

Medieval texts, and this one in particular, often existed in various versions, either simultaneously or through transmission by way of subsequent redaction, editing, correction, or fanciful poetic license taken by scribes and other writers. The search for an "original" version of any medieval work is usually futile, not only because the originals have been lost, but also because it is doubtful that a medieval readership felt the need for such a single, authoritative edition. It is now generally accepted that no such original version of the *Nibelungenlied* existed, whether in some early kind of oral production or later in its written forms. There were most likely several versions of various parts of the story circulating at the same time, and if there ever was a single, first version of the Middle High German poem, then it was soon eclipsed by various redactions that apparently were in communication with each other, which is to say that new and different versions appeared as reactions to or combinations of various previous "editions." An important piece of evidence for this is contained in manuscript fragment E (Berlin, Fragm. 44). The same scribe also copied part of the St. Gall manuscript (B). The E manuscript, however, was not copied from B, which represents the so-called *nôt* family of manuscripts, but contains instead a version of the story from the *liet* group. It seems likely, then, that different versions were available in the same scriptorium.

The online *Handschriftencensus* (manuscript register)[2] lists thirty-seven complete or fragmentary manuscripts that contain all or some part of the Middle High German *Nibelungenlied*, ranging in date from the thirteenth to the sixteenth centuries. This list includes several manuscripts that are either lost or contain versions of the text that are adaptations or translations of the text, and should therefore, strictly speaking, not be considered as extant repositories of our text. One is a fragment of a Dutch translation (T; British Libr., MS Egerton 2323a), and two are lost (c, H). Three manuscripts contain late adaptations (k, m, n), and an additional three fragments have only the *Klage*, although these could be assumed to have contained the *Nibelungenlied* as well (G, P, and AA). Of the remaining twenty-eight manuscripts, then, nine are complete or almost so, and nineteen exist only in fragments.[3] Scholars have further divided these manuscripts into three main groups, or families of manuscripts, based on shared textual features. They are most easily recognizable by the last word of the epic as either belonging to the *nôt* ("downfall") group or *liet* ("epic") group. A third group of manuscripts shows evidence of influence from both of these branches and can most suitably be labeled "hybrids."[4] Beginning with Lachmann's work on the text, we continue to identify three main manuscripts based primarily on their age, all of them complete and written sometime in the thirteenth century. These are given shorthand designations as A, B, and C, in the order of priority assigned to them by Lachmann based on his own estimation of their age. The evaluation

---

2. http://www.handschriftencensus.de/werke/271.

3. For further information, consult the list of manuscripts.

4. Heinzle, 1998, identifies five groups, with two separate *liet* groups (A and B), and two hybrid groups. For the sake of this overview, they are reduced here to the three main groups. See McConnell, *A Companion to the Nibelungenlied*, 119.

of age and quality has changed over the years, and we would now reverse the order starting with the oldest as C, B, and A, but the old shorthand persists. It is important to note at the outset that none of these manuscripts, indeed none that we currently possess, is the "original" manuscript, which is to say that they are all copies of older, now lost manuscripts.

Manuscript A is more properly named Cgm (Codex germanicus monacensis) 34, and is located in the Bavarian State Library (Staatsbibliothek) in Munich. It is also known as the Hohenems manuscript, based on the place of its rediscovery in 1779 in the palace library of the Austrian counts of Hohenems. The manuscript is currently dated as last quarter, thirteenth century, although this is usually further refined as not later than 1280. The modest codex consists of sixty parchment leaves in total and contains the *Nibelungenlied* text (1r–47v) along with the *Klage* (47v–58v) and a later addition of eight short religious texts (58v–60r). The manuscript itself is fairly plain and shows traces of considerable use. The text was written in southern Germany or Austria in two columns, with large, red uncial initials separating sections of the text, especially the beginnings of each of the thirty-nine chapters of the *Nibelungenlied*, with short chapter titles or descriptions annotated above the start of that section. In the opening of the poem (str. 1–87), the strophes are not indicated as distinct, instead each long-line is written as a separate line, in a form we would recognize as the more standard rhyming couplets. Starting with str. 88 (4v), however, the form changes and each strophe is separated with a single initial at the strophe beginning while still retaining the separation of long-lines. We also categorize manuscript A as part of the *nôt* family, based on the last line of the epic.

Manuscript B has been assigned a prominent role as the lead manuscript for most editions since Karl Bartsch (1866), including the revised edition by Helmut de Boor (1956) and the latest by Joachim Heinzle (2013). Its full catalog title is Codex 857 of the Abbey Library (Stiftsbibliothek) of St. Gall, Switzerland; it is also known as the St. Gall Epic Manuscript (*Epenhandschrift*). The consensus on the manuscript's date is the second third or third quarter of the thirteenth century, or most likely around 1260. The manuscript was purchased by the Abbey of St. Gall in 1768. Before 1820, a few leaves were removed from the codex and are now located in Berlin and Karlsruhe, leaving 318 leaves in the current manuscript. This is a large collection of several great works. The *Nibelungenlied* (117r–179r) and the *Klage* (179r–196v) are both complete and have been assembled with several other major works, including Wolfram von Eschenbach's *Parzival* and *Willehalm*. The manuscript was likely copied in southern Tyrol or an area around Salzburg. The *Nibelungenlied* is nicely written in two columns with nineteen larger historiated initials, but lacking chapter titles. The text is written in run-on lines, but the strophe beginnings are indicated with smaller initials and some blank space. Like the aforementioned manuscript A, B is part of the *nôt* family, although it distinguishes itself from A in that, among other things, it does not start with the same strophe. The later and somewhat anachronistic introductory strophe (*Uns ist in alten mæren . . .*) is replaced by what is more likely the earlier introduction starting with *Ez wuohs in Burgonden. . . .* This discrepancy has caused some confusion, beginning with the numbering of the strophes. In order to maintain the Bartsch/de Boor numbering system, editors since have had to fudge the numbering to correspond to a strophe 1 in manuscript B that does not exist there. So here, too, the translation begins with a strophe 1 that is separate from the actual introductory strophe, which is still numbered strophe 2. This of course allows comparison across editions and is continued despite its inaccuracy.

Manuscript C is Codex Donaueschingen 63 of the Baden State Library (Landesbibliothek) in Karlsruhe. It was purchased by the State Library and State Bank of Baden-Württemberg in 2001, some two and a half centuries after its rediscovery in Hohenems (where manuscript A was also later found) in 1755 by Jacob Obereit. In 1853 it passed into the possession of the princes of Fürstenberg in Donaueschingen, where it remained until being sold by the Fürstenberg family to the state. It is dated to the second quarter of the thirteenth century, so before 1250, and is therefore the oldest of our three main manuscripts. Made up of 114 leaves (six were lost at some point prior to the eighteenth century), the codex contains both the *Nibelungenlied* (1r–89r) and the *Klage* (89r–114v). Although it is the oldest manuscript we have of the *Nibelungenlied*, it, too, begins with the younger first strophe, unlike manuscript B. So it shares this feature with manuscript A, although unlike both A and B, C ends with *nibelunge liet*, and is therefore considered an exemplar of the so-called *liet* group. It has also divided the epic into thirty-eight chapters rather than thirty-nine, thereby rendering the two-part form more precisely in the middle, with the break at the end of the nineteenth chapter, and it includes brief headings for each chapter, as does manuscript A. The text is written in a single column, with strophe starts indicated with small capital letters. Perhaps most important for us in terms of this current translation is the fact that the C manuscript represents a redacted, one might even say "updated" version of the *Nibelungenlied*. Although it seems paradoxical, the oldest written copy of our epic actually provides us with a newer version of the story. The scribe or redactor is intent on providing his readership with emendations, explications, and reinterpretations of several key characters and episodes. He is intent on "spinning" the tale in a way that moves certain characters and their motivations into a more favorable, or unfavorable, light, as the case may be. It is hard to know exactly what motivated our manuscript C redactor to change the text in such significant ways, but it seems generally to be aimed at clarifying the often muddy waters and inconsistencies of the other, older versions of our story (as evident primarily in mss. A and B). Kriemhild is absolved of much of her guilt, Hagen is at the center of the evil conspiracy to kill Siegfried and is clearly culpable, and the ending of the first part of the epic, that part concerned mostly with Siegfried up until his murder and burial, gets a major makeover that in itself threatens to upset the entire connection to Part Two, sometimes known as Kriemhild's Revenge. All of the C redactor's interpolations seem to emanate from an interpretation based on the first part of the story; that is, the second part is interpreted through the lens of Siegfried's murder and Kriemhild's need to avenge it.

This translation attempts to make the reader aware of these two competing versions of the epic and to allow a greater appreciation for the unfixed and dynamic nature of the text. Since Ursula Schulze's superb edition and translation of the Donaueschingen manuscript (C) in 2005, there has been a greater appreciation for how this version can not only stand on its own, but also how differently key parts of the narrative are characterized as opposed to the "standard" version of the A and B manuscripts. Although this translation continues to be based primarily on manuscript B, as do almost all previous editions and translations, it marks the existence of significant additions and variations in the main text with an asterisk, then providing the C text in an addendum. This is exactly the point, of course: to move us away from the comfortable sense that a single medieval author wrote an epic based on various tales of Siegfried, Kriemhild, and others, and that, although we have lost this original autograph, we can reconstruct its original form and meaning. It is no coincidence that we have no mention of an author in our text, no one taking credit for having written this masterpiece, as we do with Hartmann von Aue or Wolfram von Eschenbach or others. There was no expectation that a single author should be responsible for such a work, nor that there was necessarily a single authoritative version, and so the reader should be confronted with, to some extent, the messy mix of both the *AB and *C (*nôt* and *liet*) versions.

The *Klage*

This brings us to our second text, the so-called *Klage*, or in English "Lament," or perhaps better, something like "The Grieving." This work should in many ways be considered the third part of the story, following directly on the heels of the *Nibelungenlied* in its two distinct parts. Although the complete text has been translated into English only once before, by Winder McConnell as *The Lament of the Nibelungen: Div Chlage*, 1994, it has not been included before in an English translation as a companion to the *Nibelungenlied*. First, it is not a well-known text, to put it mildly, the reasons for this being that it is not a particularly well told or interesting tale on its own. It reads to most of those with the patience to get though it as a long-winded recounting of the aftermath of the destruction of the Burgundian ruling house and its army. Often overlooked in this calculation, however, is the fact that the *Klage* follows the *Nibelungenlied* in all complete manuscripts, and was most likely present in more of the manuscripts for which we have only fragmentary evidence. It seems likely that this was the general intent of *Nibelungenlied* manuscript production and collection starting in the thirteenth century, and all three of our main manuscripts, A, B, and C, contain both works.

The connection between the two works is implicit in verse 71 of the *Klage*, in which the poet states that his audience has already heard tell of the events surrounding Kriemhild's rule in the kingdom of the Huns. The metrical form of the *Klage* is not, however, the same strophic form that we find in the *Nibelungenstrophe*. Instead, the *Klage* employs the more common rhyme-paired lines with four stressed syllables per line. An often overlooked but important piece of evidence that the *Klage* was conceived and certainly received as an integral part of the *Nibelungen* narrative is the fact that the graphical presentation of most manuscripts seeks to assimilate both the strophic and line verse forms into a homogeneous layout, whether in a single column (ms. C) or double column (mss. A and B) arrangement. The transition from one text and its verse form to another is seamless and visually identical.

I have decided to follow the B manuscript's text provided in Heinzle's edition, without including the major redactions from the C manuscript or others. The relationship between various versions of the *Klage* is even more complicated than with the *Nibelungenlied*, and the C redaction of the *Klage* is in many ways a different text than that offered by B. It would be too difficult within the scope of this translation to try to provide alternate readings as was possible with the *Nibelungenlied*. As for section starts and line numbering, these follow manuscript B, as McConnell has done in his translation, and the larger initials in the manuscript are indicated with a bold capital letter in this translation.

It is possible that the *Nibelungenlied* and the *Klage* were conceived at the same time as two parts of a larger project. The text could be dated closer to 1200 than later, but in any case no later than the first quarter of the thirteenth century. The text was clearly in close contact with both the *AB and *C (*nôt* and *liet*) forms of the *Nibelungenlied*. It has value as an attempt to interpret its referent in a way that brings greater clarity, and perhaps satisfaction to the reader; that is, it tells the "rest of the story," ending not with total destruction but instead with the crowning of Gunther's son as the new king and guarantor of the continuation of the Burgundian monarchy. Not only does it inform the reader of events after the downfall, but it also offers moral commentary intended to inform the reader of the main work's proper meaning. Students of the *Nibelungenlied* should find it instructive to compare the different commentaries within our three main texts, that is the primary, B version, the C redaction, and the *Klage*. The *B or *nôt* version is the most ambiguous, full of inconsistencies that have given scholars endless headaches in their attempts to explain away the obvious authorial "flaws" that had ended up somehow collected in the St. Gall manuscript. The tendency of the *liet* version, as exemplified by the Donaueschingen manuscript (C), is to smooth away the contradictions of time, place, motivation, and narrative either by changing the text entirely or by adding an explanatory strophe or two. Beyond this "correction" of the *B version, however, lies a project intended to clarify the moral ambiguity of other versions, beginning with the depiction of Kriemhild as the injured party, both in the first as well as the second part of the story. Her roles as the wife of Siegfried, queen of Netherland, and woman of the court are often in conflict. Given that she, and of course Siegfried, have been betrayed by her closest male relatives, she has no recourse but to seek the vengeance that any male would have had the right, and obligation, to exact. She is therefore left with few choices: she can either retreat to a monastery, as her mother did before her, to live out her life as a grieving widow, or she can take on the mantle of power that can be hers as the wife of a new and even more powerful king, namely Etzel, or Attila, the Hun.

Manuscript C ends Part One with the first option—a retreat to the royal monastery of Lorsch that is in the end not realized, somewhat clumsily, so that the story does not end there. Part Two must follow, although the C redactor wants to make it clear that another option did exist before the heavy hand of narrative tradition sets in. Manuscript B ends Part One with the second option—an opportunity for power and its advantages presents itself with the news that Etzel is seeking a new wife. The *Klage* goes one step further in this process, all but exonerating Kriemhild of guilt for the death of her brothers. The *Klage* not only relieves her of the characterization as a devil, but in several different arguments seeks to explain her actions as motivated by love, by lack of choice, and finally by excusing her inability to execute her plan as a flaw inherent in all women. While we might find some of these explanations unpalatable, they are valuable as insights to the reception and judgment of a readership that starts in the early thirteenth century, or very soon after the circulation of the *Nibelungenlied* begins. Furthermore, it was thought both proper and necessary by most scriptoria and their patrons to include this final critique of the *Nibelungenlied* as a companion text, seeing as how it offered a kind of commentary authorized by its own fictional patron, Bishop Pilgrim of Passau, most likely standing in for the actual patron of the *Nibelungenlied*, Bishop Wolfger of Erla (c. 1140–1218; bishop of Passau 1191–1204).

The Translation

We are confronted with our concurrent versions from the very start, even though we may not know it. There are two titles that contend with each other in the original manuscripts. The title of our book is taken from the end of the epic, where in the last line (str. 2379,4 in the St. Gall manuscript, or B; str. 2316,4 in the Hohenems manuscript, or A) the story is summarized as the *nibelunge nôt,* or downfall or destruction of the Nibelungen. In other manuscripts, most notably C (str. 2439,4), the same line reads *nibelunge liet,* or poem or epic of the Nibelungen. This has become the popular title, even though most versions and translations use the B manuscript as their text. Lachmann used *nôt* in his title, since he followed manuscript A, but Simrock used *Lied* in the title of his translation, *Das Nibelungenlied.*[5] This is the title that stuck, and it is used here as the default by which this work has become known, correctly or not, throughout the world. Other English translations have attempted to render the title in various ways, notably Lettsom's *The Fall of the Nibelungers,* Ryder's *The Song of the Nibelungs,* and the most recent translations by Raffel and Edwards with the aid of subtitles: *Song of the Nibelungs* or *The Lay of the Nibelungs.* The problem here is that MHG *liet* is neither a song nor a lay, despite the fact that modern German *Lied* is indeed in English "song." By the end of the twelfth century, *liet* designated a longer epic work and was closely related to *rede, mære,* or *buoch.* That is to say, the epic in its current book form was not meant to be sung, and therefore calling it a "song" in modern English is misleading. Similarly, the modern definition of "lay" is a short narrative poem or song. The Middle English, first Anglo-Norman, usage of *lai* in connection with, for example, the short narrative poems of Marie de France, is not related to Middle High German *liet.*

Another question to address concerns the proper rendition into English of the word *Nibelung* or its plural *Nibelungen.* It is a strange name, and not easy to pronounce. Even most Germans mispronounce the word, putting the accent on the second syllable, not the first, as required of a proper Germanic

5. The history of Simrock's translation is long and complex. Suffice it to say here that Simrock tried to have it both ways with regard to the title of his work. Simrock's original translation of 1827 is titled *Das Nibelungenlied,* but divides the work into two parts: *Der Nibelungen Noth, Erster Theil: Siegfriedens Tod* (Part One: Siegfried's Death) and *Der Nibelungen Noth, Zweiter Theil: Chriemhildens Rache* (Part Two: Kriemhild's Revenge). This first edition concludes with the line *Hie hat die Mär' ein Ende: das ist der Nibelungen Noth* (p. 223). The twelfth edition, 1859, completely revises the last strophe, however, the last line of which reads *das ist das Nibelungenlied* (p. 525). An interesting side note is that Richard Wagner's library in Dresden included Simrock's third edition (1843), as well as his *Heldenbuch* in six volumes (1843–46), volume 2 of which was the 1843 third edition of Simrock's *Nibelungenlied.* In a letter to Franz Müller dated 9 January 1856, he explicitly names this last volume as part of his reading for his own operatic *Ring* cycle.

name. As former Heidelberg professor Lothar Voetz explained to his classes, it is not a song about lungs, or a "Lungenlied." It is about the clan of the Nibelungen, stressed on the first syllable, a patronymic formed from the stem, Nibel, and the suffixes, -ung-en. The meaning of the first part is still not clear, although it may be related to the modern German word for fog, or *Nebel*. Regardless, it is meant to signify the sons or clan or people of a person named Nibel. Many German place-names still show the related ending -ingen, for example, Bopfingen, Sigmaringen, Tübingen, and so on. There are a few with -ungen, mostly in south-central Germany north of the Main River, such as Behrungen, Schonungen, and Morungen. Also related are the historical clan names of the Carolingians, Merovingians, and Thuringians, or in German *Karol-inger, Merow-inger*, and *Thür-inger*. We also see an analogy in Dietrich of Bern's clan name, the Amelungen. All of these are stressed on the first syllable. This is also true, although for us counterintuitive, for the name of the other principal clan in our epic, the Burgundians, historically an East Germanic tribe. Anglo and French usage has given us a name for a region in France and its wine that we stress on the second syllable, but the Germanic name was originally stressed on the first syllable. We would properly have to say BUR-gun-dian, but this might be asking too much. For purposes of continuity, tradition, and relative ease for English speakers, this translation uses the Middle High German form *Nibelungen* for the eponymous tribe or clan, as opposed to Nibelungers, Nibelungs, or perhaps the more correct English form Nibelungians.

The orthography employed here for names of persons or places requires a bit of explanation. Many of these Germanic names are hard to pronounce. There are certain conventional spellings for our main characters, and I have chosen for the most part the forms of names that most readers might recognize: Siegfried (rather than Sivrit, Sifrid, or Sifried), Gunther, Brunhild (not Prünhilt), Kriemhild, Hagen, Dietrich, Etzel (not Attila), and Ruediger (not Rüdiger). As you can see, I have avoided the use of the umlaut, as it seems to do little to better pronunciation and usually just acts in English as a gratuitous sign of "foreignness." In the end, my own convention of spelling names comes very close to that used by Hatto. As for tips for correct pronunciation, I would offer the following. Again, Germanic names are stressed on the first syllable. While some Germanic languages had the *th* [θ or ð] sound so common in English (*th*in or ei*th*er), Middle High German did not, nor does modern German. This can be pronounced as a *t* in Gunther. The *ch* [ç or x] sound is difficult for most English speakers, as with Johann Sebastian Bach's name, for example, but something approximating a *k* sound is quite adequate (as with Dietrich). The *tz* [ts] in Etzel is pronounced like pre*tz*el. The *v* in Volker is pronounced as an *f* (cf. *f*olk). As for vowels, the general rule in German is that *ie* and *ei* are not to be confused. What normally works for students is when I tell them that they should pronounce the second vowel in the pair as they would the name of the letter in English, that is long *e* as in s**ee**k for *ie*, and long *i* as in **eye**, for *ei*. Only the second pair is actually a diphthong. Ruediger is more difficult, since I have maintained the umlaut in the spelling (ue), but again, long *u* as in m**oo**d will do, but it is even better if the reader can raise the vowel on the palate to an *ee* with rounded lips. Finally, although the Middle High German pronunciation of *Klage* used a short "a" sound, in modern German the word is pronounced as in f**a**ther. The pronunciation of the final *e* is short, as in p**e**n (it is not silent). As for place-names, a few have retained their original spellings, while some more common names are modernized and anglicized, such as the Rhine, Vienna, Austria, Bavaria, Hungary (although not the same as the country), and Netherland (in the singular, so as not to be confused with the country). For lesser-known places, especially those along the Danube, I have kept a more original form rather than the current spelling, for example, Bechelarn (Pöchlarn), if it might help in pronunciation. I have tried to be as consistent as possible in all this, although there are certainly choices that have been made that might contravene some of these conventions. The overriding factor has always been to ease the readability for present-day English-speaking students of the text.

Final Thoughts

The challenge that this translation has tried to meet is the presentation of a medieval text with warts and all. That is to say, medieval texts were often messy and at times even contradictory, and scholarship has for the past few decades decided that this should be accepted and acknowledged. Gone are the days when we strive to retrieve the "original" text by reconstructing the exact same words that the poet must have used when he first put pen to paper. We want to acknowledge that the epic we have in the *Nibelungenlied* is a dynamic text, not a static one. This can be difficult to do in a translation, and compromises have to be made, but even if the result seems less than perfect, that is as it should be. The reader has been provided with options, alternatives, variants, all of which should give him or her pause to think about what it means to read a medieval text that in many ways was still being created in the thirteenth century. We are encountering a text on the cusp of the vernacular book culture, a text that has set itself the goal of incorporating an ancient, oral tradition into the book culture that began to flower around 1200. In order to do this, our poet, or poets, combined two separate stories, that of Siegfried the hero and his death, and the downfall of the Burgundians, and in doing so rearranged some of the "historical" facts in an effort to create a narrative with a clear motivational thread running through it. He was not always successful, and it took the C redactor, as we have called him, to create a version that dealt with many of the inconsistencies inherent in the earlier poet's undertaking. Finally, the *Klage* poet felt a need, perhaps in response to reader reactions, to continue the story and to explain many of its mixed messages. Was Hagen guilty, and of what? Was Kriemhild guilty, and if not, why not? Were the Burgundians heroes or did God punish them for their pride? The *Klage* does not answer all of our questions, but it shows how a book culture began to respond to the circulation of a story, in various versions, that attempted to mold heroic epic into a form that could compete with the more modern courtly romances of the time. We can see how our various manuscripts worked with the texts, collected them, organized them, and in doing so created something approaching a more fixed notion of what a text should be. This was in fact an exciting venture, a glimpse into a period of great transition and import for our own sense of book culture. In the end, though, the *Nibelungenlied* is also a great story, and it is hoped that this translation will provide the reader with both a sense of its medieval roots as well as hours of enjoyment and reading pleasure.

The annotation system used throughout the translation is as follows: Square brackets indicate strophe numbers in the *Nibelungenlied*, line numbers in the *Klage*. Superscript numbers point to footnotes, and finally, a significant manuscript variation or addition is indicated by an asterisk.

The Nibelungenlied

Or The Epic of the Nibelungen

[A1;C1] *We hear in ancient stories* || *wonders many told*
Of heroes rich in glories, || *of hardships manifold,*
Of joys and days of feasting || *of tears and hearts nigh broken,*
Of noble warriors battling || *may now you hear of wonders spoken.*[1]

Part One

1. Kriemhild[2]

[2] There once was a young noblewoman who came of age in Burgundy. She was more beautiful than anyone in all the world. Her name was Kriemhild. She grew to become an ideal woman, and many a man would lose his life on her account. [A3] She was clearly worthy of a man's love, and there was no shortage of willing young men who wanted her. She was beautiful beyond compare, but it was her character that set her apart from all other women.[3] [4] She was in the care of three kings,[4] each of them noble and

---

1. This introductory strophe appears in the A and C manuscripts but not in B, although all modern editions based on the B manuscript have included it. Almost certainly a later addition by the C redactor and perhaps inspired by the later *Klage*, it attempts to recreate an epic introduction in miniature, emphasizing the work's expansive range of extreme heroism and suffering, while reminding the reader of the age, oral origin, and marvelous character of the sources from which it is derived. The translation of the strophe, in verse, attempts to illustrate the internal rhyme and stylistic anomalies that point to its anachronistic form.
2. The B manuscript does not provide chapter titles, although it does indicate these divisions with large, illuminated initials. The titles used here are not original but loosely based on the titles in manuscripts A and C and those provided by most editors.
3. This additional strophe from manuscript A is used in most editions, as it fits well into the traditional presentation of the main character, with emphasis on Kriemhild's singular beauty and worthiness, the latter reflected in the former. This inner beauty, or virtuous character (*tugend*), is what makes her stand out from other women.
4. The text regularly labels the three brothers as "kings," although it is soon quite clear that the eldest, Gunther, is in fact the only king, as he performs the roles of ruler, commander, and judge of the kingdom of Burgundy. To make this clear, the translation sometimes uses the term "sovereigns" to distinguish the other brothers.

accomplished: Gunther and Gernot, praiseworthy knights, and their younger brother Giselher, himself a skilled warrior. Kriemhild was their sister, and her brothers were responsible for her upbringing. [B7;C4] Her mother's name was Ute, a wealthy queen in her own right. Her father's name was Dancrat, and he had left his sons their inheritance after his death. He, too, was incredibly accomplished and had gained much honor in his youth.[5] [5] These men of noble birth were charitable and aspired to greatness, and Burgundy was the name of their kingdom. They were later to accomplish great feats of courage in Etzel's lands.

[6] The lords lived with their mighty court in Worms on the Rhine. They were served until the end of their days and throughout their lands by a powerful and honorable knighthood, and yet they were to experience a miserable death on account of the hatred of two women. [8] As I have already mentioned, the three sovereigns were splendid warriors. They commanded the very bravest warriors known to man, all of them tough and unwavering and steadfast in the heat of battle. [9] There was Hagen of Troneck along with his brother, the sharp-witted Dancwart. From Metz there was Ortwin, then the two margraves Gere and Eckewart, and finally Volker of Alzey, at the height of his strength and courage. [10] Rumolt was the kitchen master, but an extraordinary warrior as well. Sindolt and Hunolt also served the court and upheld its eminence. And then there were many other warriors whose names escape me at the moment. [11] Dancwart was the marshal, and his nephew, Ortwin of Metz, was the king's seneschal. Sindolt, a high-ranking officer, was the cupbearer, and Hunolt was the chamberlain.[6] They all knew well how to serve with honor. [12] There really is no one who could adequately describe the court's greatness, its far-reaching power, or its grand reputation and its illustrious chivalry, which these lords practiced happily until the end of their days.

[13] Growing up amongst all this splendor, Kriemhild once had a dream.[7] She dreamed that she had trained a falcon that was strong, beautiful, and wild,

---

5. This strophe, placed here based on its order in manuscript C, completes the introduction of Kriemhild's immediate family.

6. These four traditional court offices were introduced in the twelfth century, and so represent the "contemporary" face of the tale in the midst of a court supposedly existing in the distant past. This is one of several points where the past and present are seamlessly blended into a new narrative reality. The role of kitchen master is added to the other four. It is important to note that Rumolt is also identified as a great warrior and hero, despite his more domestic administrative tasks.

7. Since antiquity, dreams have been interpreted as portents, and here Kriemhild's dream functions as a means to project the narrative into the distant, dark future. That future will bring love and loss. The necessary coexistence of these two sides of the same coin is a theme that pervades the entire epic. In a sense, Kriemhild is also foreshadowing her life as a cloistered widow, which is avoided at the very end of the first part by a fateful message from the East.

only to have it viciously destroyed by two eagles. She could not have imagined a more horrible sight. [14] She told her mother Ute about her dream, but she could provide no comforting explanation.

"The falcon you will tame is a noble man. May God protect him, for you will surely lose him."

[15] "Why are you talking to me about a man, mother? I want to live my life without a man's love. I want to stay carefree until I die, without the pain that a man's love will surely bring."

[16] "Don't make any hasty vows," her mother replied. "If you ever want to be truly happy, then that can only happen with the love of a man. You will grow into the beauty of womanhood if God grants you a truly virtuous knight."

[17] "Please don't say that, mother. It is only too evident that many women have been rewarded with suffering for their love. I want to avoid them both, and live happily ever after."

[18] In her mind Kriemhild had renounced love. She lived like this for quite some time without ever coming across anyone whom she might have loved. But later she would happily become the wife of a valiant warrior. [19] He was indeed that same falcon that she had seen in her dream, the one her mother had told her about. The revenge she was to exact on her dearest family members, those who murdered him, was terrible. His death would bring with it the demise of countless men.

2. Siegfried[8]

[20] There once was the son of a noble king who came of age in Netherland.[9] His father's name was Siegmund, his mother's Sieglinde. They lived in Xanten, a prosperous and illustrious town on the lower Rhine. [21] The name of this talented young man was Siegfried. He traveled throughout foreign lands boldly seeking to test his strength against others, and he was later to find many of his equals in Burgundy.* [22] Everyone had a story to tell

---

8. The second chapter begins as did the first, both in substance and style, and this parallel construction is another reason why the first strophe of mss. A and C has been rejected as an authentic part of the epic's introduction. Siegfried is introduced as being endowed with an innate nobility, which is furthered and refined through a courtly education. What connects him with Kriemhild from the start is his *tugende*, or virtues and abilities, here rendered as an inherent quality we might think of as character.

9. I am following Heinzle's convention in the translation by rendering the original plural, *Niderlande*, in the singular, to avoid any association with the name of the modern country. While this location at the Lower Rhine places it geographically with some specificity, Siegfried is not associated with a historical court or dynasty, unlike the Burgundians.

about the amazing feats he had already accomplished at such a young age. People talked about his fame and reputation, as well as his good looks. Many a beautiful woman wanted him. [23] He was educated with the kind of attention that befits someone of his lineage. It was through his own character, however, that he developed a virtuous way of life. His father's lands later flourished on account of his superior abilities in all things.

[24] Siegfried had reached the age where he could appear before the court, and people liked to see him around. A number of women, married or not, hoped that he would want to be seen in their company more often. The prince was already well aware that he had attracted the attention of so many. [25] The young man still had to have an escort when he went out riding, and his parents made sure that he was always well dressed.[10] He was also constantly surrounded by his teachers, men who knew how to raise a young man in the ways of honor. With this education he was able to win over people and lands. [26] He was soon strong enough to carry arms and armor, and he certainly had what it took to do so. It was his intention to impress beautiful women, and they thought it honorable to love him.

[27] King Siegmund declared to his vassals that he intended to host a great festival for all his dear friends. The invitations were sent out far and wide to the lands of other kings. The king rewarded his guests, familiar and unfamiliar alike, with fine horses and expensive wardrobes. [28] Young men, who, on account of their noble birth were destined to become knights, were especially sought out across the lands and invited to travel to the festival. Along with the young prince Siegfried, they were all knighted together. [29] Incredible tales of that feast have since been told. Siegmund and Sieglinde knew well how to increase the fame of their court through ample gift giving. Their generosity was legendary, and strangers came to live with them from far and wide because of it.[11] [30] Four hundred young men received their surcoats as knights alongside Siegfried. Many young women worked incessantly to provide these garments, because they were looking for his favor. The women

---

10. The inconsistency of a young hero described as still needing an escort when he leaves the court clashes with the hero of songs who has already achieved wondrous and fantastic feats of arms on his own. The inconsistency is unimportant, however, as the portrayal of Siegfried is meant to satisfy the audience's two primary expectations of the main hero: he is a mirror of courtly decorum and a prime candidate for the "modern" convention of *minne*, and at the same time he represents an uncourtly but still vital aspect of the warrior ethos. His success can therefore be attributed both to his prowess and strength as well as to his education and good looks.

11. The Xanten court is depicted as legendary in its munificence, a theme that will be repeated throughout, primarily in the characters of Ruediger and Etzel. Excessive gift giving was the seemingly paradoxical means to greater wealth and power, as it developed a court's reputation, or honor, and therefore attracted more adherents, who also acted as the primary military force available to a ruler.

affixed countless jewels into the gold embroidery [31] which they wanted to work into the clothing for the proud young men. This was as it should be. The king, their host, had them all seated together at the time of the summer solstice, when his son was to become a knight.

[32] They then went to church, all of the splendid young aspirants and many a noble knight. The older, more experienced among them had by custom to serve the younger, inexperienced men, as it had once been their place. They were all impatient and expected some excitement to follow soon. [33] A Mass was sung to honor God, and people began to crowd around as the ceremony of knighthood was performed according to ancient rite, as is not likely to be seen again with such honors. [34] They ran to where the horses had been saddled for them, and the tourney that followed in Siegmund's court was so fierce that the entire castle shook. The boisterous young knights made a joyous noise. [35] The veterans and novices alike gave blows as good as they got, and the air was filled with the crack of breaking lances. Splinters flew from their hands as they did their best, a sight visible even from the palace. [36] The king finally put an end to the melee, and the horses were led away. Strewn all over the field of battle were the broken shield bosses and precious stones that had been torn from shield plates by the forceful impacts. [37] The guests were then led to their seats, where their exhaustion was eased with the very best of the host's food and wine, served to everyone's fill. Strangers and locals were served with honor enough. [38] And so they passed away the rest of the day, while the traveling entertainers seemed to be constantly in motion. They played tirelessly for the rewards that were amply bestowed on them all.[12] Siegmund and his entire country grew in renown on account of such munificence. [39] The king allowed the newly knighted Siegfried to bestow lands and towns as fiefs, as he had once done himself. To his brothers in arms he gave freely, and they were exceedingly glad that they had made the long journey.

[40] The entire festival lasted seven days. Sieglinde, according to ancient custom and out of love for her son, distributed red gold all around. She did what she could to make them all beholden to him. [41] Not a single performer was left wanting. The hosts gave away horses and clothing as if there was no tomorrow. I seriously doubt that any clan ever displayed such great generosity. [42] The guests and their hosts parted with great honor. It was heard from the more high ranking of the men that they would gladly have Siegfried as their lord, but Siegfried declined, and he was admired all the more because of it. [43] As long as his father and mother were alive, their dear

---

12. The poet, here and elsewhere, can't seem to help but put in a plug for his brethren entertainers and singers and the rewards that they deserve for their part in making the festivities memorable.

son refused to wear the crown. But Siegfried, bold and brave, took it upon himself to defend his land against any enemy that might threaten it.*

3. Siegfried Arrives at Worms

[44] Siegfried lived without a care in the world, until he heard tales of a beautiful young woman living in Burgundy, from whom he would later gain so much joy and also so much suffering. [45] Her incredible beauty was known far and wide, but at the same time it was her temperament that attracted so many men to Gunther's lands.[13] [46] Despite all the men vying for her love, Kriemhild said to herself that she didn't want any of them as a husband. She hadn't yet met the one who would later become her husband. [47] Sieglinde's child turned his thoughts to noble love. No one else stood a chance against him, and it was easy for him to win a beautiful woman. Noble Kriemhild later became bold Siegfried's wife.

[48] Since he was determined to find true love, his family and many of his men advised him to seek out a woman of equally noble birth. Siegfried boldly replied: "Then I will take Kriemhild, [49] the beauty of Burgundy. She is beautiful beyond description, and there was never an emperor so rich who would not have been thrilled to have her for his queen." [50] Siegmund heard people talking, and he was very concerned by what he heard about his son's intentions to try to win this beautiful young woman's affections. [51] Sieglinde, the wife of that noble king, also heard the talk. She was concerned for her son's safety, because she knew the reputation of Gunther and his men.[14] Everyone tried to talk Siegfried out of going.

[52] Siegfried then said, "Dear father, if I can't follow my heart and win the woman I love, then I relinquish the love of all other women for all time. Nothing that you or anyone else could say would keep me from my realizing my dream."

[53] "If you won't give up your plan," said the king, "then I welcome your intent and will support you in any way that I can, but be forewarned that King Gunther has more than a few proud men in his court. [54] Even if you only had to contend with Hagen, someone who is as self-satisfied and full of

---

13. Kriemhild's emotional energy (*hochgemuot*) is highlighted here. When characterizing men, the term often describes a confidence and self-assurance that borders on pride yet remains a positive quality required for proper masculine and noble behavior. For Kriemhild, the term is used to describe her poise and social vitality as a quality that affirms her inner nobility.

14. The danger that the Burgundian court poses seems to emanate from its royal family, and particularly from certain members of the household, specifically Hagen, who here for the first time is described as proud or arrogant (*übermuot*) in a clearly negative characterization.

himself as they come, I fear that we might run into problems with the courtship of this beautiful woman."

[55] "Who can stop us?" Siegfried replied. "Whatever I can't get by asking nicely I'll just take by force. I'm pretty sure I can have whatever I want of Gunther's properties and people."

[56] Noble Siegmund replied, "I don't like your attitude. If anyone along the Rhine got wind of your intent, you wouldn't be able to set foot in Burgundy. I know Gunther and Gernot too well to think otherwise. [57] You won't win this young woman with bloodshed," said King Siegmund, "of that I'm sure. But if we want to undertake this journey with the support of a strong army, then we'll need to call on our best allies as soon as possible."

[58] Siegfried answered, "I don't have any intention of being accompanied to the Rhine by an army. I don't want to win this woman in a military campaign. [59] I want to earn her love by my deeds alone. I will lead eleven of my best men to Gunther's lands. This is how you can help me, father." His companions were outfitted with the very best coats and fur pelts.[15]

[60] His mother Sieglinde had heard the whole discussion. She worried about her dear son, because she had reason to fear Gunther's might. The noble queen started to cry. [61] Seeing this, Siegfried went to her and gently said to his mother, "Please don't cry on my account. I'm not worried about any warrior. [62] You could help me a great deal with this journey to Burgundy, so that my friends and I are properly outfitted as is befitting of proud heroes. I say to you that I would be forever grateful."

[63] "Since you won't give up on this," Sieglinde said, "then I will do everything that I can to help you, my only son, and I will provide you and your companions with the best provisions that knights ever had. You'll have more than enough to take with you."

[64] Siegfried bowed before his queen and said, "There will only be twelve warriors on this expedition who will need to be outfitted. I can't wait to see what Kriemhild is like."

[65] The most talented women sat day and night without rest until Siegfried's wardrobes had been completed. He was anxious to get started on his journey. [66] His father made sure that all arms and armor were in excellent condition, as he prepared to depart his father's lands. Bright chainmail and iron helmets were prepared along with shields firm and broad.

---

15. There is a fundamental conflict here between chivalrous and heroic approaches to the bridal quest. While Siegfried's father advocates for a strong military escort, he relies on the symbolic nature of this force to represent the greatness of his court, and by extension, his son's worthiness as a knight. Siegfried, on the other hand, assumes the role of solitary hero, insisting on a quest that follows the heroic concept of might makes right. This will lead to a clash of custom and law at his arrival in the Burgundian capital, Worms.

[67] The day of their departure drew near. All those left behind began to wonder if they would ever return home. The command went out to load up their arms and equipment. [68] Their mounts were superb, and their bridles and harnesses gleamed with gold stitching. There would be little reason for anyone to have been more confident than Siegfried and his men, and he asked to take his leave for Burgundy.

[69] The king and his wife sadly resigned themselves to his leaving. He tried with tenderness to comfort them both. He said, "Please don't cry on my account. You will never have to worry about my safety." [70] The leave-taking was painful even for the men, and all the young women were in tears. I think that they knew in their hearts that many of their friends might not return. They were right to be afraid. Their worst fears did come true.[16]

[71] On the morning of the seventh day they arrived on the riverbanks at Worms. Their clothing shone like red gold and their equestrian equipment was equally stunning. Siegfried's men rode in an orderly formation. [72] Their shields were not yet battle scarred; they were broad and light, and their helmets gleamed as Siegfried rode into Gunther's territory. Never before had heroes been outfitted so splendidly. [73] The tips of their swords reached down to their spurs, and these knights also carried spears with them. Siegfried actually carried a spear that was two hands wide and had an incredibly sharp blade. [74] They led their horses with the golden bridles in their hands; their breast collars were made with silk. This is how they made their appearance in that land. The people just stared at them, and many of Gunther's men ran to greet them. [75] These eager men, knights and squires, went up to the noblemen and welcomed them respectfully to their country, as they should. They took their horses and their shields from them. [76] They wanted to lead the horses off to groom them, but Siegfried quickly told them, "Leave the horses here awhile longer, since my men and I don't intend to stay very long. [77] Whoever knows where I might find Gunther of Burgundy should not keep it from me."

One of the men told him where to go. [78] "If you want to find our ruler, then we can certainly oblige you. I saw him just now in the great hall with his retinue of heroes. This is where you will find him along with many other outstanding men."

[79] The king was told that a group of stately knights had arrived, outfitted in gleaming chainmail and splendid clothing. None of the Burgundians recognized them, however. [80] The king wondered where these well-armed

---

16. This must foreshadow the final, still distant, outcome in the second part, since Siegfried and his men are clearly successful in Burgundy and able to return at the end of the bridal quest (cf. str. 260).

knights had come from, with their gleaming gear and such splendid shields. Gunther was irritated that no one could tell him anything.

[81] Ortwin of Metz, himself eminent and courageous, replied to the king, "Since we don't know who these people are, let's ask my uncle Hagen. He should have a look at them. [82] He knows everything there is to know about notable foreign lands. If he knows who they are, he'll tell us."

The king told them to bring Hagen and his men. He soon made an impressive appearance at court along with a troop of warriors. [83] Hagen asked how he could be of help to the king. "Some foreign knights have arrived at our gates and no one knows who they are. If you recognize them, Hagen, I'd like you to tell me all about them."

[84] "I would be happy to do so," Hagen replied. He went over to a window and looked out over the foreigners. He was impressed by their mounts and their equipment, but he had never seen them in Burgundy before. [85] He said that wherever these knights came from to the Rhine, they must surely be princes or the emissaries of princes. Their horses were impressive, and their dress was costly, to say the least. Wherever they were from, they certainly were sure of themselves.[17]

[86] Hagen went on to say, "I will admit to never having seen Siegfried, but I would be willing to bet that, from the looks of him, he's the one who presents himself with such splendor. [87] I'm sure he is here to bring us important news from his own lands. This hero conquered the bold Nibelungen clan, Schilbung and Nibelung, sons of a mighty king.[18] Since then he has accomplished many amazing feats of strength. [88] I have heard tales of how he went out into the mountains completely by himself and came upon Nibelung's treasure, guarded by a strong army. He had no idea who they were until he met them face-to-face. [89] Nibelung's treasure had been carried out of a cavernous mountain, and, believe it or not, the men of Nibelungen had decided to divide it up as Siegfried looked on with amazement from afar. His curiosity got the better of him. [90] So he crept up closer to see these warriors, and they caught sight of him.

One of them proclaimed, 'Here comes mighty Siegfried, the hero of Netherland.' He was to experience strange adventures there with the Nibelungen.[19] [91] Schilbung and Nibelung welcomed the warrior courteously, and after

---

17. This confidence (*hochgemuot*) is in every way appropriate to their appearance.

18. This is the first mention of the clan name that gives this work its modern title. Here the name is introduced in the plural, so that both of the brothers, Schilbung and Nibelung, and their men are reckoned as descendants of the Nibelung dynasty. Their father, King Nibelung, was the former owner of a vast treasure.

19. Heroes are quickly recognized in this alternate heroic space, even as they try to hide, whereas no one in Burgundy except Hagen, who straddles both worlds, has ever seen or heard of Siegfried.

discussing the matter amongst themselves, the young noblemen decided to ask Siegfried to help them divide the treasure evenly. It took a bit of convincing, but Siegfried finally agreed. [92] The story tells us that he saw more precious stones than even a hundred wagons could haul, and the amount of red gold from the land of the Nibelungen was greater still. Siegfried was supposed to figure out how to divide all of this between them. [93] As a reward for his trouble they gave him Nibelung's sword. But it turned out that they were ill served by Siegfried, and in the end he gave up in failure. They were not at all happy.*

[94] Among their followers were twelve men who were giants, but this did them little good when faced with Siegfried's wrath, and he killed each one along with another seven hundred of the land of Nibelungen's best soldiers [95] with that great sword called Balmung. Many of the young warriors surrendered themselves, their lands and castles, on account of their fear of that sword and the man who wielded it. [96] On top of it all, Siegfried killed the two mighty kings. It was Alberich, though, who later put him in considerable danger. He had hoped to avenge his lords swiftly until he realized the great strength that Siegfried possessed. [97] The powerful dwarf was unable to overcome him. Like wild lions they fought each other up and into the mountain, where Siegfried took the cloak of invisibility from Alberich. Siegfried was then the uncontested owner of the treasure. [98] Anyone who had dared to fight him lay dead.

He ordered that the treasure be taken back inside the mountain from where it had been removed by the Nibelungen. Alberich was appointed the treasure's chamberlain. [99] He had to swear an oath of allegiance as a vassal, and he was prepared to serve in every way."

So Hagen concluded his report: "He accomplished all these things. There is no mightier fighter than he. [100] I remember now that there is even more to the story. This great hero once killed a dragon and then bathed himself in its blood. As a result, his skin turned into a kind of armor that no weapon can penetrate, something that has been demonstrated time and again. [101] We should greet this lord courteously, so as not to earn his displeasure. He's a fearless man, and we don't want to get on his bad side. He's accomplished some extraordinary things with his great strength."

[102] Then the mighty king spoke: "I'm sure you are right. Just look at how bravely he stands ready for battle, he and his fellow warriors. What a fearless man. We will go to meet him down where the hero is standing."

[103] "This you may well do with honor," said Hagen. "He is from a noble family, the son of a rich king. So help me God, it looks to me as if the purpose of his journey is not insignificant."

[104] The king of the land declared: "Then he shall be welcome. He is noble and brave, that I can see for myself. He will be treated accordingly here in Burgundy." Gunther went down to where he could greet Siegfried.[20]

[105] The host and his warriors welcomed the guest with courtesies that left little to be desired. The bold man bowed his head in appreciation for the extraordinarily friendly welcome.* [106] The king came right to the point: "I would like to hear tell, noble Siegfried, where you have come from to this land, and what it is that you seek here in Worms on the Rhine."

The visitor replied to the king: "I have nothing to hide. [107] I heard it told in my father's land that the bravest warriors ever assembled by a king were to be found here with you. I had to come and see for myself if everything that I had heard was true. [108] I also heard it said that you were the bravest king of them all, bar none. People from all parts say the same. I won't rest until I've had a chance to find out for myself. [109] I, too, am a warrior and can claim a crown. I will do what it takes to be recognized by rights as the ruler of my lands and people. For this I pledge my honor and my life. [110] If you are as brave as I've heard said, then I am determined to take from you what is yours, whether anyone likes it or not. Your lands and castles will all belong to me."

[111] The king and his men couldn't believe what they were hearing. It seemed that Siegfried was intent on depriving them of their lands. Gunther's men heard this and were furious. [112] "What did I do to deserve this?" said Gunther. "How is it that we should lose by force of arms what my father long held with honor? We would obviously not be worthy of being called knights."[21]

[113] "I won't change my mind," replied bold Siegfried. "If you don't have the strength to maintain peace in your own land, then I'll take it for myself. If, on the other hand, you should be the stronger, then all my lands will belong to you. [114] Your lands and mine are both equally on the line. Whoever should defeat the other, he will rule all of it, the lands and the inhabitants."

Hagen and Gernot were quick to object.* [115] Gernot said, "We have no intention of conquering other lands and having men killed as a result. We have prosperous lands that are ours by right and to which no one else can lay claim." [116] His companions stood by him with grim determination.

---

20. The fact that the king goes to, that is descends down to, where Siegfried is impatiently waiting signifies a considerable concession in the protocol for welcoming a stranger at court, and is based on Hagen's advice not to offend the guest, who has a reputation for great strength and violence.

21. Gunther is referring to the code of chivalry, that is, the constant practice of the ideals of knighthood (*ritterschaft pflegen*).

Among them was Ortwin of Metz, who said: "I am opposed to letting this go unanswered. Bold Siegfried has insulted you without cause. [117] Even if you and your brothers were incapable of defending yourselves, and even if he had an entire imperial army to back him, I would bet that I could make this brash man take leave of his inflated pride."

[118] This only made the hero of Netherland angrier. He said: "Don't you dare raise your hand against me. I am a powerful king, you are but the king's man. Twelve of your kind wouldn't stand a chance against me."*

[119] Ortwin of Metz raised a cry to draw swords. He was truly Hagen of Troneck's sister's son. The king was annoyed that Hagen had remained silent for so long.

Gernot, a knight both bold and confident, stepped in. [120] He said to Ortwin: "Calm yourself. Lord Siegfried has done us no harm that can't be dealt with in a civilized manner.[22] Take my advice and let's make an ally of him. This would be to our advantage."

[121] Then valiant Hagen spoke up: "It is an insult to all of us, your warriors, that he ever chose to come here to the Rhine intent on conquest. This would have been better left undone. My lords gave him no provocation."

[122] Siegfried, that powerful man, answered: "Lord Hagen, if you are upset by what I have said, then I will gladly show you that I intend to take Burgundy by force of arms."

[123] But Gernot interjected: "I will make sure that doesn't happen." He ordered his men to refrain from boastful speeches aimed at insulting Siegfried, who by that time had already turned his thoughts to the lovely girl.

[124] "What would be the point of fighting you?" replied Gernot. "No matter how many warriors lose their lives, we would gain no honor and you no advantage."[23]*

To this Siegfried, Siegmund's son, responded, [125] "Why do Hagen and Ortwin hesitate to join the fight, along with their men, who are so plentiful here in Burgundy?"

---

22. Gernot is the peacemaker here and advocates the civilized superiority of courtly upbringing and education (*zuht*) to settle matters of dispute. Making a potential enemy into an ally corresponds to the language of diplomacy, as opposed to Siegfried's rather blunt threats of single combat to settle a claim of sovereignty.

23. Gernot offers a definition of honor here not based on victory in battle but rather on the prestige and acclamation derived from courtly, i.e., diplomatic behavior and peaceful outcomes. This kind of honor emphasizes the importance of protecting patrimony rather than expansion through new conquests. Siegfried will be co-opted, or one could say civilized, at the Burgundian court with entertainment and the finer things of life. This allows him to turn his attention to that other courtly game, love (*hôhe minne*), first mentioned in str. 131,4, and again by the C redactor in str. C138,4. This process is already foreshadowed in Kriemhild's dream, where the falcon, who is Siegfried, is first described as strong, handsome, and wild. It is ultimately Kriemhild who will tame him.

They refused to answer, as Gernot had advised. [126] Ute's son said: "You are welcome among us, along with your companions who traveled with you. I and my family, we are gladly at your service." The king's wine was ordered up for the guests.

[127] The ruler of the land then said: "Everything that we have is at your disposal. Should you choose to act honorably, we will share all that we own." Siegfried was somewhat appeased by this.

[128] An order went out that all their baggage should be looked after. The best lodging was made available, and Siegfried's men were made comfortable. Siegfried was from then on a welcome guest among the Burgundians. [129] For days on end, he was shown the greatest honor in more ways than I can describe. This he had earned with his courage. You may be assured that no one wished him ill. [130] The sovereigns and their men all passed the time with games and entertainment, and Siegfried was always the best. Whatever game was being played, no one could beat him. Whether hurling stones or throwing a javelin, his strength was incredible. [131] Whenever the spirited knights spent their time with courtly pursuits under the watchful eyes of the ladies, the hero of Netherland was a welcome guest. He was consumed with thoughts of courtly love.* [132] Whatever others engaged in, he was willing to go along. He carried a beautiful girl in his heart, and likewise she, a princess, thought of him, although they had never seen each other. In private she often spoke well of him.

[133] When young men, knights and their squires, were engaged in games in the courtyard, Kriemhild, that noble princess, would gaze down at them through the windows. She was happy just to watch for hours on end. [134] If he had known that the one he held dear in his heart was watching, he would have been satisfied enough. If he had been able to lay eyes on her, I venture to say that he would not have had a care in the world. [135] Any time he stood down in the courtyard along with the other knights, as some still do today to pass the time, Sieglinde's son stirred the hearts of many women with his good looks and charm.

[136] He continually asked himself: "How can I manage to see this girl with my own eyes? The one that I have loved with all my heart is a complete stranger to me, and I can't stand it anymore."

[137] Every time the mighty sovereigns rode out into their lands, the knights had to accompany them. Siegfried had to go along as well, which pained the young princess. He, too, suffered great hardships on account of her love.* [138] And so he lived with the sovereigns, this is true, there in Gunther's land for a whole year. During that entire time he never once saw the one he loved, for whose sake he was to experience much happiness, but also much sorrow.²⁴

---

24. The hardship that Siegfried will suffer on love's behalf thematizes the struggle (*arbeit*) that ennobles a knight in his pursuit of an unseen and potentially unobtainable goal. The necessary

4. The War against the Saxons and the Danes

[139] Disturbing reports carried by messengers from some unknown enemy were received in Gunther's lands. This news caused great consternation. [140] I will tell you who the enemy was: it was Liudeger of Saxony, a powerful noble, along with King Liudegast of Denmark. They had gathered together a mighty army. [141] Their emissaries had traveled to Gunther's lands, sent by his enemies. The strangers were asked what news they carried and were soon escorted to appear before the king.

[142] He greeted them most courteously: "You are welcome! I do not know who sent you. By whose authority do you come here?" asked the noble king.

They were fearful of Gunther's fierce temper. [143] "If by your leave, oh King, we may proclaim the news we have brought, then we will gladly answer. We can tell you who sent us. Liudegast and Liudeger are preparing to attack your lands. [144] You have earned their wrath.[25] We have been told that both these lords are your enemies and that they want to wage war against Worms on the Rhine. They have a great many men, you have my word on that. [145] Their campaign will begin in twelve weeks' time. If you have allies, then call them quickly, so that they might help protect your strongholds and your lands. They intend to destroy many a helmet and shield. [146] However, should you choose to negotiate, then make them an offer. The great legions of your mortal enemies will then not ride up to your walls to do you great harm, which would surely be the end of many a brave and proud knight."

[147] "Please wait a while," said the noble king, "and let me have some time to consider. I will declare my intent once I have been able to share this grave news with my faithful friends and allies."

[148] Gunther the powerful was greatly distressed. He kept this information close to his heart and had Hagen and his other counselors summoned. He asked that Gernot urgently join them as well. [149] The best of the land were all gathered when Gunther spoke: "A great army is intent on invading and attacking us. This should be an affront to every one of you!"

Gernot, that brave and proud knight, replied: [150] "We will defend ourselves with steel. Death will find those so fated, and they will fall on the

---

coexistence of happiness (*liebe*) and sorrow (*leit*) is a result of the potentiality of love, but also the value of its quest.

25. There is apparently no need for further justification for the attack of these two brothers from the north against the Burgundian kingdom. The C redactor emphasizes that the threat is made without provocation, but even Hagen counsels a measured approach given the enemy's initial superiority. Gernot, who had counseled conciliation when threatened by Siegfried, is now the warrior recommending a military response in defense of honor, whatever the outcome.

battlefield. I will not sacrifice my honor to avoid this fate. Let our enemies know that they are welcome!"

[151] Hagen of Troneck then spoke: "I have to disagree. Liudegast and Liudeger are arrogant and self-assured. We won't be able to gather our troops in such a short time." The great hero continued, "Why don't you confer with Siegfried?"

[152] The emissaries were then quartered within the town. Regardless of their enmity, mighty Gunther commanded that they be well cared for. This was the right thing to do, at least until he found out which of his allies would come to his aid. [153] The king was nevertheless sorely troubled. A proud knight who had no idea what was happening saw him in his despair. He asked King Gunther to reveal what was troubling him.

[154] It was Siegfried who said, "I am shocked to see how suddenly the joy and pleasures that we always shared are so soon reversed."

Gunther, that mighty warrior, answered him, [155] "Here deep in my heart is a secret, a trouble that I can't share openly. It is said that only true friends can share in one's innermost secrets."

Siegfried first turned pale, then bright red. [156] He said to the king: "I have never denied you anything. I will help you repair any misfortune. If you are looking for a friend and ally, then I am here, and I pledge to remain so with honor to the end of my days."

[157] "My dear Lord Siegfried, may God reward you. I am well pleased by what you have said, and even if I should never need to call on your courage, I am gratified to know that you are so inclined. If I have yet some while to live, you will be well rewarded. [158] I will tell you why I am so distressed. I have been informed by my enemy's emissaries that they are preparing to launch an attack against me. We have never before suffered such an invasion in these lands."

[159] "Don't let that worry you," said Siegfried. "Just follow my advice, and you can rest easy. Allow me to win honor and glory for your sake, and command your troops to rush to your defense. [160] And even if your mighty enemies should have thirty thousand warriors, I would stand against them, and if I had but a thousand. You can rely on me completely!"

King Gunther responded, "I am forever in your debt."

[161] "Give the command and have a thousand men follow me, since I have only twelve. Then I can defend your land. This, my hand, will always prove your true servant. [162] Hagen and Ortwin, Dancwart and Sindolt, these your dear warriors, we will need as well. And courageous Volker should ride alongside us. He will be our standard bearer. We could choose no one better. [163] And command the emissaries to return to their lords' lands. Let them know that we will not be far behind them, and that our fortified places will be left in peace."

Gunther called on his kindred and vassals to gather their forces.

[164] Liudeger's envoys appeared at court and were overjoyed that they could now return home. Noble King Gunther provided them with lavish gifts and an escort, for which they felt honored.

[165] "Tell my mighty enemies," Gunther said, "that they had better call off their campaign. But should they decide to invade my lands, they will soon learn the meaning of adversity, as long as I still have friends close at hand."

[166] Expensive gifts were given to the envoys, and Gunther had plenty more where those came from. Liudeger's men did not dare refuse and took their leave in good spirits.

[167] When the emissaries returned home to Denmark, King Liudegast heard for himself the news from the Rhine, and when they told him how arrogant and boastful they were there, he became angry. [168] They reported that they had many bold men and that one among them was named Siegfried, a warrior from Netherland. Liudegast was stunned once he grasped the true meaning of this. [169] After the Danes had heard all this, they redoubled their efforts to gather more troops, until they had gathered some twenty thousand of Liudegast's bravest for the impending war. [170] King Liudeger of Saxony likewise gathered his army until he had more than forty thousand altogether for the invasion of Burgundy.

King Gunther had also been busy gathering his forces for war, [171] his relatives and the vassals of his brothers, along with Hagen's own men. Every one of them was sorely needed, and some of them would die as a result. [172] They hastened to prepare themselves for battle. The colors were entrusted to Volker as they broke camp and prepared to leave Worms and cross the Rhine. Hagen of Troneck was given command of the column. [173] Sindolt and Hunolt were part of the company, and they were worthy of Gunther's gold. Dancwart, Hagen's brother, and Ortwin were also honorable participants in that campaign.

[174] "Dear King, you should stay here at home," said Siegfried. "Your warriors will follow me into battle, so stay with the ladies and rest assured that I can be trusted to protect your honor and your wealth. [175] I mean to stop those who intend to invade your home at Worms on the Rhine. They would do well to stay at home. We will strike them first in their own lands so that their arrogance soon turns to fear."[26]

---

26. Siegfried's advice to Gunther to stay at home with the women would seem at first glance intended to diminish the king's honor and increase his own. There is still a sense that Siegfried is out for his own fame as a solitary hero, as he later separates himself from the main force to probe the enemy's defenses. Rumolt will famously offer similar advice in the second part of the epic as the Burgundians are about to depart for the land of the Huns. Here, Gunther takes Siegfried's advice; in the second part he does not, and that in itself is a significant difference

[176] They and their heroes rode from the Rhine, first through Hessen, then to the Saxon border. The fighting began there as the land was plundered and burned. Soon both foreign lords learned the meaning of suffering.

[177] The [Burgundian] squires were held back as they reached the border, whereupon bold Siegfried asked, "Who will watch over these boys?" Never before had the Saxons been dealt with so harshly.

[178] Others replied: "Let noble Dancwart take the young ones under his wing. He is an accomplished fighter. Liudeger's troops will be able to do them little harm. Let him and Ortwin command the rear of the column."

[179] "I will ride out alone," said Siegfried, "to reconnoiter the enemy positions until I have found the main army."

Siegfried, Sieglinde's son, was then quickly outfitted and armed. [180] As he departed, the main body of troops was put under Hagen's and Gernot's command. Siegfried then rode alone into the Saxon lands. On that day, many a helm was battered by him. [181] He spied the main army as it stretched out on the field. It greatly outnumbered his own force, and there were forty thousand men and more gathered there. Siegfried's fearlessness and eagerness only grew at the sight.

[182] One of the enemy's combatants, who was heavily armed, had also ventured out to locate the opposing force. Siegfried caught sight of him, and he in turn saw Siegfried. They each followed the other with a wary gaze. [183] I will tell you who had ventured out on patrol. He held a shield of gleaming gold in his hand: it was none other than King Liudegast. He was intent on keeping his army forewarned. Siegfried, that noble intruder, charged at him with all his might. [184] Liudegast saw him at that moment and prepared to defend himself. They both dug their spurs into their horses' flanks and skillfully aimed their spears at the opponent's shield. The great king was fearful for his life. [185] Following the collision the horses carried the two royal sons apart as swiftly as the wind. With great skill they were able to rein in and turn their mounts. The two combatants now turned on each other with swords drawn. [186] Noble Siegfried let loose a blow that shook the earth. Fiery sparks flew from their helmets as if from great torches, but neither one would give way to the other. [187] For his part, King Liudegast gave Siegfried as good as he got. They each brought their entire strength to bear on the other's shield.

Suddenly there appeared a squad of thirty of Liudegast's men, but they were too late. Siegfried had already defeated his foe. [188] He had inflicted three great wounds on the king, clear through his gleaming chainmail, which was incredibly tough. His sword had cut into flesh, and blood gushed from

---

between both parts, the first focused on Siegfried as warrior and king, the second on Gunther as warrior king, a role he hardly embraces in the early parts of the epic.

the gashes. King Liudegast lost all hope. [189] He begged him to spare his life in return for his lands and told him that his name was Liudegast. His guard then arrived, for they had seen exactly what had transpired there between the two lone sentinels. [190] Siegfried was leading him captive from the field when he was attacked by these thirty men. The hero defended himself and his valuable hostage with incredible blows. That great warrior was to inflict even more damage later. [191] He killed all thirty with his immense strength, except for one whom he left alive, and he rode as fast as he could and reported what had happened to everyone in the camp. The truth of the matter was apparent to all who could see his blood-stained helmet. [192] The Danes were shocked and disheartened when they heard that their lord had been taken captive. It was reported to his brother Liudeger, who raged against this insult. [193] Liudegast was taken forcefully by Siegfried back to Gunther's army, where he was handed over to Hagen. When he was told that this was the king, Hagen seemed not at all disappointed.

[194] The Burgundians received the command to raise their banners. Siegfried shouted, "Forward! There is more to be done before this day is done, if I may live to see it through. Many Saxon ladies will grieve tonight. [195] Heroes of the Rhine, keep your eyes on me! I will lead you into Liudeger's ranks. Witness as these strong hands smash one helmet after another. Before we leave the field of battle, the enemy will know the meaning of fear!"

[196] Gernot and his men ran to their mounts. The banner was raised by that courageous minstrel, Lord Volker.[27] He rode out in front of the army. All the troops were heavily armed for battle. [197] They had barely a thousand men, and twelve mighty leaders. The roads were soon covered in clouds of dust. They rode over fields and meadows, and one could see their shields shining brightly from afar.

[198] The Saxons and their legions had arrived on the field as well, their swords at the ready, as I was later told. Their swords could do a lot of damage in the hands of a skilled warrior. They were determined to defend their castles and lands against the intruders. [199] The Saxon army was led on by each of its commanders as Siegfried and his men from Netherland arrived. On this day many hands would be soaked in the blood of battle. [200] Sindolt and Hunolt and also Gernot would slay many a warrior in that fight before the enemy realized how powerful their opponent really was. Noble women would later shed tears on that account. [201] Volker and Hagen and also Ortwin

---

27. Volker will play a much more prominent role in Part Two, but here he is introduced as both warrior and poet, or minstrel (*spileman*). This would not have presented any kind of contradiction to the reader, since many poets and singers of the period were knights and therefore bound to serve in their lord's military retinue. Just one example is the *Minnesänger* Friedrich von Hausen, killed in the battle of Philomelium in 1190. Volker here even takes the place of honor, leading the troops into battle.

dimmed the glint of helmets with blood in that battle. They were eager for a fight. Dancwart performed real miracles out there.

[202] The Danes fought well. Shields could be heard ringing out as they collided with the keen blades that were being wielded everywhere. The battle-hardened Saxons did considerable damage themselves. [203] The Burgundians waded into the ranks, cleaving great gaping wounds as they went. One could see blood flowing over the riders' saddles. This is how honor was won by knights both eager and courageous. [204] Others heard the steel swords sing out in the hands of the heroes from Netherland as they followed their lord into the dense ranks. The warriors advanced alongside Siegfried. [205] No one from the Rhine could keep up. Siegfried's hands caused rivers of blood to flow from bright helmets until he found Liudeger at the head of his army. [206] Siegfried had ridden the length of the army from one end to other three times. Hagen arrived on the scene and soon helped him quench his thirst for battle. Many brave knights had to give up their lives to them on that day.

[207] Liudeger saw Siegfried wielding his great sword Balmung on high, slaying his troops. This made him furious and even more determined. [208] There was a great crush as the clash of swords rang out loud and their forces pressed forward. The two fighters both gave their best as the ranks began to give way, and a bitter contest arose. [209] It had been reported to the Saxon leader that his brother had been captured, which only increased his agony. He believed that Siegfried was responsible. It had been said that it was Gernot, but later he learned the truth.

[210] Liudeger's blows were so strong that Siegfried's mount began to give way under him. Once the horse had recovered some, bold Siegfried renewed his terrible onslaught. [211] Both Hagen and Gernot were at his side, as were Dancwart and Volker. They were surrounded by the dead. Sindolt and Hunolt, and brave Ortwin, too, cut down the enemy by the score. [212] The daring nobles were inseparable. Spears were launched by the hands of heroes, finding their mark in bright shields, and the magnificent shields soon turned red with blood. [213] Riders found themselves on foot in the middle of that massive struggle. Siegfried, always fearless, and Liudeger ran at each other as missiles and sharp spears flew overhead.* [214] Siegfried's blows tore his opponent's shield out of his hand. The hero of Netherland sought to claim victory over the brave Saxons, many of whom now lay wounded. How Dancwart shattered those suits of glittering armor!

[215] King Liudeger then noticed that the shield in Siegfried's hand had a crown painted on it. He recognized that this was the mighty hero. The king shouted to his companions: [216] "Men, stop your fighting! I see before me the son of Siegmund, Siegfried the invincible. He has been sent by the foul devil to our Saxon lands." [217] He ordered the banners to be lowered. In the

19

middle of the battle he sued for peace, and peace was granted. He was taken captive back to Gunther's lands. Siegfried's strength alone accomplished all this. [218] They agreed to end the battle and laid down their battered helmets and shields. Every single one had been colored in blood by the Burgundians. [219] Prisoners were taken at will, as no one could stand in their way. Gernot and Hagen, both mighty warriors, called for the wounded to be carried away. They escorted five hundred prisoners back to the Rhine with them. [220] The defeated army retreated back to Denmark. The Saxons had not covered themselves with glory, which only added insult to injury. The dead were mourned by their families and friends. [221] Their weapons and armor were loaded and transported back to the Rhine. Siegfried and his companions had achieved great feats, and this was duly recognized by all of Gunther's men.

[222] Lord Gernot sent messengers back to Worms. He let it be known to those back home how he and his men had met with success. Those daring warriors had achieved great honor indeed. [223] The messengers carried the news as swiftly as they could. Those who had been waiting in agony were overjoyed out of love by the good news that reached their ears. Noble women had nothing but questions [224] concerning the fate of the mighty king's army.

One of the messengers was sent to see Kriemhild. She received him in private, as she did not dare to ask openly about one man in particular, the one whom she loved with all her heart. [225] As soon as lovely Kriemhild saw the herald come into her chamber, she greeted him. "Tell me the good news! I will pay you well if you tell me no lies. I will always be in your debt. [226] How did my brother Gernot fare in the battle? And what about my beloved friends? Were many of them killed? And who acquitted himself the best? Tell me now!"

The messenger said without hesitation, "There was not a single coward among us.

[227] "Since you have asked, my lady, I must tell you that there was no one who rode as well as our most noble friend from Netherland. Siegfried achieved incredible feats of arms. [228] Dancwart and Hagen and others in the king's army fought valiantly for honor's sake, but they paled in comparison to Siegfried, King Siegmund's son. [229] They laid low many a hero in that battle, but no one can adequately describe the marvelous feats that Siegfried performed as he charged into the ranks. He did grave harm to the many ladies whose relatives were killed. [230] Many a lady's beloved was left behind on that field. Siegfried's blows rang out loudly as they crashed down on helmets, where they caused wounds that gushed with blood. He is a knight in all ways bold, brave, and virtuous.[28]

---

28. Although the messenger has just praised Siegfried for his combat prowess and strength, these qualities are subsumed in his characterization of him as the complete knight, or perfect in all virtues (*tugende*), since his skill in fighting is just part of what defines a knight.

[231] "Ortwin of Metz achieved much there as well. Those he could reach with his sword were soon either wounded or for the most part dead. Your brother was the cause of the greatest suffering [232] that has ever been known up to now in battle. Truth be told, these extraordinary heroes, the brave Burgundians, performed so magnificently that their honor was well preserved and any shame averted. [233] Saddles were seen emptied by their attacks, and their brilliant swords rang out across the field. The heroes of the Rhine rode them down, and their enemies avoided them at all costs. [234] Those daring men from Troneck caused much misery when the two mighty armies crashed into each other. Brave Hagen brought death to many, and much more could be said about that here in Burgundy. [235] Sindolt and Hunolt, Gernot's men, and brave Rumolt, too, did so much harm to Liudeger that he will forever regret having offended your brothers in their homeland.

[236] "Without a doubt the greatest feats accomplished throughout the battle that anyone saw, from beginning to end, were by the hands of Siegfried. He is bringing many hostages to Burgundy with him. [237] That brave man overcame them all with his own courage. King Liudegast and his brother King Liudeger from Saxony have been completely defeated. My lady, listen closely to my story. [238] Siegfried captured both of them by himself. Never have so many hostages been brought into this land as he now brings to the shores of the Rhine." She could not have received more welcome news.[29]

[239] "At least five hundred of them are unhurt and coming here, along with another eighty severely wounded who are being carried. Know this is true, my lady: Siegfried defeated most of them singlehandedly. [240] Those who were so arrogant to come here to the Rhine and declare war are now Gunther's prisoners. They are being escorted into our land with joy."

She blushed while listening to his report. [241] Her beautiful face turned red as a rose at the thought that the young man, Siegfried, that brave warrior, had escaped harm in the horrific battle. She was also grateful that her friends and family had survived, as well she should be.

[242] The lovely girl said, "You have spoken well. As a reward you shall be given expensive clothing and ten marks of gold.[30] These are yours upon request."

---

29. The herald's retelling of the battle sequence and naming of individuals secures their place in the oral history of their clan. Gunther's household officers are singled out, but clearly Siegfried is the most accomplished and therefore due the greatest honor, or public recognition.

30. The messenger's reward is considerable indeed. A mark as a measure of weight at the time was generally considered to be half a pound, or eight ounces. The equivalent weight of ten marks would be something like eighty ounces of gold, a small fortune (cf. Heinzle, 2015, 1109n242,3).

It pays to give this kind of news to wealthy ladies. [243] He received his reward, the gold and the wardrobe. Pretty girls all went to the windows to look down onto the streets. There they could watch as high-spirited men rode home to Burgundy. [244] Those who were unharmed arrived, as did the wounded. They could hold their heads high as they were greeted by their loved ones. The king jubilantly rode out to meet his army. His greatest fears had turned to joy.

[245] He graciously greeted his own men and did the same to those who were foreigners. It was the mighty king's responsibility to generously thank those who had come to his aid and secured this great victory with honor. [246] Gunther commanded that his men tell him who among them had fallen in battle. The casualties totaled no more than sixty men. They were mourned, as heroes have been ever since. [247] Those who were unharmed brought home shields and helmets that had been battered and smashed. The army dismounted in front of the king's hall, where a joyous noise arose in welcome. [248] The warriors were all given quarters within the town walls, and the king had them well cared for. He commanded that the wounded be treated and made as comfortable as possible. His treatment of his enemies reflected his virtue.

[249] He said to Liudegast, "You are welcome here. I have suffered much on your account, and I will be compensated for it, if I am fortunate. May God reward my allies. They have done me a great kindness."

[250] "You have every reason to thank them," said Liudeger. "Never before did a king gain so many hostages. We will pay handsomely for our safety and for honorable treatment of us, your enemy."

[251] "Both of you can move about at will," Gunther said. "But I want to have securities so that my enemies stay and don't leave without permission." On this Liudeger gave his hand.

[252] They were brought to their quarters and given what they needed. Those who were wounded were given especially good bedsteads. Those who were healthy were given mead and good wine. Everyone could not have been more satisfied. [253] Their shattered shields were taken away from them and stored. The many bloody saddles, and there were plenty, were taken away so that the women would not see them and start to cry. Plenty of knights were utterly exhausted from the campaign. [254] King Gunther devoted all of his attention to the care of his guests. His lands were full of foreigners as well as Burgundians. He made sure that the wounded were especially well cared for. That brought an end to their stubborn pride.[31] [255] The physicians were

---

31. Here the Northerners' pride (*übermuot*) is punished not by defeat in battle but rather by generosity in victory. Gunther teaches them a lesson in courtly behavior, demonstrating by his actions that exaggerated or baseless pride is contrary to the virtues of an ideal ruler.

paid very well for their services: silver that was not even weighed, and gleaming gold, so that they might heal the warriors who had suffered so in battle. In addition, the king generously lavished gifts on his guests.

[256] Those who wanted to return home were asked to stay, as is customary among friends. The king asked his counselors how he might reward his men, since they had served him with great honor.

[257] Lord Gernot then spoke: "It would be right to let them go home. Then ask that they return in six weeks' time for a great festival. By then many of those who now lie here wounded will be restored to health."

[258] Siegfried of Netherland also asked to take his leave. When King Gunther heard his intent, he asked him kindly to remain with him. But he only agreed to stay on account of his sister. [259] Siegfried was too wealthy and powerful to be paid for his service. He was repaid with the king's gratitude. The entire royal court was grateful. They had seen what his strength had accomplished in that battle. [260] He wanted to stay a while longer for that beautiful girl in hopes of being able to see her. This did come to pass, and as he wished, he was able to get to know her. He was later able to ride back home to Siegmund's lands a happy man.

[261] The host commanded that the code of chivalry be practiced at all times, and many young men gladly obliged.[32] At the same time he had bleachers put up along the shore outside of Worms for the guests who were expected to come to Burgundy. [262] When it came time for the guests to arrive, Kriemhild had already heard the news that there was going to be a festival for their dear friends and supporters. Noble ladies were soon hard at work with preparations [263] for the clothes and headscarves that they would wear. Ute, the mighty queen, heard that proud warriors would be coming and so had great quantities of rich clothing taken out of the trunks and unfolded. [264] She commanded that more clothes be made to please her sons. Many women and girls, along with numerous young men from Burgundy, were to be well outfitted. She also had many fine garments fashioned for those from foreign lands.

5. Siegfried Sees Kriemhild

[265] Day after day the guests coming to the festival could be seen riding to the Rhine. Whoever wanted to attend out of love for the king, they were

---

32. Here, *ritterschefte pflegen* has mostly been taken to refer to "knightly sports" (Hatto, 1965), but the reference in str. 112,4 (see note 21) allows us to construe this more broadly and can be taken to mean that Gunther wants his young men to act at all times and in all ways like knights, i.e., to behave themselves.

given horses to ride and magnificent clothing. [266] We have been told that the seating arrangements had been well prepared for the noblest and most magnificent of the guests. Thirty-two high-ranking noblemen had come to attend the festivities. Ladies vied with each other as to who was the most beautiful.

[267] Young Giselher was untiring. He and Gernot along with their entire retinue greeted each of the guests, those they recognized and those they did not. They greeted them according to the honor due them. [268] The visitors brought golden saddles, valuable shields, and expensive garments with them to the Rhine. Many of those who had been wounded appeared to be completely restored to health. [269] Those who had been lying in sickbeds and had suffered from their wounds no longer had to fear death. The concern for the wounded was soon forgotten, and they looked forward to the coming festivities [270] and the hospitality that they were to enjoy. All those who had come were jubilant and full of anticipation, and this joyous mood spread throughout Gunther's lands.

[271] On the morning of Pentecost people could see many brave men in fine attire, over five thousand in all, going to the celebrations.[33] The entertainment had begun in some places, and everyone was trying to outdo each other. [272] The ruler of Burgundy was deep in thought. He well knew how much the hero from Netherland cherished his sister, even though he had never seen her. Everyone said that she was the most beautiful girl in the world.*

[273] Ortwin spoke to the king: "If you want to produce a grand and honorable festival, then you should let everyone see the beautiful girls that we are so proud of here in Burgundy. [274] What is it that gives men pleasure and happiness if not pretty girls and elegant women? Have your sister meet your guests." This counsel met with the approval of many of the warriors.

[275] "I will gladly follow your counsel," said the king. Everyone within earshot was glad to hear it. He commanded his mother, Queen Ute, and her lovely daughter Kriemhild to appear before the court with their female entourage. [276] The closets were rummaged through to find the best dresses, and whatever else could be found in the chests, including bracelets and headbands, was made available to them. Pretty girls busied themselves with their makeup. [277] Many young men would have gladly given a king's ransom for the chance to catch the eye of one of these girls. They were especially happy to see those they did not yet know.[34]

---

33. This festival is in many ways patterned after the descriptions in contemporary romances of King Arthur's Pentecost gatherings. Gunther is put forth as an ideal sovereign who increases the honor of his court by inviting and hosting important guests from far and wide.

34. Women were carefully managed by the court as important assets to be paraded in front of men, thereby increasing the court's value as a center of joy and beauty. Women and girls were generally confined to their living quarters, or certain parts of the castle, at most times and

[278] The king then commanded a hundred men to escort and serve his sister. The men of his household carried their swords aloft. This was the court of Burgundy. [279] Ute could be seen accompanying them in her majesty, and she had chosen at least a hundred beautiful women as her escort, all of them dressed in the most expensive finery. Many lovely girls also followed her daughter. [280] They could be seen emerging from one of the inner rooms. Men began to press forward in the hopes of catching a glimpse of beautiful Kriemhild. [281] The lovely young woman stepped out as does the rosy dawn from behind dark clouds. He who had long kept her in his heart was freed from care when he saw Kriemhild standing there in all her beauty. [282] Precious stones sparkled on her dress. Her rosy color shone divinely, such that no one could recall ever having seen anything so beautiful in all the world. [283] Just as the moon stands out among the stars as its radiance shines through the clouds, so, too, did she now stand out among all other women. The men's spirits were raised by the very sight of her. [284] She was preceded by noble attendants, but the high-spirited knights would not be denied and pressed forward for a better view of the lovely young woman.

Lord Siegfried was joyful and distressed at the same time. [285] He thought to himself, "How can it be that I might love you? It must be a foolish delusion. But if I had to be apart from you, I would rather die." The thought made him first go pale and then bright red. [286] Siegmund's child appeared to others as if he had been painted on parchment by a great master. Everyone agreed: never before had they seen a more handsome man.

[287] Those who were attending to the ladies made everyone clear a path for them, and the crowd of men gave way. Many were overjoyed by their heart's desire. Elegant women appeared in all their finery.

[288] Lord Gernot of Burgundy then spoke: "Gunther, dearest brother of mine, let me give you some advice that I will surely not regret. You should give a sign of service to the one who so willingly served you, here in front of all these warriors. [289] Ask Siegfried to go up to our sister, so that she might greet him. We will always profit from their meeting. She has never greeted a man before, but she should greet him now. This will surely bring the great hero over to our side."

[290] The king's retainers then went to where they found that hero. They said to the warrior from Netherland, "The king gives you permission to appear before him at court. His sister will greet you there. This he does to

---

made a special "showing" only on formal occasions or affairs of state. The potential to enhance a court's reputation was also part of a diplomatic program that would seek to marry women to the most valuable allies. Kriemhild is, of course, the greatest prize, and Siegfried the most desired ally.

honor you." [291] Siegfried's heart jumped for joy. His happiness knew no bounds, now that he was to be allowed to see Ute's daughter.[35]

She greeted Siegfried with virtuous kindness. [292] When she saw the spirited man standing before her, she could see that he was blushing.*

The beautiful girl said, "May you be welcome, Lord Siegfried, brave and noble knight!"

Her greeting made his heart soar all the higher. [293] He bowed before her, she in turn took his hand. Just look how affectionately he walked beside her. They looked at each other lovingly, he and she both, but so that others would not notice. [294] Did he press her fair hand gently as a sign of love? I couldn't say. But I don't think that it didn't happen either. She was quick to show him how much he meant to her. [295] Even compared with the joys of spring and summer, he could not have been happier than at that very moment, when she went with him hand in hand, the one whom he desired above all.

[296] The other men all thought, "Why couldn't I be there in his place, walking next to her the way he does? Or lying next to her? I wouldn't mind that a bit." Never before had any noble warrior courted a noble woman better. [297] No matter where the guests came from, they couldn't take their eyes off of that couple. She was allowed to kiss him, and he had never felt happier in all his life.

[298] The king of Denmark remarked, "Many had to suffer at the hands of Siegfried for that exceptional greeting, and it pains me still. May God prevent that he ever visits my kingdom again."

[299] The way was cleared for beautiful Kriemhild, and she was accompanied ceremoniously on her way to church by many courageous warriors. She was separated then from that handsome man [300] as she went into church, followed by all the women. Kriemhild was dressed so elegantly that the high hopes of many were bound to be disappointed. She was certainly a feast for the eyes. [301] Siegfried could hardly wait for Mass to end. He would always thank his lucky stars that she, the one he held dear in his heart, thought so well of him. He had every reason to cherish someone so beautiful. [302] After she followed Siegfried out of the church, he was invited to walk with her again. It was only now that the lovely girl thanked him for having fought so valiantly at the head of so many great warriors.

[303] "May God reward you, Lord Siegfried," the beautiful girl said, "that you have won such trust among the other warriors, as I have heard them say."

---

35. Siegfried is allowed a moment of joy without sorrow (*liep âne leit*), something the reader would have recognized as temporary, since we have been told on several occasions already that the two go hand in hand, most recently in str. 284,4.

He then looked at Lady Kriemhild with love in his eyes. [304] "I will always be at their service," he said. "And I will not rest as long as I live if I can do their bidding. This I do, Lady Kriemhild, to win your favor." [305] Day after day for twelve entire days he could be seen in the company of that praiseworthy young woman, whenever she was obliged to appear at court. Siegfried was allowed to be with her out of everyone's great affection for him.

[306] Every day in front of Gunther's hall, people could be seen enjoying themselves and having fun. The noise that some of the brave warriors made, inside and outside, was incredible. Ortwin and Hagen were putting on a great show. [307] Whatever sport was tried, those two spirited heroes played with gusto. The guests were full of praise for these two, and that brought fame to Gunther's land. [308] Those who had been wounded were getting up and going out. They, too, wanted to engage in competitions with others, to parry with their shields and to throw spears. They had a lot of strong supporters in that crowd, [309] and the lord of the land made sure that they had nothing but the best at mealtimes. He made sure to avoid anything that would have brought a king shame, and he was seen to be always friendly as he gathered with his guests.

[310] He said, "Dear knights, before you depart from here, please accept my gifts, and I will always be in your debt. I will gladly share my wealth with you, if it is not too little in your eyes."

[311] The Danes were quick to speak up. "Before we ride home to our own lands, we would like to secure a peace. We are obligated to do so, since we have lost many of our dear friends at the hands of your warriors." [312] Liudegast had recovered from his wounds, and the ruler of the Saxons was also now in good health, but they had to leave some of their dead there in that land.

King Gunther went to find Siegfried. [313] He said to him, "Tell me what I should do. Our enemies want to ride home early tomorrow and have requested that we guarantee a lasting peace. Give me your counsel, Siegfried. What do you think is best? [314] I will tell you the terms they have proposed. They have offered all the gold that five hundred pack horses can carry if I let them go."

Then mighty Siegfried answered, "It would be wrong to accept their offer. [315] Let them go without payment. And let them pledge with handshakes that they will never again invade your lands."

[316] "I will follow your advice," and with that they parted. Their enemies were informed that no one would take the gold that they had offered. The battle-weary men were sorely missed by their families at home.

[317] Countless shields were loaded up with gold and carried to where it was distributed to the king's supporters without even weighing it first. Each

received at least five hundred marks or more.[36] Bold Gernot had given Gunther this advice. [318] They requested their leave, as they all wanted to go home. The guests then went before Kriemhild and then to where Queen Ute was seated. Never had men been given leave so graciously. [319] The lodgings were emptied as they rode away, while the king and all his household, along with many noble men, stayed home at the royal court. They were seen visiting Lady Kriemhild every day.

[320] Siegfried, that brave hero, wanted to take his leave as well. He had lost all hope that he would achieve what he had set his mind to. The king heard that he wanted to leave, but young Giselher was the one who kept him from going. [321] "Where do you want to ride to, noble Siegfried? Stay here with the leaders of the court, with Gunther, the king, and also with his men. Please grant me this request. There are so many beautiful women here; you can meet any of them you like."

[322] Then mighty Siegfried commanded, "Leave the horses where they are! I wanted to leave, but now I will not. And take the shields back. I intended to go home, but Lord Giselher has changed my mind with his great friendship." [323] And so the brave hero stayed out of love for his friends. Nowhere else in the world did he have it so good. The reason is that he was now able to see Kriemhild every day. [324] He stayed on account of her immeasurable beauty. They all occupied their time with various entertainments, but his love for her held him captive and caused him pain. Because of that love the hero would later most miserably lose his life.[37]

[325] Stories were being told of beautiful women beyond the Rhine. Gunther, the good king, was determined to win one of them for his own. His spirits were raised by the very thought.*

---

36. This is clearly an exaggeration, since it would amount to something like four thousand ounces of gold, using the earlier calculation for Kriemhild's messenger gift, or two hundred fifty pounds per person. The amount seems arbitrary but meant to heighten the sense of Gunther's largesse, a key component of his reputation and honor. Only a decade or so before the composition of the *Nibelungenlied*, Richard the Lionheart was captured and subsequently ransomed (1192–94) upon his return to Europe following the Third Crusade. The astronomical sum of one hundred fifty thousand marks in silver was demanded by Henry VI, the emperor of the Holy Roman Empire, for his release, a sum said to be the equivalent of two to three years' annual income for the English crown. The amount was roughly equivalent to thirty-five tons of silver.

37. Siegfried is under love's (*minne*) spell, and while his love for Kriemhild would seem to conform to many of the popular notions of courtly love, with its unfulfilled desire, hope for eventual success, and joy/sorrow dichotomy, the Burgundian lords know how to use Kriemhild as the prize in a very real game of power politics.

6. Gunther Travels to Iceland

[326] There once was a queen who ruled beyond the sea.[38] There was no one like her anywhere as far as anyone knew. She was beautiful beyond compare, and her strength was amazing. She would contend with mighty warriors for her love in spear-throwing contests. [327] She could also hurl a stone great distances and leap just as far. Whoever wanted to gain her love had to win all three challenges against that noble woman. If he failed in even one, he would pay with his head. [328] This woman had already defeated countless opponents.

This story reached a handsome knight on the Rhine.[39] He could think of nothing else except that woman. This was later to be the cause of many a hero's death.* [329] The ruler on the Rhine said, "I intend to sail down to the sea and travel to Brunhild, to see how I might fare. I will risk my life to win her love: she will either become my wife, or I will die trying."

[330] Siegfried responded, "I would advise against that. This queen plays a terrifying game, and whoever tries to win her love puts himself in grave danger. I would advise that you abandon your plans for this voyage."*

[331] Hagen spoke up: "I would then advise that you ask Siegfried to share this burden with you. Since he seems to know so much about Brunhild, that's what I think would be best."

[332] The king asked, "Dear Siegfried, will you help me win her love? If you agree to do this, and if she becomes my wife, then I will in turn risk everything I have for you."

[333] Siegfried, Siegmund's son, replied, "If you will give me your sister, then I will do it. I want no other reward for my efforts than beautiful, noble Kriemhild."

[334] "You have my word," said Gunther. "Give me your hand, Siegfried. If Brunhild returns with me to my lands, then I will give you my sister in marriage. May you then live together with her happily ever after." [335] The great warriors swore oaths on the matter. Their hardships would increase before they could bring that woman back to the Rhine. These courageous men would later suffer greatly for it.*

---

38. This formulaic introduction, similar to the opening of Chapters 1 and 2, is meant to announce the third main character in the story of Burgundian dynastic ambitions. Gunther has decided to cement his own claim to the throne with a wife and the prospect of an eventual heir, and is now in a position to bargain with Siegfried to achieve his goals.

39. Gunther is characterized here not primarily as the sovereign of his land but as a handsome and well-formed knight. His quest will be undertaken as such, not as a journey of conquest more appropriate for a king. His preparations have much in common with those of his guide in this quest, Siegfried, when he came to Worms to win Kriemhild's hand in marriage. Siegfried counsels that Brunhild can only be won if defeated in single combat.

29

[336] Siegfried took his cloak of invisibility with him. He had taken it from Alberich the dwarf with great difficulty. The brave and mighty warriors then prepared themselves for the voyage. [337] When Siegfried wore the cloak, he had the strength of twelve men. He would defeat that remarkable woman with his own craftiness. [338] The cloak also provided the wearer with the power to become invisible. Siegfried used this to defeat Brunhild, but he himself would suffer great harm because of it.

[339] "Now tell me, mighty Siegfried, before my journey begins, would it be honorable to cross the sea to Brunhild's lands with an army? I could quickly have thirty thousand men assembled."

[340] "Regardless of how many men we would bring with us," Siegfried replied, "the queen with her terrifying powers and her pride would kill them all. Let me give you, oh brave one,[40] better counsel. [341] We should travel down the Rhine as lone heroes used to do.[41] I will tell you whom we should take along with us. Only four of us will make the journey to the sea, and we will win the lady, come what may. [342] I will be one of the travelers, you will be the other. The third will be Hagen—we will be well protected—and the fourth will be brave Dancwart. A thousand men wouldn't stand a chance against us."

[343] "I would like to know," said the king, "and I would be pleased to hear it before we leave, what kind of clothes we should wear that would be appropriate to meet Brunhild. This you should tell Gunther."

[344] "In Brunhild's land the custom is always to wear only the very best clothes known to man. We should be wearing the finest garments to meet that lady in order not to be shamed. At least, this is what people say."

[345] Then the king replied, "I will go to my dear mother myself and ask her to have her women make clothes for us that we can wear with honor in front of that noble woman."

[346] Hagen of Troneck then said in a formal tone, "Why do you want to ask your mother to do this? Tell your sister what it is that you intend to do. She will gladly serve you on behalf of this voyage."

---

40. It is difficult not to hear in this description of the king (*degen küene unde guot*) some exaggeration, given Gunther's desire to take a large army. The passage thus takes on a humorous, critical, or even ironic tone. Gunther was perfectly willing to stay at home in the war against the Danes and Saxons, but is now willing to risk life and limb against a woman who kills her suitors rather than submit to their advances.

41. This phrase (*in recken wîse*) defines the journey as heroic, and hearkens back to a time when heroes traveled alone, or in the company of a few trusted companions, to gain fame and honor. Siegfried knows that only a heroic quest can succeed where they are going, where the rules of chivalry and courtly etiquette do not apply. Gunther, on the other hand, still seems completely occupied with his wardrobe so that he can impress his bride-to-be with his wealth and sense of style. This is reinforced when he tells his sister that he and Siegfried intend to travel in the courtly fashion (*höfschen rîten*) as knights (cf. 350,3).

[347] Gunther announced to his sister that he and Siegfried wanted to see her. Before they appeared, she dressed herself splendidly; she was not unhappy to see them both. [348] Her attendants were also dressed as befitted the occasion. When she heard that the two noblemen had arrived, she got up from her seat and greeted the honored guest and her brother most courteously.

[349] "You are welcome, brother mine, and his companion as well. I would love to know," said the young woman, "your intentions in coming here so formally. Please tell me what you two have on your minds."

[350] King Gunther responded, "Dear lady, I will gladly tell you. We have noble intentions but also many concerns. We mean to ride to distant lands, and we will require the best clothing for the journey."

[351] "Dear brother, please be seated," spoke the royal child. "Tell me who these ladies are that you desire to win in far off kingdoms." The lady then took the two by the hand [352] and sat down with both of them where she had been sitting before, on a cushion most costly, I am sure, with beautiful images sewn in gold thread. [353] Siegfried and Kriemhild looked at each other with love in their eyes. He carried her in his heart, and she meant as much to him as life itself. Kriemhild would later become his wife.*

[354] The mighty king said, "My dear sister, we can't succeed without your help. We are looking for adventure in Brunhild's lands, and we will need rich garments to wear in the company of ladies."

[355] The young woman said, "My dear brother, you will see that I am prepared to offer you whatever help I can. If anyone were to deny you anything, that would make me very unhappy. [356] You, noble knight, do not need to be timid in asking anything of me. You should command me as my sovereign. Whatever you may wish, I am ready and will do it gladly," said the lovely young woman.

[357] "Dear sister, we need to have fine clothes. Your royal hand should help to measure them, and your girls can then finish them to order. We must go on this journey."

[358] The young woman replied, "Listen closely to what I say. I have silk material of my own; just make sure that we get jewel-laden shields delivered. That is how we will fashion these garments." Gunther and Siegfried were both ready to do as she asked.

[359] "Who are your companions who will wear these clothes and accompany you to the court?" asked the princess.

Gunther answered, "There will be four of us altogether. Two of my vassals, Dancwart and Hagen, will accompany me to court. [360] Listen to exactly what I tell you, dear lady. I and the other three will need to wear three different outfits on each of the four days. They must be such fine garments that we may leave Brunhild's lands with our heads held high."

[361] The lords bid a fine farewell and left. Kriemhild then commanded that thirty girls should leave their rooms and report to her, but only those who had the skills for that kind of work. [362] The Arabian silks were white as snow, those from prosperous Zazamanc were green as clover.[42] They worked precious stones into those materials and created spectacular garments. Kriemhild, that wonderful young woman, cut the material herself. [363] The furs of strange sea animals were then covered with the silk. People were astonished at what they had made. Listen to the amazing stories about those garments! [364] The best silks from Morocco and from Libya, better than any royal house had owned before, were in great supply. Kriemhild made it clear how much she wished them well. [365] Given the high stakes of the expedition, even ermine was considered an inferior fur. The most expensive silken material, black as coal, was used to cover it. Any mighty hero could still wear such clothes at a grand festival. [366] Countless precious stones shone out from Arabian gold. The women had not a little amount of work to do. They finished the clothing in the space of seven weeks, and the warriors' weapons had been prepared in that same time.

[367] Once provisions had been gathered, a sturdy boat was made ready on the Rhine that would take them down to the sea. The young women were completely exhausted by the work they had accomplished. [368] The warriors were told that the costly clothing they required for the journey was now ready, as they had ordered. Once this was done, they no longer wanted to delay on the banks of the Rhine. [369] A messenger was sent to the voyagers asking if they wanted to see their new clothes and to see if everything fit to perfection. It did, and they thanked the ladies for that. [370] Everyone who saw them had to admit that they had never seen garments so beautiful. They could gladly wear them at any court. No one could ever claim to having seen better knights' attire.

[371] They were not stingy with their thanks, and then the eager heroes took their leave. These knights acted according to chivalry's code.[43] Dry eyes soon became sad and teary.

[372] She said, "My dear brother, please don't go—you can court other ladies here. I think that would be the right thing to do. Here you would not be putting your life at risk. You could find a woman who is just as noble." [373] I believe that their hearts spoke to them about what would happen.

---

42. This name, given in the manuscript C version as the land of Zazamanc, whereas in B it seems to refer to a town, is interesting because it appears here for the first time and later appears in Wolfram von Eschenbach's *Parzival* as the name of Queen Belacane's homeland in Africa. This would provide some evidence that Wolfram knew the C version of the *Nibelungenlied*, at least this part, and that he lifted an exotic-sounding Arabian name for his own story.

43. The heroes continue to straddle the conventions of solitary heroic quest and chivalric enterprise. Here they exhibit educated and courtly behavior (*ritterlîchen zühten*).

They all cried, regardless of what anybody could say. The gold worn around their necks was dulled by tears that poured out of everyone's eyes.

[374] She said, "Lord Siegfried, by your faith and grace, please watch over my dear brother so that nothing happens to him in Brunhild's lands." The courageous man swore to Kriemhild that he would, and gave her his hand.

[375] The mighty warrior said, "As long as I am alive, you need not have any worries. I will return him alive and well back here to the Rhine. Of this you may be assured." The beautiful young woman bowed before him.

[376] Their golden shields were carried down to the shore along with all the rest of their gear. They asked for their horses, as they were ready to ride. All the beautiful women broke down and cried. [377] The young girls were all standing in the windows. A strong wind stirred the sails of their boat, and the proud warriors went down to the river and boarded.

King Gunther asked, "Who will captain this boat?"

[378] "I will," replied Siegfried. "I can guide you safely from here on the water, rest assured. I know all these waterways."

They left Burgundy in high spirits. [379] Siegfried took hold of the rudder and shoved off from shore. Bold Gunther also took turns at the rudder, and the praiseworthy knights were soon leaving their country behind them. [380] They had taken along plenty of provisions and good wine, the best that could be found on the Rhine. Their horses were well cared for, and the men were comfortable. Their boat sailed smoothly, and there were no mishaps of any kind. [381] The strong rigging was stretching in the wind, and they sailed twenty miles toward the sea before it grew dark. Their great efforts would later bring only harm to those spirited men. [382] By the twelfth morning, so we heard it said, the winds had driven them far toward Isenstein in Brunhild's lands. No one except Siegfried knew where they were.*

[383] When King Gunther saw all the castles and expansive countryside, he immediately said, "Tell me, Siegfried my friend, are these castles and this spacious land familiar to you?"*

[384] Siegfried answered, "I know it all very well. These are Brunhild's people and lands. And this is Isenstein, the fortress, as you have heard me tell. You will see many beautiful women there before the day is through. [385] And I advise you heroes to be of one mind and stick to the same story. That seems to me the best strategy. If we get to see Brunhild already today, we will need to be careful in front of the queen. [386] When we see that beautiful woman in front of her retinue, then you famous heroes should say the same thing: that Gunther is my lord, and I am his vassal. He will then be able to achieve all of his goals."*

[387] They were prepared to promise anything that Siegfried asked of them. Motivated by their overconfidence they said what he wanted them

to.[44] This worked out to their advantage when King Gunther came face to face with Brunhild.

[388] "I am saying this out of love for your beautiful sister more than for you. She means as much to me as my soul, as my very own life. I will gladly serve so that she can become my wife."

7. Gunther Arrives in Iceland

[389] In the meantime, their ship had sailed close enough to the castle so that the king could see attractive women standing above in the windows. Gunther was sorry that he didn't know who they were. [390] He asked Siegfried, his companion, "Do you know anything about the young women who are looking down on us here on the water? Whoever their lord may be, they all certainly appear to be very dignified."

[391] Lord Siegfried replied, "Take a look at all of those young women and tell me which one you would have for yourself if you could."

Gunther, a bold and courageous knight, said, "I will gladly do that. [392] I see one standing there in a window in a dress as white as snow. She is so incredibly beautiful that I can't take my eyes off of her. If I had it in my power, I would choose her to be my wife."

[393] "Your eyes have made the right choice. That is noble Brunhild, the virgin queen, the one you long for with all your heart and mind and resolve."[45] Her bearing was most pleasing to Gunther.

[394] The queen ordered all of the ladies away from the windows. They weren't supposed to be standing there in plain view of the strangers, and they did as they were told. We have since also been told what the ladies did next. [395] They readied themselves for the arrival of the strangers, as beautiful women have always done. They went to the narrow portals where they could look out at the heroes without being seen.

[396] There were only four of them who had traveled to that land. Bold Siegfried led one of the horses onto the shore. Beautiful women were looking

---

44. Siegfried's plan will eventually become clear, but here we have the first mention of the so-called rank or class deception, where Siegfried pretends to be Gunther's vassal. Although at first glance a fairly harmless lie, it will have far-reaching repercussions later in the story. To explain the grave nature of this deception, the poet attributes the motivation of the others in going along with it to the by now familiar defect of selfish pride (*übermuot*). There is some disagreement as to the actual meaning of this important passage. I follow Heinzle's (2015, 1139–40) interpretation that the other men's overconfidence or even recklessness motivates them to agree to Siegfried's plan.

45. This, too, is a typical *minne* theme, the eyes finding the most beautiful woman, followed by a longing of all three faculties: the heart, mind, and will, or emotion, reason, and intent (*herze, sin, muot*).

through windows.* King Gunther felt that this increased his own stature. [397] Siegfried held the magnificent horse for him by the reins—the horse was large and strong, a truly wonderful animal—until King Gunther was in the saddle. Siegfried performed this service for the king, something he [Gunther or Siegfried] later completely forgot.[46] [398] Siegfried then went to get his own horse from the boat. Never before had he performed this kind of service, where he held the stirrup for someone else. All of the noble women looking down through the windows were witnesses.[47]

[399] The two heroes had horses and garments equally white as snow, and their shields gleamed in the hands of those glorious men. [400] They rode up to Brunhild's hall with great pageantry. Their saddles were set with gems, their bridles were sleek and decorated with shining reddish golden bells. They had arrived in that land driven by a yearning for adventure, [401] and brought newly made spears and fine swords that reached all the way down to the warriors' spurs. The swords the brave men wore were broad and sharp. Brunhild, that beautiful woman, witnessed it all. [402] Dancwart and Hagen accompanied them. We have heard it said that these two wore impressive clothes that were raven black. Their shields were well made: large, sturdy, and broad. [403] Gems from India sparkled in the clothing they wore. The boat they left on the shore without a guard, and so the courageous men rode together up to the castle.

[404] Eighty-six towers they saw standing within that fortress, along with three large palaces and a great hall made of precious marble, as green as grass. Therein sat Brunhild along with her entourage. [405] The main gateway to the castle was wide open, and Brunhild's men ran to meet the guests who were newly arrived in their lady's land. Their horses were secured, and they were relieved of their shields.

[406] A chamberlain said to them, "Give us your swords and your bright armor."

"You may not have them," replied Hagen of Troneck. "We will hold on to them ourselves." Whereupon Siegfried explained to him what was customary there.

---

46. The text in all manuscripts simply supplies the masculine personal pronoun, so it is grammatically possible to read this as either Gunther or Siegfried who later "forgets" this crucial act. It seems improbable that either would forget such an unusual and consequential moment, but it seems more likely, given what follows, that the reference is to Gunther, who later pretends that he won Brunhild on his own.

47. Holding a lord's horse and stirrup, allowing him to more easily mount or dismount, was a visible sign of feudal vassalage, a ritual mentioned in the early twelfth century in the Charter of Homage and Fealty (dated 1110), between Bernard Atton, Viscount of Carcassonne and Leo, Abbot of the Monastery of St. Mary of Grasse: "And when the abbot shall mount his horse I and my heirs, Viscounts of Carcassonne, and our successors ought to hold the stirrup for the honour of the dominion of St. Mary of Grasse." Source: http://www.castlesandmanorhouses .com/demesnes.htm.

[407] "Let me tell you, it is the custom here in this fortress that strangers may not carry weapons. Let them take them away, that would be the right thing to do." Hagen, Gunther's vassal, very reluctantly gave in.

[408] The command went out to give the guests something to drink and to make them comfortable. Many able warriors could be seen hastening everywhere around the court, dressed in clothing fit for nobility, but all eyes were focused on the adventurers. [409] Lady Brunhild was given the news that unknown warriors had arrived by sea, dressed in the finest garments, and the noble young woman wanted to know more about them.

[410] "I want you to tell me," said the queen, "who these foreign knights are who stand so boldly in my fortress, and for whose sake they traveled all this way."

[411] One of her courtiers spoke up: "My lady, I must admit that I have never seen any of them before. One of them, though, does look a lot like Siegfried. You should definitely greet him accordingly. That would be my faithful counsel. [412] The second one in the group is indeed praiseworthy. He could well be a king if he had authority and power over a large land. He stands among the others as their superior. [413] The third one is fearsome, even if he is very handsome, my queen. His piercing looks, which he casts all around, are terrifying. It seems to me that he has dark thoughts on his mind. [414] The youngest among them is also praiseworthy. The noble man stands at ease and his courteous manners speak of innocence, but we would have reason to be afraid if someone were to do something to him. [415] As courteous and as handsome as he is, I'm sure that he could still cause women to grieve their loved ones if he were provoked. He is complete in his outward appearance and his behavior, a man of courage and daring."

[416] Then the queen said, "Bring me my robes. If Siegfried the bold has come to my land in order to win my love, then he will surely lose his life. I am not worried about becoming his wife."

[417] Brunhild was quickly dressed. She was accompanied by a hundred or more beautiful young women, and she was wonderfully adorned. These lovely women wanted to see the newcomers. [418] The warriors of Iceland, Brunhild's troops, also went along, five hundred and more with their swords drawn. The strangers were alarmed by this, and those brave and confident heroes arose from their seats.

[419] When the queen saw Siegfried, listen to what she had to say. "You are welcome, Siegfried, here in our land. What is the reason for your visit? I am curious to hear your answer."[48]

---

48. By now it is clear that Brunhild recognizes Siegfried on sight and, based on his intimate knowledge of the customs of the land, that he has been here before. There are other stories

[420] "My Lady Brunhild, you are too kind, that you, benevolent princess, should greet me first before this noble warrior, who stands in front of me. He is my lord. I am not worthy of your honor. [421] He was born on the Rhine. What else can I tell you? We have come here on your account, and he is determined to win your love, regardless of the consequences. Think it over—my lord will not leave without you. [422] His name is Gunther, and he is a powerful king. If he can win your love, he will wish for nothing else. This mighty warrior commanded me to come here with him. I could not refuse him, otherwise I would not have come."

[423] She answered, "If he is your lord and you are his vassal, and if he can compete in and win the challenges that I require of him, then I will become his wife. But if I should win, then all of you will pay with your lives."

[424] Hagen of Troneck spoke up, "Dear lady, show us these difficult contests of yours. Before my Lord Gunther would declare himself defeated, hell would have to freeze over. He would gladly compete to win such a beautiful virgin."

[425] "He must hurl a weight and jump the same distance, and then he must compete with me in throwing the javelin. Don't be too hasty! You may well lose both your honor and your heads here. Take your time and think it over," said the lovely woman.

[426] Siegfried the bold approached the king. He told him to tell the queen that he was still resolute. He need not be afraid. "I will be sure to protect you with my skills and tricks."

[427] Then King Gunther said, "Mighty queen, you may challenge me in any way you wish, and even if there were more, I would endure it for the sake of your beauty. I am prepared to risk my life to make you my wife."

[428] As soon as she had heard his reply, she commanded that the contests be prepared, as it was her right. She had a coat of armor brought, chainmail of reddish gold, along with a sturdy shield. [429] The young woman put on a shirt of silk that no weapon had yet been able to touch, made from Libyan material. It was extraordinary. One could see that the edges were finished with delicate, shimmering trim.

[430] All this time the men were being abused with threats. Dancwart and Hagen were nervous, and they were worried about how the king would fare. They thought to themselves, "This voyage is not turning out as planned."

[431] In the meantime Siegfried had gone down to the boat before anyone could notice his absence. There he recovered his cloak of invisibility. He

---

that tell of a previous relationship between the two. She immediately assumes that Siegfried is in charge, given what she knows of his background. Siegfried is anxious to correct this (mis)perception as quickly as possible. He calls Gunther "my lord" twice in short order, and his explanation for his own coming seems forced, all of this while Siegfried addresses Brunhild with the familiar you (*du*) form, something that stands out in the formal situation.

hurriedly wrapped it around him and so became invisible. [432] He quickly returned and saw a multitude of warriors gathered at the place where the queen held her high-stakes contests. He snuck up on them (that was shrewd), and no one there could see him. [433] They formed a ring for the contests, and the competition was to take place in front of many brave warriors who would witness the proceedings. There were more than seven hundred who were armed. They would confirm the winner of the games.[49]

[434] Brunhild arrived on the scene armed as if she were going to battle over all the kingdoms in the world. Over her silk shirt she wore countless golden ringlets. Her lovely skin shone forth in all its beauty. [435] Next her entourage arrived and brought a reddish golden shield with bands of hardened steel. It was broad and large and would protect the lovely woman during the competition. [436] The lady's shield strap was a costly band set with precious gems the color of green grass, and their sparkle competed with the gold. Someone would have to be courageous indeed to gain that lady's favor. [437] As we have been told, the shield under the boss was at least three spans [hands] thick, and this was carried by the maiden. It was made mostly of gold and hardened steel, and her chamberlain could barely carry it with the help of three men.

[438] When Hagen of Troneck saw that shield being carried, he said angrily, "So what now, King Gunther? We will surely all lose our lives. The one whom you hope to love is the devil's bride."

[439] Listen to what I tell you about her wardrobe. She had a large selection to choose from. Her surcoat was of silk from Azagouc,[50] costly and precious and stitched with countless jewels. The queen was radiant. [440] They brought her a large and heavy spear for throwing. It was extremely sharp, thick and strong, and its edges could cut terribly. [441] Listen to this: the spear's weight was made up of three and a half measures [masses] of metal. Three of Brunhild's men could hardly lift it. Noble Gunther began to have his doubts.

[442] He thought to himself, "How is this going to turn out? The devil straight out of hell couldn't survive this. If I were in Burgundy again and still alive, she would have to wait a good while for my love."*

[443] Hagen's brother, brave Dancwart, said, "I regret that we ever came here. We who were always called heroes, just look at how we will die here in this land, defeated by women. [444] I'm sorry that I came to this land. If my brother Hagen had his sword, and I had mine at the ready, then Brunhild's

---

49. The establishment of a ring by the community is an old Germanic custom. Later on it is also employed to witness and validate the engagements of Siegfried and Kriemhild (str. 614) and Giselher to Ruediger's daughter (str. 1683).
50. Azagouc is another place-name found in Wolfram's *Parzival*.

men would be a little less arrogant. [445] You can be sure that they would change their attitude. And even if I had sworn a thousand oaths of peace, that beautiful woman would die before I would let my esteemed lord lose his life."

[446] "We could escape this land without getting caught," said his brother Hagen. "If we had our armor and our trusty swords with us at a time like this, that mighty queen would curb her arrogance."

[447] The noble woman overheard what he had said and glanced over her shoulder with a smirk on her lips. "Since he thinks he's brave enough, then bring them their arms. Let the fighters have their weapons back."*

[448] After their weapons had been returned to them as the queen had commanded, brave Dancwart's face was flush with joy. "Now they can play whatever game they want," said the powerful man. "Gunther is safe now that we have our weapons back."

[449] Brunhild's great strength soon became apparent enough. They brought a heavy stone into the ring—it was extremely large and round. It took something like twelve strong men just to carry it. [450] She usually tossed it after she had thrown her spear. The Burgundians were more than a little uneasy. "Keep your guard up!" exclaimed Hagen. "What kind of woman has the king fallen for? She'll make a fitting bride for the devil in hell!"

[451] She rolled up her sleeves and revealed her white arms. She took her shield into one hand and raised the spear in the other. The fight was on. Gunther and Siegfried had reason to fear Brunhild's battle rage. [452] If Siegfried had not been there to help him, she would certainly have killed the king. Siegfried snuck up quietly and touched him on the hand. Gunther was startled by his ruse.[51]

[453] "Who just touched me?" thought the king. He looked around but couldn't see anyone. His companion whispered, "It's me, your friend Siegfried. You don't need to worry about the queen. [454] Give me your shield, let me carry it, and pay attention to what I tell you. You make the movements, but let me do the work." Gunther was happy to play along once he knew who it was. [455] "Cover my invisibility. Don't let anyone know what's happening. This way the queen can't have her way and brag about defeating you. Just take a look at how unconcerned she stands there."

[456] Then the amazing virgin queen threw her spear with great power and struck the broad new shield which Siegfried was holding in his hand. Sparks burst from the steel as if a gust of wind had blown life into a fire. [457] The hardened tip of the spear crashed through the shield so that sparks flew

---

51. This is Siegfried's second deception, following on the heels of his vassal lie. The entire expedition is characterized by deceit, and this will come back to haunt the heroes. While this all works to their advantage in Iceland, when they return to the courtly environment of Worms, the lies catch up with them.

off of the ringed armor below. That shot caused the two warriors to stagger backwards. If it hadn't been for the cloak, they would have both been dead. [458] Siegfried's mouth was bleeding, but he quickly took a step forward. Then the brave hero took hold of the spear that she had thrown through the shield. Mighty Siegfried sent it right back to where it had come from.

[459] He thought to himself, "I don't want to run her through with it," and so he turned the shaft around and threw the blunt end at her armor, which clanged loudly at the blow. [460] Her chainmail lit up like sparks in the wind. Siegfried had launched the spear with all his strength, and as strong as she was, the impact still threw her to the ground. King Gunther could never have accomplished that.

[461] Beautiful Brunhild, how quickly she recovered. "Gunther, noble knight, many thanks for that throw." She believed that he had managed it with his own strength, but a much stronger man had deceived her. [462] She quickly picked herself up, angry beyond measure. The noble woman raised the huge stone in the air and hurled it a great distance. Then she leaped after it so that her entire armor shook. [463] The stone had landed at least twelve clafters [about twenty-four yards] away.[52] The young woman managed to jump even farther.

Lord Siegfried went up to where the stone had landed. Gunther lifted it up, but Siegfried threw it into the air. [464] Siegfried was bold, very strong, and very tall. He threw the stone farther, and he jumped farther still. With his special powers he even had enough strength to carry King Gunther with him. [465] The jump was completed, and the stone lay on the ground. The only one to be seen, however, was Gunther. Brunhild the beautiful was ablaze with rage. Siegfried had saved King Gunther from certain death.

[466] When she saw that Gunther had landed safely at the end of the ring, she said in a loud voice to her people, "Come here quickly, all my relatives and my vassals! You are now all King Gunther's subjects."

[467] The brave men laid down their weapons and knelt in front of mighty King Gunther of Burgundy. They all believed that he had won the contest with his own strength. [468] He accepted them [or her][53] with grace, since he was a cultured man. The praiseworthy woman took him by the hands and granted him the power to rule her lands. Hagen, that bold and brave warrior, was relieved and happy. [469] She asked the noble knight [Gunther] to accompany her to the great hall. When they arrived, the champions were

52. The *klafter* measurement is generally considered to be the distance between a man's outstretched hands, or something like two meters.
53. The pronoun could refer either to Brunhild herself, or to all of her subjects. The basic meaning remains much the same either way, but again we have Gunther playing the virtuous knight, although he has clearly lied his way to victory; that is to say, the defeat of Brunhild should in no way be accorded with an increase in Gunther's honor.

granted a friendlier welcome. Dancwart and Hagen were happy enough for that.*

[470] Siegfried was both strong and clever.⁵⁴ He returned the cloak to its hiding place and then went back to the hall where the ladies were seated. He shrewdly said to the king, [471] "My lord, what are you waiting for? When is the contest with the queen going to begin? I can't wait to see what kinds of games she has prepared." That shrewd man pretended that he knew nothing.

[472] The queen said, "How could it be, Lord Siegfried, that you failed to watch the contest? Gunther was the winner."

Hagen of Burgundy answered her question. [473] He said, "My lady, we were feeling unwelcomed, and so brave Siegfried went down to the boat while you were beaten by the sovereign from the Rhine. That's why he doesn't know anything."

[474] "I'm glad to hear," said Siegfried, "that your pride has been laid low, and that there is someone still alive who is your master. Now, dear woman, you are obliged to accompany us to the Rhine."

[475] The beautiful one spoke, "That is not possible without the approval of my kin and my vassals. I can't leave my land so easily until my most trusted counselors have been gathered together." [476] She commanded that messengers ride out across the land. She called her supporters, kin, and vassals together and told them to come to Isenstein without delay. They were all given precious clothing. [477] They started arriving in groups at Brunhild's castle at all hours of the day.

Hagen complained, "What in the world are we doing here?⁵⁵ We're just sitting around waiting for her to gather her men together. [478] They're all coming here with their troops. We don't know what the queen's intentions are. What if she's so angry that she wants to kill us? This noble virgin may be the death of us yet."

[479] Bold Siegfried spoke, "I'll make sure that doesn't happen. Whatever you're concerned about, I'll make sure to prevent it. I'm going to bring the best warriors into this land to help us. You've never seen these troops before. [480] Don't ask where I'm going, but I'm leaving. May God preserve your honor in the meantime. I'll come back as soon as I can with a thousand men, the best warriors that I know."

[481] "Don't be gone too long," said the king. "We're in dire need of your help."

Siegfried replied, "I'll be back in a few days. Tell Brunhild that you sent me out."

---

54. Siegfried has both heroic qualities: brains and brawn. He is like Odysseus in that he can think his way out of danger rather than just rely on brute strength.

55. The original exclamation (*jârâjâ*) is untranslatable, but means something like, "yeah, yeah . . .".

41

8. Siegfried Travels to Nibelungenland

[482] Siegfried then left, and wearing his cloak went down to the port on the shore where he found a boat. Siegmund's child stepped into the boat completely unseen and quickly took the boat out, as if the wind were propelling it. [483] No one saw the captain. The boat moved on ahead, driven by Siegfried's strength to the point that it seemed as if a gale force wind was behind it. But it was Siegfried, Sieglinde's child.

[484] Over the course of a day and after a full night, he arrived with great effort in a land at least a hundred *raster* [about two hundred miles] away. The people there were called Nibelungen, where he kept his great treasure.* [485] The lone hero steered toward a broad coastline, where the mighty knight quickly secured the boat and went up to a castle that stood on a hill. There he asked for lodging, as travelers are accustomed to doing. [486] He came up to the gate, which was closed. They were concerned for their safety, as people still are today. The stranger began to knock at the gate, which was well guarded. He could see standing inside [487] a giant of a man who guarded the castle, with his weapons next to him at the ready.

He called out, "Who is pounding on the gate?"

Lord Siegfried answered by changing his voice. [488] He said, "I am a foreign warrior![56] Open the gate! I'll make many here wish they could have stayed in their warm beds if I'm provoked."

The gatekeeper was angered by Siegfried's reply. [489] The bold giant armed himself and put his helmet on. The huge man quickly picked up his shield and threw open the gate. He rushed at Siegfried with fury. [490] How did he dare to wake up so many brave men? He landed hard blows as the mighty foreigner protected himself with his shield. The gatekeeper was able to shatter the shield [491] with an iron staff. The hero was put to the test. Siegfried was in considerable danger and even began to fear the possibility of death as the gatekeeper kept beating him so severely. Siegfried admired him for that, since he was, after all, his sovereign. [492] The battle was so fierce that the entire castle echoed with the sound. The noise could even be heard in Nibelung's hall. Siegfried finally defeated the gatekeeper and restrained him. This story was told throughout Nibelungenland.

[493] The tough fighting was heard at the other end of the mountain by the wild dwarf Alberich. He quickly armed himself and ran to where he found the noble foreigner and the shackled giant. [494] Alberich was furious,

56. Rather than simply identify himself as the ruler of the land, Siegfried continues to delight in deception. He calls himself a lone warrior (*recke*), and so reverts to his identity traveling as a solitary hero (*in recken wîse*).

and he was certainly very strong. He was wearing chainmail armor and a helmet, and he held in his hand a heavy golden flail. He ran as fast as he could until he reached Siegfried. [495] There were seven metal balls hanging down in the front of his weapon, and with these he beat the bold man's shield so hard that it fell apart in pieces. The mighty foreigner feared for his life. [496] The shield had completely disintegrated, and he threw what little was left away. He then put his long sword back in its sheath. After all, he didn't want to kill his chamberlain with it. He acted according to his courtly upbringing. [497] He ran at Alberich with his bare hands and grabbed the old man by the beard. Siegfried pulled so hard that he let out a scream. Alberich felt the pain of the young hero's grasp.[57]

[498] The bold dwarf yelled out, "Don't kill me! I would gladly serve you to save my life," said the cunning man.[58] "But I have already sworn an oath that makes me the vassal of another warrior." [499] Siegfried bound Alberich as he had the giant. They both felt the pain of Siegfried's strength.

The dwarf asked, "What is your name?"

"My name is Siegfried," he replied. "I thought you would have recognized me by now."

[500] "That's welcome news indeed," said Alberich the dwarf. "Now I've experienced the combat skills and strength that give you the right to be ruler of this land. I will do anything you command if you let me live."

[501] Lord Siegfried spoke, "You can go immediately and bring me the best warriors that we have, a thousand Nibelungen are to report to me." He didn't tell anyone why he needed them. [502] He freed Alberich and the giant, and Alberich quickly went to where he found the warriors.

He nervously woke the men of Nibelungen and said, "Let's go, you mighty warriors! Siegfried needs you." [503] They all jumped up out of their beds and were quickly ready to go. A thousand well-equipped knights went to where they found Siegfried. Courteous greetings were exchanged in word and gesture. [504] Many candles were lit, and spiced wine was served.

Siegfried thanked them all for coming so quickly and said, "You will all accompany me across the sea." The brave and mighty warriors were ready to go. [505] At least three thousand knights had been assembled, and from these the best one thousand were selected. Their helmets and the rest of their armor were delivered to them since Siegfried intended to take them to Brunhild's lands.

---

57. There is a well-known play on words here that is difficult to translate. Alberich is pained both by Siegfried's upbringing (*zuht*), which here demands that he not use his sword but rather his bare hands, and his pulling, or tearing (*zuht*) of Alberich's beard.

58. Alberich is described with the same attribute of cunning (*list*) that his lord displays. This seems to be an important quality in mythic realms.

[506] He said, "Brave knights, this is what I have to say: you shall be wearing costly attire when we go to court. Since many beautiful women will be watching us, you should wear the very best clothing."*

[507] Early in the morning they departed, and what courageous companions Siegfried had with him. They had the best horses, as well as valuable wardrobes, and they arrived in Brunhild's lands as was appropriate for knights. [508] Beautiful young women were standing on the walls. The queen asked, "Does anyone know who those men are that I see sailing from across the sea? Their ships have beautiful sails, whiter than the snow."

[509] The king from the Rhine answered, "Those are my men. When I arrived, I had them wait for me not far from here. I have called for them, and now, my lady, they have arrived." The striking foreigners were scrutinized closely. [510] Siegfried could be seen standing in the prow of one of the ships, along with many other men, wearing the most luxurious attire.

Then the queen said, "Sire, please tell me, should I welcome these foreigners or should I not greet them?"

[511] He said, "You should go to meet them in front of the palace, so that they can see that they are welcome." The queen then did what the king commanded. She greeted Siegfried differently from all the others.[59]

[512] They were provided with lodgings and their equipment was stowed for them. So many foreigners had entered the land that they were crowded together wherever they went. The men would have liked to go home at that point.*

[513] The queen said, "I would be grateful if someone would distribute my silver and gold among the king's and my guests. I have more than enough of it."

Dancwart, noble Giselher's man, answered, [514] "My dear queen, let me take responsibility for the keys. I will distribute it all in such a way," said the bold warrior, "that any disgrace that might result will be mine alone." It soon became obvious that he was generous to a fault. [515] After Hagen's brother took over the keys to the treasury, he handed out some incredibly expensive gifts. Whoever asked for a mark was given so much that all the poor could have lived happily. [516] He gave away at least one hundred pounds worth, although he wasn't counting. Many left the hall wearing garments the likes of which they had never seen before. The queen was informed of this, and she sorely regretted it.

[517] The noble lady spoke, "Sire, I would gladly refrain from having your chamberlain leave me without any clothing. He's giving away all my gold,

---

59. The original is somewhat confusing, although the double meaning may be intentional. Siegfried is greeted differently, somehow, by Brunhild, and this can mean either that he is greeted particularly well, or that he is not greeted well at all.

and I would be forever grateful if somebody could put a stop to it. [518] He's giving such extravagant gifts—does he think I have a death wish? I would like to continue to have and use well what my father left me." A queen had never before found such a generous chamberlain.

[519] Hagen of Troneck said, "Lady, you should know that the king from the Rhine has so much gold and clothing to give away that we hardly need to take any of your wardrobe with us."

[520] The queen replied, "No, please, allow me to fill twenty chests with gold and silk that I can distribute with my own hands once we arrive in Gunther's land." [521] Precious gems were loaded into the chests, under the supervision of her own chamberlains, since she didn't trust Gunther's men to do it. Gunther and Hagen had a good laugh about that.[60]

[522] Then the queen said, "To whom should I entrust my lands? Both of us must give them a trustee."

The noble king replied, "Tell whomever you wish to appear, and we shall make him ruler."

[523] One of her most noble relatives was alongside her, her mother's brother. The lady said to him, "May my castles and all the land now be subject to you." They then prepared themselves for the journey and rode down to the shore.[61]* [525] She took eighty-six ladies with her, along with another one hundred young women, all of whom were very beautiful. They did not delay any longer and wanted to be on their way. Those they left behind broke down and cried. [526] She left her own country with her head held high. Those of her family and friends who were gathered there she kissed, and after heartfelt farewells, they departed across the sea. That lady never again set foot in her father's land.

[527] During the voyage, there were plenty of noisy games and entertainment. They had a good wind behind them, and they left the land with great joy. [528] Brunhild refused to sleep with her lord during the trip. This entertainment[62] was postponed until they got home to the castle of Worms and to a proper festival, which they would attend along with their knights.

---

60. This is one of the rare instances of explicit humor in the text. Gunther and Hagen seem to be having a laugh at Brunhild's expense. The humor is hard to follow, but the joke may simply be that Brunhild is worried about keeping control of her wealth. She is clearly intent on retaining some semblance of power, to be derived from gift giving in Burgundy. In any case, the laughter seems to emphasize Gunther's arrogance, something Hagen is already well known for.
61. Heinzle's edition skips strophe 524. Manuscripts A and B do not have this strophe (rendered as an addition in the C version), and it is possible that the scribe skipped over his source's copy because both strophes end with the same line ("and rode down to the shore").
62. Another pun, using a euphemism for sex, indicates in a humorous way that not all is well on the "love boat" and in Gunther's relationship with his bride. By rights the marriage could already be consummated after public approval and recognition of the betrothal by the two households.

9. Siegfried Goes Ahead to Worms

[529] After they had been traveling for nine days, Hagen of Troneck said, "Listen to what I have to say. We have delayed too long with bringing the news to Worms on the Rhine. Your messengers should already be in Burgundy."

[530] King Gunther responded, "You have spoken correctly. No one would be better suited for this mission than you, my friend, Lord Hagen. Go now and ride to my lands! No one can report of my adventure better than you can."

[531] Hagen answered, "I'm not a suitable messenger. Let me be the chamberlain here on board. I'll stay with the ladies and watch out for their wardrobes until we've delivered them to Burgundy. [532] Ask Siegfried to carry the message. He can deliver it best, given his great strength. If he refuses to go, then ask him nicely for the sake of your sister and as a friend."

[533] Gunther called for the warrior to come, which he did promptly. Gunther said, "Since we are getting close to home, it would be right to send out messengers to my dear sister and my mother, to tell them that we are approaching the Rhine. [534] I ask that you do this, Siegfried. Please do as I wish, and I will be forever grateful to you," said the noble warrior.

At first bold Siegfried declined until the king implored him. [535] He said, "You should go for my sake, but also for Kriemhild, that beautiful girl. I'm sure both of us will show our gratitude." When Siegfried heard that, he was quickly persuaded.

[536] "Command whatever you like, it will be done. I will gladly undertake anything for the sake of that beautiful girl. How could I deny anything to the one I hold in my heart? Whatever you command will be done."

[537] "Tell my mother, Ute, the queen, that we are in high spirits on this journey. Tell my brothers how we have fared. You should make sure that our supporters all hear what happened. [538] You should also give my regards to my dear sister, and Brunhild's, too. This you should pass on to her and also to the household and all of my vassals. I have accomplished everything that my heart set out to do. [539] And tell Ortwin, my dear nephew, that he should arrange at Worms for seating on the banks of the Rhine. And also tell my other relatives that I intend to celebrate a great wedding festival with Brunhild. [540] And finally, tell my sister that as soon as she hears that I have arrived with my guests, she should make arrangements for the reception of my beloved bride. I will be forever grateful to Kriemhild for that."

[541] Siegfried soon took his leave of Lady Brunhild and her supporters, as was proper, and rode on to the Rhine. There was no better emissary in all the world. [542] He rode to Worms accompanied by twenty-four warriors. When it was reported that he was arriving without the king, the court reacted with dismay. They feared that their lord had been killed far from home.

46

[543] They dismounted from their horses and were in high spirits. Giselher, the young prince, and his brother Gernot were quickly on the spot.

As soon as he saw that King Gunther was not among them, he said, [544] "You are welcome, Siegfried. Tell me where you have left my brother, the king. I fear that Brunhild's strength has taken him from us. In that case her noble love would be our great loss."[63]

[545] "Your fears are groundless. You and his other relatives are sent greetings by my dear brother in arms. I left him in the best of health. He sent me to you as his emissary to deliver news to your land. [546] You should quickly arrange for me to see the queen and your sister. I must give them the message that Gunther and Brunhild send. They are both in excellent spirits."

[547] Young Giselher said, "You may go to them immediately. You will bring great joy to my sister. She is very worried about our brother. She will be glad to see you, you have my word."

[548] Siegfried replied, "I am glad to serve her faithfully in any way I can. Who will tell the ladies that I intend to visit?"

Noble Giselher took the message to them. [549] Brave Giselher said to his mother and to his sister when he saw them together, "Siegfried, the hero from Netherland, has arrived. My brother Gunther has sent him here to us on the Rhine. [550] He brings us news about the king. You should give him permission to come before you, and he will tell you all that occurred there in Iceland."

The noble ladies were still very worried about what had happened. [551] They quickly looked to dress themselves appropriately and then asked that Siegfried appear before them. This he did most willingly, since he was so anxious to see them. Kriemhild spoke to him kindly.

[552] "You are most welcome, Lord Siegfried, famous knight. Where is my brother Gunther, the mighty king? I fear that we have lost him to Brunhild's power. Poor girl that I am, I curse the day that I was born!"

[553] The brave knight said, "I am happy to ask for my reward as emissary. My dear ladies, you cry for no reason. I left him in perfect health. This is what I have to report. They sent me to both of you with this message. [554] He and his bride offer you their greetings in brotherly love, my dear princess. Please, stop crying. They are very nearby." She had not received such welcome news in a long time.

[555] She wiped away her tears with the folds of her snow-white dress and began to thank the messenger for the report he had brought her. She no longer had any cause for tears or sadness. [556] She asked the messenger to be seated, which he did gladly. The lovely woman spoke, "It would be a great

---

63. The expedition is again cast in terms of courtly love (*hôhe minne*).

pleasure for me to give you my gold as your reward. But you are much too rich for that. I will always be grateful to you."

[557] "And if I had thirty lands all for myself," he said, "I would still happily accept any gift from your hands."

The virtuous woman replied, "Then let it be so." She commanded the chamberlain to retrieve the messenger's reward. [558] Twenty-four golden armbands, inlaid with precious gems, were her emissary's gift to him. The hero was reluctant to keep them and so gave them immediately to those of her closest supporters who were in the room. [559] Her mother graciously offered her services as well.

"I am tasked to bring you news," said the bold man, "that Gunther has a request of you when he arrives on the Rhine. If you can fulfill his wish, my lady, he would be forever grateful. [560] He told me that his noble guests should be well received and asked that you travel to meet them on the riverbanks before Worms. The king asks this of you in all sincerity."

[561] Lovely Kriemhild replied, "I am most happy to comply. I will serve him in any way I can, nothing will be denied. It will be done with love and devotion."

She began to turn red out of happiness. [562] A royal emissary had never been better received. If she had dared to kiss him, the lady would have gladly done so. He graciously took leave from the ladies there. The Burgundians then accomplished what Siegfried had told them. [563] Sindolt and Hunolt and Rumolt had their work cut out for them in setting up a reception area on the riverbanks near Worms—the court officials were kept busy enough. [564] Ortwin and Gere did not hesitate to send out calls for their supporters to gather, and they told them of the festival that was to be held. Pretty young women were busy making themselves ready. [565] The walls of the palace were hung with tapestries, and Gunther's hall was furnished with additional benches for the expected guests. This great festival was full of happy beginnings.

[566] Families related to the three sovereigns rode from all four corners of the kingdom. They were to form the vanguard to receive the arriving party, and many fine garments were taken out of their wrappings. [567] It was soon reported that Brunhild's entourage was on the march, which caused a great commotion among the people of Burgundy. What great warriors were seen on both sides!

[568] Kriemhild said, "All of you girls who will be part of the receiving party along with me, take the very best dresses out of the wardrobes. The foreigners will praise and honor us for this."

[569] Soon the knights arrived, carrying red-golden saddles for the ladies who were to ride from Worms to the shores of the Rhine. There was no better saddlery to be had anywhere. [570] How the gold gleamed upon their

palfreys, whose harnesses were covered with precious gems. Golden footstools were set on precious silken blankets for the ladies, who were in the best of spirits. [571] The gentle horses for the noble young ladies stood at the ready in the courtyard, as I have already told you. The horses could be seen wearing narrow breastgirths, made of silk material better than anyone could describe to you.

[572] There were sixty-eight ladies seen coming out wearing head coverings, and they paraded in their shimmering dresses to go meet Kriemhild. Many unmarried young women followed in their finest: [573] fifty-four from all of Burgundy.[64] They were the highest born of all, with fair hair and glimmering hair bands. The king's wishes had been fulfilled with great zeal. [574] Everyone who was going to be seen by those foreign warriors was wearing the most expensive materials available, and their garments were well suited to their own beauty. You would have to be an idiot to find fault with any of them. [575] People saw many dresses lined with furs and silks, and arms and hands were well adorned with rings and bracelets. It's impossible to describe how much work went into all this. [576] Busy hands wrapped many costly and long belts around gleaming waists dressed in silks from Arabia. The noble young women were full of joy and anticipation. [577] Beautiful young women were lovingly strapped into their dresses. They would have been disappointed if their fair skin didn't shine out from their clothing. No royal house today can boast of such a beautiful court.[65] [578] After the lovely ladies were dressed and ready, their escorts soon arrived. There were many bold knights present, carrying shields and spears.

10. Brunhild's Reception in Worms

[579] On the other side of the Rhine the king and his retinue could be seen riding toward the shore. People also saw many young women being led on their horses. The entire reception party was at the ready. [580] Those from Iceland and Siegfried's men from Nibelungen were in ships and with much effort arrived at the far shore, where the king's followers were waiting.

[581] Now listen to the story of how mighty Queen Ute led the women from the town down to the shore. Many knights and young women came

---

64. The distinction between married and unmarried women here is clear. Married women, the ladies, must wear head coverings (wimples) to hide their hair, unmarried young women (maidens) can show off their hair and decorate it with flowers, garlands, and bejeweled headbands.
65. The court's, and therefore the sovereign's, honor is represented through the beauty of its membership, both male and female. Here the parade of women is meant to showcase the sophistication, wealth, and good taste of the ruling house, all characterized as beauty, both to the eye of the beholder as well as in the descriptive powers of the narrator.

together there. [582] Duke Gere led Kriemhild on her horse up to the castle gate, and from there bold Siegfried was in attendance. She was a beautiful young woman, and he was well rewarded by the princess for that service later on. [583] Bold Ortwin rode alongside Queen Ute, accompanied by a large contingent of knights and young women. I can assure you that so many ladies had never before taken part in such a reception. [584] The noble knights played at one jousting game after another in front of Kriemhild all the way down to the ships; it would have been a shame if it had been otherwise. There the ladies were lifted off their horses.

[585] The king and many of his noble guests had by now come ashore, and still strong lances were being broken in front of the ladies. The din of shields colliding could be heard everywhere. What a noise those costly shield buckles made! [586] The lovely ladies were standing at the pier as Gunther and his guests disembarked from the ships. He himself led Brunhild by the hand. Precious gems and costly garments were shining, each one more so than the other.

[587] Kriemhild approached with great courtesy to greet Brunhild and her entourage.⁶⁶ As they both kissed, girls with fair hands adjusted the garlands in their hair, a gesture of courtliness. [588] Kriemhild, the young woman, then spoke politely, "You are most welcome to us here in this land, to me and my mother, and to all who are our faithful supporters." They bowed in turn. [589] The ladies embraced each other most lovingly. Such a warm welcome had not been seen before as these two ladies welcomed the new bride. Queen Ute and her daughter kissed her again and again. [590] After all of Brunhild's ladies had set foot on land, they were lovingly taken by the hand by strong warriors, and the beautiful women of Burgundy stood arrayed before Brunhild. [591] The reception went on and on as many a red mouth was kissed, and still the two royal daughters stood together. The knights were all happy to witness it.

[592] Those who heard tell of this had to see it with their own eyes and agreed that they had never seen anything so beautiful as these two women in all their lives. It was not a lie. No one could see anything of them that was not as nature intended.* [593] Those who knew a thing or two about beautiful women were full of praise for Gunther's wife. The more experienced who had observed them closely gave Kriemhild the edge over Brunhild in beauty.

---

66. The entire scene at the shores of the Rhine is characterized by courtly protocol (*zuht*), and the women, both Kriemhild and Ute, seem to be responsible for much of the production during the greeting ceremony that is meant to outwardly display Burgundy's cultural sophistication. Brunhild is welcomed by the women of the court, as she will soon take up her position as the head of the female household.

[594] Women young and old came together. Attractive women were on display there in front of the tents and pavilions that filled the fields below Worms. [595] The king's relatives all pressed closer. Brunhild and Kriemhild and all the other women were asked to remove themselves from there and find some shade, and they were escorted away by the warriors of Burgundy. [596] In the meantime, the guests had also mounted their horses. What followed were many vigorous jousts against strong shields. Dust started to cover the field as if it had been set on fire. Heroes soon proved their worth there. [597] Many of the girls observed what they were doing. I believe that Siegfried and his men rode through the columns again and again in front of the tents. He led a thousand courageous men, all of them Nibelungen.

[598] Hagen of Troneck then appeared and, as the king had commanded, kindly asked that the games come to an end, so as to keep the dust off of the pretty young women. The guests were glad to comply.

[599] Lord Gernot spoke, "Let the horses rest until it cools down. Then we'll escort the ladies down to the great hall, and you'll all be ready to mount up when the king commands it."

[600] When the martial games had come to an end across the entire field, the knights retired to the tents for entertainment to see the ladies, hoping for even greater amusement. There they spent some time until they were ready to leave. [601] As the sun was setting and evening approached, it began to cool off, and the waiting was over. Men and women began to make their way to the town. Glances followed shapely female figures. [602] Brave knights on horseback rode around practically wearing out their clothes, as high-spirited men did in that country, until the king himself dismounted in front of the great hall. Then the men turned their attention to help the ladies, as high-spirited knights should.

[603] There the two mighty queens also had to part company. Lady Ute and her daughter retired with their entourage into a large room. All around one could hear joyful noises. [604] The seating was properly arranged, and the king went to eat with his guests. Brunhild could be seen standing next to him as she wore her crown there in that land, and it was an exceedingly precious one at that. [605] Several high seats were set up along with long, wide tables, loaded with food and drink, as we were told. Whatever they wanted, it was not lacking. People saw many honorable guests sitting with the king. [606] The host's chamberlains carried in the water bowls of red gold. It would be pointless for anyone to tell you that any noble festival had been better served. I certainly wouldn't believe it.

[607] Before the ruler of the Rhineland had washed his hands, Lord Siegfried did what was his good right. He reminded the king what he had in good faith promised him before he had brought Brunhild home from Iceland. [608] He said, "I would like to remind you that you raised your hand and

51

swore to me that if Queen Brunhild were to return with you to your lands, then you would give me your sister. Is your oath still valid? I took on risks and dangers on your behalf."[67]

[609] The king replied to his guest, "You have rightly reminded me of my promise. My hand will not be raised to swear false oaths. I will arrange it as best I can."

Kriemhild was told to appear before the king. [610] She arrived in the hall along with her young ladies. Giselher came bounding down the stairs: "Tell all these girls to go away. Only my sister shall appear before the king." [611] Kriemhild was then brought in to see the king. Alongside him stood noble knights from many different lands, and they were commanded to remain there in the great hall. Queen Brunhild had already arrived at the table.*

[612] King Gunther spoke, "My dear sister, with your own goodness you can fulfill a pledge I made. I promised you to a knight, and if he becomes your husband, then you will have done my will with great faithfulness."

[613] The noble maiden replied, "My dear brother, you don't need to plead with me. I will always do as you command. Whatever it is, it shall be done. I will gladly accept whomever you, Lord, have chosen to be my husband."

[614] Siegfried turned red as she gazed at him, and he pledged his service to Lady Kriemhild. They were told to enter a circle that the others had formed, where she was asked if she would have that noble man. [615] She was embarrassed as a young woman should be, but Siegfried's happiness and well-being were complete when she did not hesitate to accept. He, the noble king of Netherland, for his part also promised to take her as his wife. [616] After they had pledged themselves to each other, Siegfried gladly took that lovely woman into his arms. Then Kriemhild was kissed in front of many great warriors.[68]

[617] The supporters then spread out, after which Siegfried and Kriemhild took their seats opposite the king and were hailed by their vassals. The Nibelungen went up to where Siegfried was sitting. [618] The king had taken his seat alongside Brunhild. She looked over and saw Kriemhild sitting close to Siegfried and began to cry. She had never before felt such pain. Hot tears ran over her rosy cheeks.

[619] The ruler of the land spoke up: "My dear lady, why are your bright eyes clouded by tears? You will soon be happy enough. My lands and towns and powerful men will all be your subjects."

---

67. Siegfried's efforts (*arbeit*) are those that would lead a knight to expect a reward under the rules of courtly *minne*.

68. Only the B manuscript has "by" (*von*) heroes, which would mean that she was then kissed in turn by those most important and high-ranking nobles present. All other manuscripts read "in front of" (*vor*), which would accord best with the practice of concluding the betrothal ceremony with a public kiss, still common practice in western marriage ceremonies.

[620] "I have every reason to be crying," the beautiful maiden said. "My heart is broken on account of your sister. I see her sitting next to a man who is your own vassal.[69] It causes me great pain to see her so debased."

[621] King Gunther then spoke, "You can stop worrying about that. I will explain everything some other time, why I gave my sister to Siegfried. She will be forever happy with him, I'm sure."

[622] She replied, "I am sorry for her beauty and her courtesy. If I could, and knew where to go, I would run away. If you don't tell me how it is that Kriemhild is Siegfried's wife, I will never sleep with you!"

[623] The noble king said, "I will tell you exactly how it is. He has towns and great lands as many as I have, of this you can be certain. He is a mighty king. That is why I gave him my sister as his wife."[70]

[624] Regardless of what the king told her, she was still miserable. Many knights soon ran from their tables to engage in jousting games until the castle echoed with the noise. The king was getting tired of his guests. [625] He thought it would be better if he could be sleeping with his wife. His heart told him that she could love him, and he began to look affectionately at Brunhild.

[626] The guests were asked to quit their games of chivalry. The king wanted to go to bed with his wife. Kriemhild and Brunhild encountered each other on the steps outside the hall. There was as yet no hatred between the two.* [627] Their entourages came rushing out behind them, and their noble attendants brought them both lanterns. The two kings' knights split up at that point, and many of the warriors could be seen following Siegfried.

[628] Both of the noble lords arrived in their own bedrooms, where they each thought about winning love's victory over their charming ladies. They were happy at the prospect, and Siegfried's enjoyment was beyond measure. [629] As Siegfried lay with Kriemhild and held the woman tenderly in love's embrace, his life became one with hers. He would not have wanted a thousand other women in her place.*

[630] I don't want to tell you more about what he did with that lady. Listen instead to how Gunther, that exemplary fighter, lay with Brunhild. He had slept with other women much more satisfyingly before. [631] His attendants had departed, both men and women, and the door to the

---

69. The fact that Kriemhild is seated next to a man already implies that something is wrong. As an unmarried woman, she would not be allowed to sit next to a man not in her immediate family, much less someone of lower rank. Siegfried is identified by Brunhild as a retainer (*eigenholde*), a legal term for vassalage, although the word is only attested in the *Nibelungenlied* here and once more in str. 803,3.

70. Gunther must essentially admit that he lied to Brunhild in order to explain that Siegfried is indeed worthy of marrying Kriemhild. Either way, Gunther loses.

bedroom was closed. He imagined how he would enjoy her beautiful body, but it was to take some time yet before she became his wife.[71] [632] She came to bed wearing a nightshirt made of whitest linen cloth. The noble knight thought to himself, "Now I have everything that I have ever wished for in my life." He couldn't help but appreciate her great beauty. [633] The noble king put out the lights as he went to bed, where he found her waiting. He lay right next to her, full of joyful anticipation, as he closed his arms around that lovely woman. [634] He was ready to love her tenderly if noble Brunhild would have allowed it, but he was shocked at how angry she was. He thought he would find an agreeable partner, instead he was confronted with hostility.

[635] She said, "My dear knight, let it be. What you were hoping for is not going to happen. You can rest assured that I'm going to stay a virgin until I've heard the whole story."

Gunther was furious at her. [636] He forced himself on her and tore her nightgown, but that remarkable women in turn grabbed a belt, a strong band that she wore around her waist. She made the king suffer with it. [637] She tied up his feet and his hands, carried him to a nail protruding from the wall, and hung him on it for disturbing her sleep. Sex was out of the question. In fact, she nearly killed him, she was that strong.

[638] Then the one who thought he should be the master began to plead. "My dear queen, please let me loose! I know that I can never get the better of you, dear lady, and I promise I'll never lie so closely beside you again."

[639] She didn't care how uncomfortable he was. She was perfectly comfortable in bed, and so he hung there all night until the morning light shone through the window.[72] If he had ever had any strength, there was no sign of it now.*

[640] The maiden asked, "Tell me now, Lord Gunther, wouldn't it be humiliating if your chamberlains found you had been tied up by a woman?"

The noble knight replied, "You would pay dearly for that. [641] But I would gain little honor, to say the least," said the great man. "By your own goodness, please let me down. Since you reject my love so strongly, I will never again lay a finger on your gown."

[642] She soon had him untied and took him down from the wall. He climbed back into bed with her and lay down so far away from her that there

---

71. The consummation of the marriage was necessary as the final legal act that bound the two people, and their lands, in matrimony, and would hopefully eventually produce an heir.
72. As Hatto, 1965, and others have pointed out, this is a reference to the typical *alba*, or dawn song, in which daybreak warns the lovers that they must part or be discovered. Wolfram von Eschenbach's famous poem, *Sîne klâwen*, dramatizes this scene in the opening lines as the sun breaks through the window, threatening with its "claws."

was no danger that he would touch any part of her nightgown. She wouldn't have allowed it in any case.

[643] Their attendants came in and brought them fresh clothing, which they wore that morning. Everyone was in a good mood except the lord of the land, who was disheartened even though he was to wear his crown that day. [644] As was their custom and according to their laws, Gunther and Brunhild went without delay to church, where Mass was being sung. Siegfried joined them there along with a great crowd of people. [645] Befitting the king's honor, everything that they needed was prepared for them there, their crowns and their robes. After being blessed, all four of them were seen happily wearing their crowns.

[646] Many young men were knighted there, six hundred and more, all to honor the king. This is without a doubt true. The land of Burgundy was filled with joy throughout, and the newly minted knights were soon breaking lances loudly. [647] Pretty young women were sitting in the windows, where they could see shields gleaming in the light. The king had already parted from his men. People could see that the king was depressed regardless of what everybody else was doing.

[648] Siegfried and he were in very different moods. The noble knight knew exactly what the matter was, and he went up to the king and asked him, "How did it go last night? I'd really like to know what happened."

[649] The host spoke to his guest, "I have nothing but shame and loss since I brought that devil into my house. When I wanted to make love to her, she tied me up. She carried me and hung me high up on a nail in the wall. [650] That's where I was left hanging the entire night until morning, when she finally untied me. And she was lying all the while as comfortably as can be. I ask you to help me as my friend."

Mighty Siegfried replied, "I'm really sorry to hear that. [651] I'll prove it to you as long as you don't hold it against me. I'll make sure that she lies close to you tonight and never again will deny you her love." Given what he had suffered, Gunther was glad to hear these words.*

[652] Lord Siegfried said, "You'll be fine. Apparently our nights were very different. Your sister Kriemhild means more to me than life itself. Lady Brunhild will become your wife this very night." [653] He continued, "I'm going to slip into your bedroom tonight wearing my cloak. That way no one will be the wiser, just be sure to send your attendants away for the night. [654] I'll put out the lamp that the servants are holding so that you'll know I'm there and ready to help. Then I'll subdue your wife so that you can have your way with her, or I'll die trying."

[655] "As long as you don't sleep with her yourself," said the king, "then I'm agreed. Do whatever it takes. And even if she happens not to survive, I'll find a way to get over it. She really is a terrifying woman!"

[656] Siegfried replied, "I promise that I won't sleep with her. Your dear sister is more important to me than any other woman I've ever known." King Gunther had faith in Siegfried's pledge.

[657] The jousting games produced both winners and losers. The fighting and noise were brought to a complete halt when the ladies were supposed to go down to the great hall. The attendants made everyone stand aside and get out of the way, and [658] the courtyard was cleared of horses and people. The two queens were each escorted by a bishop as they approached the two kings sitting at the high table. Many valiant men followed to take their seats.

[659] The king had high hopes as he sat there, as he thought about what Siegfried had promised. This one day seemed to him like thirty. All he could think about was his lady's affection, and [660] he could hardly wait for dinner to be over. Beautiful Brunhild, and Lady Kriemhild too, were taken to their respective bedrooms. It was amazing how many strong knights could be seen there in front of the kings.

[661] Lord Siegfried sat affectionately with his wife, completely content and without a care, and she in turn held his hands in hers. Then he disappeared. She wasn't sure how or when. [662] Just as she was touching him, he vanished. The queen said to her attendants, "I have no idea where the king just disappeared to. Who took his hands out of mine?"

[663] She stopped her questioning. He had gone to where the attendants were all standing with their lamps. He took each one of them out of their hands, and Gunther realized that Siegfried was there. [664] Siegfried knew exactly what he was going to do. He sent all the women away, went to lock the door himself, and hurriedly put two strong crossbars in place. [665] He quickly stashed the lamps under the bed. Mighty Siegfried and that beautiful maiden then engaged in a relentless contest. King Gunther was pleased and worried at the same time.

[666] Siegfried lay down very close to the young woman. She said, "Gunther, don't try anything if you don't want to suffer like last night." The lady was starting to hurt Siegfried.

[667] But he stayed completely silent and didn't say a word, so that she wouldn't recognize him. Although he couldn't see a thing, Gunther could hear that the two of them were not doing anything covertly. They really didn't have much pleasure in bed. [668] Siegfried pretended that he was Gunther, the mighty king, and embraced the maiden in his arms, but she threw him out of the bed and onto a bench nearby. His head smacked into a stool with a loud thump. [669] The powerful man quickly jumped back up. He wasn't going to quit so easily, but when he tried to force her down, he paid a painful price. I don't think that any other woman could have defended herself so well.

[670] When he wouldn't give up, the maiden jumped out of bed. "You tore my white gown. You'll be sorry for being such an oaf. I'll make you pay."

[671] She grabbed the great warrior in a bear hug, intending to tie him up as she had the king, so that she could go back to bed and have some peace and quiet. He paid a heavy toll for ruining her gown. [672] What good was his great strength now? She showed him who was stronger. She carried him by force—there was nothing he could do—and jammed him forcefully in between the wall and a cabinet.

[673] "Oh no," thought the warrior, "am I going to be killed by a woman? From now on all women will treat their husbands with barefaced contempt, something they wouldn't have done before."[73]

[674] The king heard all of it and was afraid for Siegfried's life, but Siegfried was ashamed and became enraged. He defended himself with superhuman strength, but it took everything he had to overcome Brunhild.* [675] The king thought it was taking a long time for Siegfried to finally overpower her. She squeezed his hands so intensely that blood spurted from his fingertips. The hero was in considerable pain, but he was eventually able to get the better of that powerful woman [676] so that she had to give up her original intentions. The king heard everything, even though Siegfried said not a word. He pushed her down on the bed, and she began to scream. His strength inflicted great pain on her. [677] She reached down to her waist, where she knew the belt to be. She wanted to tie him up with it, but he grabbed her with his hands so that every joint and tendon cracked. That decided the contest, and she became Gunther's wife.

[678] She said, "Dear king, please let me live. I will atone for what I did to you. I won't resist you anymore. You've proven to me that you know how to handle a woman."

[679] Siegfried stepped aside and left the maiden lying there, as if he was going to get undressed. He took a small gold ring from her finger without the noble queen noticing. [680] He also took her belt, which was a finely made strap. I don't know if it was his pride that made him do it.[74] He later gave it to his wife, and he came to regret that.

Gunther and his beautiful bride then consummated their marriage. [681] He had sex with her, which was his right, and she was forced to abandon her anger and her humiliation. She became pale and weak after they had finished.

---

73. Siegfried seems to imagine himself as responsible for ensuring the continued legal, social, and physical dominance of men over women. In truth, men were very much the legal custodians of "their" women and this included the right to physically assault and discipline women for their (mis)behavior, something that Kriemhild comes to experience later at the hands of her husband.

74. The term used here to describe Siegfried's moment of exuberance (*hôher muot*) is not the same as the pride displayed by Hagen and Gunther, but it does seem an unnecessarily egotistical act to take away these souvenirs of his conquest. They will certainly lead to trouble later on, since Siegfried so carelessly, or thoughtlessly, gives them as gifts to Kriemhild.

Amazingly her strength vanished after she lost her virginity. [682] She was no stronger than any other woman. He affectionately caressed her beautiful body. Even if she had tried to resist, what good would it have done? Gunther had changed all that once he slept with her.[75]

[683] She lay with him tenderly and lovingly until the morning light. Lord Siegfried had left some time ago to return to his own wife, who greeted him affectionately. [684] He refused to answer any questions that she might have had, and the gifts he had brought were kept a secret for a long time, until she had taken the crown in his own land. What he was meant to give her, he gave gladly.[76]

[685] In the morning the lord of the land was in a much better mood than the day before. As a result everyone in the entire country shared in his joy, and whoever became his guest was well taken care of. [686] The festivities lasted fourteen days, and the noise from all the different kinds of entertainment never ceased. The costs that the king incurred were considered to be very high indeed. [687] The king's relatives were commanded to give gifts of clothing and red gold, horses, and silver to complete strangers in order to increase his honor. Whoever asked for anything went away happy. [688] Siegfried, the Lord of Netherland, along with a thousand of his men, gave away everything that they had brought with them to the Rhine, all their clothing and equipment, and all their horses and their saddles. They really knew how to live extravagantly. [689] All the gift giving took so long that those who were ready to go home became restless. Guests had never before been treated so well. And so the festival finally came to an end, as Gunther instructed.

11. Siegfried Takes Kriemhild Home

[690] After the guests had all gone, Siegmund's child spoke to his followers. "We should also get ready to return home."

His wife was glad to hear the news. [691] She said to her husband, "When will we be leaving? I want to avoid leaving too hurriedly, since my brothers will first have to divide up their lands with me." Siegfried was unhappy when Kriemhild told him this.

---

75. The legendary strength attached to virgin warriors has a long history. Again, the supernatural and heroic world temporarily intrudes on the Burgundian court, and the woman Gunther previously described as the devil is now as weak and docile as all women at court are expected to be.

76. This line is filled with ambiguity, meant at once to imply that Siegfried and Kriemhild's sex life was healthy and vigorous, but also to hint at the fateful role that his gifts of the ring and belt were to play; that is to say, he had very little trouble giving her what he should not.

[692] The three lords went to him and all spoke with one voice, "Please be assured, Lord Siegfried, that we will support you faithfully until our dying day." He bowed to them in recognition of their kind offer.

[693] "We are also obliged to share with you," said young Giselher, "lands and towns that we rule, along with the vast territories under our control. You and Kriemhild should have your portion of these."

[694] After he had heard and witnessed their kind offer, the son of Siegmund replied to those nobles, "May God always bless your birthright and your people. My dear wife will not [695] accept the portion that you want to give her. She will have her own crown, and if I have anything to say about it, she will certainly be wealthier than anyone else alive. I remain at your service, however, in any other way."

[696] Lady Kriemhild then said, "Even if you want to decline a part of the inheritance, it's not as simple as that where Burgundy's warriors are concerned. A king would have good reason to take them with him back to his homeland. My dear brothers should give us our part of the fighting force."

[697] Lord Gernot then spoke up, "You can take whomever you like. You will certainly find many here who will gladly go with you. Out of three thousand we'll give you a thousand men who can form your court guard." Kriemhild immediately sent for [698] Hagen of Troneck and also for Ortwin, to inquire if they and their families wanted to serve her.

Hagen became furious at the very thought. He said, "Gunther can't give us away to just anyone. [699] You can take your other followers with you, but you know how we from Troneck are. We have to stay here at court with our three lords. We will continue to serve those whom we have always served."[77]

[700] They left things as they were and prepared to depart. Kriemhild had her courtly entourage join her, thirty-two young women in all along with five hundred men. Count Eckewart joined Siegfried's followers.* [701] They all took their leave, knights and squires alike, girls and women, as it was right and proper. With abundant kisses they soon parted and left Gunther's lands with joyful hearts. [702] Their relatives accompanied them a good distance on the journey. Their quarters were arranged for them every night, as they wished, throughout the king's lands. Messengers were quickly sent off to Siegmund, [703] so that he and his wife Sieglinde would know that their son was on his way home, along with Queen Ute's child, beautiful Kriemhild, traveling from Worms along the Rhine. The news could not have made them happier.

---

77. The complications of feudal vassalage come to the fore in this section. While Kriemhild is entitled to a share of land, property, and followers, it is her husband who has the final say in accepting these. Although Hagen and his clan of Troneck are vassals of the house of Burgundy, they apparently have a right to decide whom they serve.

[704] "I am blessed," said Siegmund, "that I have lived long enough to see Kriemhild crowned here. All my lands are honored by this. My son will himself be crowned king."

[705] The noble Sieglinde gave out much red silk, silver, and heavy gold as a reward for the envoys. She was extremely pleased by the news they brought, and her entourage hurried to dress themselves as was fitting. [706] The news included who would accompany Siegfried into their lands. They ordered that proper seats be prepared immediately, and to these he would process in front of his men once he was crowned. King Siegmund's men rode out to greet them. [707] If anyone has ever been better received than these famous heroes in Siegmund's lands, then I don't know about it. Sieglinde the beautiful rode out to meet Kriemhild with many fine ladies, followed by handsome knights. [708] It took a day's journey to meet up with the guests. It was a hardship for locals and strangers alike until they reached a large town, which was called Xanten, where they were to be crowned.

[709] Sieglinde and Siegmund joyfully kissed Kriemhild again and again, and Siegfried, too. All their sorrows had come to an end. All their followers were likewise heartily welcome. [710] The guests were led to Siegmund's great hall. The pretty young women were lifted up from their horses, and lots of men were gathered there as the young women were busily attended to. [711] As grand as the festival on the Rhine had been, the heroes here were given even better wardrobes, better than any they had ever worn before. Their wealth was legendary, [712] as was evidenced by their high honor and wondrous possessions. Their supporters wore golden clothing, adorned with pearls and precious stones. Sieglinde, the noble queen, paid close attention to their needs.

[713] King Siegmund spoke in front of his followers, "I proclaim to all of Siegfried's clan that among these warriors he shall wear my crown." Those from Netherland were happy to hear this. [714] Siegmund handed over to him his authority, crown, and properties. He was the ruler of all who appeared before him, and where he sat in judgment, all feared the man who was Kriemhild's husband. [715] In truth he lived in great honor and ruled as king for ten years, at which time that noble lady bore him a son. This was the fulfillment of all the royal family's hopes and dreams. [716] He was quickly baptized and given the name Gunther, after his uncle. It was a name he could be proud of, and if he grew up to be like his relatives, that would serve him well. He was raised with great devotion, as was right and proper.

[717] At around the same time, Queen Sieglinde died. Kriemhild, noble Ute's child, then gained all authority over the land, as it befitted such a powerful woman. Many people mourned the loss of Sieglinde, their queen.

[718] We heard it said that beautiful Brunhild also bore Gunther, the powerful, a son there in Burgundy on the Rhine. Out of love for that hero, he was named Siegfried. [719] He was doted on and watched over with great care. Noble Gunther entrusted him to relatives who knew how to raise him to be a virtuous man. Fate was to rob him of many of his family.

[720] Stories were constantly being told about how praiseworthy were the lives of those warriors that lived in Siegmund's lands. Gunther and his famous clan did likewise. [721] The land of the Nibelungen was subject to Siegfried. Never had anyone of his kin been more powerful. He was served by all the warriors of Nibelungen along with the treasure that had belonged to the two kings.* This may have been why the keen hero was so self-assured and confident.[78] [722] The greatest treasure that any hero had ever won now belonged to Siegfried, as it had to those who held it before him. He won it on the side of a mountain with his own hands and had to kill many brave knights in the process. [723] He was held in the highest esteem, but even without winning the treasure, people would have had to say that he was the best man who ever mounted a steed. They were afraid of his great strength, as they had every reason to be.

12. Siegfried and Kriemhild Are Invited to Return

[724] This whole time Gunther's wife was thinking to herself, "Why does Kriemhild hold her head so high? Her husband Siegfried is our vassal. He hasn't attended to us for a long time." [725] She carried this notion around with her and kept it from everyone. She was irritated that they had not come to visit and that she had received no fealty from Siegfried's lands.* She especially wanted to know the reason for this absence. [726] Brunhild tried to persuade the king to have Kriemhild come to visit her. She told him in confidence what was in her heart, but the king was not pleased by what he heard.

[727] "How could we get them to come here to our lands?" the king asked. "It's not possible. They live much too far away. I wouldn't want to ask them for such a favor."

Brunhild answered him cleverly, [728] "No matter how rich a man may be, if he is a king's vassal, then he has to obey what his lord commands him to do."

---

78. This is the appropriate attitude (*hôher muot*) that a king should display, not the negative, self-aggrandizing quality (*übermuot*) of someone who has forgotten that fortune's wheel turns for all.

Gunther smiled when he heard this. As often as Siegfried had been by his side, he had never considered it to be any kind of service.

[729] She said, "My dear lord, out of love for me, please help me convince Siegfried and your sister to come visit us here in our lands. I have no greater desire than this. [730] Your sister's courtesy and her manner make me happy just thinking about it. I remember how we sat together when we were first married. Siegfried can consider himself honored to be married to her."*

[731] She kept on asking until the king finally said, "You should know that there is no one I would rather have as guests. You don't need to keep asking. I will send out my messengers to the both of them and ask them to visit us on the Rhine."

[732] The queen replied, "Tell me, please, when you plan to send out your envoys or when you want our dear friends to arrive here. Let me know whom you will send."

[733] "That I will do," said the king. "I will send thirty of my men." He had them come to him and instructed them to carry his message to Siegfried's lands. To their delight, Brunhild gave them a most exquisite wardrobe.

[734] King Gunther went on to say, "Men, I want you to tell Siegfried and my sister from me—and be certain not to leave anything out—that no one in the world is more beholden to them than I. [735] And ask most kindly that they come visit us here on the Rhine. The queen and I will always be in their debt. He and his men should come before the next solstice to be greeted by many who hold him in the highest regard. [736] Offer my service to King Siegmund, and say that I and my countrymen will always think fondly of him. And also tell my sister that she must come to see her family. There was never a festival more worth celebrating."

[737] Brunhild and Ute and the other ladies sent their greetings to all the lovely ladies and courageous men there in Siegfried's lands. The envoys then made themselves on their way with the permission of the king's closest advisers. [738] They were well provisioned when they left. As soon as their horses and their equipment had all been provided, they departed. They quickly rode toward their destination, and the king had his emissaries accompanied by his royal guard. [739] In the space of three weeks they arrived in the fortress of the Nibelungen, in the Norwegian march,[79] to where they had been sent. There they found the hero. The envoys' horses were tired from their long journey.

---

79. Norway is not mentioned in C. Siegfried is assumed to have ruled in his father's capital, Xanten, on the Lower Rhine, and the Nibelungen lands are assumed to have been in the distant north, as was Isenstein, Brunhild's capital. The fact that the messengers have to travel this great distance emphasizes the effort necessary to invite the royal couple.

[740] It was reported to Siegfried and Kriemhild that knights had arrived dressed in the Burgundian custom. She leaped up from the bed on which she was resting. [741] She told one of her attendants to go to the window. There she saw bold Gere standing in the courtyard along with the other emissaries who had been sent on that mission. There was no better news to cure her homesickness.

[742] Kriemhild said to the king, "Take a look and see the men who are out in the courtyard with bold Gere. They have surely been sent down the Rhine by my brother Gunther."

Mighty Siegfried declared, "They shall be welcome here."

[743] The entire household ran down to where they were standing. They all greeted the envoys most kindly, as best they could. King Siegmund was especially happy that they had come. [744] Gere and his men were given accommodations, and their horses were stabled. The messengers then went to where King Siegfried and Kriemhild would receive them. They had been given permission to appear at court, which they did.

[745] The ruler of the land and his wife rose as soon as they came in. Gere of Burgundy and his companions, Gunther's men, were well received. Courageous Gere was asked to take a seat.

[746] "Please allow us to deliver our message before we are seated. As tired as we may be, allow us to stand a while longer. We have been directed to convey a message from Gunther and Brunhild, who rule in power and glory. [747] And your mother, Ute, has also given us a message, along with young Giselher and Lord Gernot and the rest of your kin. They have sent us on this mission and send you their humble greetings from Burgundy."

[748] "May God reward them for this," said Siegfried. "I trust in their loyalty and noble intentions, as is fitting where family is concerned. Their sister agrees with me. Tell us what is new and if our dear relatives are in good spirits. [749] Since we left them, has anyone tried to attack them, my kin? You must report the truth. I will always be a loyal defender against their enemies, who will lament my aid."

[750] Margrave Gere, a truly courageous warrior, responded, "They are in fine spirits and live nobly. They invite you to attend a grand festival on the Rhine. They would be very happy to see you again, of this you can be certain, [751] and they request that my lady should accompany you. You should arrive after winter has passed, and before the summer solstice."

Bold Siegfried answered, "That will be very difficult to accomplish."

[752] But Gere of Burgundy said, "Your mother Ute, and Gernot and Giselher beseech you not to deny their request. I hear them complain every day that you are so far away. [753] My Lady Brunhild and all her attendants would be overjoyed if they heard that they would see you again. That would cheer them up." Kriemhild was glad to hear this.

[754] Gere was family.[80] The lord of the land asked him to take a seat. He ordered that the guests be given something to drink, and his command was immediately carried out. Siegmund then joined them, and when he saw the emissaries, the lord addressed the Burgundians as friends.

[755] "You are most welcome, Gunther's men. Since Siegfried, my son, gained Kriemhild as his wife, we should have seen you more often here in this land as a demonstration of your friendship."

[756] They answered that they would gladly come anytime he wanted. They were relieved of their great weariness with excellent hospitality. The envoys were offered comfortable seats and brought something to eat. Siegfried commanded that his guests should not go hungry. [757] They stayed there nine whole days. Finally the eager knights had to complain that they weren't able to go back home. In the meantime, King Siegfried had sent for his followers to join him.*

[758] He asked them for their advice, whether they should travel to the Rhine. "Gunther, my close relative, and his family have invited me to visit them at a festival. I would gladly go, but their land is a great distance away. [759] And they have asked that Kriemhild come along with me. Please tell me, my dear counselors, how can I travel there? If I led an army for them in thirty lands, then Siegfried's hand would gladly be at their service."

[760] His men answered him, "If you want to travel to attend the festival, then we will give you our advice. You should ride to the Rhine with a thousand men, and so you will be assured of being received with honor by the Burgundians."

[761] Lord Siegmund of Netherland then said, "If you want to attend the festival, why didn't you tell me? If you don't mind, I'd like to ride along with you. I will lead a hundred warriors and so contribute to your own force."

[762] "It would make me very happy if you wanted to ride with us, my dear father," said Siegfried. "We will depart in twelve days." Everyone who wanted one was given a horse and all the necessary equipment.

[763] After the noble king had made up his mind to travel, the courageous envoys were told that they could return home. He wanted to let his in-laws on the Rhine know that he wanted very much to join them for their celebration. [764] Siegfried and Kriemhild, as we have heard said, gave the emissaries so much to take with them that their horses couldn't carry it all. Siegfried was an incredibly wealthy man. They cheerfully led their pack animals back home with them.

[765] Siegfried and Siegmund both equipped their own followers. Count Eckewart directed the search for the best women's clothing to be had or

---

80. Gere is a high official of the Burgundian court, but his relation to the ruling family is not spelled out. Here he is described as one of Kriemhild's clan (*sippe*).

acquired in all the land. [766] Saddles were gathered along with shields. Knights and ladies who were to go on the journey were given whatever they needed—they were lacking nothing. Siegfried was going to bring his relatives many noble guests.

[767] The messengers quickly made their way back home, and Gere arrived back in Burgundy. He was heartily welcomed as they dismounted from their horses in front of Gunther's great hall. [768] Young and old alike went to hear the news, as people do.

The brave knight answered, "You'll hear the news just as soon as I've told the king." He went to see Gunther along with his comrades. [769] The king leaped up from his high seat for joy. Brunhild the beautiful thanked them for returning so quickly.

Gunther said to the messenger, "How is Siegfried doing? He has always done a lot for me."

[770] Gere answered, "He and your sister were so happy, you could see it in their faces. Never has a relative received a more loyal and kind greeting than Lord Siegfried and his father send to you."

[771] The noble king's wife then spoke to the margrave, "Tell me, is Kriemhild coming? Is she still as elegant and courtly as she was before?"

Gere answered, "She will certainly be coming."

[772] Ute requested that the envoys come to see her. It was easy to tell from her questions that she was very concerned about Kriemhild's well-being. He told her how she seemed to him and that she was coming very soon. [773] They also told everyone at court about the gifts that they had received from Siegfried. Gold and costly clothing were brought out to show to all the three sovereigns' men, and they were applauded for Siegfried's great generosity.

[774] Hagen spoke up, "He can afford to be generous. He couldn't give it all away if he lived forever. He controls the hoard of the Nibelungen. If only we could get that treasure to Burgundy!"*

[775] The entire court was happy that they were going to come. The king's officers were busy day and night getting ready, preparing many high seats. [776] Hunolt the strong and Sindolt the bold were kept busy. The seneschals and cupbearers had to set up all the furniture for dining. Ortwin helped out in the effort, and Gunther thanked him for that.* [777] Rumolt the kitchen master was in charge of his staff of huge kettles, pots, and pans. There were more than you could count. They all prepared the meals for the guests who would be arriving.*

13. Kriemhild and Siegfried Return to Worms

[778] Let's leave all of their hard work behind us and talk about how Lady Kriemhild and her entourage traveled from the land of the Nibelungen to the Rhine. Never before had horses carried such expensive clothing. [779] Many wardrobe chests were packed for the journey. Siegfried and the queen rode with all their supporters to a place of joy, or so they thought. But it turned out to be a place of great pain and sorrow instead. [780] They left Siegfried's and Kriemhild's little son at home, which they had to do. Their journey to Gunther's court brought him great suffering. The little boy never saw his father or his mother again. [781] Lord Siegmund rode along with them. If he had known what was going to happen at the festival, he surely would not have attended. Nothing worse could ever have befallen him among dear friends.

[782] Messengers were sent out ahead to announce their arrival. Many of Ute's followers and Gunther's men rode out in great multitudes to meet them. The host was concerned with providing his guests a proper welcome.

[783] He went to where he found Brunhild. "Just as my sister welcomed you when you arrived in my lands, so should you receive Siegfried's wife."[81]

[Brunhild replied,] "I am duty bound to do so, for she is dear to me."

[784] The noble king said, "They will be arriving tomorrow morning. If you want to welcome them, then you'll need to get going. We don't want to be waiting for them here in town. I have never before been so anxious to welcome such dear guests."

[785] She immediately commanded her ladies and young women to pick out the best dresses they could find to wear in front of their guests. They were happy to do so, there is no doubt about it. [786] Gunther's men were also quick to do his bidding, and the lord gathered all of his warriors around him. The queen then rode out with great pomp and circumstance. The dear guests were greeted with much fanfare. [787] How the guests were greeted with great joy! It seemed to people that Kriemhild had not greeted Brunhild as well when she arrived in Burgundy. Those who had never seen her before were excited at the prospect. [788] Then Siegfried arrived with his men. The warriors could be seen riding back and forth on the field in large formations. It was impossible to avoid the dust and tumult.

[789] When the lord of the land saw Siegfried and Siegmund, he spoke to them most kindly, "May you and all my kin be welcomed most warmly! Your journey to my court brings me great joy and pride."

---

81. Gunther is making it very clear to Brunhild that both Kriemhild and Siegfried are to be considered their equals, to include sending out a greeting party to meet them before they arrive. The reader must assume that Brunhild either ignores these clear signs or remains ignorant of them for purposes of the conflict to come.

[790] "May God reward you," said Siegmund the honorable. "Ever since my son Siegfried gained you as his family I have wanted to visit you."

King Gunther responded, "That makes me very happy."

[791] Siegfried was received with great honor as suited his rank. No one wished him harm. Giselher and Gernot did their part with their courtly manners. I don't believe that guests were ever better welcomed.

[792] The wives of the two kings rode toward each other. Saddles were emptied of their ladies as men lifted them down to the grass. There were many who did their very best to serve the ladies. [793] The two lovely ladies approached, and the knights were all glad that their greetings were so courteous. Many of the knights stood next to their ladies there. [794] The noble fellowship took one another by the hand, and there were a great many bows and curtseys, and lovely ladies exchanging kisses. Gunther's and Siegfried's men were happy spectators. [795] They didn't stay there for long but rode on into the town. The king had ordered that everyone was to make his guests feel at ease in Burgundy. Many great jousts were carried out in front of the young women.

[796] Hagen of Troneck and Ortwin made it clear that they were in charge, and whatever they ordered was carried out immediately. They took great care to provide the guests with whatever they needed. [797] Shields could be heard being battered by thrusts and blows at the castle gates. The host remained outside the gates for a while with his guests before entering. With all the entertainment the time flew by quickly.

[798] They rode up to the great hall with the ladies. There were many precious and well-made fabrics seen hanging down from the ladies' saddles. Gunther's men arrived next. [799] They were told to escort the guests to their lodgings. From time to time Brunhild could be seen looking at Kriemhild, who was very beautiful. Her skin was radiant as it was set off by the gold of her dress. [800] In every corner of Worms one could hear the people celebrating. Gunther told his marshal, Dancwart, to take good care of them, and he made sure that everyone had a place to stay. [801] Food was served both inside and outside the castle. Foreign guests have never been better cared for. Anything they wanted they were provided. The king was so rich that nothing was denied anyone.

[802] They were served pleasantly, without any resentment. The host sat down to eat with his guests, as Siegfried was shown to his old seat. Many of his strongest men accompanied him to his bench. [803] There were at least twelve hundred warriors surrounding his table. Brunhild, the queen, thought to herself that a vassal could not be any more powerful. At this point she was still favorably inclined to do him no harm. [804] In the evening with the king presiding, many expensive garments were stained with wine as the cupbearers circulated among the tables. They were keen to provide the very best service

67

[805] as was the custom at such great festivities. Ladies and their servants
were then assigned to comfortable bedrooms. Wherever they came from, the
host was concerned for their well-being. They were honored with generous
gifts as well.

[806] As the night came to an end and the new day began, costly garments
embedded with precious stones were taken out of their wardrobes by the
ladies. They were looking for the most luxurious dresses of all. [807] It was
still dawn when many knights and their squires came to the hall. They raised
a noise even before the early Mass was sung for the king. The young knights
showed off their riding, and the king praised them for it. [808] The din of
the trumpets was impressive, and drums and flutes made such a noise that
all of Worms, as big as it was, echoed with the sound. The high-spirited men
were all mounted on their steeds. [809] Outside the town a tournament was
begun with a great many knights. The youngest were filled with excitement.
The knights in their armor were a spectacle for all to see. [810] Beautiful
women and young maidens sat up high in the windows in their best finery, as
they were entertained by the brave men. The lord of the land took part with
his own men.

[811] Time flew by while they were so engaged, but then the bells could be
heard ringing from the cathedral. The horses were led in, and the ladies rode
out. The noble queens were escorted by many brave men. [812] They dis-
mounted on the grass in front of the church. Brunhild was well disposed, still,
toward her guests. They entered the great church wearing their crowns. This
amity was later destroyed, and that came from great envy.[82] [813] After the
Mass they rode back and proceeded to go dine with great courtliness and joy-
fulness. The festivities were blessed with this sense of joy for all of eleven days.*

14. The Queens' Dispute

[814] One evening before vespers, a great commotion broke out among
the warriors there in the castle.[83] They were engaged in contests of knightly

---

82. For the first time we have envy (*nît*) raising its ugly head. The word can also be translated
as hatred. The term describes a mutual feeling in str. 829,4, and in str. 838,2 it expresses
Brunhild's prime motivation. In the C redactor's additional strophes, the devil comes into
play as an instigator of Brunhild's secret envy. Although taxes are mentioned again, it seems
hardly plausible that Brunhild is mostly worried about the state of Burgundy's tax collection.
Rather, she wants to get at the heart of the matter, which is Siegfried's feudal relationship to
her husband, since Gunther's status as the greatest king reflects directly on her own status as
the greatest queen.
83. Vespers is one of the eight canonical hours or offices in a day for prayer set aside in the
monastic rule. It is the hour between none and compline, and would normally, depending on

prowess for fun. Men and women alike went down to have a look. [815] Both of the mighty queens sat there together as they discussed two exemplary warriors.

Beautiful Kriemhild said, "I have a husband who should by rights be lord of all these lands."

[816] Brunhild answered her, "How is that possible? If you and he were the last two people on earth, then he might have some claim to these lands, but as long as Gunther lives, that's just impossible."

[817] Kriemhild continued, "Just take a look at how he stands there, how he shines among his warriors, just like the bright moon among the stars. This is why I am content."

[818] Lady Brunhild said, "As powerful as your husband may be, however noble and handsome, you must still acknowledge that Gunther, your noble brother, is the greatest. He stands above all other kings, of this you should have no doubt."

[819] Kriemhild answered her, "My husband is so mighty that I cannot exaggerate my praise for him. His honor and reputation are great in many ways. You can rest assured, Brunhild, that Siegfried is Gunther's equal in every way."

[820] "Don't take this the wrong way, Kriemhild, but I'm not making this up. When I first saw them, after the king had defeated me, I heard them say, [821] when he won my love in a contest of arms, that he was the king's vassal. I therefore consider him to be in Gunther's service, since I heard him say it myself."

Beautiful Kriemhild replied, "That would make me the butt of a cruel joke. [822] How is it possible that my brothers would have given me to a retainer? My dear Brunhild, please, for my sake I beg you to stop this kind of talk."

[823] "I'm sorry, but I can't," said the king's wife. "Why should I abandon my claim on the service of Siegfried's many brave knights?" This infuriated beautiful Kriemhild.

[824] "You will have to abandon your claim. He will never serve you. He is more powerful than that most noble of men, my brother Gunther. Spare me any more of this nonsense. [825] I have to say I'm surprised, since he is your vassal, and since you apparently have complete power over us, that he has neglected to pay you any taxes. Your arrogance is completely out of place."

[826] "You really are reaching too high," said the king's wife. "I'd like to see who will be shown the most honor, you or me." Both women were furious.

---

the season, be read at about 6 p.m. or sunset. It was also commonly associated with the hour of the evening meal, and the term is still used in southern Germany for a light afternoon snack.

[827] Queen Kriemhild then spoke, "We will see soon enough. You have claimed that my husband is a vassal, but the supporters of both kings will appreciate the truth when I dare to enter the church before the king's wife. [828] Today you will see for yourself that I am a free and noble woman and that my husband is more powerful than yours. No one will blame me for saying so. You will witness this evening how this liege woman [829] makes her appearance before the Burgundian court. I declare that I am more powerful than any queen who has ever worn a crown."[84] Envy and hatred gripped the two women.

[830] Brunhild spoke, "If you don't want to be a liege woman, then you and your entourage will have to make your way to the church separately."

Kriemhild answered, "Rest assured, that's exactly what will happen."

[831] "Girls, put on your finest!" said Siegfried's wife. "My honor is at stake. Let people see what fine dresses you have. Brunhild will have to eat her words."

[832] They were eager to please and looked for their very best garments. Many young women and ladies were well adorned there. Brunhild, the noble king's wife, left with her attendants. Kriemhild was also beautifully outfitted. [833] She was accompanied by forty-three young women who had come with her to the Rhine. They wore precious fabrics made in Arabia, and so the beautiful ladies arrived together at the church. All of Siegfried's men were waiting for them there. [834] People were surprised that the two queens were separated and that they weren't walking together as was their custom. Many a warrior was later to suffer as a result.

[835] Gunther's wife was already standing in front of the church. The knights were enjoying watching the ladies pass by. Lady Kriemhild soon arrived with her large entourage in tow. [836] The dresses that daughters of noble knights wore long ago cannot be compared with what those ladies were wearing. Kriemhild was able to afford more than what thirty other queens put together could muster. [837] What her attendants were wearing was beyond anyone's wildest dreams. Kriemhild made sure of that, just to vex Brunhild.

[838] The two groups ran into each other in front of the great church. Motivated by a great hatred, Brunhild, the queen of the land, commanded Kriemhild to stop. "A liege woman shall never go before the king's wife!"

[839] Beautiful Kriemhild, filled with anger, responded, "It would have been better for you if you had kept still. You have only insulted yourself. How could a concubine[85] ever become the wife of a king?"

---

84. Kriemhild's challenge is to be made public with an open display of hierarchy that the entire court will witness. Such displays are often meant not only to demonstrate fact, but to establish it as well by public acclaim. Brunhild's counterclaim is made in the public sphere as well, since the situation has escalated well beyond a dispute between two individuals.

85. Brunhild's repeated insult, now made in public, of calling Kriemhild an unfree vassal (*eigen*) by virtue of her marriage to Siegfried, is escalated by Kriemhild's rejoinder that

[840] "Who are you calling a concubine?" said the king's wife.

"You," said Kriemhild. "Siegfried, my dear husband, was the first to enjoy your pretty body. My brother was not the one who took your virginity. [841] Were you out of your mind? It must have been an evil trick. How else would you have let your vassal sleep with you? All I hear is you making false accusations."

Brunhild shot back, "Trust me, Gunther will hear about this."

[842] "I couldn't care less. Your arrogant pride has betrayed you. You have publicly claimed that I am your servant. You can rest assured that this hurt cannot be repaired. My loyalty and friendship to you are over."

[843] Brunhild was crying. Without hesitation, Kriemhild entered the church with her attendants before the king's wife. This was the beginning of their great enmity. Her bright eyes were to become dim and misty. [844] Regardless of how heartfelt the prayers or hymns, Brunhild felt as if the service wouldn't end. She had been deeply hurt, and many brave and strong knights would later have to pay for that. [845] Brunhild took her place with her ladies in front of the church. She thought to herself, "I need Kriemhild to tell me more about what she said out loud. If Siegfried bragged to anyone about that, it will cost him his life."

[846] Kriemhild arrived on the scene, accompanied by many strong men. Lady Brunhild said to her, "Wait! You[86] called me a concubine. You'll have to prove that. You should know that your outburst has harmed me."

[847] Lady Kriemhild replied, "You should let me pass. I can prove it with the gold here on my hand. My husband brought it to me after he slept with you."

This was indeed Brunhild's darkest day. [848] She said, "That costly gold ring was stolen from me, and it has been kept hidden from me all this time. I will find out who took it from me." Both women were extremely upset.

Brunhild first had sex with a vassal before being with the king. This is the argument of the lowest common denominator, which is to say, "if I'm a vassal's woman, then you are no better." This is emphasized again in str. 851,4, where Brunhild restates Kriemhild's accusation that she was "Siegfried's woman." The term *kebse*, often glossed in Latin as *concubina*, is translated here as concubine. It has enjoyed great variation in English translations: whore (Edwards, Mowatt, Raffel), harlot (Needler), paramour (Hatto, Lettsom), consort (Lichtenstein), mistress (Ryder), and leman (Lettsom). Regardless, the point that Kriemhild makes is that Brunhild gave herself out of wedlock to a lowly "vassal," Siegfried, and is therefore no better than Kriemhild herself, who gave herself, or was given, to a vassal of Gunther's. The complication, of course, is that Brunhild does not know that Gunther had Siegfried's help in bed, nor does she know that Siegfried bragged to Kriemhild about conquering Brunhild, nor does she know that Siegfried and Gunther lied about their relationship. Either way, the dispute is founded on a web of lies. 86. Brunhild reverts to the formal you (*ihr*) address, a clear sign of their new and estranged relationship. Kriemhild replies in kind with a formal you.

[849] But Kriemhild answered, "Well, I could hardly be the thief. It would have been better had you kept silent, if your honor means anything to you at all. I can prove that I'm telling the truth with this belt that I'm wearing. My Siegfried was your first."

[850] She was wearing a band of silk from Nineveh, set with precious jewels, and it was extremely valuable. When Lady Brunhild saw it, she broke down in tears. Gunther and all the men of Burgundy would hear about that.

[851] Queen Brunhild said, "Tell the ruler of the Rhine to come here. I want him to hear how his sister has shamed me. She has declared publicly that I slept with Siegfried."

[852] The king arrived in the company of his officers and saw that his wife was in tears. He spoke gently, "Tell me, my dear wife, who has done you wrong?"

She answered the king, "I have every reason to be unhappy. [853] Your sister wants to destroy my reputation. I am charging her with declaring that I was her husband Siegfried's concubine."

King Gunther responded, "She is wrong in doing so."

[854] "She is wearing the belt which I lost, and my red-golden ring. I will be sorry that I was ever born if you, King, don't defend me against this great dishonor. Oh King, I will be forever grateful to you for that."*

[855] King Gunther spoke, "Tell him to come here at once. If he has been boasting about this, then the hero from Netherland will have to admit it, or he must deny it publicly." Kriemhild's husband was called to appear.

[856] When Siegfried saw the stern faces, he wondered what had happened. He quickly asked, "Why are these ladies crying? I would like to know. And why did the king send for me?"

[857] King Gunther said, "I am deeply troubled. My wife Brunhild has reported to me that you have been bragging that you were the first to sleep with her. Kriemhild, your wife, has said so."

[858] Bold Siegfried replied, "And if she has been saying this, then she'll be sorry by the time I'm through with her. And I will swear a sacred oath before you and all your men that I have said[87] no such thing."

[859] The king of the Rhine said, "I want proof. If you swear this oath that you offer here and now, then I will declare you innocent of all charges."

The proud Burgundians were told to form a circle. [860] Bold Siegfried raised his hand to swear the oath. The mighty king quickly said, "I am convinced of your[88] innocence, sir. I pronounce you free of any guilt regarding what my sister has claimed. I know you did not do this."

---

87. Most other manuscripts aside from B include "to her" (*irʾz* or *ir*), a small difference, but still of consequence.

88. Formal address is used to denote the legal and impersonal aspects of the oath and judgment.

[861] Siegfried spoke, "I will be sorry indeed if my wife is not punished for insulting Brunhild." The brave knights who were gathered there looked at each other.[89] [862] "Women need to be taught," said Siegfried the warrior, "that they should not engage in idle gossip. You must keep your wife from doing so, and I will do the same. I am ashamed of her misbehavior."

[863] Many women stopped speaking to each other. Brunhild was miserable, and Gunther's court felt sorry for her. Hagen of Troneck went to see his lady and [864] asked her what was bothering her. She was crying when he arrived. She told him the whole story, and he promised her there and then that he would never be content until Kriemhild's husband paid for what he did. [865] Ortwin and Gernot joined the discussion, and the nobles began to plot Siegfried's death. Giselher, Ute's youngest, arrived later, and when he heard what they were talking about, spoke with a loyal heart.

[866] "My dear comrades, why do you talk of this? Siegfried never deserved such enmity that he should have to forfeit his life. It's a fact that women are easily upset."

[867] But Hagen replied, "Are we supposed to just ignore this false friend?[90] There's not much honor for warriors in that. Bragging about being with my dear lady will cost me my life, or him his."

[868] Then the king himself spoke up, "He never did anything that was not good or honorable. He should be allowed to live. What would I gain by being his enemy? He was always loyal and supportive."

[869] Ortwin of Metz spoke next, "His great strength won't help him now. If my lord permits it, I will kill him myself." These heroes declared Siegfried an enemy, without reason.

[870] No one pursued the matter except Hagen, who constantly kept reminding Gunther that if Siegfried were dead, he would rule over all his lands. The king became sullen and dejected. [871] The matter was left at that. There were games and jousts by Siegfried's men, and sharp lances were broken there from the church to the great hall, all of it observed by Siegfried's wife. Gunther's men were apprehensive.

---

89. Various editors and translators have disagreed as to whether this refers to the knights gathered around to witness the proceedings, and the looks would therefore be some kind of acknowledgment of the presence of the court, or that Gunther and Siegfried exchange some sort of meaningful glances (Hatto, 1965,). I have taken the former interpretation for the more likely. There is nothing in the original text that warrants reading anything into the fact that Gunther and Siegfried look at each other at this particular moment.

90. The original term is somewhat difficult to understand, but most think that the term "to raise a cuckoo" (*gouche ziehen*) refers to the propensity of the cuckoo to lay eggs in other nests and then have them raised by unsuspecting hosts, even at the expense of their own offspring. This would mean that Siegfried is an interloper who has falsely insinuated himself into the ruling house of Burgundy and deserves to be expelled, and in this case, killed, for his deception and falsehood.

[872] The king said, "Stop all this talk of murder! His life here only increases our fortune and honor. And besides, he is so powerful that no one could lay a hand on him if he knew about it."

[873] "He won't find out," replied Hagen. "You have to keep this to yourself. I'm sure that I can keep the plot secret and see that Brunhild's tears will be his undoing. He will forever be Hagen's enemy."

[874] King Gunther spoke, "How is that possible?"

Hagen answered, "I will gladly tell you. We will have messengers that no one knows here ride into our lands and declare war. [875] Then you pronounce in front of the strangers that you and your army intend to campaign against them. When that is done, Siegfried will promise to help you. This will seal his death. I'll find out more about him from his wife."*

[876] The king wrongly followed Hagen, his vassal. This act of deceit and disloyalty was planned by these great knights, and no one else found out. The quarrel of two women was to result in the death of many heroes.

15. Plotting Siegfried's Death

[877] Four days later, thirty-two men were seen riding into court. It was announced to mighty Gunther that war had been declared. This deception was later to cause Lady Kriemhild great sorrow. [878] The men were given leave to appear, and they declared that they were Liudeger's men, whom Siegfried had once defeated and brought to Gunther's lands as a hostage. [879] The king greeted the emissaries and asked them to take their seats.

One of them spoke, "Sire, may we be allowed to stand until we have delivered our message to you? You should know that you have many enemies abroad. [880] Liudegast and Liudeger have declared war against you. Long ago you did them grave harm, and they intend to invade your country with an army."

The king became enraged when he heard this message.* [881] The impostors were then sent off to their lodgings. How could Siegfried, or anyone else for that matter, defend himself against their plot? They were themselves later to suffer greatly for it. [882] The king and his fellow conspirators conferred in secret. Hagen of Troneck never let up. There were others among the king's men who would have looked for a peaceful resolution, but Hagen would not give up on his plan.

[883] One day, Siegfried discovered them conferring in secret. The hero from Netherland started by asking, "Why are the king and his men so glum? If anyone has done anything to you, I will gladly help to avenge it."

[884] Lord Gunther replied, "I have every reason to be concerned. Liudegast and Liudeger have declared war and want to invade my lands."

That brave warrior said, "I, Siegfried, [885] will defend your honor at all costs. I will deal with those two the same way I did before. I will lay waste to their towns and lands before I'm through. My life is my pledge. [886] You and your army should remain here at home, and let me ride out against them with my forces. I will prove to you that I am gladly at your service. Rest assured that your enemies will suffer at my hands."

[887] "This is wonderful news," said the king, as if he were truly glad for the assistance. The traitor insincerely bowed down to him.

Lord Siegfried replied, "Don't worry, your problems are over."

[888] The logistics for the campaign were quickly set in motion. They did this openly so that Siegfried and his men could see it. He commanded his troops from Netherland to get ready, and Siegfried's warriors gathered their armor.

[889] Mighty Siegfried said, "My dear father, Siegmund, you should stay here. We will be back on the Rhine soon enough, if God goes with us. Stay here and enjoy the king's company."

[890] They raised their banners and were prepared to ride. Many of Gunther's men were there as well, but they didn't know what was behind it all. They could see that Siegfried had gathered a great force. [891] They secured their helmets and their armor on their horses, as many brave knights prepared themselves. Hagen of Troneck then went to find Kriemhild and asked her for permission to leave. They were ready to depart.

[892] "I am very fortunate," said Kriemhild, "to have a husband who has the courage to defend my family the way that Siegfried is standing up for my kin. I am proud of that," said the queen. [893] "My dear Hagen, please remember that I gladly serve you and have never thought ill of you. Please consider this when dealing with my husband. He should not have to pay for what I did to Brunhild. [894] I'm sorry for that now," said that noble woman. "He beat me because of it, and if I ever said anything that caused her pain, then that brave and noble hero has evened the score."

[895] Hagen replied, "I'm sure that you will be reconciled with her soon enough. Kriemhild, my dear lady, please tell me how I may best serve your husband Siegfried. I am happy to do this for him, my lady, more than anyone else."

[896] "I wouldn't worry," said the noble woman, "that he could be killed in battle, if it weren't for his own recklessness.[91] Otherwise he is completely invincible."

---

91. Siegfried's invulnerability is actually a liability here, because it leads him to take reckless chances. The term is the same pride or arrogance that Hagen displays (*übermuot*), and although this does not equate Siegfried's actions with Hagen's duplicity, they share a sense of overconfidence in their own abilities that ultimately leads to disaster. Siegfried has exhibited this quality in the past, from the moment he set foot in Worms to win Kriemhild to his theft

[897] "Dear lady," said Hagen, "if you think that he might be harmed, then you must let me know how I can prevent that. I will be his constant guard, on horseback and on foot."

[898] She said, "You and I are family. I trust you completely with my husband's life, and that you will protect my dearest." She then confided in him a secret that she had better left unsaid. [899] She continued, "My husband is brave and extremely powerful. When he killed the dragon on the mountain, the hero bathed himself in its blood. Since then no blade can harm him in battle. [900] But I am still worried that, when he goes into battle and the fighters are using all their spears, I might lose my dear husband. I worry about Siegfried all the time. [901] I will tell you in strictest confidence, my dear trusted friend, so that you may continue to be loyal to me. The spot where my dear husband can be wounded I will tell you. I know I can trust you. [902] As the hot blood was flowing from the dragon's wounds, and the brave knight was immersed in it, a leaf from a linden tree fell between his shoulder blades. This is where he can be wounded, and that is the source of my worries."

[903] Hagen of Troneck spoke, "You should sew a small sign on his blouse that will show me where I need to protect him when we are in battle." She thought she would be saving the hero, but instead she had sentenced him to death.

[904] She said, "I will sew a small, discreet cross on his clothing. There is where your hand can shield my husband when you are in the thick of battle and he is facing his enemies."

[905] "I will do that," said Hagen, "my dearest lady."

She thought it would all be for the best for Siegfried. Instead, Kriemhild's husband had been betrayed. Hagen took his leave and went away in the best of spirits.*

[906] The king's man was contented. I don't think that any knight ever committed greater treason than was committed by him, after Kriemhild the queen had confided in him.

[907] The next day, Siegfried rode out with a thousand of his men, completely at ease, thinking that he would be able to avenge the wrong done to his friends. Hagen rode so close to him as to be able to see his shirt. [908] After he had made out the sign there, he had two of his men leave the group secretly. They were to return and report that Gunther's lands would be left in peace, and that Liudeger had sent them to see the king. [909] Siegfried rode back again unhappy at not having been able to avenge the wrong done to his

---

of Brunhild's ring and belt to commemorate his conquest. Kriemhild recognizes that his pride or self-confidence can sometimes get the better of him.

friends. Gunther's men could hardly convince him to turn around. He rode back to the king, who thanked him.

[910] "May God reward you for your efforts, dear Siegfried. The fact that you are so willing to do what I ask puts me forever in your service, as it should. I trust you more than any of my friends. [911] Since the campaign has been called off, I intend to go hunting for bear and boar in the Vosges Mountains, as I have often done before." This was Hagen's idea, that traitor.[92]

[912] "All of my guests should be told that we will ride out early in the morning, and whoever wants to ride out with me should make himself ready. Whoever wants to stay behind can entertain the ladies, which is fine with me as well."

[913] Lord Siegfried then spoke nobly, "If you're going hunting, then I want to go with you. Please loan me a tracker and a couple of dogs, and then I'll ride into the forest."

[914] "If you would like to take more than one," said the king quickly, "then I'd be happy to give you four trackers who know the forest and the trails where animals can be found. They will make sure that you don't return to camp empty handed."

[915] The mighty warrior then went to see his wife. Hagen had quickly told the king how he would be able to defeat the famous knight. This kind of betrayal should be beneath any man.*

16. Siegfried's Murder

[916] Gunther and Hagen, those two daring warriors, deceitfully called for this hunt in the forest. They said they wanted to hunt for boar, bear, and bison with sharp pikes. What could be more enticing? [917] Siegfried accompanied them in grand style, and they had plenty of provisions along with them. It was at a cool spring that he was to lose his life. This was what Brunhild, King Gunther's wife, had instigated.

[918] The bold hero went to see Kriemhild. His valuable hunting equipment, and those of his followers, had been loaded onto pack animals, and

---

92. The appellative of traitor (*ungetriuwe man*) has now become Hagen's main attribute. The concept of loyalty and faithfulness (*triuwe*) is the driving force behind the murder that is being plotted. The concept itself is complicated, however, in that Hagen sees himself as fulfilling his role as a loyal vassal of the king and queen, his lady, and sees it as his duty to avenge the wrong done to them by Siegfried and Kriemhild. This split in loyalty in which Hagen clearly betrays Kriemhild's confidence, is not thematized in its complexity, since Hagen's pride naturally leads him to be disloyal to his lord's sister, with the added motivation, already addressed, of securing the Nibelungen hoard for the house of Burgundy.

they intended to cross the Rhine. Nothing could have been more painful to Kriemhild.

[919] He kissed his wife on the mouth. "May God grant, dear lady, that we see each other again alive and well. Stay here and enjoy your family's company. I need to leave for a while." [920] She didn't dare say anything, but she had to think about what she had told Hagen. The noble queen began to regret that she had ever been born. Siegfried's wife broke down and cried relentlessly.

[921] She said to her husband, "Don't go on this hunt! I had a nightmare last night. Two wild boar were running across the fields and all the flowers turned red. I can't help crying about it. [922] I am terrified that something is going to happen. Who knows if we have insulted one of them so that they have some reason to hate us. Please stay, dear sir, that is my faithful wish."

[923] He said, "My love, I will be back in a few days. I don't know anyone here who hates me. I am in favor with all members of your family. And I have earned nothing less."

[924] "No, Lord Siegfried, I foresee your death! I had another dream last night, how two mountains came crashing down on you, and you disappeared from my sight. If you leave me, it will break my heart."

[925] He embraced that virtuous woman and kissed her lovingly. He said goodbye and was quickly gone. She was never to see him alive again.

[926] They rode from there into a great forest looking for sport. Many daring knights followed Gunther and his men. Gernot and Giselher stayed at home. [927] The packhorses had preceded them across the Rhine, carrying food and drink, meat and fish, and other provisions for the hunting party, basically everything a mighty king needs. [928] Those daring hunters set up camp at the edge of the green forest, on a large meadow, where the quarry could exit and where they intended to start the hunt. Siegfried had come along with them, a fact that was reported to the king.

[929] The hunters took up their positions in a circle, and Siegfried, that courageous and powerful man, said, "Who is going to show us the trail of the game through the woods, you keen heroes?"

[930] "Do we want to divide ourselves up," asked Hagen, "before we start the hunt? That way we, my lords and I, can determine who the best hunters are. [931] We'll divide up the people and the hounds. Then everyone will take off whichever way he wants. Whoever has the best result will be rewarded." The hunters all soon departed separately.

[932] Lord Siegfried spoke, "I don't need any dogs, except one good hound that has had a taste of its reward and can find the game's trail through the woods. We'll have a great hunt," said Kriemhild's husband. [933] An old hunter took a good hound that quickly brought the lord to a spot with plenty of game. Whatever was flushed out was quickly dispatched, as good hunters

still do today. [934] The animals that the hound scared up were killed by Siegfried's own hand, the hero of Netherland. His horse was so swift that nothing could outrun it. He was declared the best of all on that hunt.

[935] He was talented in everything he tried. He was the first to kill an animal with his own hands, a very large wild horse.[93] Right after that he encountered a lion. [936] When the hound had flushed him out, he shot him with a bow, using an especially large arrow. The lion managed another three steps before he fell dead. The other hunters praised Siegfried for that shot. [937] After that he killed a bison and a moose, four strong aurochs, and a dreadful elk.[94] His horse was so fast that nothing could outrun it. Stags and hinds could not escape him.

[938] The tracking dog came upon a great boar. Just as it was trying to escape, the master of the hunt came up. He attacked him on the trail, and the boar reared up and attacked the hero. [939] Kriemhild's husband dispatched it with his sword. Any other hunter would have had difficulty. After the boar was killed, they put the hound back on the line. The Burgundians soon found out about his great catch.

[940] His hunters said, "If it wouldn't dishonor you, Lord Siegfried, we ask that you leave us a few animals. You're clearing the mountains and the forests today." That made the brave and daring warrior smile.

[941] Suddenly they all heard shouting and lots of noise. The uproar from people and dogs was so loud that it echoed throughout the mountain and the forest. The hunters had let loose twenty-four packs of hounds. [942] Many animals lost their lives there. The men hoped that they could still earn the prize for best hunter, but that was impossible, since Siegfried had already been seen back in camp.

[943] The hunt was almost finished. Those who were coming back to camp brought with them hides from different animals and meat as well. It was amazing how much they brought to the king's kitchen. [944] The king commanded that all these excellent hunters should be signaled that it was time to eat. The horn was given one long blast, which indicated that the lord had returned to camp.

[945] One of Siegfried's hunters said, "Sir, I hear a horn sounding that means we should return to camp. I'll answer it." Many horns were heard recalling their comrades.

[946] Lord Siegfried said, "Let's leave this forest." His horse carried him easily from there, and his men hurried back along with him. Their noise had

---

93. The manuscripts are corrupted here, and the identity of this animal (*halpful* or *halbswuol*) is uncertain. Other suggestions have been "half-grown boar," and "half-wolf."

94. While others hunt for bison and boar, this list of animals seems somewhat fantastic and is certainly meant to exaggerate Siegfried's prowess and skill. The aurochs is an extinct kind of wild cattle, whereas the identification of the elk (?) (*schelch*) is still a matter of debate.

roused a huge and terrible animal—it was a wild bear. The hero called back behind him, [947] "I want to have some fun with my fellow huntsmen. Let the hound loose, I see a bear. We'll drive him all the way back to camp. Unless he escapes right away, he'll have no choice."

[948] The hound was released, and the bear bounded away. Kriemhild's husband wanted to catch him on horseback, but he came into difficult terrain and could go no farther. The powerful animal thought that it could escape from its pursuer, [949] but the brave knight jumped from his horse and pursued on foot. The creature never stood a chance. It could not escape, and he caught it on the spot. The hero was able to bind it without hurting it [950] so that it couldn't bite or scratch him. He tied it to the saddle, mounted up, and then brought it back to camp to show off and have some fun.[95]

[951] How nobly he rode to the encampment. His spear was powerful, strong and broad, and a beautiful sword hung down to his spurs. He also carried a precious horn made of red gold. [952] I have never heard of any more costly hunting outfit. He was seen wearing a coat of black material and a fur hat that was itself extremely valuable. He even had exquisite straps for his quiver [953] that was covered with the skin of a panther, on account of its fragrance. He also had a bow that would have required a winch for others to draw, but not him. [954] His complete attire was made of fur, and he was covered from head to toe with ornaments. This master of the hunt had on a gleaming pelt that was set off by rows of gold clasps. [955] He was carrying Balmung, a broad and handsome sword. It was incredibly sharp and never failed him when he brought it down on someone's helmet. Its blade was exceptionally keen edged. The mighty hunter was high spirited and proud. [956] Since I should tell you everything I know, I want to add that his precious quiver was filled with excellent arrows, with golden quills as broad as a hand. Whatever he aimed them at was soon dead.

[957] That noble knight was a sight to behold. Gunther's men saw him as he rode in, and they ran to receive him and to take the reins of his horse. Attached to the saddle was a large and terrifying bear. [958] After he had dismounted, he removed the ties from its paws and snout. As soon as they saw the bear, the hounds started barking and howling. The bear wanted to escape back into the forest, and there was a great panic. [959] The bear, driven on by the noise, found itself in the kitchen area. It drove the kitchen knaves from their fires. The pots were overturned and the fires scattered, and many a tasty dish was left lying in the ashes. [960] The lords and their attendants jumped up from their seats. The bear was enraged. The king commanded that all the hounds be let loose. They would have had a good time if it had gone according

---

95. Siegfried's need to show off is still motivated by his exuberance (*hôher muot*) and his sense of entertainment and fun. There is no indication that this kind of behavior should cause others to be envious of his accomplishments.

to plan. [961] Those who dared chased after the bear with their bows and pikes, but there were so many dogs around that no one could take a shot. The entire mountain reverberated from all the noise. [962] The bear was trying to get away from the hounds, but only Kriemhild's husband was able to keep up. He caught up with it and killed it with a single stroke of his sword. [963] Everyone who saw that had to admit that he was an amazingly powerful man.

The entire hunting party was then called to dinner. They were gathered on a great meadow, and the noble hunters were all served wonderfully tasty meals. [964] Missing were the servants who were supposed to bring the wine. The nobles could not have been better served. If it hadn't been for the treason in their hearts, they could have remained free from dishonor.*

[965] Siegfried said, "I'm wondering where the servants are with the wine, since everything else seems to be flowing out of the kitchen. If thirsty hunters can't be better served, then I don't want to be one. [966] I've earned better treatment than this."

The king called over from his table, with feigned sincerity, "Everything will be done to make up for this oversight. It's all Hagen's fault. I think he wants us to die of thirst."

[967] Hagen of Troneck spoke up, "My dear lord, I thought that the hunt today was going to be in the Spessart forest. I sent the wine over there. We may go thirsty today, but I'll make sure it doesn't happen again."

[968] King Siegfried replied, "Damn them! They were supposed to bring seven loads of mead and wine here for me. And when that couldn't happen, they should have positioned us closer to the Rhine."

[969] Hagen of Troneck said, "Dear noble knight, don't be upset. I know a cool spring not too far from here. Let's go there instead." This proposal led to the death of many warriors.

[970] Siegfried the bold was tormented by thirst, and so he ordered that the table be cleared. He wanted to find the spring up on the mountain. The others had given treacherous advice. [971] The game that Siegfried had bagged was sent to Worms in wagons, and everyone who saw it praised him greatly for that accomplishment. Hagen had initiated his betrayal of Siegfried.

[972] Just as they were ready to leave for the broad linden tree, Hagen of Troneck said, "I have often been told that no one can keep up with Kriemhild's husband in a foot race. Would he be willing to give us a demonstration?"

[973] Bold Siegfried of Netherland replied, "You can certainly give it a try. If you want to race me to the spring, then let's do it. Whoever gets there first is the winner."

[974] "I'm willing to give it a go," said Hagen.

Siegfried the bold said, "I'll start by lying down in the grass here in front of you." When Gunther heard him say that, he was very pleased. [975] The bold hero went on to say, "I'll go you one better. I will carry all of my gear with me, my spear and shield and all my hunting equipment." He also strapped on his quiver and sword on the spot.

[976] Hagen and Gunther took off most of their clothing. Both of them were seen wearing white undershirts. Just like two wild panthers, they took off through the clover. But Siegfried was the first to be seen at the spring. [977] He was clearly superior to any man. He untied his sword, took off his quiver, and leaned his spear up against the linden tree. The noble foreigner waited there at the bubbling spring. [978] Siegfried was the paragon of virtue. He put down his shield at the fountain, but as thirsty as he was, the hero didn't drink until the king had gone first. He was repaid for this gesture with little thanks. [979] The spring was cool, clear, and clean. Gunther knelt down to the water. After he drank he got up, and Siegfried then did likewise.

[980] He was to pay dearly for his chivalry.[96] Hagen removed the bow and the sword and then ran back to where he found Siegfried's spear. He looked for the sign on his shirt. [981] As Siegfried was drinking from the spring, he drove the spear through the cross and into his heart. Blood spurted out of the wound and onto Hagen's clothing. Never since has anyone committed such a heinous crime. [982] He left the spear sticking through his heart. Hagen had never tried so desperately to get away from anyone. As Siegfried realized that he had been mortally wounded, [983] he leaped up from the fountain in a rage. The spear was still protruding from his back, as the lord was grasping for his bow or sword. Hagen would have met his well-deserved end had he found them.

[984] When the mortally wounded man failed to find his sword, he had nothing left but the edge of his shield. He lifted it up from the spring and went after Hagen. Gunther's man could not escape him now. [985] Despite his mortal wound, he struck so fiercely that the jewels fell left and right as he destroyed the shield. The noble foreigner was desperate to avenge himself. [986] Hagen was struck down, and the fields echoed with the sound of that stroke. If Siegfried had had his sword at hand, Hagen would surely have been killed. He was in a rage, as well he should be. [987] He turned completely white and could no longer stand. All of his life force was drained from him, and death was marked on his handsome face. He has since been mourned by many beautiful women.

[988] Kriemhild's husband tumbled into the flowers. The blood from his wound could be seen flowing out. He began to curse those who had committed this treasonous murder, as well he should. [989] The mortally wounded man said, "You evil cowards, what good did my service do me now that you have killed me? I was always loyal to you, and now I've had to pay the price. You've done this misdeed to your own family. [990] Your offspring are cursed

---

96. Siegfried's courtly upbringing and chivalrous manner (*zühte*) now lead to his death. In this moment, Gunther and Hagen's betrayal is shown to be more than just disloyalty to an individual, but rather a renunciation of all that knighthood is supposed to stand for.

for all eternity for this. Your hatred against me has found its revenge, but you will be cast out by all brave warriors."

[991] The knights all ran to where he was lying. For many it was a wretched day, and whoever was still loyal to him lamented his death. That bold and noble knight deserved no less. [992] The king of Burgundy lamented his death. The dying man said, "It is needless to lament a loss if one caused it. He deserves to be cursed instead. It would be better left unsaid."

[993] Then Hagen the terrible spoke, "I have no idea what he's going on about. Everything is now over, our worries and our grief. No one will dare attack us now. I'm glad that I put an end to his power."

[994] "You can praise yourself now," said Siegfried. "If I had known that you were nothing but a murderer, I would have protected myself. I'm sorry mostly for my wife Kriemhild. [995] May God have mercy that I have a son who will be damned for his family's treachery and murder. If I could, I would lament that."* [996] The dying man spoke through his pain, "If you, noble king, want to show your faithfulness to anyone in the world, then let my dear wife receive the benefit of your grace. [997] And let her profit from the fact that she is your sister. For the sake of nobility's virtues, stay true to her. My father and my men will have to wait a long time for my return. And no wife has been harmed more by the death of her dear husband."*

[998] The flowers all around him turned moist with his blood as he fought his final battle with death. It did not last long, for the sharp edge of death had cut all too deep. The bold, noble hero was finally silenced. [999] When the nobles saw that the hero was dead, they placed him onto a shield of reddish gold. They agreed how they would go about concealing Hagen as the perpetrator.

[1000] Many of them said, "Evil has befallen us. Everyone needs to keep this quiet and say that when Kriemhild's husband was hunting alone he was ambushed by robbers as he rode through the forest."

[1001] Hagen of Troneck spoke up, "I'll take him back to town. I couldn't care less if she finds out about this. She's the one who insulted Brunhild. I really don't care how much she cries about it."*

17. Kriemhild's Lament and Siegfried's Burial

[1002] They waited until morning and then crossed the Rhine. There was never a more evil hunt perpetrated by heroes. Noble children would continue to lament the prey they had slain, and many brave warriors had to make the ultimate sacrifice for that deed.

[1003] You will now hear a tale of boundless arrogance and terrible vengeance. Hagen ordered that the corpse of Siegfried of Nibelungenland be placed at the threshold of Kriemhild's bedroom. [1004] He instructed that he should secretly be left at her door so that she would find him as she left to go to Mass first thing in the morning, which Lady Kriemhild never missed.

[1005] The bells were rung for Mass as was the custom. Lady Kriemhild the beautiful awakened her household and asked for a light and for her clothes. One of the attendants hurried over and chanced upon Siegfried. [1006] He saw him soaked in red blood, but he didn't recognize him as his lord. He carried a light into the room and told Lady Kriemhild of his terrible discovery.

[1007] She wanted to go to church with her ladies, but the attendant yelled, "Stop! There is a dead knight lying at the door." Kriemhild cried out loud. [1008] Even before she had seen that it was her husband, she remembered Hagen's question about how he could protect him. She was overwhelmed by grief. His death meant the end of her joy forever. [1009] She fell to the ground and was still, and everyone saw that silent, joy-ridden woman lying there. Her pain was immeasurable, and when she awakened from her shock, she screamed so that the entire room shook.

[1010] The attendants all said, "Maybe it's a stranger."

Blood ran from her lips, fed by her broken heart, and she cried, "It's Siegfried, my beloved husband. Brunhild started this, Hagen finished it." [1011] The lady wanted them to lead her to where they had found the body. She lifted his handsome face in her pale hands, and even though he was covered in blood, she recognized him immediately. The hero of Nibelungenland lay there, a pitiful sight.

[1012] That charitable lady cried out in her sorrow, "What grief and pain! Your shield has not even been touched by swords. You have been murdered in cold blood. If I knew who did this, I would never cease to seek his death."

[1013] All of her household sobbed and cried along with their dear mistress, since they, too, were grieved by the loss of their lord. Hagen had grimly avenged Brunhild's anger.

[1014] She said in her sorrow, "Chamberlains, go immediately to waken Siegfried's men. You should also tell Siegmund of my sorrow, and ask him to help me grieve for bold Siegfried."

[1015] A messenger ran quickly to where they were all sleeping, Siegfried's heroes from the land of the Nibelungen. He took all their joy with the horrific news. They didn't want to believe it, but then they heard the crying. [1016] The messenger also rushed to King Siegmund's bed, but he was not asleep. I think that his heart had already told him what had happened, that he would never see his son Siegfried alive again.

[1017] "Wake up, Lord Siegmund. My Lady Kriemhild told me to come find you. She is in great pain, her heart is broken. You should help her grieve, because this affects you as well."

[1018] Siegmund sat up. He said, "What is this pain of Lady Kriemhild that you speak of?"

The messenger spoke through his tears, "I can't withhold the truth. Bold Siegfried of Netherland has been murdered."

[1019] King Siegmund responded, "Stop making things up and telling lies, for my sake, and don't say that he has been murdered. I couldn't bear it if he were gone."

[1020] "If you don't believe what I'm telling you, then you should come hear Kriemhild and her household bewailing Siegfried's death." Siegmund recoiled, as was only natural.

[1021] He jumped out of bed and gathered a hundred of his men. They all grabbed their sharpest swords and ran with grim thoughts to where the wailing was coming from. They were joined by a thousand of Siegfried's men. [1022] When they heard the women crying so mournfully, some of them thought they ought first to change into more proper clothing, but they were out of their minds with suffering. Their hearts had all been broken.

[1023] Bold Siegmund came up to Kriemhild and said, "Curse the journey we made here to this country. Who has taken my son and your husband from us with such treason here among friends?"

[1024] "If I knew who it was," said the noble woman, "I would hate him with my whole being. I would do him such harm that his friends would mourn and regret my act."

[1025] King Siegmund took the man in his arms. The wailing of those around him was so terrible that the sound shook the entire castle all the way to the town of Worms itself. [1026] Siegfried's wife was inconsolable. They undressed the corpse, washed his wounds, and laid him out. His people were deeply saddened and in great anguish. [1027] The Nibelungen warriors said, "We will avenge him ourselves. The murderer is here in this castle," whereupon all of Siegfried's men ran to arm themselves. [1028] These excellent fighters came back armed with their shields, eleven hundred in all. King Siegmund had command of this fighting force, and he would have gladly avenged his son's death, as he had every right. [1029] But they did not know where the enemy was, except for Gunther and the men who had gone hunting with Siegfried. Kriemhild saw them all fully armed, and she was upset. [1030] As great as her sorrow and her devastation were, she feared even more that the Nibelungen would be killed by her brother's men, and she had them stand down. She warned them out of her concern for them, as good friends do for others.

[1031] Kriemhild spoke, full of grief, "My Lord Siegmund, what do you plan to do? You don't know the state of affairs here. King Gunther has a great many capable men, and you will all be lost should you attack them."

[1032] With their shields at the ready, they were desperate to fight. The noble queen begged and pleaded with these brave men not to go into battle. She was terrified that they would not back down. [1033] She said, "Lord Siegmund, please wait until the circumstances are in your favor. I will avenge my husband alongside you. Whoever has taken him from me, once I can prove who it is, he will have to deal with me. [1034] There are many self-righteous and arrogant men here on the Rhine, which is why I advise you not to fight. They have at least thirty for every one of your men. May God grant them what they have earned on our account. [1035] Please stay here and share my grief with me. When it is morning, my heroes, help me to place my dear husband in his casket."

The men all said, "It will be done."

[1036] No one could adequately describe for you the spectacle of knights and ladies and how they mourned, and how their wails were heard down in the town. Noble citizens came running out of their houses. [1037] They joined the foreigners in their mourning, for they, too, were greatly saddened. No one told them what Siegfried had done wrong and why the noble knight had to lose his life. The wives of the good burghers joined the ladies with their tears. [1038] Craftsmen were told to build quickly a large and durable casket of silver and gold. It was to be reinforced with bands of steel all around. The entire population was downcast and dejected.

[1039] When the night was through and morning had been announced, the noble lady ordered that her dear husband Siegfried be carried to the church. The friends he had there followed him and cried for him. [1040] As he was being brought to the church, many church bells could be heard ringing, and numerous priests were heard chanting and singing. King Gunther, in the company of his men and hardhearted Hagen as well, joined the mourners.

[1041] He said, "Dearest sister, your loss pains me greatly. If only we could have been spared this great disaster. We will always mourn Siegfried's death."

"You do so without reason," said the sorrowful woman. [1042] "If you were truly sorry, then this would not have happened. You weren't thinking of me, that I can now say for sure, as my dear husband and I were separated. If God had only ordained," said Kriemhild, "that I should be the victim."

[1043] They were quick to deny it. Kriemhild then continued, "Whoever says he is innocent, let him prove it. He should walk up to the bier in front of witnesses. This will soon bring the truth to light."[97]

[1044] This is a kind of miracle that still occurs often to this day. Whenever a man stained by murder comes close to his victim, the wounds will open and bleed anew. This is what happened there, and everyone saw that Hagen

---

97. As a legal instrument this method of determining a guilty party only became commonly known in Germany in the fourteenth century, so this is usually thought to be the first literary mention of the procedure in German. A similar event, although not as part of an accusation, occurs in Hartmann von Aue's *Iwein* (around 1200), where the wounds of a dead man begin to bleed again in the presence of his killer. There is no way to determine a relationship between the two texts.

was guilty. [1045] The wounds started bleeding again, as they had before. Those who had been wailing loudly now did so even more.

King Gunther spoke, "I say to all of you: robbers killed him. Hagen is innocent."

[1046] "I know all about these robbers," she said. "May God grant that someday his friends can avenge him. Gunther and Hagen—you are his murderers!" Siegfried's men were prepared for battle, [1047] but Kriemhild said, "You should share my grief with me."

Then two others walked up to the dead man, Gernot and Giselher, her brothers. They mourned sincerely along with the others. [1048] They cried for Kriemhild's husband with all their hearts. The time for Mass had come, and women, men, and children were all going down to the church. Even those who did not know Siegfried shed tears for him.

[1049] Gernot and Giselher said, "Dear sister, you must console yourself now, it is right for you to do so. We will strive to compensate you for this loss as long as we live." But no one in all the world could console her.

[1050] The casket was completed around the middle of the day, and Siegfried was lifted up from the bier on which he had been placed. The lady did not yet want him to be buried, and this made it hard for everyone. [1051] The corpse was wrapped in costly material. I don't think there was anyone there who wasn't weeping. Queen Ute, a noble woman, and her entire household mourned for that magnificent man. [1052] When everyone heard that Mass was being sung in the church and that Siegfried had been laid to rest in the casket, there was a great gathering. Large donations were offered there for his soul. He still had plenty of friends in the land of his enemies.

[1053] Poor Kriemhild said to her attendants, "I ask that those who want to honor him and me should share this hardship with me. For the sake of Siegfried's soul, his gold should be given as an offering."

[1054] Everyone, young and old alike, went to give alms. Before he was buried, at least a hundred masses had been sung daily as Siegfried's friends crowded all around. [1055] After the masses had been sung, people began to disperse.

Lady Kriemhild said, "Please don't let me watch over this great hero alone tonight. All of my joy has been destroyed along with him. [1056] I will have him lying in state here for three days and three nights before I can tear myself away from my dear husband. What would happen if God decided that I, too, should die? At least it would end my suffering."

[1057] The townspeople returned to their homes. Priests and monks she asked to stay, along with all of his men, so that they could keep watch over him. They experienced difficult nights and trying days. [1058] Many of them went without food or drink, but those who wanted something were well looked after. King Siegmund made all the arrangements. The men from

Nibelungen took on many hardships. [1059] As we've heard, those who were able to say Mass toiled ceaselessly those three days. What alms were given there! Those who were poor became wealthy. [1060] The poor who had nothing to contribute were given gold from his own treasure house to make their offerings. After his death, many thousands of marks were given for the sake of his soul. [1061] They distributed properties throughout the land to monasteries and pious people. Significant amounts of silver and clothing were given to the poor. She demonstrated to everyone how much she loved him. [1062] On the morning of the third day the churchyard was filled at Mass with mourners from around the land. They served him even after death, as one does for dear friends. [1063] People have said that in those four days thirty thousand marks or more were given to the poor for his soul's sake, but his power and his life now counted for nothing.[98]

[1064] When the church service had ended, people were left to deal with their great pain. He was carried from the church to his grave. Those for whom parting was unbearable could be seen weeping and lamenting. [1065] People accompanied his body with loud wailing, and no one, man or woman, felt any joy that day. Before he was buried, they recited psalms and sang antiphons. There was an abundance of good priests present at his burial. [1066] Before Siegfried's wife was able to approach the grave, the faithful woman had to try to overcome her great grief, and people kept splashing water on her face. Her pain and grief were overwhelming beyond measure. [1067] It was actually a miracle that she survived at all. Other ladies were there to join her in mourning.

The queen said, "Siegfried's men, you should grant me one request out of loyalty. [1068] Please grant my small wish that after all this sorrow I may see his lovely face one more time." She pleaded so long and so vehemently that finally they had to break open the casket. [1069] The lady was then led to where he was lying. She lifted his handsome face in her pale hands and kissed that noble knight once more. Her suffering caused her clear eyes to cry tears of blood. [1070] That was a parting most sorrowful. They had to carry her away from there because she couldn't walk on her own. This marvelous woman had fallen unconscious, and she could have easily died from her anguish.

[1071] After the noble lord had been laid to rest, all those who had accompanied him from the land of the Nibelungen could be seen in great distress. Siegmund would never again experience joy. [1072] There were those among them who had had nothing to eat or drink for three whole days of mourning.

---

98. The practice of giving alms for the sake of the departed's soul is meant both to aid the soul through purgatory and to demonstrate the faithfulness of those left behind. The poor were not given gold for their own needs but rather so that they might also demonstrate their piety in offering a donation. The church benefited through the land donations made to monasteries and other sacred institutions, in return for those same institutions offering supplications and prayers to God on behalf of the deceased.

But they couldn't completely deny the body's needs and had to eat again after their suffering, as it still happens to many today.*

18. Kriemhild Remains in Worms

[1073] Kriemhild's father-in-law went to Kriemhild and said to the queen, "We should go back to our own country. It seems to me that we are unwelcome guests here on the Rhine. Kriemhild, my dear lady, please come back with me to my lands. [1074] It was treason here in this land that took your noble husband from you, and you should not continue to suffer here for it. I remain devoted to you for my son's sake, of this you can be assured. [1075] You will have, dear lady, all of the authority that Siegfried, that brave warrior, once bestowed on you. The land and its crown shall be subject to you, and Siegfried's men will gladly serve you."

[1076] The squires were told that they should make preparations to depart, and everyone rushed to get the horses together. They didn't want to stay a minute longer amongst their bitter enemies. Ladies and young women were told to get their wardrobes in order. [1077] As soon as King Siegmund was ready to leave, Kriemhild was asked by her relatives to stay there with her mother. The regal lady replied, "That's impossible. [1078] How could I stand to look him in the eyes after what he did to me, a lowly woman?"

Young Giselher said, "My dearest sister, you should stay here with your mother out of devotion to her. [1079] You don't need to depend on those who have done you wrong and caused you to be sad. You can share in my wealth."

She said to the warrior, "It just can't be. I would die from the pain of having to see Hagen."

[1080] "I can protect you from him, my dear sister. You can stay with your brother Giselher. I will compensate you for the loss of your husband."

The unfortunate woman answered, "That would indeed be necessary."

[1081] While young Giselher was tenderly imploring her, Gernot and Ute and her faithful relatives began to plead with her to stay as well. She didn't have any relatives among Siegfried's men.

[1082] "They are all strangers to you," said Gernot. "Everyone has to die sometime, no matter how strong he is. Think about this, dear sister, and console yourself. Stay here with your friends. This is what is best for you." [1083] She promised Giselher that she would stay.

Siegmund's men collected their horses, since they wanted to ride back to the Nibelungen lands. Their equipment was packed up as well. [1084] Lord Siegmund went to see Kriemhild. He spoke to the lady, "Siegfried's men are waiting with their mounts. We want to depart. I would rather not stay here with the Burgundians."

[1085] Lady Kriemhild answered him, "My family has advised me to stay here with those who are still faithful to me. I don't have any family in the land of the Nibelungen."

Siegmund was sorry to hear her say this. [1086] King Siegmund said, "Don't ever let anyone tell you that. Above all the rest of my family, you shall wear the crown as mightily as before. You will not have to suffer from the fact that we have lost our hero. [1087] Come back home with us for the sake of your little son. You can't allow him, dear lady, to become an orphan. When your son matures he will be your consolation. But in the meantime you will be served by many brave and bold warriors."

[1088] She answered, "My Lord Siegmund, I'm sorry, but I can't go. I have to stay here with my family, regardless of what happens to me. They can help me in my mourning." These explanations displeased the brave men.

[1089] They all spoke as one, "Now we can say that a catastrophe has really befallen us if you want to stay here with our enemies. Never have warriors undertaken a more tragic journey to another court."

[1090] "You can travel safely in God's hands, and you will be given safe passage all the way to Siegmund's lands. I will make sure of it. I give my little one over to your care."

[1091] When they realized that she was not going to go, all of Siegmund's men wept. Siegmund's farewell from Lady Kriemhild was unhappy indeed. He was overcome by sadness.

[1092] "May this celebration be damned!" said the noble king. "Never again will a festival of joy end this way for a king and his household as it has for us. We will never again show our faces here in Burgundy."

[1093] Siegfried's men declared before all who were assembled there, "We may yet lead a military campaign into this land if we find out who has killed our lord. They have made grave enemies of his family."

[1094] Siegmund kissed Kriemhild goodbye. Since he saw that she was determined to stay, he said with great sadness, "We will ride home then, bereft of joy. Only now can I see the extent of all my sorrows." [1095] They rode from Worms to the Rhine without an escort. They could rest assured that the courageous men from Nibelungen would know how to defend themselves if attacked. [1096] They said farewell to no one. Gernot and Giselher were seen going up to Siegmund in friendship. They were sorry for his loss. These two bold and brave knights demonstrated their sincerity.

[1097] Lord Gernot spoke courteously, "God in heaven knows full well that I had nothing to do with Siegfried's death. I never heard his enemies plotting against him. I honestly mourn him."[99]

---

99. Gernot seems to go out of his way in meeting with Siegmund and lying to him. Giselher is depicted as innocent, even though he, too, heard of the plots against Siegfried. Gernot's

[1098] Young Giselher rode with the king and his men out of his lands all the way to Netherland. Joy had deserted his supporters and kin there. [1099] I don't know what happened to them after that. In Burgundy, Kriemhild could be heard in ceaseless mourning, and no one could console her except for Giselher. He alone remained faithful and true. [1100] Brunhild, the beautiful, reigned with self-satisfaction and arrogance. No matter how much Kriemhild cried, she couldn't have cared less. She wanted nothing to do with her. Later on Lady Kriemhild would make her suffer as well.

19. The Treasure of the Nibelungen

[1101] After Kriemhild was widowed, Count Eckewart stayed with her in Burgundy, along with his men. He served her every day and joined with his lady in mourning the death of his lord. [1102] Close to the church there in Worms a house was built for her. It was large and roomy, stately and expansive. There she lived with her household, bereft of joy. She gladly went to church and was a pious worshipper. [1103] She often went to visit the gravesite of her beloved, and in her great sorrow she went there whenever she could. She prayed to God almighty that he would protect his soul. That man was mourned faithfully day in and day out.

[1104] Ute and her attendants consoled her constantly, but her heart was so broken that no amount of consolation could repair it. The pain she felt for her friend and dear husband was greater [1105] than any woman had ever suffered. This was a measure of what a virtuous woman she was. She grieved her entire life, right up to the very end. She was later to avenge Siegfried's death with great courage.*

[1106] This is how she lived after the tragedy of her husband's death for three and a half years, all this is true. She never once spoke with Gunther and never saw her enemy Hagen during that entire time. [1107] The hero from Troneck said, "If you could arrange it with your sister that she would again be your ally, then the gold of the Nibelungen could be transferred to our land. You would have much to gain if we were in the queen's good graces."

[1108] Gunther replied, "We can try. My brothers see her on a regular basis. We can ask them if they would try to gain her friendship for us. Maybe we can get her to agree to this."

"I really don't believe," said Hagen, "that could ever happen."

---

blatant lie at this juncture, however, when Siegmund and his troops are already leaving, serves to heighten the culpability and wrongdoing even of those who did not have a direct hand in Siegfried's murder, i.e., Gunther and Hagen. Even Brunhild's callous and arrogant snub of Kriemhild at this point seems to involve her as one of the guilty party.

[1109] The king first had Ortwin and Margrave Gere pay her a visit. After that, he sent Gernot and young Giselher. They tried to gain Lady Kriemhild's trust and friendship. [1110] Bold Gernot of Burgundy spoke up, "Lady, you have been mourning Siegfried's death for too long now. The king will swear an oath to you that he did not kill him. Everyone hears only your constant lamentations and weeping."

[1111] She said, "No one is accusing him of the killing. Hagen is the one who killed him. When he found out from me where Siegfried was vulnerable, how was I to know that he despised him? I should have been more careful," said the queen, [1112] "not to endanger his life. The poor woman that I am, I wouldn't need to be crying now. I will never forgive the one who did this." Giselher, that courageous man, resorted to pleading with her.*

[1113] "I will meet with the king." After she had promised him this, the king appeared before her with his most loyal supporters, but Hagen did not dare let himself be seen. He well knew his guilt and what pain he had caused. [1114] Since she was willing to reconcile with Gunther, it would have been more appropriate for him to kiss her, if he had not caused her such great suffering. He could have then gone to Kriemhild with his head held high.* [1115] Never before had there been such an emotional reconciliation among family. Her loss still caused her pain. She forgave them all, except for one man. No one would have murdered Siegfried, had Hagen not done it himself.

[1116] Not long after these events they convinced Lady Kriemhild to have the great treasure transported from Nibelungenland all the way to the Rhine. It was her dowry and belonged to her by law. [1117] Giselher and Gernot rode out to retrieve the treasure. Kriemhild then commanded eight thousand men to remove the treasure from its hiding place, where Alberich watched over it with his most trusted lieutenants. [1118] As the men from the Rhine were seen coming, Alberich said to his comrades, "We cannot dare to deny them the treasure, since the noble queen demands it as her dowry. [1119] But I wouldn't do it," said Alberich, "if we had not sadly lost both the invisibility cloak and Siegfried. The husband of beautiful Kriemhild always had it with him. [1120] Siegfried has had to pay for the fact that he took the cloak from us and that this entire land became subject to him."

The chamberlain then left to get the keys. [1121] Kriemhild's men and some of her relatives stood in front of the mountain, and the treasure was brought down to the sea and loaded onto ships. From there it was transported by sea all the way to the Rhine.

[1122] Now you will hear amazing things about that treasure.[100] It was so immense that it took twelve wagons four days and nights to remove it from

---

100. There are echoes of the opening strophe in manuscripts A and C of the *Nibelungenlied* in this line, as the poet prepares to amaze his readers with the wonders they are about to hear told.

the mountain, and each wagon had to make the trip three times each day. [1123] It was made up entirely of gold and precious gems. And if the entire world had been paid its due, the treasure would not have lost a mark's worth of its value. Hagen had every reason to lust after it. [1124] The greatest single piece was hidden underneath: a small rod of gold. If someone had been able to discern its use, he could have ruled the world and every single person in it.[101] Many of Alberich's men joined up with Gernot.*

[1125] Once they had brought the treasure to Gunther's lands and the queen had taken possession of it, it was removed to various rooms and towers. Never before had such amazing things been said about riches. [1126] Yet even if it had been a thousand times greater, Kriemhild would have given it all up if Lord Siegfried could have been brought back to life. Never did a hero have a more faithful wife. [1127] Now that she had the treasure, it attracted many foreign warriors to that country. The lady's own hands distributed so much that no one before had seen such generosity. She was noble and virtuous, this is what people said of her. [1128] She gave so much to rich and poor alike that Hagen speculated that if she lived much longer she could gather enough men into her service to pose a threat.

[1129] King Gunther said, "She has rights and property. Why should I prevent her from doing with it whatever she wants? It was difficult enough just to achieve a reconciliation. It's none of our business what she does with her own silver and gold."

[1130] Hagen replied to the king, "A real man would not allow a woman to have sway over a treasure horde.[102] Her gift giving will someday lead many brave Burgundians to regret it."

[1131] King Gunther responded, "I swore an oath to her that I would do her no more wrong, and I aim to keep my word. She is my sister."

But Hagen replied, "Just let me be the guilty party."

[1132] Several of them broke their oaths when they took the great treasure horde from the widow and Hagen took possession of all the keys. When he heard about this, her brother Gernot became enraged.

[1133] Lord Giselher said, "Hagen has made my sister suffer a great deal. I should put an end to it. If he weren't part of our family, he would surely die." Siegfried's wife began to weep.

[1134] Lord Gernot spoke, "Before we have even more trouble on account of the gold, we should have it all thrown into the Rhine. That would be the

---

101. This small but apparently extremely powerful implement is never mentioned again, but in a sense it further represents the vast power of the treasure as a symbol of world rule.

102. Hagen has to remind the king of his duties not only as king but also as a man. The concept is translated here as "real" man (*vrumer man*), since even though Kriemhild has a legal right to her dowry, Gunther should, as her brother and guardian, but also as a man, provide an example of the proper relationship between a man and a woman.

right thing to do."* Kriemhild went to see her brother Gunther and complained loudly.[103]

[1135] She said, "My dear brother, you should have my best interests at heart. As my guardian, you should protect me and my property."

He answered the lady, "That will be done when we return, but right now we are going out riding."

[1136] The king and his household left the land with the best men he could find, all except for Hagen. He remained there, motivated by his hatred for Kriemhild.* [1137] Before the mighty king returned, Hagen had collected the entire treasure. He sank it all into the Rhine near Loche.[104] He was hoping someday to make use of it.*

[1138] The nobles returned with all their men. Kriemhild, along with all her ladies and maidens, protested her great loss. She had suffered a grave injustice, but Giselher alone wanted to remain loyal to her.*

[1139] The nobles all said the same thing, "He was in the wrong." Hagen avoided the angry nobles for a while until he was back in their good graces, and they did him no harm. Kriemhild's hatred could not have been greater. [1140] Before Hagen had hidden the treasure, they had sworn solemn oaths to each other to keep the location a secret as long as one of them was still alive. They were not to have any of it for themselves nor give any of it to others. [1141] Kriemhild was tortured by the loss of her husband, and after they had robbed her of the treasure as well, she never ceased to protest and lament until the end of her days. [1142] After Siegfried's death, and this is the truth, she lived in sorrow and pain for thirteen years. She could not forget the hero's death, and she remained faithful to him, as everyone acknowledged.**

---

103. Only manuscript B has Kriemhild going to Gunther to complain, all other manuscripts have her going to Giselher instead. However, it seems more plausible that she should go to Gunther, given the dialogue that follows and Kriemhild's reminder that there are responsibilities that go along with being a legal guardian (*vogt*). This applies mostly to Gunther.

104. There has been much speculation about the treasure's location, and the site of the burial has been either equated with a place-name (*Loche*) or its more literal meaning, "in a deep hole or cave." Needless to say, the treasure has never been found, the search for which of course assumes that it actually existed. Some have speculated that the treasure serves as representative of other great historic treasures in Germany, for example various Roman hoards known to exist, or in fact as a metaphor for Roman troops or the Roman empire as a whole.

Part Two

20. King Etzel Asks for Kriemhild's Hand

[1143] It happened around this time that Lady Helche died, and King Etzel began to search for another wife. His advisers directed his attention to Burgundy and a proud widow by the name of Kriemhild. [1144] After the beautiful Helche died, they said, "If you want to have a noble woman at your side again, the best and most noble that any king has ever had, then you should have this lady. Mighty Siegfried was her husband."

[1145] The great king asked, "How will that be possible, since I have not been baptized? The woman is Christian and will therefore never consent. It would take a miracle, if it happens at all."

[1146] But his chief advisers replied, "She might agree on account of your fame and riches. It would be worth the effort for the noble woman and to your advantage to wed this beauty."

[1147] The noble king then said, "Which one of you knows the people and lands of the Rhine?"

Bold Ruediger of Bechelarn[105] spoke up, "I have known the lords there since I was a child, [1148] Gunther and Gernot, brave and highborn knights. The third is named Giselher. Each one of them conducts himself in a most honorable and chivalrous manner, and their ancestors did likewise."

[1149] Etzel said, "Friend, please tell me if she is fit to wear a crown in my lands, and is she really as beautiful as they say? If so, I'm sure that my most powerful supporters will have no objections."

[1150] "She is every bit as beautiful as my dear Lady Helche was. There is definitely no wife of a king who could be any more beautiful. Whomever she chooses to love may consider himself lucky."

[1151] He said, "Make it happen, Ruediger, as you value my friendship. And if I ever get Kriemhild into bed, then I'll be sure to reward you as well as I can, for then you will have fulfilled my every wish. [1152] I will take from my treasure house everything you and yours will need to live a good life. Everything you need now, from horses to clothing, I'll make sure that it's ready for your trip."

[1153] Margrave Ruediger answered, "It would be dishonorable to ask anything of you. I will gladly be your ambassador to the Rhine, but funded by my own wealth, which you have made possible."

---

105. This is modern-day Pöchlarn, situated on the Danube about one hundred kilometers west of Vienna.

[1154] The wealthy king said, "When will you leave to see this lovely woman? May God watch over you along the way and guard your honor, and my lady as well. May I have the good fortune that she is inclined to grant my wish."

[1155] Ruediger replied, "Before we depart, we have to prepare our weapons and equipment so that we can appear before these lords with dignity. I want to take five hundred capable men with me to the Rhine. [1156] When they see me and my men in Burgundy, I want everyone to say that a king never sent out so many well-equipped men as far as you did to the Rhine. [1157] That is, if you, mighty king, are still determined to see this through. She was bound to Siegfried, the son of Siegmund, in a great love. You saw him here once. People had every right to honor him as they did."

[1158] The noble king said, "If she was that hero's wife, and given how well regarded that noble was, then I don't see any reason to criticize her on that account. And I am intrigued by her great beauty."

[1159] The margrave said, "Then I say to you that we will depart in twenty-four days. I will send word to my wife Gotelind that I am leading the embassy to Kriemhild myself."

[1160] Ruediger sent out messengers to Bechelarn. The margravine was sad and happy at the same time. He let her know that he was to find the king a new wife, but she still had loving memories of the beautiful Helche. [1161] When the margravine first heard the news, she was very unhappy and had to cry as she wondered if her new lady would be like the former. She was still saddened whenever she thought about Helche. [1162] Seven days later, Ruediger departed Hungary, and King Etzel was pleased and proud to see him off. In Vienna he stopped to be outfitted with a larger wardrobe, but he was anxious to resume his journey.

[1163] Gotelind was waiting for him in Bechelarn, and the young margravine, Ruediger's daughter, was happy to see her father and his troops, and many other young women waited there in anticipation as well. [1164] Before noble Ruediger left Vienna for Bechelarn, their entire wardrobes had been loaded onto pack animals, and these were escorted in such a way that they would not be attacked. [1165] When they arrived in the town of Bechelarn, Ruediger, as host, gave orders that his men be given comfortable accommodations. Gotelind was thrilled to see her husband. [1166] The same was true for his dear daughter, the little margravine. Nothing could have given her more joy than his arrival, and she was also happy to see all the warriors from the land of the Huns.

The highborn maiden said gleefully, [1167] "You are most heartily welcome, father, and also your men." Many gracious knights gave their most courteous thanks to the young margravine.

Gotelind knew well what her husband Ruediger was thinking about. [1168] As she was lying next to Ruediger during the night, she asked tenderly where the king of the Huns was sending him. He answered, "My Lady Gotelind, I will gladly tell you. [1169] I am supposed to find a new wife for my lord, since the beautiful Helche has died. I am riding to see Kriemhild on the Rhine. She is meant to be the new queen of the Huns."

[1170] "May God grant," said Gotelind, "that this will come to pass. Since we have heard so many good things said about her, I hope that she will replace our lady for many years. We would be delighted if she were to wear the crown in the land of the Huns."

[1171] The margrave said, "My love, please be so kind as to share some of your wealth with the men who are accompanying me to the Rhine. When such warriors ride in luxury, then they are filled with enthusiasm."

[1172] She said, "Anyone who would like to receive something from me before you and your men leave can have what best suits him."

The margrave replied, "That pleases me."

[1173] Amazingly rich fabrics were taken from her stock rooms, and the noble knights received their share of garments, which were sumptuously lined from top to bottom. Ruediger had chosen his men well for this mission. [1174] On the morning of the seventh day, Ruediger and his men departed Bechelarn. They carried ample weapons and clothing through the land of the Bavarians, where they were left undisturbed by brigands on the roads.*

[1175] In twelve days they reached the Rhine, a fact that could not remain hidden. The king and his counselors were told that foreign troops had come into his lands. The sovereign said that [1176] if anyone knew who they were, he should tell him. People could see that their pack animals were weighted down, and so it was obvious that these were very prosperous men. They were immediately given lodgings in the town. [1177] After the strangers had been lodged, people began to scrutinize them more closely. They wondered where they had come from to the Rhine. The king asked that Hagen be called, since he might know them.

[1178] The hero of Troneck said, "I haven't looked at them yet, but as soon as I do, I can tell you where they've come from to this land. They would have to be from very far away if I don't recognize them immediately."

[1179] The foreigners had by now taken up their lodgings. The ambassador and his escorts were handsomely dressed as they rode to the court, with garments that were both costly and exotic-looking.

[1180] Hagen the strong said, "If I'm not mistaken, and I haven't seen him in a long time, it looks to me like it's Ruediger, the bold and mighty warrior from the land of the Huns."

[1181] "Am I to believe," said the king promptly, "that the Lord of Beche-larn has traveled to our lands?"

As soon as King Gunther had finished speaking, Hagen recognized Rue-diger. [1182] He and his men all ran out of the hall and watched as five hundred men dismounted from their horses. Those from the Hunnish ter-ritories were warmly welcomed. Never before had emissaries worn such pre-cious garments.

[1183] Hagen of Troneck spoke in a booming voice, "May these warriors be most welcome here among us, the Lord of Bechelarn and all his men!"

The reception of the mighty Huns was conducted with full honors. [1184] The king's closest relatives came next, and Ortwin of Metz said to Ruediger, "We have not been so happy to see guests in many years. I can assure you of that."

[1185] The Huns were grateful for the many salutations they received. They all went together into the great hall, where they saw the king sur-rounded by many important men. The king got up from his seat as a sign of great courtesy, [1186] and he approached the party most respectfully. Gun-ther and Gernot greeted the guest and his men courteously, as was their due, and Gunther took noble Ruediger's hand. [1187] He brought him to the very seat that he had been sitting in. The guests were eagerly served the very best mead and wine available anywhere in all the lands along the Rhine. [1188] Giselher and Gere joined them there, and Dancwart and Volker had also heard about the guests. Everyone was pleased as they greeted the brave and noble knights in the presence of the king.

[1189] Hagen of Troneck said to his sovereign, "The margrave should be repaid for what he has done for us with our support. The husband of the beautiful Gotelind deserves abundant reward."

[1190] King Gunther spoke out, "I can't hide my curiosity. Tell me how Etzel and Helche are doing, far away in Hun land."

The margrave answered, "I am glad to inform you." [1191] He got up from his seat, and all of his men did the same. He said to the king, "If I may be permitted by you, my lord, then I will not delay in willingly telling you the news that I bring."

[1192] The king said, "You may deliver the message that has been sent to us in your person. I don't need to consult with my advisers in this regard. Let me and my men hear what you have to say. I want very much that you have success with your mission."

[1193] The trustworthy messenger continued, "My great lord sends his faithful greetings to you here on the Rhine, along with all of your support-ers. This mission is a sign of his great trust. [1194] The noble king has com-manded that his grief be proclaimed. His people are bereft of joy. My Lady Helche, my lord's wife, has died. Many young women are now left orphans,

[1195] the daughters of wellborn nobles she had raised.[106] The reason there is so much grief in his lands is that the people now have no one who can look after them with compassion. And I think this is why the king's cares will not go away."

[1196] "May God reward him," said Gunther, "that he sends such sincere greetings to me and to my people. I receive his greetings here with gratification. My family and my men will gladly return the favor."

[1197] Gernot of Burgundy then spoke, "He will certainly always be pained by the death of Helche, because she knew well how to practice true courtliness." Hagen agreed with what he said, as did many others there.

[1198] Ruediger, that noble and highborn ambassador, said, "If you permit me, dear king, I would like to continue with the message that my lord has entrusted to me, since his life has become so unhappy after Helche's death. [1199] My lord was told that Kriemhild was now without a husband and that Siegfried was dead. If this is indeed true, and if you allow it, then she may wear a crown in the presence of Etzel's men. This is what my lord commissioned me to communicate."

[1200] The mighty king responded in his most courteous fashion, "If she wishes, then she will hear my opinion on the matter. You will have my answer in three days' time. Until I have heard what she thinks, I won't turn Etzel down."[107]

[1201] In the meantime the guests were provided with comfortable accommodations. They were served so well that Ruediger realized that he had the support of Gunther's men. Hagen also assisted him just as Ruediger had done for him previously.[108] [1202] And so Ruediger waited until the third day. Gunther called for his counselors, which was a wise thing to do, and asked if they thought it was right for Kriemhild to take King Etzel as her husband.

[1203] They all agreed that it was, except for Hagen. He said to Gunther, "If you are sensible, then you should refuse the offer, even if she agrees to it."

[1204] "Why," asked Gunther, "should I not agree? If the queen desires something, I would like her to have it. She is after all my sister. We should pursue whatever increases her honor."

---

106. Just as sons were often sent to a foreign court to be raised to manhood by relatives or powerful allies, so too were girls sent into the care of a noblewoman who filled the role of mother, teacher, and advocate. The girls in Helche's care are therefore not literally orphans, but they could be considered such since their welfare and future had been placed in the former queen's hands.

107. Gunther may simply be stalling for time here, or he may be taking his sister's legal rights into consideration. Since she is a widow, she has certain rights to property and to marital consent. The text later makes it clear, however, that Gunther would still have the final say.

108. This is most likely a reference to another tradition that has Hagen and Ruediger sharing a previous exile together in Etzel's court.

[1205] But Hagen said, "Stop this talk. If you knew Etzel the way I do, and if she were to marry him as I've heard you suggest, then it would only be the start of your troubles."

[1206] "I don't understand," said Gunther. "I can make sure to keep my distance. I wouldn't have to worry about an attack if she became his wife."

Hagen replied, "I advise against it, now and in the future."

[1207] Gernot and Giselher were called for, and they were asked if they thought that Kriemhild should marry the powerful king. Hagen alone kept counseling against it.

[1208] Giselher of Burgundy spoke, "My dear friend Hagen, this is an opportunity for you to do something good. Let her be compensated for the pain you have caused her. If it makes her happy, you should not stand in the way. [1209] You have done enough harm to my sister already." Giselher, the brave knight, continued, "She has every right to hate you. Never before has a man taken so much joy from a woman."

[1210] "That is certainly true, I say it openly. If she marries Etzel and lives to see the day, she will do us great harm, however she manages it. She will have a great many courageous men at her beck and call."

[1211] Bold Gernot answered Hagen, "We can agree that we will never ride into Etzel's lands as long as both are still alive. We should remain loyal to her; our honor demands nothing less."

[1212] But Hagen said, "Everyone knows I'm speaking the truth. If noble Kriemhild wears Helche's crown, she'll find some way to harm us. It would be better for nobles like you to leave this deal undone."

[1213] Giselher, beautiful Ute's son, responded heatedly, "Not all of us have to act deceitfully. We should be happy about any honor that comes her way. Regardless of what you may say, Hagen, I will continue to serve her faithfully."

[1214] Hagen was infuriated when he heard this, but Gernot and Giselher, both brave and prominent knights, and powerful Gunther all agreed that if Kriemhild should say yes, they would not stand in her way.

[1215] Lord Gere said, "I will tell her that she should give King Etzel's proposal positive consideration. Many warriors serve him out of fear, and he can well compensate her for all the pain that she has had to endure."

[1216] The valiant noble went to where he found her. She received him warmly, and he quickly got to the point. "You can greet me happily and provide me with a messenger's reward. A lucky turn of events will soon save you from all your distress. [1217] My lady, someone has asked for your hand, and he is one of the very best that ever ruled a mighty kingdom and wore a crown. Noble knights have brought this proposal, and your brother wanted you to be told."

[1218] She replied, full of grief, "May God forbid that you and all my family should make fun of such a poor woman as myself. What would a man want with me if he had ever enjoyed the love of a good woman?"

[1219] She refused to consider the offer, but then her brother Gernot came to see her, along with young Giselher. They tried lovingly to assuage her by saying that it would really be to her advantage to accept the king's offer. [1220] No one could talk her into taking another husband. The nobles then asked her, "If nothing else, then you could at least listen to what the messenger has to say."

[1221] "I won't refuse," said the noble woman, "to see Ruediger, because he is such a good man. If he had not been sent, I would never agree to see any other messenger." [1222] She said, "Please ask him to come see me tomorrow morning here in my rooms. I want him to hear my decision, and I want him to hear it from me." With that she once again broke into tears.

[1223] Noble Ruediger wanted nothing more than to visit the highborn queen, and he thought that if anyone could convince her, he could. [1224] Early the next morning after Mass, the noble emissaries gathered together in a great throng, all of those who wanted to accompany Ruediger to the court. People could see many of them dressed in their finest. [1225] Kriemhild, sad but regal, was waiting for Ruediger, that noble ambassador. He saw her wearing her everyday clothes, even though her attendants were all dressed resplendently. [1226] She met him at the door and received the noble knight most warmly. He had gone to see her with only eleven others and was treated very well, as they had never received such a high-ranking emissary before.

[1227] The lord and his men were invited to be seated. They could see the two margraves, Eckewart and Gere, both noble knights, standing in front of her. Everyone was somber, in respect for the feelings of the lady of the house. [1228] They also saw many beautiful ladies seated in front of her. Kriemhild felt nothing but sorrow, and her blouse had been soiled by her hot tears. The noble margrave certainly recognized these signs.

[1229] The dignified emissary said, "Your Majesty, please allow me and my comrades who have accompanied me to stand before you and deliver to you the message that we have brought this great distance."

[1230] "You have my permission," said the queen, "to present to me what you will. I am well inclined to hear your communication, since you are a well-respected emissary." Others in the room could tell that she said this only half-heartedly.

[1231] Lord Ruediger from Bechelarn said, "Dear lady, Etzel, a great king, sends to you in this land assurances of his loyalty and love. He has sent a good many knights here to ask for your hand. [1232] He promises you love without sorrow. He is prepared to abide in faith and friendship, as he had once with Lady Helche, whom he loved dearly. He grieves daily still because of her many fine qualities."

[1233] The queen replied, "Margrave Ruediger, anyone who knew how much I suffer would not ask me to marry another man. I lost the very best husband that any woman ever had."

[1234] "What can replace sorrow," said the audacious man, "if not heartfelt love, provided that one can give love and is seeking for a suitable mate as well. Nothing else is as effective against heartfelt sorrow.[109] [1235] And if you were to decide to take my noble lord as yours, you would hold sway over twelve kingdoms. In addition, my lord would grant you thirty principalities, all of which were conquered by his own hand. [1236] You would also be sovereign over many men of the nobility, who were subjects of my Lady Helche. And there are also many ladies whom she commanded, all from noble houses," said the bold knight. [1237] "In addition, my lord wants you to know that he will give you the crown to wear alongside his, if you agree, that is, all the power that Helche once had. This is the power you will have over Etzel's people."

[1238] The queen replied, "How could I ever want to be the wife of a hero again? The death of one has caused me such grief that I can never gain happiness again."

[1239] The Huns responded, "Mighty queen, your life with Etzel will be so wonderful that you will never cease to be amazed, should it come to that. The mighty king has many brave warriors. [1240] Helche's ladies and your maidens, should they together be a single household, would give warriors something to cheer about. Dear lady, we ask you to consider this offer, as it is for your own good."

[1241] She answered in her courteous way, "That's enough for now. Why don't you come back tomorrow morning? I'll give you an answer to your proposition then." The bold men had to acquiesce.

[1242] After they had all returned to their lodgings, the noble lady asked that Giselher and her mother be brought to her. She told them both that mourning was the only thing that she was fit to do.

[1243] Her brother Giselher then spoke, "Sister, I have been told, and I believe it as well, that King Etzel could take away your sorrow if you took him as your husband. Whatever others may say, this is what I think is the right thing to do. [1244] He can completely compensate you for your loss," said Giselher. "From the Rhone to the Rhine, from the Elbe to the [Mediterranean]

---

109. This is decidedly not a message of *minne*, given the emphasis instead on friendly *liebe* and the ability of love to mitigate pain, rather than to cause it. Etzel's embassy and Ruediger's role as messenger fit into dynastic match-making strategies and not the more fashionable, but unrealistic pleas for unrequited love that characterized the courtly game of *minne*.

Sea, there is no king as powerful as he. You can soon be happy again if he makes you his wife."

[1245] She said, "Brother dearest, why are you telling me this? I am fated to tears and mourning. How could I possibly appear before the court and its men there? I may have been beautiful once, but that was long ago."

[1246] Lady Ute then spoke to her daughter, "My dear child, you should do what your brothers advise. Listen to your family and you will always do the right thing. I've seen you in mourning now for too long."

[1247] Kriemhild prayed to God that he might provide her the means to give away gold, silver, and clothing as she and her husband had once done while he was still alive. She was never as happy as she had been then. [1248] She thought to herself, "If I should give myself to a heathen as a Christian woman, my reputation would be ruined forever. Even if he gave me all the riches in the world, I couldn't do it." [1249] This was what she resolved. Throughout the night until the next morning, the lady lay in bed thinking. Her bright eyes did not dry until she got up to go to Mass first thing in the morning.

[1250] The sovereigns arrived for morning Mass, and they started in on their sister again, telling her that she should take the king of the Huns as her husband, but there was no joy to be found in her by anyone. [1251] Etzel's men were called in. They were ready to go home, regardless of the outcome. Next Ruediger arrived at the court, and he and all his men [1252] wanted to know Gunther's decision forthwith. They were all in agreement in this, as their way home was a long one. Ruediger was led to see Kriemhild, and [1253] he asked the noble queen most kindly if she would tell him what answer he could take back to Etzel's lands. She refused to believe [1254] that she could ever love another man.

The margrave spoke, "That is not the right way to think about this. How can you let such beauty go to waste? You can still be the wife of an important man."

[1255] There was no convincing her until Ruediger managed to speak with the mighty queen in private. He told her that he would personally answer to her for whatever might happen. She started to think more sympathetically about things.

[1256] He said to the queen, "Please don't cry anymore. If you had no one else in the land of the Huns except me, my faithful kin, and my men, then anyone who harmed you in any way would have to pay dearly."

[1257] The lady's mind was greatly eased. She said, "Then swear an oath to me, that whatever anyone does to me, you will be the first to avenge the injury."

The margrave responded, "Dear lady, to this I will agree." [1258] Along with all of his men, Ruediger swore to serve her faithfully and always, and

that the highborn warriors from Etze
that would increase her honor. Ruedi

[1259] The faithful woman then
allies, I can let people say whatever
Perhaps my dear husband can still b
"Since Etzel has such a large army, if
wanted. He is also so wealthy that I w
hateful Hagen robbed me of my own

[1261] She said to Ruediger, "If I
would gladly come along wherever he

The margrave replied, "You should
many knights who are Christian that
you are with the king. Perhaps you
would be reason enough to become F

[1263] Her brother said, "Say yes
end to your mourning." They kept at her until the woeful woman finally
agreed, in the company of those nobles, to become Etzel's wife.

[1264] She said, "I will follow you, poor queen that I am, and ride to
the land of the Huns, just as soon as possible, if my friends will accompany
me there." Beautiful Kriemhild raised her hand to swear in front of the
nobles.

[1265] The margrave said, "If you had only two men, then I would have
many more to add. We can easily escort you across the Rhine honorably.
You need not, lady, remain here in Burgundy any longer. [1266] I have five
hundred men and kin who will serve you here and also at home, however
you may command them, dear lady. I will do the same, and whenever you
call, it will be my honor.[111] [1267] Have your horse saddled. You will never

---

110. The theme of conversion is thrown into the mix, as it could be considered a noble motive
to try to convert a non-Christian through marriage. Similar themes are found in Wolfram's
Willehalm in which Willehalm marries Arabel, whose Christian name then becomes Gyburg.
In his *Parzival*, Wolfram has Belacane, Gahmuret's heathen wife, declare that she would gladly
be baptized if it could bring about her husband's return. We are also told in the *Klage* that Etzel
had once been converted to Christianity but had subsequently renounced his baptismal vows.
111. Translators and editors have read this important oath quite differently. Ruediger promises
his own personal service as well as that of his five hundred men, both in Worms as well as at
Etzel's court. Option 1 translates the oath: "I shall do likewise, underline{unless it should dishonor me,}
my lady, whenever you remind me of what was said here" (Hatto, 162; similarly Edwards,
Lichtenstein), and Option 2: "underline{may I have no cause for shame} whenever you remind me of
my promise" (Mowatt). The critical phrases have been underlined. Helmut de Boor makes a
note in his edition that reads as does Option 1, Schulze follows this in her translation of C.
Heinzle takes Option 2, translating "es wird mir eine Ehre sein" (it will be my honor). I have
opted for the second reading as well, mainly because Ruediger in fact never makes use of this
so-called escape clause ("unless") in his oath, and providing such an out would have the effect

regret having followed Ruediger's counsel. And alert the women who will be going with you. A great many outstanding warriors will join us along the way."

[1268] They still had saddlery that they had used for riding in Sieg-fried's time, when they would take many young women with them hon-orably whenever they wanted. The saddles they had for the women were amazing. [1269] Those who had ever worn expensive dresses prepared them now for their journey, since they had heard much said about this king, and they opened up the wardrobes that had remained closed for so long. [1270] They were busy for four and a half days and took out of the chests everything that had been folded up. Kriemhild opened up her trea-sury so as to make all of Ruediger's men wealthy. [1271] She still possessed gold from the land of the Nibelungen, and it was her intent to distribute it in the Hunnish lands. There was so much that a hundred horses couldn't carry it all.[112]

Hagen heard about Kriemhild's intentions. [1272] He said, "Since Queen Kriemhild will never forgive me, then Siegfried's gold must stay here. Why would I let my enemies keep so much wealth? I know very well what Kriem-hild intends to do with this treasure. [1273] If she takes it with her, I'm sure that it will be handed out to set people against me. They don't have enough horses to carry it all. Tell Kriemhild that Hagen is going to keep it."

[1274] When she heard the news, she was stunned. The three sovereigns were also informed and wanted to reverse the decision, but when they failed to do so noble Ruediger said lightheartedly, [1275] "Mighty queen, why do you lament the loss of gold? King Etzel will be so beholden to you that when he sees your eyes he will give you more than you could ever spend. Dear lady, I can swear to that."

[1276] The queen replied, "Dear noble Ruediger, never before has a king's daughter possessed a greater treasure than what Hagen has taken from me."

---

of making his oath less than absolute. It is his absolute loyalty to this oath that in the end causes his own death. The pledge can also be compared to Eckewart's (str. 1283), who places no conditions on his straightforward pledge of loyalty. Grammatically it is also the simplest solution of the subordinate clause introduced by *daz*, with a literal rendition being "that I may never be ashamed of it."

112. There is an obvious inconsistency here between what we are told at the end of the first part of the epic and what is revealed here in the beginning of the second part. In str. 1137 we read that Hagen sinks the entire treasure in the Rhine, a fact that Kriemhild protests in the strongest terms. Here in str. 1277 we have in a sense a reenactment of that earlier seizure, with Hagen and Gunther even offering the remains of the treasure to Ruediger, which he refuses. That Kriemhild has to endure the theft of her property twice serves to emphasize her unjust loss and will resurface when Hagen and the Burgundian court arrive in Etzel's court empty handed.

Her brother Gernot went to her rooms [1277] and with the king's authority placed the key in the lock. Kriemhild's gold was removed, at least thirty thousand marks of it. He told the Huns to take it, which Gunther approved.[113]

[1278] The Lord of Bechelarn, Gotelind's husband, said, "If my Lady Kriemhild had all that was taken out of the land of the Nibelungen, neither I nor the queen would touch any of it. [1279] Keep it, I don't want any of it. I have brought enough of my own, and we will have more than enough along the way. Our expenses for the return are more than covered."

[1280] In the meantime, her attendants had filled twelve chests with the best gold that could be found anywhere. These they took with them and used them to dress many of the women on their journey. [1281] She was stunned by Hagen's ruthlessness, but she still had about one thousand marks of her own gold, which she donated for her dear husband's soul. That seemed to Ruediger to be done with great loyalty.

[1282] The mournful lady spoke, "Where are my friends, who out of love are willing to endure exile? They may ride with me to the land of the Huns and use my money to buy horses and clothing."

[1283] Margrave Eckewart spoke to the queen, "Since I first became part of your household, I have served you faithfully, and I pledge to continue to do so to the end of my days. [1284] I will take five hundred of my men along with me, and I place them at your service as a sign of my loyalty. We are one, until parted by death." Kriemhild bowed to him in thanks for his speech, as well she should.

[1285] Then they retrieved the horses and were ready to ride. Friends shed many tears, while Ute the powerful and many pretty young women showed how much they would miss Kriemhild. [1286] One hundred highborn women went with her, outfitted as was appropriate for them, but their clear eyes were filled with tears.

She was later to experience much happiness with Etzel. [1287] The lords Giselher and Gernot appeared along with their households, as courtesy demanded. They wanted to escort their sister part of the way, and they took along a thousand of their best men, [1288] with bold Gere and Ortwin joining them. Rumolt, the master of the kitchen, was there, too. They arranged for daily lodgings all the way to the Danube. Gunther only rode out a short way from the town.*

---

113. Gunther apparently approved of the notion that Ruediger and his accompanying force be given what remains of the Nibelungen treasure as a show of good will and support. Presumably if it were in the hands of a man, Kriemhild would lose the opportunity to gain supporters through a generous distribution of her own wealth. Ruediger rejects the offer, both for himself as well as for Kriemhild, as a sign that Etzel can more than make up for the loss, and that Ruediger's allegiance is clearly given to Etzel and his new wife.

[1289] Before they left the Rhine, they sent out their fastest messengers to the Hunnish lands. They were to tell the king that Ruediger had successfully won the noble queen to be his wife.*

21. Kriemhild Travels to the Land of the Huns

[1290] We'll let the emissaries be on their way. We should tell you how the queen traveled through the land, and where Giselher and Gernot, who escorted her out of loyalty, left her. [1291] They rode to the Danube and to Vergen [Pförring], where they asked the queen to give them leave to ride back to the Rhine. Many tears were shed among friends.

[1292] Giselher spoke to his sister, "If you, my lady, should ever need me, if you have any problems, let me know. I will come to Etzel's lands to give you my support."

[1293] She kissed her relatives on the mouth. The parting from Margrave Ruediger's men there was warm and loving. The queen took many beautiful young women along with her, [1294] 104 altogether, all of them wearing costly garments made of colorful and rich materials. Many broad shields were carried alongside the women on the way, but many excellent warriors turned around at that point and left her. [1295] The rest moved on quickly down through Bavaria. People there heard reports that a large group of foreigners had been seen where a monastery [Niedernburg] still stands today and where the Inn flows into the Danube.*

[1296] There was a bishop in the town of Passau. The houses and the noble court were emptied as people rushed to meet the foreigners up in Bavaria, where Bishop Pilgrim greeted Kriemhild.[114] [1297] The knights of the region were not at all displeased when they saw so many pretty young women, and these daughters of highborn knights were greeted with loving glances. The guests were given excellent lodgings.* [1298] The bishop rode back to Passau with his niece. The townspeople prepared a great reception for her when the citizens of the town were told that Kriemhild, the sister of kings, was coming.

---

114. There was a Bishop Pilgrim of Passau attested in the late tenth century (971–91). A cult developed around this figure in the late twelfth century in Passau, and it was the bishop at the time of the composition of the *Nibelungenlied*, Wolfger von Erla (1191–1204), who encouraged the veneration of his predecessor. This Bishop Wolfger is known to have patronized the poet Walther von der Vogelweide around the same time, before moving on to take the patriarchate of Aquileia in northern Italy. In the story, Pilgrim is Queen Ute's brother, making him Kriemhild's uncle. He plays an even larger role in the *Klage* as the authority that had the entire *Nibelungen* epic written down, supposedly first in Latin to establish its veracity, then translated into other languages.

[1299] The bishop hoped that they might be able to stay, but Lord Ecke-
wart said, "That is not possible. We have to travel on to Ruediger's lands. Many
men are waiting for us, since our arrival is already known to everyone there."

[1300] By now beautiful Gotelind had heard the news as well, and so she
readied herself and her daughter. Ruediger sent her a message saying that he
thought it would brighten the queen's mood [1301] if she rode up to the Enns
River with his own men to meet her. After the message had been delivered,
the roads were filled, and everyone rode and walked out to meet the guests.

[1302] The queen arrived in Eferding. If the Bavarians had attacked them
along the way, as they are accustomed to doing, then they could have caused
the travelers a good deal of harm. [1303] The mighty margrave was able to
prevent that, however, since he was leading more than a thousand knights.
Gotelind, Ruediger's wife, arrived at around the same time, with many noble
and impressive knights attending her. [1304] Once Kriemhild's company had
crossed the Traun River and arrived on the fields near the town of Enns, they
could see tents and pavilions set up where they were to spend the night. The
costs were all covered by Ruediger. [1305] Beautiful Gotelind left her lodg-
ings, so that the road was packed with handsome horses with bells on their
harnesses. The reception was a great success, and Ruediger was very pleased.

[1306] Those who came from all directions to meet them were excellent
horsemen, including many knights, and they engaged in contests watched
by the young women. The queen was also pleased by their attention. [1307]
When Ruediger's men met the foreigners, people saw spears shattered by the
knights, as is common in such chivalrous sport, and they jousted for prizes
there in front of the women. [1308] When they stopped, many of the men
greeted each other warmly. They escorted beautiful Gotelind to where Kriem-
hild was staying, so that those charged with serving the ladies were kept busy
indeed.

[1309] The Lord of Bechelarn rode out to meet his wife. The noble mar-
gravine was by no means unhappy about his safe return from the Rhine, and
all her cares were swept away by great joy. [1310] After she had greeted him,
he asked her and all her ladies to dismount on the grass. Many noble men
were energetically helping out, and the ladies were served with great enthu-
siasm. [1311] Lady Kriemhild saw the margravine standing there along with
her household, and so she rode no further, bringing her horse to a halt by
pulling on the reins, and commanded that she be helped out of the saddle
on the spot. [1312] People then saw the bishop and Eckewart escorting his
sister's daughter to see Gotelind, whereupon everyone immediately stepped
aside. The queen, far from home, kissed Gotelind on the mouth.

[1313] Ruediger's wife said affectionately, "I am honored, dear lady, that I
may lay eyes on your beauty here in these lands. I can think of nothing that
would be more pleasing."

[1314] "May God bless you, noble Gotelind," replied Kriemhild. "If I and the son of Botelung [Etzel] live in health, then you may well be pleased that you saw me today." Neither one knew what was going to happen later.

[1315] Many young women approached one another courteously, and knights were readily at their service. After exchanging greetings, they sat down together on the meadow, where many of them made friends with complete strangers. [1316] Refreshments were ordered for the ladies as it was around noontime, but the noble entourage did not stay there much longer, instead riding on to where they found many large pavilions. Here the noble guests were served lavishly, [1317] and then they rested through the night until morning. The people of Bechelarn were prepared to receive all the foreign guests, as Ruediger had made sure that nothing would be lacking.

[1318] The windows in the town walls were all open, and the gates to the castle of Bechelarn were unlocked as well. The guests entered there, as they were all most welcome, and the lord ordered that they be made comfortable. [1319] Ruediger's daughter went up to the queen with her attendants and greeted her kindly. Her mother, the margrave's wife, was there as well, and many young women were welcomed with affection. [1320] They took each other's hands and went to the great hall, which was incredibly beautiful, in fact, the Danube ran right beneath it. They all sat near the windows and enjoyed the company of others. [1321] I can't say what else they did.

Kriemhild's men complained that they were spending too much time there, and they weren't happy about it. There were a great many brave warriors who rode on with her from Bechelarn. [1322] Ruediger kindly offered them his support. Gotelind's daughter received twelve armbands of red gold along with the most precious dress that the queen had brought with her. [1323] Even though the Nibelungen gold had been stolen from her, she gave what little she had left to whomever she saw, and they were grateful for it. The lord's household was amply rewarded.

[1324] In return and to her honor, Lady Gotelind was so generous to the guests from the Rhine that there was no one among them who did not wear some jewel or precious garment of hers. [1325] After they had eaten and were preparing to leave, the lady of the house offered Etzel's wife her loyal support.

Kriemhild in turn showed her young daughter great affection. [1326] She said to the queen, "If you think it's a good idea, I know that my father will gladly send me to visit you in the land of the Huns." Kriemhild thought that the young woman had spoken with true devotion.

[1327] The horses were prepared and brought outside of Bechelarn. The noble queen took her leave there from Ruediger's wife and his daughter. Many beautiful young women also said their goodbyes. [1328] They never saw each other again after that day.

In the streets of Melk the foreigners were served wine in precious gold goblets and were heartily welcomed. [1329] There was a local lord there whose name was Astolt, and he showed them the road to Austria down the Danube toward Mautern. The queen was later to be well served there. [1330] It was here that the bishop affectionately parted company with his niece. He advised her to stay positive and to gain honor, as Helche had done before her. She won great honor indeed in the land of the Huns.

[1331] The foreigners were then brought to the Traisen River. Ruediger's men kept them safe until the Huns came riding up to meet them, and the queen was treated most honorably there. [1332] In the lands surrounding the Traisen River the king of the Huns possessed a mighty castle known far and wide called Traismauer. Lady Helche had lived there so respectably, that it would be hard for anyone to match, [1333] with the exception of Kriemhild, who in turn was so generous that she was able to enjoy life after her suffering. Etzel's men gave her the recognition and honor she deserved. [1334] Etzel's power was so widely recognized that one could always meet the greatest warriors at his court, those acclaimed by both heathens and Christians, and they all attended him. [1335] Christians and heathens lived side by side under his rule, something that will surely never happen again. Regardless of religion, the king was generous to everyone alike.

22. Kriemhild Marries Etzel

[1336] She spent four days in Traismauer. The dust along the roads never settled, and the entire time it looked as if a fire were burning. King Etzel's men were on the move throughout Austria. [1337] It was also faithfully reported to the king that Kriemhild was riding majestically through the lands. This made any hint of sorrow disappear, and the king quickly set out to meet the beautiful woman. [1338] Many skillful warriors were seen riding ahead of him, all speaking different languages, leading large troops of men, both Christian and heathen, and they met up with the queen in a splendid procession. [1339] Numerous men from Russia and Greece were riding there, men from Poland and Wallachia could be seen on powerful and swift horses, all of them showing off their own customs and traditions. [1340] From the land of Kiev there rode scores of men, and the wild Pechenegs, who were skilled at shooting birds with their bows, joined them. They could pull back an arrow all the way to the tip.

[1341] There is a town in Austria on the Danube named Tulln, where Kriemhild became familiar with foreign customs that she had never seen before. She was greeted by many who were later to suffer on her account. [1342] Part of Etzel's court rode out before him, all of them in good spirits and strong, courtly and proud, in total twenty-four of the highest and mighti-est nobles. They wanted nothing more than to see their future lady. [1343] Count Ramunc from Wallachia hurried up to her with seven hundred men, who looked as swift as birds when they rode. Then came Lord Gibeche with a large and powerful force. [1344] Hornboge the strong separated himself from his king with a thousand men to meet his lady, and they made a great noise, as is custom in that land. Those related to the Huns were also vigor-ous riders. [1345] Bold Hawart from Denmark was there, along with Irinc, strong and always true, and Irnfried of Thuringia, a most formidable man. They greeted Kriemhild in a way that certainly increased her honor, [1346] with twelve hundred men in their company. Next came Lord Bloedelin, King Etzel's brother, from Hunnish lands with three thousand men. He arrived with great ceremony as he met up with the queen. [1347] Finally King Etzel arrived along with Lord Dietrich and all his comrades. Present were many famous knights, all of them virtuous and brave. This spectacle helped to lift Lady Kriemhild's spirits.

[1348] Lord Ruediger spoke to the queen, "Dear lady, I want to greet the mighty king here. You should kiss those whom I point out to you, since not all of Etzel's men can be greeted equally."

[1349] The distinguished queen was then lifted off her horse. Mighty Etzel could wait no longer. He dismounted along with his enthusiastic men, and he was seen cheerfully walking up to Kriemhild. [1350] We were told that two powerful nobles accompanied the queen to carry her train as King Etzel approached her, and that she greeted the noble lord graciously with a kiss. [1351] She lifted her head covering, and her beautiful skin shone out from the surrounding gold material. Many of the men there said that Lady Helche had not been any more beautiful.

The king's brother, Bloedelin, was standing close at hand. [1352] Ruedi-ger, the powerful margrave, directed her to give him a kiss, along with King Gibeche. Dietrich was also standing there. Etzel's wife kissed twelve heroes altogether, but many of the knights were greeted otherwise.

[1353] The entire time that Etzel stood there next to Kriemhild, the young men did as they still do today. They could be seen jousting, Christians and heathens, each according to his own custom. [1354] Dietrich's men, those courageous knights, were particularly adept at shattering their lances high above the shields, and the German troops ran through many a shield.[115]

---

115. It is not clear if Dietrich and his men are referred to as German *gesten* (guests), or if this is a separate contingent. It is possible that this refers to Irnfried of Thuringia and his men, men-tioned in str. 1345, or that Dietrich, originally an Ostrogothic king (Theoderic, d. 526), could have been characterized as a German serving Etzel as a foreign exile. This is the only reference in the text to the Germans (*tiusch*) as a distinct group.

[1355] The noise from the splintering shafts was deafening, now that all the country's warriors, along with the king's allies, had arrived.

The mighty king escorted Lady Kriemhild away from there. [1356] They saw a large and magnificent pavilion nearby, and the entire field was filled with tents where they could rest after their toil and travail. The knights escorted [1357] the queen and many beautiful women to their tents, and the queen took her place in an elegant chair. The margrave had made sure that Kriemhild's seat was the best possible, and Etzel was pleased. [1358] I don't know what Etzel said there. Kriemhild's fair hand rested in his own hand, and they sat together affectionately, although Ruediger did not want to leave the king alone with her. [1359] The command went out to stop the jousting altogether, whereupon the great tumult was honorably brought to a close. Etzel's men retired to their tents, spread out over a wide area. [1360] The day finally came to an end, and they slept comfortably until the next day dawned, when many of the men were already at their horses again. These games and contests all increased the king's honor.

[1361] The king commanded the Huns to form a grand procession, and so they rode from Tulln to Vienna. There they met many elegant women who greeted King Etzel's wife with great honors. [1362] Anything at all that they desired was abundantly available, and the men, eagerly anticipating the clamor and commotion, retired to their lodgings. The king's festival was off to a joyous start.

[1363] They weren't all able to find a place to stay in town. Ruediger asked those who were local to take their lodgings outside of the walls. I think [1364] that Dietrich and other warriors could be seen spending all their time with Kriemhild. They gave up their rest and made a great effort to amuse the guests, so that Ruediger and his men were fully entertained.

[1365] The festival took place at Pentecost, and King Etzel slept with Kriemhild there in the town of Vienna. I don't think that she had as many men at her command with her first husband. [1366] Whomever she did not know, she introduced herself to them with gifts. Some of them said to the foreigners, "We thought that Lady Kriemhild had lost all of her possessions. Now she is doing wonders with all her gift giving."

[1367] The festivities lasted for seventeen days. I don't think that anyone can claim that another king had a more magnificent festival; we certainly never heard of any. Everyone there went away wearing something brand new. [1368] I don't think that she had as many warriors by her side even in Netherland. And I also believe that Siegfried, as wealthy as he was, never had as many noble men as she saw standing in front of Etzel. [1369] And no one had ever, at his own festival, given away so many costly full-length robes or excellent clothes, of which they had plenty. All this was done to honor Kriemhild. [1370] Her friends and strangers alike were all of one mind, that they would spare nothing they owned, and if someone wanted something, then it was willingly given, until many a generous warrior stood there with nothing left to wear.

[1371] Kriemhild thought back on how she had lived on the Rhine along with her noble husband, and her eyes filled with tears, although she was able to hide her crying so that no one could see it. After so much suffering she had been greatly honored.

[1372] Whatever others were giving away, it was nothing in comparison to what Dietrich was bestowing. What Botelung's son [Etzel] had given him was all gone. Open-handed Ruediger was also performing sheer wonders. [1373] Lord Bloedelin from Hungary ordered several travel trunks to be emptied of silver and gold, which was all given away. The king's heroes were all in joyful spirits. [1374] I think both Werbel and Swemmel, the king's minstrels, received at least a thousand marks at the festival, where beautiful Kriemhild sat in majesty with Etzel.

[1375] On the eighteenth morning they departed Vienna, where the knights had destroyed many a shield with their spears during their chivalrous contests. Etzel then arrived in the land of the Huns. [1376] They spent the night in the old town of Hainburg. No one could guess how large the army was that was traveling across the land. They were happy indeed to see such beautiful women in their homeland. [1377] In the prosperous town of Miesenburg they boarded ships. The river was covered with horses and people, as if it were solid ground, as far as the eye could see. The travel-weary ladies finally had some rest and comfort. [1378] Many of the large ships were lashed together so that they were less vulnerable to the waves and the currents, and the decks were covered with pavilions as if they were still on land.

[1379] News arrived in Etzelnburg that they were on their way. Every woman and man in the town was overjoyed. Helche's household, which had once served that lady, was still to experience happy times with Kriemhild. [1380] Many highborn women were standing there in anticipation, though still sad over the death of Helche. Kriemhild met seven royal daughters who were still there, and they were an adornment for all of Etzel's lands. [1381] The young lady Herrat was the head of the household. She was Helche's niece and beyond reproach. She was Dietrich's bride, the daughter of Nentwin, a powerful king, and she was destined to achieve great acclaim. [1382] She was especially looking forward to the arrival of the guests, and no expense was spared in preparation for the reception. Who could describe to you how the king ruled? They never had it better in the land of the Huns even during Queen Helche's days.

[1383] After the king had ridden away from the riverside with his wife, noble Kriemhild was told who everyone was so that she could greet each one appropriately. Since taking Helche's place, she had assumed a prominent position. [1384] She was served faithfully, and in turn the queen distributed all the gold and gowns, silver and precious stones that she had brought with her from the Rhine to the Huns. [1385] Later all the king's kin and all his men would give her their support. Even Lady Helche had never ruled with the power of all those who would serve Kriemhild unto death. [1386] The court and the entire land were held in such esteem that people could find whatever kind of amusement they desired there, out of love for the king and the benevolent queen.[116]

23. Etzel and Kriemhild Send a Message

[1387] They lived together for seven years with great honor, and this is the truth. During this time the queen gave birth to a son, and King Etzel could not have been happier. [1388] She would not relent, however, until Etzel's child had been baptized according to Christian rites. He was named Ortlieb, and all of Etzel's lands were filled with great joy.

[1389] Kriemhild strived to match Helche's great virtue. Herrat, a foreign lady, helped her in this endeavor, although she still secretly mourned for Helche. [1390] Kriemhild was well known among both native inhabitants and foreigners, and they said that never before had a royal land possessed a finer and more generous lady, something on which they all agreed. She enjoyed this kind of acclaim in the land of the Huns for a full thirteen years.

[1391] She knew that no one could oppose her, as sometimes happens still today when warriors of the king stand up against his wife. At all times she had twelve kings at her service, and yet she still thought about all that she had suffered at home. [1392] She also remembered the honors of the land of the Nibelungen that she had possessed and that Hagen had taken from her with Siegfried's death. She wondered if she might still have the opportunity to make him suffer.

[1393] "That could happen, if I could get him to come here to this land."* She often dreamed that she and her brother Giselher were walking hand in hand, and she kissed him often in her gentle slumber. But they would later have to endure many hardships. [1394] I believe it was the malevolent devil

---

116. Ms. A and others have a text that translates ". . . for love of the king and for the queen's wealth (*guot*)" (Edwards). Hatto, 1965, follows this line, although the text in B and C states clearly ". . . and for the good (benevolent) queen." It seems a stretch to use a reading from ms. A when both B and C agree and there is no reason to diverge simply for the sake of supporting the notion that Kriemhild's remaining wealth is somehow motivation alone for the loyalty, and ultimately demise, of the Huns.

who counseled Kriemhild to sever the friendship with Giselher[117] that she had sealed with a kiss in Burgundy.

Again her gown was dampened by her hot tears. [1395] She agonized in her heart from morning till night how it was that she had been talked into becoming the wife of a heathen. Hagen and Gunther were responsible for her anguish. [1396] She was constantly obsessed in her thoughts with a single purpose: "I am so powerful and have so much money that I could destroy my enemies, above all Hagen of Troneck. [1397] How my heart often longs for those who are faithful. If I were now near those who had caused me such grief, then I could well avenge my husband's death, something I long for," said Etzel's wife.

[1398] All the king's men and Kriemhild's warriors loved her, as they should. Eckewart was the chamberlain, which won him many friends. No one refused to do Kriemhild's bidding. [1399] She constantly thought to herself, "I will ask the king," that he should allow her to invite her relatives to visit the land of the Huns. No one guessed the queen's ill intent. [1400] One night she was lying with the king, with his arms around her as was his custom when they slept together, since she was as dear to him as life itself. The formidable woman's thoughts were on her enemies.

[1401] She said to the king, "My dear lord, I wanted to ask you kindly, if it meets your favor, that you would show me, that is if I deserve it, whether my family is dear to you or not."

[1402] The mighty king responded with devotion. "I will prove to you that whatever goodness and kindness these warriors can gain would make me happy. I have never gained better friends by way of a woman's love."

[1403] The queen said, "As you have been told, I have many great relatives. This is why it is so painful to me that they have never visited me here before. I hear people talking about me, saying that I am nothing but an exile here."[118]

[1404] King Etzel replied, "My dear wife, if it is not too far for them, I would invite everyone from the Rhine whom you would want to see here in my lands." The lady was glad to know his state of mind.

---

117. Some manuscripts have Gunther in place of Giselher, and this seems at first glance more logical, although the reading from A and B (C diverges here and does not name one of the brothers) of Giselher can be defended as representative of all three brothers who were reconciled with Kriemhild.

118. The term *ellende* has different shades of meaning, and is here often translated as foreigner or stranger. In this instance the meaning is more specific, in that a distinction is being made between a voluntary "guest" in Etzel's court versus someone banished and living outside the law as an exile. Kriemhild seems to be trying to convince Etzel that people are beginning to doubt that she comes from a powerful family at all and that she was instead forced to seek out Etzel's protection, which he has provided to many other exiles, such as Dietrich of Bern.

[1405] She said, "If you want to show me your faithfulness, my lord, then send emissaries to Worms on the Rhine. That way I can tell my family about my intentions, and many noble knights will travel here to this land."

[1406] He said, "Your wish is my command. You can't want to see your family any sooner than I, those noble sons of Ute. It has greatly concerned me that they have been absent for so long. [1407] If it's alright with you, my dear wife, then I'll send my minstrels to your family in Burgundy." He ordered that the minstrels be brought to him immediately. [1408] They hurried to where he was with the queen, and he told both of them that they were to serve as ambassadors to Burgundy. He had costly garments made for them. [1409] Clothes were also prepared for twenty-four men. They were given the message by the king how they were to invite Gunther and his men, but Kriemhild the queen then spoke with them alone.

[1410] The mighty king said, "I will tell you what your mission is. I send my relatives good and kind wishes and ask that they might ride here to my lands. Never before have I wanted more to have such dear guests. [1411] And if they, Kriemhild's family, will agree to grant my wish, then they should not fail to come here for our summer festival. My wife's family is the source of all my joy."

[1412] Proud Swemmel, the fiddler, asked, "When will the festival take place, so that we can tell your relatives?"

King Etzel replied, "At the next summer solstice."*

[1413] "We will do as you command," said Werbel.

The queen then had them secretly brought to her rooms, where she spoke to them. Little good came of this later for many warriors. [1414] She said to both of the emissaries, "You can earn a large reward if you do as I command and take this message back to my homeland. I will make each of you rich and provide you with precious garments. [1415] Anyone in my family you should meet at Worms on the Rhine, don't tell them that you have ever seen me unhappy. And be sure to offer my services to those daring and brave heroes. [1416] Ask that they do what Ruediger requests of them, and so release me from all my suffering. The Huns still think that I have no family and friends. If I were a knight, I would certainly travel here once in a while.[119] [1417] And please also tell Gernot, my dear brother, that no one in the world is more devoted to him, and ask that he bring with him our very best friends into this land, so that my honor might be increased. [1418] Say also to Giselher that he should remember that I suffered no harm through his doing. I would be overjoyed to see him with my own eyes, and I would love to have him here on

---

119. Kriemhild hopes to shame her brothers into accepting, saying in effect that if she were a man, and a knight, she would have no fear of traveling such a great distance to enhance her reputation and honor.

account of his great devotion. [1419] And tell my mother that I am greatly honored here. Finally, if Hagen of Troneck wants to stay behind, then ask them who will lead them through unfamiliar lands. He knows the way to the Huns from his childhood."

[1420] The messengers had no idea why Hagen of Troneck was not supposed to stay behind on the Rhine. They later regretted it, because along with him many other warriors would come to a bitter end. [1421] They had now been given letters and messages and rode out well provisioned and lacking nothing. Etzel and his beautiful wife sent them on their way, outfitted with precious garments.

24. The Messengers Arrive

[1422] After Etzel had sent his emissaries to the Rhine, the invitation quickly spread from land to land. He sent out his fastest heralds and requested or ordered others to attend his festival. Many of them were to die as a result. [1423] The emissaries left the land of the Huns and rode on to Burgundy. They were sent there to invite three noble kings and their men to visit Etzel, and they were in a great hurry.

[1424] They rode up to Bechelarn, where they were happily received and where nothing was neglected. Ruediger and Gotelind, along with their child, sent their best wishes to the Rhine.

[1425] They made sure not to let them leave without gifts, so that Etzel's men could travel in style. Ruediger asked them to tell Ute and her children that no margrave was more devoted to them than he was. [1426] They also sent Brunhild their support and best wishes, their steadfast loyalty and dedication. The emissaries were ready to leave as soon as they heard the message, and the margravine prayed to God in heaven to protect them.

[1427] Before the emissaries left Bavaria, Werbel the strong went to find the good bishop. I don't know what words he sent along to his friends on the Rhine, I just know that he gave his red gold [1428] to the messengers as a sign of his affection.

As he sent them on their way, Bishop Pilgrim said, "I would be pleased to see my sister's sons here, since it is not possible for me to travel to the Rhine."

[1429] I'm not sure what roads they took on their way to the Rhine. No one robbed them of their silver and equipment, since people feared their lord's wrath. The noble king was in fact very powerful. [1430] Werbel and Swemmel reached Worms on the Rhine in twelve days. The sovereigns and their men there were told the news that foreign messengers had arrived. Gunther wanted to know more.

[1431] The ruler on the Rhine said, "Who can tell us where these strangers who are riding into our lands come from?"

No one knew until Hagen of Troneck saw them. He said to Gunther, [1432] "We have received news that I want to report to you. I've seen Etzel's minstrels. Your sister sent them here to the Rhine, and we should welcome them warmly on account of their sovereign."

[1433] By that time they had already ridden up to the palace. Never before had a ruler's minstrels traveled in such splendor. The king's household greeted them immediately, they were given fine lodgings, and their equipment was stowed away. [1434] Their travel clothes were so well made that they could have appeared before the king as they were, but they didn't want to come to court in them, so the messengers asked if someone else wanted to have them. [1435] They found people who were happy to take them, and so the clothes were passed on. The guests then put on even better clothes, the kind that would be appropriate for royal emissaries to wear.

[1436] Etzel's retainers were then allowed to appear before the king, which made everyone glad. Hagen rushed up to greet the messengers kindly and courteously, and the squires thanked him for that. [1437] Hagen asked for news about how Etzel and his men were faring.

The minstrel replied, "The land has never been better nor the people happier, rest assured."

[1438] They went on to see the king in the great hall, which was full. The guests were then welcomed, as one should by rights welcome others in a foreign kingdom. Werbel saw many warriors there with Gunther.

[1439] The king greeted them politely. "May you be welcome, Hunnish minstrels, along with your comrades. Did Etzel the powerful send you here to Burgundy?"

[1440] They bowed before the king, and Werbel spoke first, "My dear lord sends his best wishes to you in this land, along with your sister Kriemhild. They sent us here to you nobles in good faith."

[1441] The mighty king replied, "I am glad to hear this news. How is Etzel doing?" asked the noble. "And Kriemhild, my sister, in the land of the Huns?"

The minstrel answered, "I can report to you [1442] that no one has ever been better than those two, that is certain. And it is also true for their supporters, their kin, and their troops. They were happy about our journey as we departed."

[1443] "Thank him for the wishes that he has sent me, and my sister's, too, since they live in happiness, the king and his men. I was concerned when I first asked about them."

[1444] The two young sovereigns had also arrived by now and had just heard the news. Giselher the young, because he loved his sister, was happy to see the messengers and said to them affectionately, [1445] "Ambassadors, you would be most welcome here with us if you visited us more often on the Rhine. You would find friends here that you would be happy to visit, and no harm would come to you in this land."

[1446] "We trust that you want the best for us," said Swemmel. "I can't express in words how sincerely Etzel salutes you, as does your highborn sister, who is in the highest standing. [1447] The king's wife recalls your benevolence and devotion, and the fact that you were always sympathetic to her in thought and deed. But we were sent here first and foremost to the king to invite you to ride to Etzel's lands. [1448] Etzel the powerful has commanded us that we convey his entreaty. He would like to know, if you do not want to visit your sister, what it is that he has done to offend you, [1449] to make you avoid him and his land this way. Even if the queen were a complete stranger to you, he would still deserve that you should want to see him. If this came to pass, he would be very pleased."

[1450]* King Gunther responded, "In seven days' time I will let you know how I and my counselors have decided on this matter. In the meantime you may return to your lodgings and enjoy a comfortable rest."

[1451] But then Werbel asked, "Would it be possible that we might first see our Lady Ute, the mighty, before we retire to our accommodations?"

Giselher the noble then replied most courteously, [1452] "No one will prevent that. If you appear before her, then you are doing exactly what my mother would want, because she would gladly see you for the sake of my sister, Lady Kriemhild. You will be welcomed by her."

[1453] Giselher brought them to where the lady was waiting. She was pleased to see the emissaries from the Hunnish lands and greeted them affectionately in her courtly manner. The ambassadors, courteous and skilled, then conveyed their message to her.

[1454] "My lady offers you," said Swemmel, "her service and loyalty. If it could be that she could see you more often, then you may believe that there would be nothing in the world that would make her happier."

[1455] The queen said, "That is not possible. As much as I would like to see my dear daughter more often, the noble king's wife unfortunately lives much too far away. May she and Etzel be blessed forever. [1456] Please let me know before you leave when you intend to depart. I haven't been happier to see messengers in a long time."

The courtiers promised that they would let her know. [1457] The men from the land of the Huns then left for their lodgings.

The mighty king had called for his counselors. Noble Gunther asked his advisers what they thought about the matter, and they started to answer all at once. [1458] The most senior men among them told him that he should certainly ride to Etzel's lands. Only Hagen disagreed, as he thought it would be a grave mistake.

He said to the king in private, "You have become your own worst enemy. [1459] You know very well what we did. We should always be cautious of Kriemhild. I killed her husband with my own hands. How could we dare to ride to Etzel's lands?"

[1460] The mighty king spoke, "My sister has forgotten her sorrow. Before she left she forgave us with a loving kiss for all that we had done to her. It is possible that you alone, Hagen, are her enemy."

[1461] "Don't let yourself be fooled," said Hagen, "regardless of what they may say, these envoys from the Huns. If you want to see Kriemhild, you may well lose your honor and your life in the process. King Etzel's wife is obsessed with revenge."

[1462] Lord Gernot then spoke to the council, "It would be a grave mistake for us to forsake visiting our sister even though only you rightly fear death in Hunnish lands."

[1463] Lord Giselher spoke to the assembly, "Since you know that you are guilty, friend Hagen, then you should remain here and save your own skin, and let those who dare to go visit their sister."

[1464] This made Hagen of Troneck furious. "I don't want you to take anyone to this foreign court who is more daring than I.[120] Since you won't change your minds, then I'll prove to you that I'm right."

[1465] Rumolt, the master of the kitchen, chimed in, "You have enough wealth here to host foreigners and locals alike as you wish. I don't think that Hagen has ever held you here against your will before. [1466] If you don't want to follow Hagen's counsel, then listen to what Rumolt, your most loyal servant, advises you. Do me the favor and stay here, and let King Etzel stay with his Kriemhild. [1467] Where in the world could you be more comfortable than here, where you are safe from your enemies? Wear your best clothes, drink only the best wine, and love beautiful women! [1468] In addition you have the best cuisine that any king ever enjoyed. And if that weren't the case, then you should stay on account of the beautiful women, rather than risk your life so childishly.* [1469] This is why I advise you to stay: your lands are rich and you can more easily collect what you are owed here than in the land of the Huns. Who knows what the situation is like there. You should stay here, that is Rumolt's advice."[121]

---

120. In a rather convoluted way, Hagen is saying that he wouldn't want anyone to claim the honor of being more daring in undertaking this venture than he; that is to say, that he is as willing to risk everything as are they. In this way he is responding to Giselher's accusation that he is thinking only of his own safety and that the brothers will prove their daring by traveling to Etzel's court. Hagen wants to prove that he is right, not just that he has the most at stake, but that their acceptance of Kriemhild's invitation will lead them all to their deaths.
121. This well-known passage, known as Rumolt's Counsel (*rât*), provides evidence that this text was known to Wolfram von Eschenbach around 1204/1205, who references the scene in

[1470] "We will not stay," said Gernot, "since my sister and mighty King Etzel have so kindly invited us. Why should we not go? Whoever does not want to go can stay here at home."*

[1471] Hagen replied, "Don't misunderstand what I am saying. Whatever happens to you, let me give you this loyal counsel. If you want to live, then take every precaution in traveling to the Huns. [1472] Since you won't change your minds, gather together only the very best men that you can find. I will choose the best thousand knights from all of them. Then evil Kriemhild's intentions can do you no harm."

[1473] "This is advice that I will follow," said the king straightaway. He commanded messengers to go out far and wide in his lands, and three thousand or more men were gathered together, but they had no idea what great agony awaited them. [1474] They rode into Gunther's lands without a care. All those who were to ride out from Burgundy were given horses and clothing, and the king found many who were eager to go. [1475] Hagen of Troneck had his brother Dancwart bring eighty knights to the Rhine, prepared for war. These courageous men brought their armor and equipment with them to Gunther's lands.

[1476] Then an enthusiastic Volker joined the expedition with thirty of his men. He was a noble singer and poet. They had clothing with them fit for a king, and he let Gunther know that he wanted to ride to the Hunnish lands. [1477] I will tell you who this Volker was. He was a lord born of nobility, and many skilled warriors of Burgundy were under his command. Because he knew how to play the fiddle, he was known as "the minstrel."[122]

[1478] Hagen selected a thousand of them altogether. He knew them all well and had often seen their accomplishments in battle and elsewhere for himself. Everyone had to agree that they were all courageous.

Parzival, Book VII. It is now generally assumed that his source was most likely the C redaction, since the additional information given there, especially the mention of special cuts of meat cooked in oil (*sniten in öl gebrouwen*), is reflected in Wolfram's reference. This would establish an early date for the C redaction, placing it close to the B version's supposed time of composition around or shortly before 1200.

122. Although this is not the first introduction of Volker (he was introduced briefly in the very beginning of the epic, str. 9,4), it is the first description of his qualities as both a member of the nobility and as a poet/song maker (*herre* and *spilman*). The latter sobriquet was given to him because "he could play the fiddle." This in no way limits his abilities as a fighter, as will become evident in the final battle scenes, and the two sides of his character are perfectly compatible. The appellation *spilman* is complicated, in that this clearly involves both playing an instrument and some ability to write and perform songs as the occasion warrants. This will later be evident at Ruediger's court, where Volker plays and sings to compliment his host Ruediger (str. 1670; 1673), and for Gotelind (str. 1705). Werbel and Swemmel, Etzel's messengers, are also called *spilman* and *videlaere*, but Volker has no function as an emissary in this tale.

[1479] Kriemhild's messengers were getting nervous. They were afraid of their lord, and they wanted to take their leave to go home, but Hagen did not allow it because he had a secret plan.

[1480] He said to his lord, "We should not allow them to ride away until we are ready to leave for Etzel's land in seven days' time. If someone means to do us harm, we will know about it all the sooner. [1481] This way Kriemhild will also not be able to make preparations or order someone to attack us. If that is her intent, she will fail. We have in our company only the very best men."

[1482] Shields and saddles and all the equipment that they wanted to take with them to Etzel's lands were made ready for the many eager men. Kriemhild's messengers were ordered to appear before Gunther.

[1483] Once the emissaries had appeared, Gernot spoke to them, "The king will accept Etzel's invitation. We will happily travel to his festival to see our sister, rest assured."

[1484] King Gunther then said, "Can you tell us when the festival will take place, or at what time we are to arrive?"

Swemmel replied, "It will take place at the next summer solstice."

[1485] The king then allowed them to see Lady Brunhild, should they so desire—this had not yet happened. Volker prevented this from happening, and she was grateful for that. [1486] "My Lady Brunhild is unfortunately not feeling up to seeing you now," said the good knight. "Wait until tomorrow morning, then you will be able to see her." But when they thought they could finally see her, it still proved impossible.

[1487] The wealthy king, who was well disposed toward the messengers, by virtue of his own generosity ordered that gold be brought on broad shields, of which he had many. They were also richly rewarded by others of his household. [1488] Giselher and Gernot, Gere and Ortwin proved that they, too, were generous. They offered the emissaries such rich gifts that they refused to take them out of fear of their lord.

[1489] Werbel the envoy said to the king, "Lord King, please keep your gifts here in this land. We could not possibly take them with us. My lord has forbidden us to take your gifts. And we have no need of them."

[1490] That they would reject gifts from such a powerful king angered the ruler of the Rhine, and in the end they had to accept his gold and garments and take them along to Etzel's lands.[123] [1491] Before they left, though, they asked to see Ute. Giselher the brave brought the minstrels to his mother Ute,

---

123. The strange reaction of the emissaries to receiving gifts is an aberration that may point to some present or future conflict. That Etzel would not allow members of his court to receive gifts should not in itself impinge on his honor, in fact, it should increase it. There is no indication that Etzel gave any such order. Gunther's angry reaction is understandable, as his own honor is called into question by their refusal, and in the end they accept anyway. Exactly what

and the lady asked them to pass on this message: she was happy as long as Kriemhild was held in high esteem. [1492] The queen then commanded that bracelets and gold be given out to the minstrels for Kriemhild's sake and for Etzel's, because she cared deeply about her. They were happy to receive such gifts, given out of devotion.

[1493] The emissaries took their leave from both women and men and happily rode on toward Swabia. Gernot had his troops escort them so that they would be safe along the way. [1494] After their escort had departed, Etzel's power gave them safe passage the rest of the way. No one took their horses or their equipment, and they hurried to reach Etzel's lands. [1495] Wherever they had allies, they told them that the Burgundians were following closely behind, on the way from the Rhine to Etzel's lands. Bishop Pilgrim heard the news as well. [1496] As they rode past Bechelarn, they made sure to let Ruediger and Gotelind, the margrave's wife, know that they would soon see the Burgundians, and they were very pleased about that.

[1497] The minstrels were seen hurrying along with their report and found Etzel in the town of Gran [Esztergom]. They passed on to the king all of the many compliments and greetings that the others sent, and the king positively glowed with joy. [1498] When the queen heard the news that her brothers were coming to their land, she was content. She rewarded the minstrels with large gifts, thus increasing her own honor.

[1499] She said, "Now tell me both of you, Werbel and Swemmel, who among my kin will be coming to the festivities, and who is the highest ranking of those we invited? And tell me what Hagen said when he heard of the invitation."

[1500] He said, "He came early one morning to take part in the council. He had nothing good to say about it, and when they agreed to make the journey here into Hunnish lands, fierce Hagen thought that they had uttered his death sentence. [1501] Your brothers are coming, all three of them, and they are filled with joy. I have no detailed knowledge of everyone else who is coming with them. Volker, the bold poet, also pledged to come along."

[1502] "I could easily do without seeing Volker again," said the king's wife. "I value Hagen, though. He is a brave hero. I'm excited that I will be able to see him."[124]

---

motivated the original refusal is not clear, since it does not seem to have any lasting or significant impact on the chain of events.

124. Kriemhild is clearly lying to maintain the fiction that she has invited her brothers out of love, but her complimentary words about Hagen can also be read with a view to the fact that she is encouraged that her plan is working and that Hagen was compelled to come along. In some way her comments about Volker can also contain some foreshadowing, in that Volker will be one of her most determined and deadly opponents.

[1503] The queen then went to see the king. Kriemhild spoke lovingly, "What do you think of the news, my lord? What I have always wished for will now be fulfilled."

[1504] "Your wish is my joy," said the king. "I was never so happy to see even my own family come to visit. My joy over your family's visit has erased all my cares."

[1505] The king's officers had seats set up everywhere in the palace and hall in anticipation of the dear guests who were on their way, but these guests were later to rob the king of all his happiness.

25. Departure for the Land of the Huns

[1506] We will leave out the rest of what happened there. Never before had such self-assured men traveled in such luxury into another king's land. They had everything they could desire, including weapons and equipment. [1507] The ruler of the Rhine gave his men, and I heard that there were 1,060, along with nine thousand squires, suitable clothing for the festivities. Those who stayed at home later shed tears on that account. [1508] The equestrian equipment was carried across the courtyard there in Worms, as the old bishop of Speyer said to beautiful Ute, "Our friends are ready to depart for the festival. May God preserve their honor there."

[1509] Noble Ute then said to her children, "Brave heroes, you should all stay here. I had a terrible dream last night that all of the birds throughout the land were dead."[125]

[1510] "Whoever relies on dreams," said Hagen, "can never know when a true opportunity to win honor presents itself. I want my lord to take his leave from the court. [1511] We should ride to Etzel's lands willingly, because it is there that brave heroes can serve kings well, and there we will join in Kriemhild's festivities."

Hagen was now all in favor of the journey, a viewpoint he later regretted. [1512] He would have advised against it if Gernot hadn't goaded him with his harsh words. He reminded him of Siegfried, Lady Kriemhild's husband, by saying, "This is the reason that Hagen wants to cancel this great expedition."

[1513] Hagen of Troneck replied, "I do nothing out of fear. If you heroes want to do this, then march on. I am happy to accompany you to Etzel's lands." He later shattered many a helmet and shield.

---

125. As once before, a dream about birds being killed is deemed a particularly bad omen. Kriemhild first dreamed of a falcon being destroyed by two eagles. A later dream of two mountains crashing down (str. 924) and another of two boars in a field of red flowers (str. 921) all foretold Siegfried's death.

[1514] The ships were ready to sail, and huge numbers of men were standing by. All of their equipment was stowed on board. They were kept busy until day's end but were full of good cheer afterwards. [1515] Tents and pavilions were set up on the meadows on the far side of the Rhine. After that was completed, the king's beautiful wife Brunhild asked him to stay the night, and she slept with him one more time.

[1516] Early in the morning could be heard the sound of trumpets and flutes, and everyone prepared for their departure. Whoever had a lover embraced her one last time, but Etzel's wife was to bring an end to this and cause suffering for many.

[1517] The sons of beautiful Ute had a vassal who was diligent and trustworthy. As they were getting ready to leave, he told the king what he thought in private. "I'm sorry that you are undertaking this expedition." [1518] His name was Rumolt, a brave champion. He said, "Whom will you entrust with your people and lands? Can no one change your minds? I have always thought that any news from Kriemhild can never be good news."

[1519] "The land is in your care, as is my little son. Take good care of the women: this is my command. If you see anyone crying, give them comfort. Etzel's wife won't harm us."*

[1520] The horses were made ready for the king and his men, many of whom said goodbye with passionate kisses. But they were filled with a sense of adventure, and many a beautiful woman would later lament their enthusiasm.*

[1521] As the brave men were mounting their horses, many of the women could be seen sadly standing by. Their intuition told them that their long leave-taking would eventually lead to much suffering. Their hearts were broken. [1522] The strong Burgundians soon got on their way, but the entire countryside was in an uproar, and people were in tears on both sides of the mountains. They ignored their people's sentiments, however, and happily embarked on their journey. [1523] The men of Nibelungen were with them in a thousand coats of armor.[126] They had also left many beautiful women

---

126. The Nibelungen named here must be synonymous with the just-mentioned Burgundians, given that one thousand men were chosen by Hagen to undertake the task of armed escort. Heinzle's note, 2015, 1358–59, tries to explain that some contingent of original Nibelungen must be meant, but the mention of Nibelungen who are clearly Burgundians just a few strophes on (str. 1526,1–2) makes this distinction effectively meaningless, and furthermore there is no mention of other Nibelungen anywhere in Etzel's lands. Much has been written about this shift in identity, but it would not necessarily have been out of place to equate the Burgundians with one of their other subject lands and people, as they have for some time been the rulers of both the Nibelungen treasure and the inhabitants of that land. The Burgundians are the heirs to Siegfried's properties outside of Netherland. Their theft of the treasure will figure in their destruction, just as its possession did for Siegfried.

at home and would never see them again. Siegfried's wounds still pained Kriemhild.*

[1524] Gunther's men took the road toward the Main River and through East Franconia. Hagen was their guide since he knew the way, and the marshal was Dancwart, a Burgundian hero. [1525] As they were riding from East Franconia to the Schwalbfeld, people marveled at the magnificence of the nobles and their company of famous heroes. The king arrived at the Danube on the morning of the twelfth day. [1526] Hagen of Troneck rode out front, a welcome reassurance for the Nibelungen. The astute warrior dismounted at the river's edge and tied his horse to a tree branch.

[1527] The river had breached its banks, and the ships were all gone. The Nibelungen were concerned about how they would cross, because the river was too wide at that point. Many of the brave knights dismounted there.

[1528] Hagen said, "You may well suffer losses here, Lord of the Rhine. As you can see for yourself, the river is flooding, and its current is extremely swift. I fear that we could still lose many good men here today."

[1529] "What are you saying?" said the noble king. "Take heart and stop making things sound so hopeless. Find a ford to the other side so that we can get our horses and equipment away from here."

[1530] Hagen replied, "I'm not so tired of living that I want to drown in this broad river. My firm intent is to kill plenty of warriors in Etzel's lands first. [1531] Stay here at the river, all you brave knights, and I'll go find the ferrymen along the shore who can bring us over to Gelfrat's lands."

With that mighty Hagen picked up his broad shield. [1532] He was well armed and took his shield and fastened his helmet, which gleamed brightly. Along with his coat of mail he carried a broad sword that had two extremely sharp edges. [1533] He went up and down looking for the ferrymen. He could hear water splashing in a beautiful pool, so he listened more closely. Women with second sight were making that sound as they were bathing to cool off.[127] [1534] Hagen caught sight of them and quietly crept up on them, but they started to flee as soon as they noticed him. They would have been glad to escape from him. He took their clothes, though, but did nothing else to them.

[1535] One of the mermaids, her name was Hadeburg, said, "Hagen, dear noble knight, if you give us back our clothes we will foretell how your expedition to the Huns will turn out."

---

127. What might be called mermaids (*mêrewîp*) were associated with second sight or the ability to foresee the future, and are here referred to as *wîsiu wîp*. They are actually the only supernatural characters to play a role in the text, not including the tales told about Siegfried and the dragon.

[1536] They hovered like birds before him on the waves, and this convinced him that they could foretell the future. Whatever they would tell him, he believed it would be true, and so they told him what he wanted to know.

[1537] She said, "You may ride into Etzel's lands with confidence. I pledge on my faith that this is true. Never before have heroes journeyed to another kingdom and achieved such honor. This you may believe."

[1538] Hagen was glad in his heart to hear such talk. He gave them back their clothes and was ready to go, but after they had put on their enchanted garments, they told him the whole truth about the trek to Etzel's lands.

[1539] The other mermaid then spoke, her name was Sieglinde. "I want to warn you, Hagen, Aldrian's son. My aunt lied to you in order to get our clothes back. If you make it to the Huns, then you will be betrayed. [1540] Turn back. It is still not too late. You brave heroes were invited to Etzel's lands to be killed. Whoever rides there faces certain death."

[1541] Hagen replied, "You don't need to lie. How is it possible that we will all die by our enemy's hand?" They then told him the whole story.

[1542] One of them said, "It is meant to be that not a single one of you will survive, with the exception of the king's chaplain. This is well known to us. He alone will return to Gunther's lands unscathed."

[1543] Bold Hagen said angrily, "It would be difficult to tell my lord that we are all destined to die with the Huns. Still, tell us, all-knowing woman, how we should cross this river."

[1544] She said, "Since you won't listen to our warnings about the journey, there is an inn upstream, and inside is the ferryman, and nowhere else." His question had been answered truthfully, he thought.

[1545] One of them called to Hagen as he was leaving, "Wait a minute, Lord Hagen, you're in too big a hurry. You should hear the story of how you make the crossing. The lord of this march is named Else. [1546] His brother's name is Gelfrat, and he is a lord in Bavaria. Traveling through his march will be a great challenge, so take care, and treat the ferryman courteously. [1547] He is so terrifying that he might leave you barely alive if you're not nice to him. If you want him to take you across, be sure to pay him his fare. He watches over this land and is in Gelfrat's service. [1548] And if he does not appear right away, then yell over at him across the river and tell him that your name is Amelrich. He was a brave hero who left this land because of a feud. The ferryman will come out if he hears this name."

[1549] Hagen, overly confident, bowed to the ladies and had nothing more to say. He walked along the banks of the river until he found the lodging on the other bank. [1550] He started to shout over to the other side. "Come bring me across, ferryman [informal *du*]," the brave man yelled. "As a fare I will give you a bracelet of red gold. I urgently need your help."

[1551] The ferryman was so wealthy that he didn't need to answer to anyone, which is why he never took a fare. His servants were also very self-assured, and so Hagen remained standing alone on the other side of the river. [1552] He then shouted across with a force that shook the waves, so great was that hero's strength. "Come get me, I am Amelrich! I am Else's man, who fled from this land on account of a feud."

[1553] He held up a bracelet on the tip of his sword as payment to take him to Gelfrat's land.[128] It was bright and beautiful, and made of red gold, and so the proud ferryman manned the rudder himself. [1554] The ferryman was newly wed.[129] The desire for more wealth always ends badly. He wanted to have Hagen's red gold but paid the ultimate price for it at the end of the hero's grim sword.

[1555] The ferryman made his way to the other side in haste. When he failed to find the one he thought was there, he became furious. When he saw Hagen, he said to him in his wrath, [1556] "Perhaps your name is Amelrich, but you are not at all like the one I expected to find here. He was my brother, we shared both mother and father. Since you have deceived me, you will have to remain on this side."

[1557] "No, by God Almighty!" said Hagen. "I am a foreign warrior and responsible for other men. Kindly accept my payment and take me across. I am truly in your debt."

[1558] But the ferryman replied, "This is not possible. My dear lords have enemies, and I will not bring foreigners into these lands. If you value your life, then get out and go back up to the bank."

[1559] "Don't say that," said Hagen. "I'm not in a very good mood. Now take my good gold out of kindness and ferry a thousand horses and as many men across."

The dreadful ferryman replied, "That will never happen."

[1560] He picked up a strong rudder board, large and broad, and swung it at Hagen, who was not at all happy about that and had to duck inside the ship. The man from Troneck had never before encountered such a ferocious ferryman. [1561] The ferryman did his best to further enrage the arrogant stranger and broke a pole over Hagen's head. He was certainly a strong man, but Else's ferryman would come to some harm on that account. [1562] Hagen was furious, quickly reaching for his scabbard and drawing his sword. He lopped off the ferryman's head and threw it into the deep waters. The proud Burgundians soon heard about that deed.

128. This presentation of a golden bracelet on the edge of a sword brings to mind a similar scene in the *Hildebrandslied* (c. 830), where a bracelet is offered on the tip of a spear. This would seem to be a gesture common to heroes.

129. The fact that he is newly wed could explain why he is eager to accept the gold to impress his new bride. Most manuscripts read instead: "he was a tough character" (*müelich gesit*).

[1563] At the instant that he killed the ferryman, the ship started to drift, which concerned him a great deal, and it took him considerable effort to get it back under control. King Gunther's man worked the rudder with all his might. [1564] The foreigner was able to bring the ship around with mighty strokes until the sturdy rudder broke in his hands. He wanted to reach the other men on the opposite shore, but since there was no other rudder, he quickly patched it up [1565] with a band from his shield. It was really just a small strip of leather. He steered toward a forest downstream, where he found his lord standing on the shore. Many powerful men met him there. [1566] The brave knights all greeted him heartily, but they could see the blood steaming in the ship from the deadly wound that he had given the ferryman. The men peppered Hagen with questions.

[1567] When Gunther saw the hot blood sloshing around in the ship, he said right away, "So tell me, Hagen, what happened to the ferryman? It seems to me that your great strength took his life."

[1568] He lied in response. "When I found the ship along the marshy bank, I cut it loose. I haven't seen a ferryman all day. I haven't done anyone any harm today either."

[1569] Lord Gernot of Burgundy spoke, "I'm worried that we will lose those dear to us today. We don't have anyone around who can get us across, and I have to say that worries me."

[1570] Whereupon Hagen yelled, "Squires, lay down the saddles on the grass! I seem to remember that I'm the best ferryman there ever was on the Rhine. I trust that I can bring you all across safely to Gelfrat's lands."

[1571] To cross even more quickly they drove the horses into the river, and they all swam across without the strong current sweeping a single one away. Some of them did end up far downstream as they tired. [1572] Then they loaded their gold and their equipment onto the ship, since they had no other means to cross. Hagen was in command and ferried many noble warriors across to the other side into foreign territory. [1573] First he brought a thousand mighty knights across, and then his own champions.[130] But that wasn't all. He then took nine thousand squires and attendants to the other side. The man from Troneck was kept busy the whole day.*

[1574] After he had brought everyone safely across the river, the brave fighter thought about the strange prophecy that the otherworldly mermaids had told him. That almost cost the king's chaplain his life. [1575] He found the priest with the church baggage, where he was leaning on the holy relics,

---

130. There is a clear distinction made here between the regular cavalry troops, or knights (*ritter*), and the leading warriors, here *recken*. This distinction is usually not made, and terms for warriors are used fairly indiscriminately, but those who stand out are in a separate class of heroes or champions. According to the original tally given, there were sixty *recken* in this company explicitly chosen by Hagen (mentioned again in str. 1806).

not that they helped him any. When Hagen caught sight of him, the poor priest had to pay dearly. [1576] Hagen threw him overboard, while others shouted, "Grab him, lord, grab him!" Young Giselher was furious, but Hagen prevented anyone from intervening.

[1577] Lord Gernot of Burgundy spoke, "What is the point of killing the chaplain, Hagen? Anyone other than you would face harsh consequences. What did the priest do to you?"

[1578] The priest tried to swim to save his life until someone could help him. That didn't happen. Mighty Hagen was furious and pushed him under the water, which no one thought was right. [1579] Since the priest couldn't find anyone to help him, he made his way over to the other side. He was in real distress, since he couldn't swim, but God's hand protected him until he arrived safely on the shore. [1580] There the poor priest stood and shook out his clothes. Hagen could then see that the mermaid's prophecy was bound to come true. He thought to himself, "All of these warriors will lose their lives."

[1581] After the ship had been unloaded and everything that the three sovereigns had brought with them was on dry land, Hagen hacked the ferry up into pieces and threw it into the river. The brave men could not figure out what this meant.

[1582] "Why are you doing this, brother?" asked Dancwart. "How will we get across again when we come back from the Huns on our way to the Rhine?" Hagen told him later that they would not be returning.

[1583] The hero of Troneck said, "This is the idea: if we have any cowards on this journey who might want to escape and run away, they will most certainly meet a shameful death here at the river."

[1584] They had along with them a hero from Burgundy who was named Volker. He was able to artfully express what was on his mind. This fiddler thought that everything that Hagen did was for the best.*

[1585] Their horses had been saddled and the pack animals loaded up. Their expedition had so far not encountered any major losses, except for the king's chaplain. He had to walk back all the way to the Rhine.

26. Dancwart Kills Gelfrat

[1586] After they had all arrived on the other side of the river, the king started by asking, "Who will guide us through this land on the right roads so that we don't lose our way?"

Brave Volker answered, "I can make sure we don't get lost."

[1587] "Wait just a minute, knights and squires," said Hagen. "It is right that we support our friends, but I have bad news to share with you. We will never go back to the lands of Burgundy. [1588] This morning two mermaids told me that we would never return. Let me advise you on what we should do next: arm yourselves well and take good care. We have many powerful enemies here, so let us continue with extra caution. [1589] I hoped that I could catch the wild mermaids in a lie. They said that not one of us would return home, except the chaplain. That's why I tried to drown him today."

[1590] The news spread like wildfire from formation to formation. Strong warriors turned white at hearing it and started to think about the death that awaited them on this journey. They had every reason to be concerned.

[1591] They had crossed over at Mehring, where Else's ferryman was murdered. Hagen said, "Since I have made enemies of others along the road here, we will most certainly be attacked. [1592] I killed the ferryman this morning, and now you know the whole story. Prepare yourselves, heroes, so that when Gelfrat and Else attack us today they will go down in defeat. [1593] I know them, and they are both so bold that they won't wait. Let the horses walk at a slow pace, just so no one thinks we are trying to run away from them."

"That is good counsel, and that is exactly what I will do," said Giselher. [1594] "Who will lead us through this land?"

Everyone said, "Volker will lead us. That bold minstrel knows all the roads and paths around here."

Even before they had finished saying this, they saw the courageous fiddler [1595] standing there, fully armed. He had strapped on his helmet, his battle tunic shimmered in many colors, and he attached a red banner to his spear. Later he was to suffer greatly alongside the sovereigns.

[1596] In the meantime Gelfrat had received word of the ferryman's death. Mighty Else had also heard the news, and they were both outraged. They rallied their troops, which were quickly assembled. [1597] In almost no time at all (I will give you all the details), they could be seen riding to answer the call. These powerful fighters had caused many losses in hard battles. More than seven hundred made their way to Gelfrat. [1598] They were led by their lords as they rode after their determined enemy. But their leaders were too hasty to catch the bold foreigners and avenge their anger, and as a result of all the noise they made, more of their troops would end up dead.

[1599] Hagen of Troneck had made excellent preparations. No hero could have protected his own kin any better. He led the rearguard himself, along with his brother Dancwart, which turned out to be a wise decision. [1600] The day had nearly run its course, and they had only a little of it left. He was worried that his troops would suffer losses, so they rode through Bavaria fully armed. The force was attacked soon afterwards. [1601] On both sides of the road and not far behind them they heard the thunder of hooves. They were in too great a hurry.

Bold Dancwart spoke, "They want to challenge us here. Fastening your helmets now would be advisable, I think."

[1602] They stopped and got into formation, since they had no other choice. They could see the shields shimmering in the darkness. Hagen could no longer stay silent, "Who is chasing us on this road?"

Gelfrat had his answer. [1603] The margrave from Bavaria replied, "We are in search of our enemies, and we have pursued them this far. I don't know who killed my ferryman today, but he was a brave man, and I am injured by his loss."

[1604] Then Hagen of Troneck spoke, "Was that your ferryman? He didn't want to take us across. You can blame me, I killed him. I really had no choice, because he would have otherwise killed me. [1605] I offered him gold and robes in payment for taking us to the other side, sir, into your lands. He became so angry that he attacked me with a huge rudder board. Then it was my turn to get angry. [1606] I reached for my sword and put an end to his wrath with a fatal wound. That's how he died. I will offer you compensation in whatever amount you decide." That's when the fighting started, and everyone was determined to see it through.

[1607] "I was sure," said Gelfrat, "that when Gunther and his men rode through here Hagen of Troneck would do us some harm. He will not survive. That hero must pay the price for the ferryman's death."

[1608] Both Gelfrat and Hagen lowered their spears above their shields for the charge, and each had his sights on the other. Else and Dancwart likewise charged brilliantly. They wanted to see who the better man was, and both were unwavering in battle. [1609] Have heroes ever been more tested? Hagen was thrown from his horse by Gelfrat's powerful thrust. His horse's breast-strap had torn. He found out what a hard fight meant. [1610] Their troops also let loose a great crashing of lances. Hagen recovered from his fall to the ground, but I think he was not happy with Gelfrat. [1611] I have no idea who held their horses for them, as they had both been unhorsed into the dirt. Hagen and Gelfrat ran at each other, and their comrades fought hard as well. [1612] No matter how fiercely Hagen charged at Gelfrat, the noble margrave managed to hack a large piece out of his shield, making sparks fly. Gunther's courageous retainer almost lost his life there.

[1613] He called to Dancwart, "Help me, brother! I'm being attacked by a bold knight who wants me dead."

Fearless Dancwart called back, "I'll get you out!"

[1614] The hero [Dancwart] got close enough to slash him [Gelfrat] with his sharp sword, a wound that killed him. Else wanted to avenge him, but instead he and his troops retreated with losses. [1615] His brother had been killed, and he himself had been wounded. Eighty of his warriors were left there dead on the field. The lord had to turn and flee from Gunther's men. [1616] After the Bavarians left the battlefield, terrible clashes could still be heard as the men of Troneck chased after their enemies. They had thought they had nothing to worry about but now couldn't get away fast enough.

[1617] As they were fleeing, Dancwart said, "We should make our way back soon. Let them go. They're already wet with blood. Let's get back to our own comrades, that's my best advice."

[1618] After they returned to the site of the battle, Hagen of Troneck said, "Warriors, take a look around to see who is missing, who we have lost here in this battle on account of Gelfrat's fury."

[1619] They had lost four men. They were mourned, but they had also been avenged. They had killed at least a hundred or more of the Bavarians. The shields of the men from Troneck were smashed up and soaked with blood.

[1620] The moonlight was partly visible through the clouds as Hagen spoke, "No one is to tell my lord what happened here today. Let's not worry them until tomorrow."

[1621] As those who had fought rode to catch up with the others, some of the troops began to complain of fatigue. "How much longer are we supposed to ride?" asked some of the men.

Bold Dancwart replied, "We won't be able to make camp. [1622] You'll all have to ride until daybreak."

Brave Volker, who was leading the group, asked the marshal, "Where will the horses and the nobles rest?"

[1623] Bold Dancwart said, "I don't know, but we can't rest until the day dawns. Wherever we are then, we'll rest on the ground."

When they heard that, they were dismayed. [1624] No one noticed the warm red blood on them until the sun's light rose up above the mountains, when the king saw that they had been in a battle. The noble angrily inquired, [1625] "What's this, dear Hagen? It seems to me that you didn't want me along when your chainmail was soaked with blood. Who did this?"

He answered, "That was Else. He attacked us last night. [1626] They attacked us on account of his ferryman. My brother Dancwart killed Gelfrat, but Else got away. It was all he could do to escape. They lost a hundred, we lost four in battle."

[1627] We don't know where they made camp. All the people in the land found out that the sons of noble Ute were marching through. They were well received in Passau. [1628] Bishop Pilgrim, the sovereigns' uncle, was very pleased that his nephews had traveled to his lands with so many warriors. They quickly realized how supportive he was. [1629] They were welcomed by friends all along the way. They couldn't all be accommodated in Passau but had to be taken to the fields across the river,[131] where tents and pavilions had been set up. [1630] They stayed there an entire day and through the night

---

131. They crossed the Inn River, over which a wooden bridge had stood in Passau since 1143, so that this would have been a relatively easy movement of forces.

and were well cared for. They had to continue on to Ruediger's lands, who soon heard that they were on their way.

[1631] After the travel-weary men had gotten some rest, they approached the border and came upon a man who was asleep. Hagen of Troneck took his stout sword from him. [1632] That strong and courageous knight was named Eckewart, and he was unhappy that the heroes' trek had cost him his sword. They found Ruediger's borders to be poorly guarded.

[1633] "Disgrace!" cried Eckewart. "The Burgundians' journey is my downfall. Ever since I lost my Lord Siegfried, my happiness has vanished. Lord Ruediger, I have disgraced you."

[1634] Hagen could hear the warrior's laments. He gave him back his sword, along with six gold bracelets. "Take these as a sign of my friendship. You are a brave warrior, even if you are alone here on the border."

[1635] "May God repay you for your gift," exclaimed Eckewart. "But your journey to the Huns worries me greatly. You killed Siegfried, and you have enemies here. My honest counsel to you is to be on your guard."

[1636] "May God protect us all," said Hagen. "The only concern these warriors, the nobles, and their men have at the moment is where in this land they should camp for the night. [1637] Our horses have been spent on the hard ride, and our supplies have run out," said Hagen the warrior. "There is nothing here to buy. We have need of a host who, out of generosity, would give us something to eat this very night."

[1638] Eckewart replied, "I can lead you to a host who will receive you better than anyone in any other land, that is, if you want to visit Ruediger the brave. [1639] He lives here along this road, and he is the best host who ever had a home. His heart is filled with virtues as plentiful as sweet May has fields of flowers. Whenever he is called on to be of service to others, he is happy to do so."

[1640] King Gunther spoke, "Please be my emissary and inquire if my dear friend Ruediger will provision us, my household and my men, out of regard for me. I will be in his debt always, to repay as best I can."

[1641] "I will gladly serve as your ambassador," Eckewart replied. He set out with great enthusiasm to convey to Ruediger what he had been told. It had been a long time since Ruediger had heard such welcome news.

[1642] People could see a warrior rapidly approaching Bechelarn. Ruediger recognized him and said, "Eckewart, one of Kriemhild's men, is racing down the road toward us." He thought that perhaps his enemies had attacked him. [1643] He went down to the gate to meet the messenger, who took off his sword and put it aside. The message that he brought was communicated to the lord and his companions as quickly as possible.

[1644] He said to the margrave, "Gunther, the ruler of Burgundy, and his brothers Giselher and Gernot have sent me to you. These men offer you their support. [1645] Hagen and Volker likewise offer you their complete loyalty. There is more. The king's marshal requested me to tell you that these brave men are in need of your accommodations and provisions."

[1646] Ruediger answered with a smile, "This news does me good, that these highborn nobles would accept my services. They will not be denied. If they come to my town, I would be most happy and gratified."

[1647] "Dancwart, the marshal, wants you to know who needs these accommodations. There are sixty brave champions and a thousand knights, along with nine thousand attendants and squires." He was pleased to hear this.

[1648] "I am honored to have such guests," said Ruediger, "who come to my home, these great warriors, whom I have not yet had the pleasure to serve. Ride out to meet them, the nobles and their men!"

[1649] Knights and squires rushed to mount their horses. They were pleased to obey their lord's command and determined to serve as best they could. Lady Gotelind was not yet aware of all this, as she was in her rooms.

27. Arrival in Bechelarn

[1650] The margrave then went right away to see the ladies, his wife and his daughter, to tell them the good news he had received, that her lady's brothers would be guests in their home.

[1651] "My love," said Ruediger, "please welcome these highborn nobles well when they come to our court with their household. And please greet Hagen, Gunther's man, as well. [1652] There is someone else in his company, his name is Dancwart. There is another who is called Volker, a most courtly man. These six you and our daughter should kiss, and treat the other men as befits their station."

[1653] The ladies were in agreement and did so gladly. They took the most costly garments out of the wardrobes and planned to meet the men in these. Many beautiful women were busy with the preparations. [1654] The ladies all appeared without makeup, wearing bright golden bands and costly headdresses to keep their hair from being blown around by the wind. It's true.

[1655] Now let's leave the ladies alone to do their work. Outside, Ruediger's supporters rode out swiftly across the fields to meet the nobles, who were warmly received in the margrave's lands.

[1656] When the margrave saw them approaching, brave Ruediger said happily, "You are welcome, my lords, along with your men. I am happy to see you."

[1657] The warriors bowed to him to show their friendship. He in turn demonstrated his readiness to serve them. He greeted Hagen especially warmly, since he knew him from earlier times.[132] He did likewise with Volker of Burgundy. [1658] He also welcomed Dancwart. This bold warrior said, "Since you have welcomed us, who will take care of all the men we have brought with us?"

The margrave replied, "You will sleep well tonight, and so will [1659] your men. Everything else that you've brought with you, your horses and equipment, I will have guarded so that nothing goes missing, not even a single spur. [1660] Squires, set up the tents on the field. Whatever you may lose here I will replace. Unsaddle the horses, let them run loose." No other host had treated them this well along the way.

[1661] The nobles and guests were contented, and once everything had been taken care of, they continued on. The squires spread out over the grassy field where they were comfortable. I don't think they had it so good anywhere else on this journey.

[1662] The noble margravine came out of the castle with her beautiful daughter, and alongside her one could see lovely ladies and beautiful young women, wearing all sorts of bracelets and costly robes. [1663] Precious gems shone brightly from their expensive garments, they were a sight to behold. The guests then arrived and quickly dismounted. Everyone thought that the Burgundians were most refined. [1664] Thirty-six young girls and many other women, who were all exceptionally beautiful, went out to meet them along with many gallant men. These noble women greeted everyone most courteously.

[1665] The noble young margravine kissed all three sovereigns, and her mother did the same. Hagen was standing there as well, and her father commanded her to kiss him. She took one look at him, and he seemed to her so frightful that she would have gladly disobeyed. [1666] She had to do what she was told, but her face turned red and then pale. She also kissed Dancwart, and after him the poet. He was greeted in this special way on account of his bravery. [1667] The young margravine took Giselher of Burgundy by the hand, and her mother did the same with brave Gunther. They led the heroes away with great joy. [1668] The host entered a great hall at Gernot's side. Knights and ladies were seated there, and the guests were served fine wine. Never before had heroes been treated better.

[1669] Ruediger's daughter was admired with loving eyes. She was most beautiful, and many a brave knight thought of love. She deserved it, for she had a most noble attitude. [1670] They could think what they wanted, but in the end it was not to be. Glances were exchanged, back and forth, with the young women and ladies, and there were many sitting there. The highborn poet was complimentary of the host.

---

132. This most likely refers to Hagen's already mentioned sojourn at Etzel's court as a young man (see str. 1756).

[1671] As was custom, men and women then separated, and knights and ladies went their own ways. The tables were set up in the great hall, where the foreign guests were served most splendidly. [1672] The noble margravine, in order to please the guests, joined them at their table. She left her daughter sitting with the children, as was appropriate, but the guests could not see her and were unhappy about that. [1673] After everyone had enough to eat and drink, the beautiful women were brought back into the hall. There were plenty of jokes and speeches. Volker, that bold and proud knight, was in especially good form.

[1674] The highborn poet said loudly, "Dear mighty margrave, God has blessed you with a beautiful wife and a fulfilling life. [1675] If I were a king," said the poet, "and if I had a crown, then I would want your lovely daughter as my wife. This would be my heart's desire, for she is lovely to behold, and also noble and virtuous."

[1676] The margrave replied, "How could it be that a king would want to marry my daughter? We are but outsiders here, my wife and I. What good is beauty for such a girl?"

[1677] Gernot, that well-mannered man, answered, "If I could have my choice of love, then I would always be glad of such a woman."

Hagen added in good fun, [1678] "It's about time my Lord Giselher took a wife. The young margravine is of such noble birth that I and his other men would gladly serve her, if she wore the crown in Burgundy."

[1679] Ruediger and Gotelind were delighted by what they heard. The nobles all agreed right then and there that noble Giselher would take her as his wife, and that she was befitting of a king. [1680] Who can stand in the way of two who should be together? The young woman was called to the court, where oaths were made that he [Giselher] would be given the beautiful woman. He in turn swore that he would love her. [1681] The young woman was given towns and land, and noble King Gunther, by his own hand, along with Lord Gernot, guaranteed with oaths that this would be so.

The margrave spoke, "I have no castles or towns, [1682] but I will pledge my loyalty to you. For my daughter's dowry I will give gold and silver, as much as one hundred pack animals can carry, a price worthy of this hero's family and honor."

[1683] Both of them were then placed in a circle as was customary. Many young men stood around them cheerfully, thinking about what young people still tend to think about. [1684] When the lovely young woman was asked if she wanted to have him, she was a bit uncomfortable, even though she really did want him. She was embarrassed by the question, as is common with young women. [1685] Her father Ruediger advised her to say yes and to do so gladly. Right away noble Giselher was there with his gentle hands to embrace her. Oh how little she would have of him.

[1686] The margrave then spoke, "Mighty nobles, when you ride back this way to Burgundy, I will give you my child, as it is custom, to return with you."

On this they all agreed. [1687] As loud as the festivities got, they eventually had to come to an end. The young women were told to return to their rooms, and the guests were invited to go to bed and rest until the morning. Then they provided breakfast and all were well fed. [1688] After they had eaten, they were eager to continue riding to the Hunnish lands.

"I won't allow that," said the noble host. "You should stay, as I've never had more welcome guests here."

[1689] Dancwart answered him, "I'm afraid that's just not possible. Where would you get the provisions, the bread and the wine, so that you could feed all of these warriors again tonight?"

When the host heard that, he said, "You needn't say that. [1690] My dear lords, please don't refuse my offer. I could feed all of you at least fourteen days, including all the men that have come with you. King Etzel hasn't taken anything away from me yet."

[1691] As much as they resisted, they had to stay until the fourth morning. The host then gave his guests so many gifts, including horses and robes, that people spoke of it far and wide.

[1692] When it could be postponed no longer, they had to ride on. Bold Ruediger had little left given his generosity. Whatever anyone wanted, he gave it to them, and so everyone was satisfied. [1693] The noble [Burgundian] squires brought many saddled horses to the town gate. They were joined by many of the foreign warriors who carried their shields at the ready, for now they were riding into Etzel's lands. [1694] The host distributed gifts to all of the noble guests before they left the great hall. He earned great honor through his generosity, including giving his beautiful daughter to Giselher. [1695] He gave Gunther, that praiseworthy knight, a coat of armor that the wealthy noble could wear with honor, even though he rarely accepted gifts. Gunther bowed to Ruediger in thanks. [1696] He then gave Gernot a fine sword that he later used in battle to great effect. The margrave's wife approved of that gift, although it would later cost brave Ruediger his life. [1697] Gotelind offered Hagen, as was fitting, a gift in friendship, since the king had already accepted one. She didn't want him to leave the festivities without a gift, but he refused her offer.*

[1698] "Of everything that I have ever seen," said Hagen, "I have never wanted to have anything more than that shield hanging there on the wall. I would want to carry it into Etzel's lands."

[1699] When the margravine heard what Hagen had said, she was reminded of past grief and had every reason to cry. She thought sadly of Nudung's death. He was slain by Witege, and that was a painful memory for her.

[1700] She said to that warrior, "I will give you that shield. If only God would grant that the one who carried it would still be alive, but he died in battle. I must always cry for him, and as a poor woman I have every reason to do so."

[1701] The noble margravine stood up from her seat and grasped the shield with her delicate hands. The lady brought it to Hagen, who took it into his hands. The hero was a worthy recipient of this gift. [1702] A layer of precious material covered the shield and its precious gems. A better one had never seen the light of day. If anyone had been interested in buying it, it surely would have cost at least a thousand marks. [1703] Hagen had the shield carried away, and then Dancwart entered the hall. The margrave's daughter gave him costly robes, which he later wore proudly in the land of the Huns. [1704] All the gifts they had accepted would not have become their own but for the generosity of their host, who gave it all in friendship. Later they were to become enemies, and they had to kill him.

[1705] Bold Volker presented himself with his fiddle to Gotelind and played sweet melodies and sang his poem for her. This was his farewell as he left Bechelarn. [1706] The margravine commanded that a wardrobe chest be brought before her. You may now hear tell of a gift of true friendship. She took out twelve bracelets and placed them over his hand. "These you should carry into Etzel's lands [1707] and wear them for my sake at the court. Then, when you return people can tell me how well you served me there at the festivities." He later gladly did what the lady asked of him.

[1708] The host then addressed his guests, "You will travel more safely as I will escort you myself to make sure that no one can harm you along the way."

His pack animals were immediately loaded up. [1709] The host made himself ready along with five hundred men, their horses, and equipment. He proudly led them to the festival himself, but not a single one of them would return alive to Bechelarn. [1710] The host took his leave with loving kisses, and Giselher did the same, as his courtliness demanded. They embraced beautiful women, and many young women would later shed tears remembering that farewell. [1711] All the windows in the town were opened. The host and his men prepared to mount their horses, but I think that their hearts already knew what disaster was to follow. Many ladies and beautiful girls broke down in tears. [1712] Their friends and relatives all showed their concern for those who would never be seen in Bechelarn again, but they rode down to the shore joyfully, downstream along the Danube, into Hunnish lands.

[1713] Noble Ruediger, that proud knight, spoke to the Burgundians, "We should send out news that we are on the way to the Huns. King Etzel will never have received such a welcome message."

[1714] The messenger rode swiftly down through Austria, and people all around were told that the heroes from Worms on the Rhine were on their way. The king's retainers could not have been happier. [1715] The messengers rode out with the news that the Nibelungen were in the land of the Huns. "You should welcome them most warmly, my Lady Kriemhild. Your dearest brothers are coming and will increase your honor."

[1716] Lady Kriemhild stood waiting at a window. She was watching for her relatives, as people still look out for the ones they love. She saw a mass of men from her father's country. The king had also received the news and laughed out loud for joy.

[1717] "Oh what joy!" exclaimed Kriemhild. "My friends and family are carrying new shields and gleaming armor. Whoever wants gold should remember my suffering, and I will always remain beholden to him."*

28. The Nibelungen Arrive

[1718] After the Burgundians had arrived in Etzel's lands, old Hildebrand of Bern [Verona] heard the news and informed his lord, who was troubled by it.[133] Nevertheless he ordered him to greet the bold and courageous knights as friends. [1719] Bold Wolfhart ordered men to fetch the horses, and many other strong warriors rode out with Dietrich to greet the Burgundians in the fields, where they had unloaded many magnificent tents.

[1720] When Hagen of Troneck saw them riding toward them in the distance, he politely said to his lords, "Valiant nobles, you should rise from your chairs and ride out to greet those who want to meet you. [1721] A company of men approaches that is well known to me. They are courageous warriors from the land of the Amelungen. Dietrich of Bern leads them, and they are proud men. You should not disregard the support they offer."

[1722] Along with Dietrich, the knights and their squires dismounted, as they should. They approached the foreigners and the heroes among them, greeting those from Burgundy as friends. [1723] As Dietrich saw them coming toward him, you may want to hear what the warrior said to Ute's sons. He was sorry that they had come. He thought that Ruediger would have known and would warn them.

[1724] "You are welcome, my Lords Gunther and Giselher, Gernot and Hagen, as are you Volker and Dancwart the bold. Do you not know? Kriemhild still mourns the hero of the land of the Nibelungen."

---

133. The hero Hildebrand is introduced here. He is the constant companion of Dietrich of Bern and is the central character in the short lay that has come down to us in an early ninth-century manuscript as the *Hildebrandslied*. He is depicted as an aging warrior, past his glory days, but still able to match any of the younger men in combat. Wolfhart is also part of Dietrich's company from the land of the Amelungen, and his role tends to be that of the young upstart and hothead.

[1725] "She can cry as long as she wants," said Hagen. "He was killed years ago, and she should cherish the king of the Huns now. Siegfried is not coming back. He was buried a long time ago."

[1726] "Let's leave Siegfried's wounds out of this for now. As long as Lady Kriemhild is alive, she can cause a lot of harm." This is what Lord Dietrich of Bern had to say: "Protector of the Nibelungen, watch out for yourself."

[1727] "Why should I have to protect myself?" asked the mighty king. "Etzel sent us emissaries—why should I question them?—and they asked us to travel to them here in this land. My sister Kriemhild also included many entreaties."

[1728] "Let me give you some good advice," said Hagen. "Please ask Dietrich and his brave men to tell you more about the situation and what they know about Lady Kriemhild's intentions."

[1729] The three powerful rulers, Gunther, Gernot, and Dietrich, then stepped aside to speak privately. "Tell us, noble knight of Bern, what do you know about the queen's plans?"

[1730] The Lord of Bern answered them, "What more can I tell you? All I hear every morning is Etzel's wife crying and lamenting in the worst way to almighty God in heaven about her brave Siegfried."

[1731] "We can't change now what we've just heard," said bold Volker, the poet. "Let's ride on to the court and see what happens to brave warriors here in Hun land."

[1732] The bold Burgundians rode on to court and arrived in splendid form, as was the custom of their land. Many of the Huns were curious to see what Hagen of Troneck looked like. [1733] The story was already well known that he had killed Siegfried of Netherland, the strongest of all heroes and Kriemhild's husband, and so there were lots of questions about Hagen at court. [1734] Hagen was tall, that's certainly true, with a broad chest, and his hair was greying. He had long legs, and his gaze was petrifying. He had a real swagger about him.

[1735] Lodgings for the Burgundians were ordered, and Gunther's household was accommodated separately. This was done at the queen's behest, for she held a deep hatred for him, and this is why the squires were later all killed in their quarters.[134] [1736] Dancwart, Hagen's brother, was the marshal, and the king had put the army under his command to ensure that they were well cared for and well provisioned. The hero of Burgundy was mindful of their welfare.

---

134. The squires and servants were all housed away from the fighting men, and so they were particularly vulnerable to attack. It hardly seems to be Kriemhild's intent at this point, however, to exact revenge by killing all the defenseless young squires. It does explain why they were not protected.

[1737] Beautiful Kriemhild went along with her attendants and greeted the Nibelungen, feigning cheerfulness. She kissed Giselher and took him by the hand, but Hagen of Troneck watched closely, and he tightened his helmet straps.

[1738] "After this greeting," said Hagen, "brave warriors should consider their next move carefully. The nobles are being greeted differently than their men. The journey to this festival was a mistake."

[1739] She said, "You are welcome to those who are happy to see you. I myself do not greet you out of friendship. Tell me what you bring me from Worms on the Rhine that would make you welcome here."

[1740] "If I had only known," said Hagen, "that warriors were supposed to bring you gifts. I have the means, if I had thought it a good idea to bring you a gift here in this land."

[1741] "You should tell me what I want to know: what did you do with the treasure of the Nibelungen? It was my property, something you know all too well. You should have brought it with you to Etzel's land."

[1742] "By my faith, my lady, it was a long time ago that I had my hands on the Nibelungen fortune. My lords told me to throw it into the Rhine. That's where it will stay until the end of time."

[1743] The queen said, "That's what I thought. You brought me nothing of it even though it belonged to me and was once mine to dispose of. I have endless days of nothing but unhappiness."

[1744] "What I bring to you is the devil," replied Hagen. "I have enough to carry with my shield, my armor, my bright helmet, and my sword. I couldn't really bring anything else."[135*]

[1745] The queen addressed all the men, "Weapons are not allowed into the great hall. Warriors, give them to me, and I will have them held for you."

"Certainly," said Hagen, "that's not going to happen. [1746] I will forgo the honor, kind lady, that you should carry my shield and my other weapons to the storeroom. You are, after all, a queen, and my father taught me better. I will be my own attendant."

[1747] "I am cursed!" cried Lady Kriemhild. "Why do my brothers and Hagen not want their shields stored? They must have been warned. If I knew who it was, he would soon have to die."

[1748] Lord Dietrich answered her angrily, "I am the one who warned the mighty and noble kings, along with Hagen, the bold Burgundian. Do your best, you fiend! Don't think that you have to go easy on me."

---

135. I'm following Heinzle, 2015, in taking the sword as the final element in a list of equipment that Hagen has had to carry all the way from Worms, and so basically he had his hands full, i.e., this is another attempt at Hagen's grim humor. Other translators see a specific refusal of Hagen to give up his sword, which is in fact Siegfried's old sword, Balmung.

[1749] Etzel's wife was put to shame. She feared Dietrich, and so quickly departed in silence, looking on her enemies with hatred. [1750] Two heroes then took each other by the hand, one was Dietrich, the other Hagen. The noble said most courteously, "I really am very sorry that you traveled to the Huns, [1751] especially after what the queen just said."

Hagen of Troneck replied, "Everything will turn out alright." This is how these two bold men spoke to each other. King Etzel saw this and began to ask questions.

[1752] "I would like to know what's going on," said the powerful king. "Who is that warrior whom Dietrich is greeting so cordially? He appears to be very self-assured. Whoever his father may be, he seems to be a great hero."

[1753] One of Kriemhild's men answered the king's questions. "He comes from Troneck, and his father was Aldrian. As relaxed as he may appear here, he's really a cruel man. I can prove to you that I'm not lying."

[1754] "How do I know that he's really so terrible?" [Etzel asked]. At this point he didn't yet know anything about the dreadful treachery that the queen would later perpetrate on her relatives, and that not a single one would leave the land of the Huns alive.

[1755] "I knew Aldrian well, he was a vassal of mine, and he won acclaim and much honor while he was here. I made him a knight and gave him my gold. Faithful Helche was especially fond of him. [1756] Since then I came to know all about Hagen. He was a hostage of mine, along with Walther of Spain, two impressive young men who grew up here. I sent Hagen home, and Walther fled with Hildegund."[136]

[1757] He thought about old stories that happened long ago. He now recognized his friend from Troneck who had served him so well in his youth. In his old age he would kill many other dear friends.

29. Hagen Confronts Kriemhild

[1758] The two famous warriors, Hagen of Troneck and Lord Dietrich, parted. Gunther's man looked over his shoulder and saw one of his comrades, whom he recognized immediately. [1759] He saw Volker standing next to Giselher, and so he asked the clever fiddler to follow him, because he knew what a temper he had. He was in all ways a bold and brave knight. [1760]

---

136. This is a reference to the story told in the Latin poem *Waltharius*, transmitted to us in a text from the ninth or tenth century. Hagen, Walther, and Hildegund are sent by the rulers of the Franks, Aquitania, and Burgundy as hostages to secure an accord with Attila (Etzel). It was a common practice to send young sons and daughters to live as captives at a foreign court. Their lives would serve as guarantees that the agreement would not be broken by their parents back home.

They left the lords standing in the courtyard, and the two of them could be seen walking well beyond the courtyard to a large palace. These great warriors feared no one. [1761] They sat down on a bench in front of the building across from a hall, which belonged to Kriemhild. Their magnificent armor glimmered in the light. As they sat there, many wanted to know who they were. [1762] The Huns gawked at the proud heroes as if they were wild animals, and Etzel's wife looked at them through a window. Beautiful Kriemhild was saddened by that sight. [1763] It reminded her of her loss, and she began to cry. Etzel's men wondered what had suddenly made her so sad.

She answered, "You bold and brave warriors: it's Hagen's fault."

[1764] They asked the lady, "How did that happen? We saw you just a short while ago and you were happy. Whoever did this to you, no matter how bold he may be, we will make him pay with his life if you so command us."

[1765] "I would be eternally grateful to anyone who would avenge my loss, and I will give him anything that he asks. I throw myself at your feet!" cried the king's wife. "Give me revenge against Hagen! Make him pay with his life!"

[1766] Sixty brave men quickly armed themselves, who, for Kriemhild's sake, were prepared to kill Hagen, that courageous man, as well as the fiddler. They wanted to ambush them.

[1767] When the queen saw that their troop was so small, she spoke angrily to the warriors, "You should give up your plan. You would never survive an attack on Hagen with so few. [1768] As strong and bold as Hagen of Troneck is, the one sitting next to him is even stronger. Volker the fiddler is a fearsome man. It's not so easy to attack these two heroes."

[1769] When they heard that, more of them armed themselves, four hundred men in all. The highborn queen was intent on causing both of them grievous harm. This would later create great suffering for these warriors. [1770] After she saw that her troops were well armed, the queen commanded the keen warriors, "Wait! Stand fast! I first want to go to my enemies as Queen.[137] [1771] Then you can hear what Hagen of Troneck, Gunther's man,

---

137. Kriemhild is intent on making the confrontation with Hagen both public and a matter of honor, since she tells her men that she will meet her enemies "under her crown," that is under the authority that she enjoys as queen, including the respect that her position should engender. An insult to her at this point becomes an insult to her husband, Etzel, who would be obliged to respond, as Gunther was once obliged to respond to the insult to his wife, Brunhild. Hagen takes the bait, so to speak, and responds with a gesture of open disrespect, laying Siegfried's sword across his lap, unsheathed, in a gesture of both judgment and open defiance. Symbolically the sword prevents him from standing, thus forcing others to stand in his presence. This is the posture of the medieval ruler as judge. Hagen is putting himself above the queen's jurisdiction and posing as the true judge of the matter at hand, that is Siegfried's death and Kriemhild's loss.

did to me. I know that he is so arrogant that he won't lie about it, and I don't care what happens to him as a result."

[1772] The fiddler, that bold minstrel, saw the noble queen walking down the steps from a house. Seeing that, bold Volker said to his comrade, [1773] "Take a look, friend Hagen, here she comes, the one who brought us to this land through deceit. I've never seen a king's wife accompanied by so many men with swords drawn and ready for battle. [1774] So tell me, friend Hagen, are these your enemies? Let me give you some advice. Guard yourself and your honor, that would be wise. If I'm not mistaken, they look like they're angry. [1775] And some of them have such broad chests, whoever must defend himself, he should do it now. I think they must be wearing chainmail underneath. I have no idea who they have it in for."

[1776] Bold Hagen spoke, filled with anger, "I know that all of this is directed at me, that they're carrying glimmering swords openly. They couldn't stop me from riding back to Burgundy. [1777] Now tell me, Volker, my friend, will you stand by me when Kriemhild's men attack? Let me know now, if I mean anything to you. I will always faithfully fight at your side."

[1778] "I will certainly come to your aid," said the poet, "even if the king himself with all his army is against us. As long as I am still alive, I will not move an inch from your side."

[1779] "May God in heaven reward you, noble Volker. If they attack me, what more do I need? Since you're with me, as I've just heard, then these warriors will need to take care as they approach."

[1780] "Let's stand up," said the poet. "She is a queen, and we should let her pass. Let's give her the honor she deserves as a noble woman. This will also reflect honorably on us."

[1781] "No, not on my account," said Hagen. "These warriors would otherwise think that I am acting out of fear if I step aside. I will never stand up for any of them. [1782] It would be better for us to do nothing. Why should I honor my enemies? I refuse to do so as long as I live, and I couldn't care less if King Etzel's wife hates me."

[1783] Hagen arrogantly placed a naked sword across his legs. On its pommel was a gleaming jasper, greener than any meadow. Kriemhild recognized it immediately as Siegfried's sword. [1784] As soon as she recognized the sword, she was overcome with grief. Its hilt was pure gold, the sheath wrapped with a red strap. It reminded her of her loss, and she started to cry. I think that's exactly why Hagen did it. [1785] Shrewd Volker pulled the strong bow from his instrument closer to him. It was large and quite long, just like a sharp and broad sword.[138] There these two heroes sat, completely unafraid. [1786]

---

138. The poet introduces the metaphor of Volker's sword as his "instrument." This becomes more plain during the following fight scenes (e.g., str. 1966; 2004; 2007), but it also serves

The two bold men thought they were so superior that they would not get up from their seats out of fear of anyone, and so the noble queen stepped right up to them and greeted them as foes.

[1787] She said, "Hagen, who asked you to come that you dared to ride to this land, knowing what you did to me? If you had any sense, you would have let it be."

[1788] "No one asked me to come," replied Hagen. "Three noblemen were invited here to this land. They are my lords, and I am their vassal. I have always accompanied them on every court visit."

[1789] She said, "Tell me more about why you did what you did to deserve my hatred? You killed Siegfried, my beloved husband, something that I will mourn to the end of my days."

[1790] He answered her, "What more do you want to know? Enough of this talk. I am Hagen, and I killed Siegfried, the brave hero. He had to pay the price for beautiful Kriemhild's insult to Lady Brunhild. [1791] There is no denying it, mighty queen. It is all because of me, all the great loss. Avenge it, whoever will do so, man or woman. I don't want to lie—I have certainly caused you much pain."

[1792] She said, "Listen to me, you warriors. He does not deny the pain he has caused me. You, Etzel's warriors, whatever happens to him is not my concern." The two proud warriors looked at each other. [1793] If anyone had started a fight, these two men would certainly have come out of it with honor, because they had always proven themselves in battle. Whatever the Huns had intended, they had to leave it undone out of fear.

[1794] One of the men said, "Why are you all looking at me? I take back what I said. I won't lose my life for any reward. King Etzel's wife wants to lead us to doom."

[1795] Then another spoke up, "I feel the same way. Even for towers of red gold I wouldn't want to fight this fiddler. I've seen the way he looks with that piercing gaze. [1796] I recognize Hagen from his younger days, and no one needs to tell me anything about him. I saw him in twenty-two battles where many ladies suffered from the results. [1797] He and the one from Spain [Walther] traveled everywhere fighting wars for Etzel and increasing his honor. He has fought a great deal, which is why Hagen deserves respect. [1798] Back then he was still a young man. Those who were young back then are grey now. He has experience and is hardened. He also carries the sword Balmung, which he won with deceit."

---

to emphasize Volker's two main qualities: artist and warrior. These qualities as combined in Volker are not at all incompatible, and one might imagine that the poet seeks to strengthen his colleagues' reputations as fighters as well as singers.

[1799] The matter was decided then, and no one attacked. The queen was dismayed. The warriors turned around because they feared death at the hands of the fiddler. They were right to be afraid.

[1800] The fiddler spoke, "Now we've seen for ourselves that we have enemies here, just as we were told. We should go see the nobles at court so that no one dares to attack our lords."

[1801] Men will often decline to act out of fear. But when a friend stands at one's side, as friends should do, and he decides not to act out of good sense, then many men can be spared harm through wisdom.[139]

[1802] "That sounds like good advice to me," said Hagen. They went to where they found the brilliant nobles, surrounded by a great throng in the courtyard.

Bold Volker then spoke with a loud voice [1803] to his lords, "How much longer are you going to stand here and let yourselves be shoved around? You should go to court and find out what the king's intentions are."

The nobles paired up with others. [1804] The Lord of Bern took mighty Gunther of Burgundy by the hand. Irnfried joined up with bold Gernot. Ruediger walked to court with Giselher. [1805] As they went to court, Volker and Hagen stuck together. They were never separated except in their final battle together. Noble women would later bemoan their fellowship. [1806] The kings were accompanied on their way to court by their household troops, a thousand courageous men. In addition there were sixty great champions who had accompanied them on their journey. Hagen had brought them along from his own lands. [1807] Hawart and Irinc, two famous men, were seen in the kings' company. Dancwart and Wolfhart, a mighty warrior, could be seen as virtuous examples among the others. [1808] As the ruler of the Rhine entered the palace, Etzel the powerful hesitated not a moment and jumped up from his seat when he saw him coming. He was greeted courteously by the three sovereigns.

[1809] "You are welcome, Lord Gunther, and also Lord Gernot and your brother, Giselher. I sent to you in Worms on the Rhine my faithful offer of support. All of your household is welcome as well. [1810] You are also most welcome, you two heroes, bold Volker and Hagen, by me and my wife here in this land. She sent numerous messengers to the Rhine."

[1811] Hagen of Troneck spoke, "I heard quite a lot about that. If I had not come here to the Huns on account of my lords, I would certainly have come to this land to honor you."

---

139. This proverbial interpolation from the poet seeks to find the right balance between Hagen's and Volker's fearlessness (but not recklessness) and the heroes' wisdom that counsels steadfast friendship and loyalty as a counterbalance to rash action. Some editors and translators have taken this as a continuation of Volker's speech (Schulze, 2005, Mowatt, 1962), but I follow Heinzle, 2015, although he, too, admits that either interpretation is possible.

The noble host then took his dear guests by the hand. [1812] He led them to where he himself had been sitting. The guests were then quickly served mead, berry wine, and grape wine in large golden goblets. The foreigners were given a great welcome.

[1813] King Etzel spoke, "I must tell you that nothing in the world could please me more than to have you heroes come to visit me. It has lifted a great sadness from the queen. [1814] I still have to wonder what I did to you that you never wanted to come to my lands before. I've had many noble guests in the past. It is a great pleasure finally to see you now."

[1815] Ruediger, that proud knight, answered him, "You may well be glad to see them. The loyalty of my lady's family is irreproachable. They bring many strong warriors to your house."

[1816] The lords had arrived at Etzel's court on the eve of the solstice. It is rarely heard that anyone was greeted more respectfully than those nobles there. When it was time to eat, the king accompanied them to their table. [1817] Never before had a host dined so well with his guests. They were given their fill to drink and eat, and anything that they wanted was provided to them. Wondrous tales were told about those heroes.*

30. Hagen and Volker Stand Guard

[1818] The day had come to an end, and night had fallen. The weary warriors were thinking about when they could get to bed and get some rest. Hagen brought up the subject, and an answer was soon forthcoming.

[1819] Gunther said to his host, "May God grant you a long life. We would like to retire now. Please give us permission to do so, and if you like, we can return in the morning." Etzel parted with his guests in good spirits.

[1820] The guests were being jostled on all sides, so bold Volker said to the Huns, "What's gotten into you, why are you stepping on everyone's feet? Back off, or you'll be sorry. [1821] I'll give each of you a stroke of my bow so hard that your loved ones will be moved to tears. When will you all finally make room for real warriors? Not soon enough. Everyone's a warrior here, but I think some more than others."

[1822] After the fiddler had vented his anger, bold Hagen looked behind him. He said, "The bold poet knows what he's talking about. You heroes of Kriemhild, you should all go to bed now. [1823] I don't think anyone is going to actually do what you've planned. If you want to start something, then come back again in the morning, and give us foreigners some peace and quiet tonight. I think that's the way it has always worked among heroes."

[1824] The guests were taken to a large hall that had been prepared for the warriors with costly beds that were long and wide. Lady Kriemhild intended to do them great harm there. [1825] They could see many beautiful sheets along with lustrous materials from Arras and bed covers of Arabian silk, which is the best silk by far. These were decorated with strips of wonderfully sparkling material. [1826] Many of the blankets were fur, both ermine and black sable, and they rested comfortably through the night until the light of day. A king and his household had never before had such an exquisite resting place.

[1827] "These night lodgings be damned," said young Giselher, "as are my comrades who have come with us. As much as my sister invited us in friendship, I'm afraid that we will all owe our deaths to her."

[1828] "Stop worrying," said Hagen. "I'll take the first watch myself tonight. I have faith in my ability to keep us all safe and sound until daytime, so have no fear. After that, everyone can look out for himself."

[1829] They all bowed to him showing him their gratitude and then went to bed. It didn't take long before the strong men had all settled in. Hagen, the bold hero, armed himself.

[1830] Volker the fiddler spoke up, "If you don't mind, Hagen, I'd like to stand guard with you tonight until daybreak." The hero kindly thanked Volker.

[1831] "May God in heaven reward you, dear Volker! Given all my cares, there's no one I'd rather have at my side in time of need than you. I'll be sure to try to repay you if death doesn't prevent it."

[1832] Both of them put on their gleaming chainmail and took their solid shields into their hands. They went outside the hall and positioned themselves at the door. There they watched over the guests, an act of loyalty. [1833] Talented Volker put down his shield, leaned it up against the wall of the hall, then went inside and retrieved his fiddle. He played for his friends as only that hero could. [1834] He sat down in front of the door on the stones. There was never before a fiddler more bold, and as the strings sang their sweet melody, the proud foreigners thanked Volker. [1835] His strings rang out and echoed in the whole hall. He was courageous and talented. His playing grew sweeter and sweeter, and many a careworn man fell asleep in his bed.

[1836] After he noticed that they had all fallen asleep, the warrior took his shield into his hands again, went to the hall, and placed himself in front of the tower to protect the foreigners from Kriemhild's men. [1837] Sometime around the middle of the night, I don't know, it could have been earlier, bold Volker saw a helmet glimmering in the darkness. Kriemhild's men were intent on attacking the guests.*

[1838] The fiddler spoke, "Dear friend Hagen, it looks like we'll have to carry this burden together. I see armed men standing near the house. If I'm not mistaken, I think they want to attack."

[1839] "Keep quiet," said Hagen. "Let them come closer. Before they know that we're here, we'll adjust a few helmets with the swords in our hands. They'll be sent back to Kriemhild somewhat worse for wear."

[1840] One of the Hunnish warriors immediately saw that the main door was guarded. He hurriedly said, "What we had planned isn't going to work. I see the fiddler standing guard with his shield. [1841] He's wearing a brilliant helmet on his head, bright and strong, solid and without fault. His chainmail is flashing like fire. Hagen is standing next to him. The foreigners are well guarded."

[1842] They quickly turned around. When Volker saw that, he angrily said to his comrade, "Let me go out to the front of the house and have a word with Lady Kriemhild's men."

[1843] "No, leave it be for my sake," replied Hagen. "If you get too far from the house, those clever fighters will soon have you in trouble with their swords. Then I'll have to come and save you at the risk of losing the rest of my household. [1844] If we both get into the fight, then two or four of them could easily run to the house and do harm to those who are sleeping. We would always regret that."

[1845] But Volker answered, "Then at least allow me to let them know that I've seen them, so that Kriemhild's men can't deny that they wanted to commit an act of treachery." [1846] Volker straightaway called out to them, "Brave men, why are you fully armed? Are Kriemhild's men going out on a raiding expedition? My brother in arms and I will gladly help."

[1847] No one answered him, and he was furious. "Shame on you, cowards," said the brave hero. "Did you want to murder us in our beds? That's never happened to such brave heroes."

[1848] It was reported truthfully to the queen that her messengers had achieved nothing. She was rightfully upset, but she changed tactics. She was determined, and the bold and brave heroes had to die because of it.

31. Confrontation

[1849] "My chainmail is giving me chills," said Volker. "It seems to me that the night is coming to an end. I can feel it in the air, dawn is near."

They woke up all of those who were still sleeping. [1850] The bright dawn shone upon the guests in the hall, and Hagen started to awaken all the knights so that they could get up and go to church and to Mass. The bells were ringing, as is the Christian custom. [1851] They sang different tunes, Christians and heathens, and it was plain to hear that they weren't in harmony. Gunther's men wanted to go to church, and they were already out of bed. [1852] The warriors put on their Sunday best, of a sort that heroes had never before brought with them into any king's land.

Hagen was not pleased. He said, "You warriors should really wear something else. [1853] You all know what's going on here. Instead of carrying flowers you should be carrying swords, instead of bejeweled laurels you should wear bright and solid helmets. We know exactly what evil Kriemhild's men have planned. [1854] I'm here to tell you that we will go into battle this very day. Instead of silk shirts you should put on your chainmail, and strong, broad shields instead of expensive coats. You should be well armed if someone attacks you. [1855] Dear nobles, kinsmen, and vassals, go into the church and proclaim your troubles and anguish to almighty God. Know this: death approaches. [1856] And don't forget to confess your sins, whatever you may have done, and stand before God with remorse. I am warning you, great warriors. Unless God in heaven wills otherwise, you will not attend another Mass."

[1857] So the nobles and their men went to the church. Bold Hagen had them stop at the hallowed churchyard to keep them all together. He said, "No one yet knows what the Huns have in store for us. [1858] My friends, put your shields down on the ground, and if someone wants to harm you, repay him with fatal wounds, that's my counsel. You will be praised as you are worthy."

[1859] Volker and Hagen both went on to the front of the church to see if the king's wife would cross their path. Her anger was terrifying. [1860] The lord of the land came toward them along with his beautiful wife, who was wearing costly garments and accompanied by many strong warriors. People could see all the dust kicked up by Kriemhild's troops.

[1861] When the mighty king saw the nobles and their household fully armed, he said right away, "Why do friends of mine go about wearing helmets? Truly I am sorry if anyone has done anything to them. [1862] I will gladly compensate them, as they wish, if anyone has insulted them, and show them that I am truly sorry. Whatever they may want, I am prepared to provide it."

[1863] Hagen answered him, "No one has done us any harm. It is the custom of my lords that they go fully armed to all festivals for a full three days. If anyone had done anything, we would certainly tell Etzel."

[1864] Kriemhild heard everything that Hagen said and then looked at him with unbridled hatred. But she didn't want to comment on the customs of her land, even though she had lived in Burgundy for so many years. [1865] As much as she hated them, if only someone had informed Etzel of the true situation, he could have easily prevented what was to come, but because of their stubborn pride, everyone kept silent.[140]

---

140. This line of reasoning is emphasized in the *Klage* as well. Etzel should have been able to prevent the bloodshed at his court if he had been informed of his wife's secret plan to attack Hagen and the other Burgundians.

[1866] The large crowd continued on with the queen, but the two men [Volker and Hagen] refused to budge an inch. This upset the Huns as they had to jostle with the proud heroes. [1867] Etzel's attendants thought this was a problem. They would have confronted the two warriors, but they did not dare do so in the presence of the mighty king. There was a huge commotion, but that was all. [1868] After the church service, they all wanted to leave, and many of the Huns raced to their horses. Many beautiful young women were with Kriemhild, and at least seven thousand men rode along with the queen.

[1869] Kriemhild took her place in the window niche next to Etzel, and her ladies followed suit, which pleased Etzel. They all wanted to see the proud heroes ride by. What an amazing number of foreign fighters there were in that courtyard. [1870] Bold Dancwart the marshal had also come along with the squires, having gathered his lords' entire household from Burgundy. The horses had been well prepared for the bold Nibelungen. [1871] Once the sovereigns and their men mounted the horses, mighty Volker suggested that they ought to joust as was customary in their lands. The warriors were eager to show off their riding skills. [1872] The hero's suggestion pleased them. The joust and its accompanying noise were enormous. Many men gathered there in the castle's large square, and Etzel and Kriemhild watched the games.

[1873] Six hundred of Dietrich's warriors rode out against the foreigners to join the joust. They wanted to try themselves against the Burgundians, and if he had allowed it, they would have gladly done so. [1874] What a great many skilled warriors rode after them. Once Dietrich became aware of this, he prohibited his men from competing with Gunther's. He was concerned for their safety, as he had every right to be.

[1875] After the men from Bern had withdrawn, Ruediger's men from Bechelarn, five hundred of them, all well armed, came riding out in front of the palace. The margrave had hoped that they would avoid doing so. [1876] He had the presence of mind to ride out in the middle of the troop to tell his warriors to be mindful that Gunther's men were looking for trouble, and he wanted them to leave the joust. [1877] After the proud heroes had departed, next came those from Thuringia, as we have been told, and then those from Denmark, at least a thousand bold men altogether. The lances shattered and splinters flew into the air as they collided. [1878] Irnfried and Hawart rode into the joust. The men from the Rhine were waiting for them in their pride and rode numerous jousts against the Thuringians. Many fine shields were filled with holes from the thrusts. [1879] Then Lord Bloedelin arrived on the scene with three thousand men. Etzel and Kriemhild could see him perfectly well, because the contests were taking place right in front of them. The queen was hoping that it would end badly for the Burgundians.* [1880] Schrutan and Gibeche rode into the fray, along with Ramunc and Hornboge.

They lined themselves up against the Burgundians in a Hunnish formation. The spear shafts flew high over the roof of the king's hall.

[1881] Everything that they did created a lot of noise. People heard how Gunther's men caused the palace and hall to resound from the crash of shields. His retinue won great honor and praise. [1882] The games became so large and drawn out that the chargers the warriors were riding were drenched in sweat, even through their saddle blankets. They weren't about to let the Huns steal the show.

[1883] Volker the bold poet said, "It seems to me that these men don't dare stand up to us, but I always heard it said that they hated us. They won't find a better opportunity than this. [1884] We should have our horses taken back to the stables," said Volker, "and then in the evening we can ride out again. We'll see if the queen gives the prize to the Burgundians."

[1885] Then they saw one of the riders proudly cavorting about unlike the other Huns. He must certainly have been in love with one of the ladies, and he was dressed as finely as any noble knight's bride.[141]

[1886] Volker spoke up, "I can't let this go. That lady's man needs to be taught a lesson, and no one can prevent me from putting him to the test. I don't care if Etzel's wife is upset by it."

[1887] "No, please don't, for my sake," said the king quickly. "The people will blame us if we attack. It would be better to let the Huns make the first move."[142] King Etzel was still sitting next to the queen.

[1888] Hagen said, "I'm going to join the joust. Let's show the ladies and the men how we ride, that would be the thing to do. They won't be awarding King Gunther's men any prizes anyway."

[1889] Skillful Volker turned and rode back into the joust, and many ladies were to be saddened by his actions. He drove his lance straight through that boastful Hun. Girls and women alike could be seen crying after that. [1890] Hagen and his men, he went out with sixty of his knights, rushed after the fiddler where the action was taking place. Etzel and Kriemhild could see everything perfectly clearly. [1891] The three kings didn't want to leave their poet in the midst of the enemy without protection. A thousand knights did as they saw fit and confidently raced out on their mounts.

[1892] After the mighty Hun had been slain, his family could be heard crying out in lament. The entire retinue cried out, "Who did this?" "It was the fiddler, Volker, the bold minstrel." [1893] The Hunnish margrave's relatives

---

141. This Hunnish champion is thought by Volker and Hagen to be effeminate in his appearance and actions, and therefore needs to be "taught a lesson" in masculinity.

142. Volker disobeys his king's orders in the next moment, and he is joined by Hagen in this disobedience, who has gone against his king in other instances. The provocation that Gunther tries to avoid is provided by Volker and Hagen, and it ends badly, as Gunther had feared.

quickly called for their swords and shields because they wanted to kill Volker. The king left his seat at the window in great haste.

[1894] The people all began to shout and make noise. The kings and their retinue dismounted in front of the hall, and the Burgundian men drove the horses back. Then King Etzel arrived and separated the two sides. [1895] He ripped a great sword out of the hands of one of the Hun's relatives who was standing next to him and forced everyone back on account of his great anger. "I would have been wrong to honor these heroes [1896] if you had killed the poet in my court," said King Etzel. "That would have been a crime. I saw exactly how he rode as he pierced the Hun. The horse was startled, and it wasn't his fault. [1897] My guests will be left in peace!"

He then personally led them away, and their horses were taken to the stables. There were many squires ready to perform any service required. [1898] The host entered the palace with his friends and would not allow the hostilities to continue. The tables were set and water was brought out, but the men from the Rhine had plenty of enemies there.* [1899] It took a while before the lords could take their seats.

Kriemhild was deeply troubled. She said, "Lord of Bern, I need your counsel, help, and good will. I am in a difficult situation."

[1900] Hildebrand, that praiseworthy warrior, answered her, "Whoever kills the Nibelungen on account of treasure will have to do it without me, and they'll be sorry they did. These courageous knights are still undefeated."*

[1901] Lord Dietrich spoke in his polite manner, "Please don't ask me to do this, almighty queen. Your family has done nothing to me that would give me cause to stand against them in combat. [1902] This request of yours does you little honor as the wife of a great noble, if you are looking to harm your kin. They came here to this land out of trust. Siegfried will not be avenged by Dietrich's hand."

[1903] Since she could find nothing treasonous in the Lord of Bern, she immediately promised Bloedelin rich lands once possessed by Nudung. He was later to be killed by Dancwart, and he soon enough forgot his prize.[143]

[1904] She said, "You must help me, Lord Bloedelin. My enemies are in this house, those who murdered Siegfried, my dear husband. I will always be indebted to whoever can help me avenge him."

---

143. Bloedelin is Etzel's brother, first introduced in the welcome and opening ceremonies of Etzel's festival (str. 1346). Nudung, Gotelind's brother, had been previously mentioned in Bechelarn when Hagen had requested his shield as a gift. There it was stated that he had been killed by Witege. Nudung's widow is then promised by Kriemhild to Bloedelin. It is not quite clear how Kriemhild has the authority to give away Nudung's property and his wife, or why Bloedelin would be so eager for these possessions, given his position as the king's brother. Nevertheless, the point is that greed motivates him to engage in treasonous behavior.

[1905] Bloedelin answered her, "Lady, you should know that I don't dare start a fight with them out of fear for Etzel. He is so happy to have your relatives here, Lady. If I were to harm them, the king would not be happy with me."

[1906] "But no, Lord Bloedelin, I will always support you. I will give you silver and gold as a reward, along with a beautiful young woman, Nudung's wife. You'll be able to enjoy that lovely woman. [1907] I will give you lands and castles, and you, noble knight, will be able to live a carefree life once you possess the border lands that Nudung formerly ruled. All that I have promised you today, I will faithfully deliver."

[1908] When Lord Bloedelin considered the reward, and because the lady's beauty suited him, he resolved to serve the lovely woman in battle. This was to be his demise.

[1909] He said to the queen, "Go back into the hall. I will let out a battle cry before anyone notices anything. Hagen will have to pay for what he did to you. I will deliver Gunther's man to you in bonds."

[1910] "All my men, arm yourselves!" commanded Bloedelin. "We will seek out the enemy in his lodgings. Etzel's wife has commanded me to do so, and for this we warriors must risk our lives."

[1911] After the queen had left Bloedelin ready to do battle, she went to have dinner with the king and his men. She had laid evil plans for the guests.*

[1912] Since there was no other way to incite the conflict, and since Kriemhild's old sorrow was buried deep in her heart, she had Etzel's son brought to the table. How could a woman have done something so terrible out of vengeance?* [1913] Etzel's men then went out and carried Ortlieb, the young prince, back to the nobles' table, where Hagen was also seated. And so the child would have to die on account of Hagen's murderous hatred.

[1914] When the powerful king saw his son, he spoke kindly to his wife's family, "Look, my friends, this is your sister's and my only son. This is all to your advantage. [1915] If he takes after his kin, he will become a bold man, powerful and noble, strong and handsome. Should I live a while longer, I will give him twelve lands. Then noble Ortlieb will be a great supporter to you. [1916] And so, my dear friends, I ask you kindly that when you return to the Rhine, take your sister's son with you, so that you might give the child your favor [1917] and educate him in the ways of honor until he becomes a man. If anyone in your land has done you wrong, then he will help avenge it when he grows to adulthood." Kriemhild, King Etzel's wife, also heard this speech.

[1918] "These warriors could certainly have faith in him, if he were to become a man," said Hagen. "But the young prince looks as if he is doomed to die. I certainly won't be attending Ortlieb's court."

[1919] The king stared at Hagen, and his speech upset him greatly. The proud lord said nothing, but his heart was saddened and his mood darkened.

155

Hagen was not disposed to making jokes. [1920] All of the nobles had been offended, as had the king, by what Hagen said about his son, and they found it difficult to keep quiet about it. They didn't know what that hero would do later.*

32. Dancwart Kills Bloedelin[144]

[1921] Bloedelin's men were ready for battle. They ran forward in a thousand coats of mail to attack Dancwart and the squires as they sat at the dinner table. This started the greatest battle ever between heroes.

[1922] As Lord Bloedelin approached the tables, Dancwart, the marshal, greeted him most courteously, "You are welcome here in this house, my Lord Bloedelin. I'm surprised by your appearance. What is the purpose of your visit?"

[1923] "There's no need to greet me," said Bloedelin. "My entrance is your exit. Your brother Hagen murdered Siegfried. You and others will have to pay for that here among the Huns."

[1924] "I don't think so, Lord Bloedelin," replied Dancwart. "We would soon have to regret our journey here. I was still a small child when Siegfried died.[145] I don't know what King Etzel's wife blames me for."

[1925] "There's nothing more I can say about that. Your relatives, Gunther and Hagen, were responsible. Now defend yourselves, foreigners! You are doomed to die. Your deaths will be Kriemhild's reward."

[1926] "So there's nothing that will change your mind?" asked Dancwart. "Well then, I'm sorry for my appeals. I should have spared myself the trouble."

The bold and skilled warrior sprang up from his table and drew his sharp blade, a great and mighty sword. [1927] He struck Bloedelin such a powerful blow with that sword that his head was quickly lying at his feet.

"Take that as your dowry," said Dancwart, "for Nudung's bride. And you thought you would get to sleep with her. [1928] Tomorrow she can be given to another. If anyone wants to take a dowry, he'll get the same from me." A trustworthy Hun had told him earlier that the queen wanted his death.

[1929] Bloedelin's men saw their lord lying there, slain. They were determined not to take that from the foreigners and charged at the young squires with their swords drawn and hate in their hearts. Many would soon regret that.

---

144. The following action takes place in a separate hall where the squires and Dancwart are having their dinner.
145. Cf. str. 359. Dancwart is one of Gunther's and Siegfried's companions on the journey to Brunhild's court. The two statements cannot be squared.

[1930] Dancwart shouted loudly at the company, "Noble squires, you can see what awaits. Defend yourselves, you wretched foreigners. Truly, we must do this to match noble Kriemhild's friendly invitation."

[1931] Those who didn't have a sword reached under the tables and pulled out the chairs by their legs. The Burgundian squires were prepared to defend themselves, and many a helmet was bashed in by thick chairs. [1932] How those young foreign men defended themselves with determination! They drove their armed opponents out of the hall, but still over five hundred of them died there inside. The squires were stained red and soaked with blood.

[1933] The terrible news soon reached Etzel's warriors. They were stunned that Bloedelin and his men had been killed. Hagen's brother and his squires had accomplished that. [1934] Before the queen heard the news, the Huns, more than two thousand of them, had armed themselves in their rage. They went to where the squires were, there was no way to stop it, and they killed every last one of them. [1935] The faithless men brought a large force to the front of the hall, and the foreign squires defended themselves well. But of what use was their courage? They all had to die. A short time afterwards a great battle was to unfold.

[1936] Now you can hear tell about a horrific spectacle.[146] Nine thousand squires lay dead, along with twelve of Dancwart's knights. He could be seen standing alone against the enemy. [1937] The noise was now quieted, the din was done. Dancwart the warrior looked back over his shoulder and said, "Oh, what friends I have lost. I am left to stand alone against my enemies."

[1938] Many sword strikes fell on this lone survivor. The women of many a hero later had to lament that. He raised his shield ever higher, the neck strap ever lower. He drenched many coats of mail in blood.

[1939] "What a catastrophe!" exclaimed Aldrian's son. "Get back, you Hunnish fighters. You'll have to let me outside, where the air can cool off this battle weary man." The warrior could be seen leaving with great courage. [1940] As the weary man ran out of the building, new blows rained down on his helmet. Those who had not seen the feats of arms he accomplished launched themselves against the Burgundian.

[1941] "If only God willed it," said Dancwart, "that I had a runner who could let my brother Hagen know that I am in dire need here against these fighters. He would help me or die alongside me."

[1942] Hunnish warriors spoke, "You will have to be your own messenger, when we carry your body to your brother. Then Gunther's man will see something that causes him pain. You have caused King Etzel much trouble here."

---

146. This is another of the "wonders" that are heard tell, as announced in the first strophe of the A and C manuscripts.

[1943] He said, "Take your threats and go to hell! I'll still moisten plenty of chainmail. I'll bring my message personally to court and complain to my lord of my great suffering."

[1944] He frightened Etzel's men so much that they did not dare attack him with their swords, but they threw so many spears into his shield that he could no longer hold it upright because of the weight. [1945] They thought they could defeat him without his shield. It was amazing how many deep wounds he still inflicted through their helmets. Many bold men ended up lying dead in front of him. Brave Dancwart gained great praise for his actions. [1946] They attacked him from two sides, but they had all come to the fight at a bad time. In the face of the enemy he fought like a wild boar in the forest beset by hounds. He could not have been bolder. [1947] His trail was once again wet with blood. A single combatant could never have fought more fiercely against his enemies than he did there. Hagen's brother could be seen bravely marching to the court. [1948] Stewards and cupbearers could hear the clatter of swords, and many of them dropped the food and drink they were serving the nobles. He [Dancwart] encountered many enemies at the foot of the staircase.

[1949] "What is this, you stewards?" said the weary warrior. "You should serve the guests courteously and bring the nobles fine foods. And let me give my report to my lords."

[1950] He met everyone who bravely challenged him on the stairs with such determined sword strokes that they had to retreat out of fear. His great courage achieved wondrous feats of arms.

33. The Burgundians Battle the Huns

[1951] As bold Dancwart came through the doorway, he commanded Etzel's household to withdraw. His clothing was completely soaked in blood, and he carried a naked sword in his hand.*

[1952] Dancwart shouted to the nobles in a loud voice, "Brother Hagen, you've been sitting for far too long. I declare our tragedy to you and to God in heaven. Knights and squires lie dead in their quarters."

[1953] Hagen shouted back at him, "Who did this?"

"Lord Bloedelin and his men. But he also had to pay for it dearly, I can tell you that. I lopped off his head with my own hands."

[1954] "There's little harm," said Hagen, "in news about a warrior when he is killed by another warrior. Beautiful women should lament him all the less for that. [1955] Now tell me, brother Dancwart, why are you all red? It seems to me that you have been gravely wounded. If whoever did that to you is still here in this land, he will certainly have to die, unless the devil himself can save him."

[1956] "You can see that I don't have a scratch. My clothes are soaked with blood, that's all from other men's wounds. I've laid low so many today that I couldn't swear to the total number."

[1957] Hagen said, "Brother Dancwart, then guard the door for us, and don't let any of these Huns back out. This disaster requires that I have a word with these warriors. Our squires did not deserve to die."

[1958] "If I am to play doorman now," said the bold man, "then I can serve mighty kings. I will guard the stairway according to my honor." Nothing could have been worse for Kriemhild's warriors.

[1959] "I would like to know," said Hagen, "what the Huns are muttering about. I think they would rather avoid the one who's standing at the door, the one who brought the Burgundians the news from the court. [1960] I've heard Kriemhild saying for a long time now that she wouldn't lay her sorrow to rest. Now drink up and let's pay the bill for the king's wine.[147] The young prince of the Huns will have to be the first to pay."

[1961] Hagen, the famed hero, struck young Ortlieb a blow so that the blood ran down the sword to his hand. The boy's head landed in the king's lap.* A great slaughter of warriors commenced. [1962] Next he swung a great two-handed stroke at the boy's tutor, and his head fell to the ground at the table's end. He made the teacher pay a terrible price.

[1963] He saw a minstrel at Etzel's table. Hagen, in his rage, walked up to him and cut off his right hand as he held his fiddle. "Take that as a message to the land of Burgundy."

[1964] "Ahhh, my hand!" cried Werbel, the minstrel. "Hagen of Troneck, tell me what I did to you? I came to the land of your lords in good faith. How can I play now that I've lost my hand?"

[1965] Hagen couldn't have cared less if he ever played the fiddle again. In his murderous rage, he killed scores of Etzel's warriors in that hall. Plenty of men in that hall met their end. [1966] Volker, the shrewd one, bounded up from the table. His fiddle's bow rang out loudly in his hands. Gunther's minstrel made terrible music there, and he made plenty of enemies among the bold Huns.

[1967] The three mighty kings jumped up from their table as well. They wanted to separate the sides before more damage was done, but they were unable to use reason once Volker and Hagen had started the carnage. [1968] The ruler of the Rhine realized that he could not end the battle. The king

---

147. The original text is not entirely clear. Literally this is a toast to love (*minne*), which is a particular toast, often to a saint, on some special occasion or celebration. Hagen's words are ironic in that he toasts the slaughter that is about to occur. The price to be paid for the wine is also ironic, in that Hagen may mean that the price to be paid for Etzel's hospitality will be death, both his and as many as he and Dancwart can take with them, starting with the king's young, and innocent, son.

159

himself then struck many deep wounds through the shining armor of his enemy. He was a real hero, and he proved it to everyone. [1969] Brave Gernot entered the fight next, killing many of the Hunnish heroes with the sharp sword that Ruediger had given him. He did great harm to Etzel's men. [1970] Queen Ute's youngest son rushed into battle, and his sword rang clearly through the helmets of Etzel's Hunnish warriors. Bold Giselher performed great feats there.

[1971] The kings and all their men, how accomplished they were! But in front of all of them, Giselher could be seen toe to toe with the enemy. He was a great hero and wounded many who fell onto the bloody ground. [1972] Etzel's men also knew how to defend themselves, but the foreigners were seen blazing a path through the king's hall with their bright swords. Everywhere one could hear a great hue and cry. [1973] Those outside wanted to get in to help their allies. They took heavy losses at the tower. And those inside wanted only to get out of the hall. Dancwart would let no one get up or down the stairs. [1974] There was a large clamor at the battlements, and helmets rang out from sword strokes. Bold Dancwart was hard pressed, which concerned his brother, as loyalty required.

[1975] Hagen called loudly to Volker, "Comrade, do you see over there my brother standing among the Huns, with blows raining down on him? Friend, save my brother for me before we lose that hero!"

[1976] "I will certainly do that," said the minstrel. He began to "fiddle" as he waded through the palace. A solid sword sang out often in his hand, and the warriors from the Rhine were incredibly thankful.

[1977] Bold Volker said to Dancwart, "You've experienced great trials today. Your brother asked me to come over and give you a hand. If you take the outside entrance, I'll take the one inside."

[1978] Clever Dancwart stood just outside the door and defended the staircase against all who approached. The heroes' swords could be heard ringing out. Volker of Burgundy did the same inside.

[1979] The bold fiddler cried out over the throng, "The hall is secure, my friend Lord Hagen. Etzel's door is sealed off by two heroes, like a thousand bolts."

[1980] When Hagen of Troneck saw the door guarded this way, the legendary hero threw his shield on his back. His revenge was only just beginning, and his enemies soon found out that their lives were worthless.

[1981] When the Lord of Bern saw that mighty Hagen was smashing countless helmets, the king of the Amelungen jumped up on a bench and said, "Hagen is pouring out the very worst kind of drink."

[1982] The host was in great distress, as he should be, since his dear friends were being taken from him before his very own eyes. He had to fear for his life among his enemies. He was horrified. What good did it do him that he was king?

[1983] Mighty Kriemhild called out to Dietrich, "Help me, noble knight from the land of Amelungen, for the sake of all that is noble. If Hagen reaches me, I'll be dead on the spot."

[1984] "How can I help you, noble queen?" spoke Dietrich. "I'm concerned for myself at the moment. Gunther's men are in such a rage that I can't protect anybody else right now."

[1985] "No, Lord Dietrich, noble knight. Let your excellence shine out today by helping me get out, or else I am lost!" Kriemhild was right to be so alarmed.

[1986] "I will do what I can to help you. In many years I haven't seen so many good knights in such a bitter rage." He could see the blood spurting out from helmets struck by swords. [1987] That extraordinary warrior called out with such great force that his voice thundered out like a bison's horn, resounding throughout the spacious castle. Dietrich's strength was beyond measure.

[1988] Gunther heard this man calling out in the heat of battle. He stopped to listen and said, "I hear Dietrich's voice. I think our warriors have killed one of his men. [1989] I see him on top of the table, waving his hands. Friends and family from Burgundy, stop your fighting. Let's listen and look at what my men have done to this hero."

[1990] When King Gunther commanded it, they put down their swords in the midst of battle. His authority was so great that they stopped fighting. He immediately asked the Lord of Bern what had happened. [1991] He said, "Noble Dietrich, what have my friends done to you here? I am determined to compensate you. Whatever anyone did to you, I am truly sorry."

[1992] Lord Dietrich spoke, "Nothing has been done to me. Let me and my men walk out of this hall and this tough fight with your guarantee of safe passage. I would be forever grateful for that."

[1993] "Why are you pleading with them?" asked Wolfhart. "The fiddler hasn't blocked the door completely—we could still get out."

"Silence!" shouted Dietrich. "You will do nothing!"

[1994] King Gunther then spoke, "I will allow you to take out as many of your men as you want, but don't let my enemies go with you. They must stay. They have done me great harm here in Hunnish lands."

[1995] When Dietrich heard that, he put one arm around the noble queen, who was in fear for her life. On his other side he led out Etzel. Along with Dietrich went another six hundred strong men.

[1996] Noble Ruediger, the margrave, then said, "If more people want passage out of this hall, then let those who would gladly serve you speak up. True friends will have a secure peace."

[1997] Giselher of Burgundy answered him, "You and your men will have peace and reconciliation from us for your tireless loyalty. You may leave with your friends without fear."

[1998] As Ruediger was leaving the hall, five hundred or more men from Bechelarn followed him out, both allies and vassals. King Gunther would later do him great harm. [1999] A Hunnish fighter saw Etzel leaving with Dietrich. He wanted to take advantage of that and leave, but the fiddler gave him such a blow that his head ended up at Etzel's feet.

[2000] When the ruler of the land had come out in front of the building, he turned around and looked at Volker. "I am cursed by my guests. It is a great disaster to have all of my warriors killed by them. [2001] Curse these festivities!" cried the mighty king. "Someone's fighting inside like a wild boar. His name is Volker, and he's a minstrel. I thank my good fortune that I escaped that devil. [2002] His songs have a terrible sound, his bow strokes are red, and his melodies are killing many a hero. I don't know what this poet has against us, but I've never had a more terrifying guest."*

[2003] Everyone they wanted to let go got out of the hall, but inside a great noise arose. The guests brought down a terrible vengeance for what had happened to them. Bold Volker busted one helmet after another.

[2004] Gunther, the mighty king, turned toward all the racket. "Hagen, do you hear the tunes that Volker is fiddling with the Huns as they go to the battlements? He's painting broad red strokes with this 'fiddle' bow."

[2005] "It causes me great regret," said Hagen, "that I ever sat in the hall above that hero.[148] I was his comrade in arms, and he was mine. And if we should ever get home again, we will remain so faithfully. [2006] Take a look, mighty king. Volker is loyal to you. He has diligently earned your silver and gold. His fiddle bow cuts through hardened steel, and he smashes shiny ornaments from helmets. He should be riding fine horses and wearing expensive clothes. [2007] I never saw a musician perform so wonderfully as that warrior Volker does today. His melodies ring out loudly through helmets and shields."

[2008] Whatever Huns were once in the hall, there were none left alive now. The clamor abated and the fighting ended, and the bold warriors let their swords fall from their hands.

---

148. Hagen regrets that he sat at a higher position at table than Volker, thus claiming greater honor, something he now sees was presumptuous.

34. The Dead Are Thrown Out [combined
with Chapter 33 in ms. C]

[2009] Exhaustion forced the nobles to sit down on the ground. Volker and Hagen went out in front of the hall, where the brash men leaned on their shields and conversed in a scornful tone.

[2010] Giselher of Burgundy, said, "It's too soon to rest, dear friends. You'll have to pull the bodies out of the hall. We will certainly be attacked again, I can assure you of that. [2011] They shouldn't be lying around here under foot. Before the Huns can beat us in battle, I'm looking forward to causing many more wounds. This I am determined to do," said Giselher.

[2012] "It's great to have such a lord," said Hagen. "The leadership that my young lord has shown today can only come from a true warrior. All of you Burgundians can be happy about that."

[2013] They carried out the order and threw seven thousand dead out of the building. They fell to the ground at the bottom of the hall's staircase. There the relatives cried out in loud lament. [2014] Some of them were only somewhat wounded, and with more gentle treatment they might have lived, but the fall from that height certainly killed them. Their friends complained bitterly about this, as they had every right to do.

[2015] The fiddler Volker, a proud hero, said, "Now I see that what I've always heard is true. Huns are worthless and complain like women. They should take care of their own wounded."

[2016] One of their margraves thought that was sound advice and, seeing one of his clan lying in blood, wrapped his arms around him so that he could carry him away. But the bold minstrel killed him with a spear, which he threw over the wounded man. [2017] When the others saw that, they all fled and cursed the poet. He grabbed a sharp and solid spear from the ground that a Hun had thrown at him. [2018] He threw it far across the courtyard, well over the heads of the troops. He made sure that Etzel's men would take their positions farther from the hall. People feared his strength and fearlessness above all. [2019] There were thousands standing in front of the building, but Volker and Hagen started to speak to King Etzel in their anger. This would bring the bold and mighty heroes trouble later on.

[2020] "It would be appropriate, oh great defender," said Hagen, "for the lords to fight in the front rank, as each of my lords has done here. They split helmets, and blood flows under their swords."

[2021] Etzel was so bold that he grabbed for his shield. "Be careful!" cried Lady Kriemhild. "You should instead offer our warriors shields laden with gold. If you are within Hagen's range, you'll be dead on the spot."

[2022] The king was so bold that he did not want to stay his hand, some-thing that happens rarely to the powerful lords of today.[149] They had to pull him back on his shield strap, but terrible Hagen began to mock him.

[2023] "The kinship was apparently not very close," said Hagen, "that connected Etzel and Siegfried. He loved Kriemhild before she ever laid eyes on you. Oh powerless king, why do you come after me?"

[2024] The noble king's wife heard this, and Kriemhild was upset that he would insult her in front of Etzel's men. This is why she continued to press for an attack on the foreigners.

[2025] She said, "Whoever kills Hagen of Troneck for me and brings me his head, I will fill Etzel's shield with gold for him. What is more, I will reward him with great castles and lands."

[2026] "I don't know what they're waiting for," said the poet. "I've never seen heroes so hesitant when offered such a great reward. Etzel will never forgive them for that.* [2027] Those who eat their lord's bread so shamefully and then desert him in his hour of need, I see them all wavering here. They all want to be brave, but instead they will live in infamy forever."

35. Irinc Is Killed

[2028] Margrave Irinc of Denmark then cried out, "I have for a long time strived only for honor, and I was often the best in battle. Bring me my arms! I will fight Hagen."

[2029] "I would advise against that," replied Hagen. "But if you want to fight alone, then tell the Huns to back off. If two or three of them run into the hall, I'll send them back down the staircase in poor health."

[2030] "That won't stop me," said Irinc. "I've had difficult fights before. I challenge you to single combat with the sword. All your arrogant boasting won't help you now."

[2031] Irinc was quickly armed, as were Irnfried of Thuringia, a bold young man, and Hawart the strong, along with another thousand men. Whatever Irinc got involved in, they wanted to support him. [2032] The fiddler then saw a great contingent accompanying Irinc, fully armed and wearing strong helmets. Bold Volker was furious.

[2033] "Do you see Irinc over there, friend Hagen, the one who challenged you to single combat with the sword? Are heroes supposed to lie? I think it's a disgrace. There are a thousand or more armed warriors escorting him."

---

149. The poet is on occasion critical of contemporary nobility, as here, where he points out that few rulers of his day would stand in the front ranks and risk their lives along with their men.

[2034] "Don't call me a liar," said Hawart's vassal. "I will gladly hold to what I promised, and no fear could keep me away. As terrible as Hagen may be, I will fight him alone."

[2035] Irinc pleaded with his clan and his men to let him fight Hagen alone, but they were reluctant to comply, because they knew all about arrogant Hagen from Burgundy. [2036] He kept at them until they finally gave in. When his retainers realized that he was intent on winning honor, they let him go, and a hard-fought battle between the two ensued.

[2037] Irinc of Denmark raised his spear. The famous hero protected himself with his shield and ran toward Hagen all the way up to the hall. The two fighters clashed loudly. [2038] They both launched their spears with great force. Piercing their solid shields all the way through to their gleaming armor, the spears traveled in a great arc. Then the two bold and determined men drew their swords. [2039] Bold Hagen's strength was amazing, but Irinc struck him so hard that the entire hall resounded. The sound of their blows echoed off of the palace and its towers, but the warrior could not achieve his goal.

[2040] Irinc was unable to inflict any wounds on Hagen. Then he charged toward the fiddler, hoping that he could force him back with his hard blows, but Volker knew how to protect himself with his shield. [2041] The fiddler struck so hard that the rim of Irinc's shield burst, and Irinc had to withdraw from his terrifying opponent.

He ran instead toward Gunther of Burgundy. [2042] They were both powerful fighters. Gunther and Irinc rained down blows on each other, but they remained unharmed. Blood was kept from flowing by their dense and solid armor.

[2043] Next he abandoned Gunther and charged at Gernot, who began to strike sparks on his chainmail. Mighty Gernot of Burgundy nearly beat Irinc to death. [2044] He then leapt away, he was certainly quick. The hero quickly killed four Burgundians, retainers of the ruler of Worms on the Rhine. Giselher could not have been more furious.

[2045] "God knows, Lord Irinc," said young Giselher, "you will have to repay me for those who now lie dead before you." He rushed at him and hit the Dane so hard that he was stunned. [2046] He collapsed under the blows into his own blood, and everyone thought that the great hero would never again deliver a stroke in battle. But Irinc lay in front of Giselher unwounded. [2047] His brain had been rattled by the crash of the sword and the clanging in his helmet, and the bold warrior lay unconscious. Mighty Giselher had accomplished that with his strength.

[2048] When the buzzing in his head, caused by that great blow, had stopped, he thought, "I'm alive, and not injured. Now I know how strong Giselher really is."

[2049] He heard his enemies standing all around him. If they had known his condition, worse would have happened to him. He heard that Giselher was close by and asked himself how he could escape from his enemies. [2050] In a frenzy, he sprang up out of the blood. Thanks to his swiftness, he sprinted out of the building but ran right into Hagen, dealing him a massive blow with his mighty hand.

[2051] Hagen thought, "You're going to have to die. You won't survive unless the devil himself protects you." With his mighty sword Waske, Irinc wounded Hagen through his helmet. [2052] When Lord Hagen felt the wound, the sword in his hand began to flail wildly. Hawart's man had to retreat from him as Hagen pursued him down the staircase. [2053] Bold Irinc raised his shield above his head, but even if the staircase had been three times as long, Hagen would not let him return a single stroke. The red sparks flew around his head!

[2054] Irinc finally returned to his own side alive, and Kriemhild found out what had happened and how he had fared in his fight with Hagen. The queen gave him high praise and thanks.

[2055] "May God reward you, Irinc, mighty and illustrious hero! You have consoled me and given me hope. I see that Hagen's armor is red with blood." Out of gratitude, Kriemhild herself took his shield from his hand.

[2056] "You can save your thanks," said Hagen. "A real warrior would be ready to try again. Then if he escaped unharmed, he would indeed be a daring man. The injury he gave me won't do you much good. [2057] The red you see on my chainmail from my wounds only inspires me to kill more men. Now I'm really mad, and still fearless. Irinc has done me no harm."

[2058] Irinc of Denmark stood in the breeze, cooled himself in his armor, and took off his helmet. Everyone praised him for his great courage. The margrave's spirits were raised by this.

[2059] Irinc then said, "My friends, pay attention, you must rearm me immediately. I will try again to defeat that arrogant man."

His shield was hacked to pieces, and so he got a new one. [2060] The combatant soon had new weapons and armor and in his rage chose a strong spear to attack Hagen, who glared at him with death in his eyes. [2061] Hagen was not going to wait. He charged down the stairs at him [Irinc], throwing and swinging and filled with rage. Irinc's strength did him little good. [2062] They hammered through each other's shields, creating a firestorm as they did. Hawart's man was severely wounded by Hagen's sword despite his shield and chainmail, and he never recovered. [2063] When Irinc felt his wound, he moved his shield higher above his head. He thought that he had survived the worst of it, but King Gunther's vassal had more in store for him.

[2064] Hagen found a spear lying at his feet and threw it at Irinc, the hero from Denmark. It penetrated his skull and remained stuck there. Hagen bestowed on him a terrible end. [2065] Irinc fled back to the Danish troops, who had to pull the spear out of his head before they could remove his helmet. Death was near. His clan wept, and they had good cause. [2066] The queen came to stand above him and mourned for Irinc the strong. She wept over his wounds and felt the bitter loss.

The bold and proud warrior spoke in front of his troops, [2067] "Dear noblewoman, please leave your lament. What good will your crying do? I will die from these wounds. Death will no longer allow me to serve you and Etzel." [2068] He said to those from Thuringia and those from Denmark, "None of you will earn the queen's reward, her gleaming red gold. If you fight Hagen, you will surely die."

[2069] His face turned white. Bold Irinc was marked by death. They were all greatly saddened, as Hawart's vassal could not survive. The men from Denmark were intent on doing battle. [2070] Irnfried and Hawart rushed to the hall with a thousand men. A great noise arose that could be heard all around. It was unbelievable how many spears were launched at the Burgundians. [2071] Bold Irnfried charged the minstrel, who repaid him dearly for that attack. The noble fiddler struck the count right through his helmet. He was terrifying indeed. [2072] Irnfried in turn struck at the bold minstrel so that his chainmail burst and red sparks streamed down over the armor. Nonetheless the count ended up dead at the fiddler's feet.

[2073] Hawart and Hagen were locked in combat. All who saw it were witness to a great spectacle. Sword strokes rained down from each hero, but Hawart was killed by the man from Burgundy. [2074] When the Danes and the Thuringians saw their leaders dead, a terrible battle began in front of the building before they bravely reached the door. Countless helmets and shields were battered.

[2075] "Pull back!" cried Volker. "Let them get in! They won't stand a chance. Inside they'll all die in no time at all. They will pay for the queen's reward with their lives."

[2076] As the overly confident men broke into the hall, many of them had their heads battered by swift strokes to the point of death. Bold Gernot fought well, as did the combative Giselher. [2077] One thousand and four men entered the hall. People could see swords flashing back and forth, but in the end all of the warriors in the hall were killed. Fabulous wonders were recounted about the Burgundians there. [2078] Afterwards silence returned and the noise ceased. Blood from the dead flowed all around and seeped out through holes to the pavement. This had all been accomplished with great courage by those from the Rhine. [2079] The men from Burgundy sat down to rest and put down their swords and shields. The bold minstrel still stood in front of the battlement, waiting to see if anybody else wanted to take him on.

[2080] The king cried out in grief, as did his wife. Young women and ladies beat their own bodies. I believe that death itself had conspired against them. Many warriors were still to be lost there on account of the foreign guests.

36. The Queen Orders the Hall Set Ablaze

[2081] "Take off your helmets!" commanded Hagen. "My companion and I will watch out for you. And if Etzel's men dare to try us again, then I will warn my lords as quickly as I can."

[2082] Many of the brave knights removed their helmets and sat down on the corpses that had been laid low in the blood by their own hands. The guests had been poorly cared for.

[2083] Before the evening, the king and the queen ordered the Hunnish warriors to make another attempt. They could see at least twenty thousand men standing before them, and they all had to enter the fight. [2084] They charged into battle against the foreign guests. Dancwart, Hagen's brother and a clever man, ran from his lords toward the enemy in front of the door. The Huns thought that he had died, but he came out of it in fine shape. [2085] The battle lasted until the darkness of night put an end to it. The foreigners had defended themselves against Etzel's men the entire long summer's day, as heroes should. There were to be many more bold warriors that would lie at their feet. [2086] The great bloodbath took place on the summer solstice, in order that Lady Kriemhild might avenge her grief against her closest relatives and many others. As a result, King Etzel was to lose happiness forever.*

[2087] The day had ended, but their cares had not. They thought that a quick death would be a better fate than suffering a long and terrible end, and the proud knights wanted to sue for peace. [2088] They asked to see the king. The three highborn kings, covered in blood, grime, and rust walked out of the hall, but they did not know to whom they could make their great suffering known.

[2089] Etzel and Kriemhild both appeared before them. They were the rulers of the land, and the size of their army was constantly increasing. Etzel said to the foreigners, "Tell me, what do you want from me? You want peace, but this is hardly possible [2090] given the great harm you have done to me. You will not rest as long as I am alive. You killed my son and many more of my kin. Peace and reconciliation will elude you."

[2091] Gunther answered, "We have been forced to sue. My entire household has been killed by your warriors inside their quarters. How did I deserve this? I came here to you in good faith. I thought that you respected me."

[2092] Young Giselher of Burgundy then spoke up, "You heroes of Etzel, those of you still alive, what do you accuse me of? What have I done to you? I rode to this land out of friendship."

[2093] They [the Huns] said, "The entire castle and all the land are full of the sorrow and pain from your friendship. It would have been better for you if you had never crossed the Rhine from Worms to come here. You all, you and your brothers, have decimated this land."

[2094] Gunther said angrily, "If you would agree to put aside this hatred and reconcile with us foreigners, it would be good for both sides. We don't deserve what Etzel has done to us."

[2095] The host then replied to his guests, "My sorrow cannot be compared to yours. The great anguish over the harm and shame that I have suffered means that none of you will leave here alive."

[2096] Mighty Gernot spoke to the king, "Then do as God has commanded, and have mercy. Slaughter us as exiles and let us come out to you in the open. That would be the honorable thing to do. [2097] Whatever may happen to us, make it quick. You still have so many fresh troops, and if they dare to attack us, we won't survive. We're exhausted from battle. How much longer are we supposed to take this agony?"

[2098] Etzel's troops were all in favor of letting them come out to gather in front of the palace. Kriemhild heard that and it mispleased her greatly, and so the truce was therefore rashly denied the foreigners.

[2099] "Stop, Hunnish warriors, don't go through with it. I only have your best interests at heart, that you not let the butchers out of the hall. Your friends and family will be put to death. [2100] And if none of them were alive except Ute's sons, my noble brothers, and they got out into the open and cooled off their armor, then you would all be lost. The world has never seen fighters more bold."

[2101] Young Giselher spoke, "My dearest sister, I would never have believed that you would invite us from the Rhine here to this land to such great ruin. What have I done to the Huns that I deserve to die? [2102] I was always faithful to you. I never did you any harm. I rode here to this land thinking that you cherished me, my dearest sister. Have mercy on us. It's our only hope."

[2103] "I can show you no clemency. I have no mercy left to give. Hagen of Troneck has done such terrible things to me that, as long as I am alive, there can be no reconciliation. You will all have to pay," said Etzel's wife. [2104] "If you hand over Hagen alone to me as a hostage, I would consider letting you live. You are my brothers, and we are children of the same mother. Then I would counsel these heroes here to accept reconciliation."

[2105] "May God in heaven prevent that!" said Gernot. "If there were a thousand of us from the same clan, we would rather be dead than give up one man as a hostage. It will never happen."

[2106] "We all have to die sometime anyway," said Giselher. "No one will keep us from defending ourselves as knights. If someone wants to fight us, here we are. I have always been loyal to all of my friends."

[2107] Then it was bold Dancwart's turn to speak. "My brother Hagen does not stand alone. Those who deny us a truce may yet regret it, I assure you of that. This I say in truth."

[2108] The queen replied, "You proud heroes, move to the staircase and avenge my pain! I will always be grateful for this, as I should. I will repay Hagen for his arrogance. [2109] Don't let any of them out of the building. I command that the hall be put to the torch at all four ends. This will avenge all of my grief." Etzel's troops were quickly armed and ready.

[2110] Those Burgundians who were still standing outside the hall were now driven inside with blows and missiles. The noise was deafening. But the nobles and the men were not to be separated, and they stayed together as their loyalty demanded. [2111] Etzel's wife ordered that the hall be put to the torch, and the warriors inside were tortured by the fire. The flames were fanned by the wind and soon the entire building was ablaze. I don't think that any army ever experienced more terror.

[2112] Many of those inside yelled, "This is the end! We would rather all die in combat. May God have mercy, we are all lost. The queen has unleashed her anger on us."

[2113] One of them inside said, "We will all die. What good is the king's friendly welcome now? The heat in here is making me die of thirst, but I think that death will soon enough put an end to this agony."

[2114] Hagen of Troneck spoke, "You noble knights, if you are thirsty, then drink from the blood here. It is better than wine in this heat. Right now it is the best we have."

[2115] One of the men went up to one of the corpses. He kneeled down, took off his helmet, and drank from the flowing blood. As strange as it was, it seemed to him to be exceptionally good.

[2116] "May God reward you, Lord Hagen," said the exhausted man, "that I have drunk from your good counsel. I have never before had better wine. Should I live a bit longer, I will always be in your debt."

[2117] When others heard that he thought it was good, then more drank blood and gained great strength. Many beautiful women would lose their dear friends on that account. [2118] In the hall they were showered by embers, but they used their shields to deflect them to the ground. The smoke and the heat made them suffer greatly. I don't think that heroes will ever again suffer so much.

[2119] Hagen of Troneck said, "Everybody stand against the wall! Don't let the embers fall on your helmets. Stamp them out in the blood. The queen has offered us a cruel feast."

[2120] The night finally came to an end after such misery. The bold minstrel still stood in front of the building, along with Hagen, his companion, both leaning on their shields. They were prepared for more trouble from those from Etzel's land.*

[2121] Then the fiddler spoke, "Let's go back into the hall so that the Huns will think that we were all killed by this torture they subjected us to. But they'll still have to fight some of us."

[2122] Young Giselher of Burgundy said, "I think the day is dawning. There's a cool wind blowing. May God in heaven grant us better times. My sister Kriemhild has prepared an evil feast for us."

[2123] Somebody else said, "Day has arrived. Since things aren't going to get any easier for us, it's time to arm and defend yourselves, heroes. King Etzel's wife will soon enough visit us again."

[2124] The ruler of the land was convinced that the foreigners were all dead from their ordeal and the fire, but six hundred bold men were still alive. No king ever had better warriors. [2125] The Hunnish guards could see that the foreigners were still alive, despite the injury and suffering they had endured, the lords and their men. They could be seen alive and well, standing inside the hall.

[2126] Kriemhild was told that many of them had survived. The queen said that it was impossible that anybody could have survived the fire. "I'm sure that all of them are lying there dead."

[2127] The nobles and their men still wanted to live, if someone had shown them any mercy. But they found none in the land of the Huns, and so they avenged their own deaths with their brave defense. [2128] They were greeted in the morning with a hard fight. The heroes were hard pressed by the many sturdy spears thrown at them. They all defended themselves as bold and brave knights should. [2129] Etzel's forces were intent on earning Kriemhild's reward, and they were also determined to carry out the king's command. Many Burgundians were soon to lose their lives on that account. [2130] Marvelous stories can be told about what was given and what was taken. She had shields heaped up to the rim with red gold and gave it to all who wanted to take it. Never before had so much been paid to fight an enemy. [2131] A great armed force came up to meet them.

Bold Volker said, "Here we are. I never enjoyed seeing men ready to fight more than now, especially those who have taken a king's ransom to kill us."

[2132] Many of the Burgundians called out, "Closer, heroes, onward! Let's get on with it, the sooner the better! Everyone left here is destined to die." Their shields were soon filled with spear tips.

[2133] What more can I say? At least twelve hundred men fought each other, surging back and forth. The foreigners cooled their inner fire with the wounds they slashed. No one could separate the two sides. Blood could be seen flowing [2134] from deadly wounds inflicted left and right. People could hear how they were all crying out for their friends. The mighty king lost all of his bravest warriors, and they were mourned by their loving families.

37. Ruediger Is Killed

[2135] The foreigners had fought well that morning. Gotelind's husband [Ruediger] arrived at court and could see for himself the great suffering inflicted on both sides. Noble Ruediger was brought to tears.

[2136] "I wish that I had never been born!" he cried. "That no one can stop this tragedy! I wish I could reconcile everyone, but the king won't budge. His injury is ever growing."

[2137] Ruediger then sent a message to Dietrich to see if they could still change the great kings' minds. The Lord of Bern replied, "Who could end it? King Etzel refuses to let anyone try."

[2138] A Hunnish warrior saw Ruediger standing there with tears in his eyes, he had been weeping for a while. He said to the queen, "Just look at how he's standing there. He is the most powerful of all here at Etzel's court [2139] and everyone answers to him, the people and the land. How does Ruediger control so many castles, all of them given to him by the king? He hasn't lifted his sword once in this battle. [2140] It seems to me that he really doesn't give a damn about what's happening here, since he already has everything he wants. According to his reputation he's more courageous than anyone else, but in this struggle none of that has been apparent."

[2141] The faithful hero looked sadly at the man he heard saying this. He thought to himself, "You'll pay for calling me a coward. You've been spreading your words around the court too loudly."

[2142] With his hand clenched in a fist, he ran up to the Hun and hit him so hard that he instantly dropped dead at his feet. This only added to King Etzel's loss.

[2143] "Take that, you coward!" said Ruediger. "I have enough pain and loss. How dare you blame me for not fighting. I have every right to hate the foreigners, [2144] and I would have done all that I could, if I had not been the one who led the warriors here. I was their escort into my lord's lands. As a foreigner here myself, I can't fight them."[150]

---

150. Ruediger's reluctance is not based on a strict legal prohibition, but seems instead to come from his own sense of conflicting loyalties. He is Etzel's vassal, and he pledged to support Kriemhild, but like many others, he remains apart from the Huns in faith and tradition. Etzel's court may be what we would consider a multicultural, tolerant center of power, but Ruediger clearly still feels that he is an outsider who identifies mainly with other outsiders.

[2145] Mighty King Etzel spoke to the margrave, "How has this helped us, noble Ruediger? We have so many casualties here, we don't need any more. You have acted in bad faith."

[2146] The noble knight responded, "He insulted me and questioned my honor and wealth, so much of which I have from your hands. That did little to help the liar's case."

[2147] The queen joined them. She had seen what the hero's rage had done to the Hun and complained about it bitterly and began to weep. She said to Ruediger, "How do we deserve this, [2148] that you increase the pain for me and the king? Noble Ruediger, you have always said that you would risk your honor and your life for us. I have heard many a warrior praise you. [2149] I remind you of the oath you swore to me, great knight, when you counseled me to become Etzel's wife, that you would serve me until one of us dies. I am a poor woman very much in need of help now."

[2150] "That is the truth. I swore to you, noble woman, that I would risk my honor and life for you. But I did not swear to sell my soul.[151] I invited these highborn nobles to this festivity."

[2151] She said, "Think, Ruediger, about your great loyalty and constancy, and the oath you made that you would always avenge any harm and pain I have suffered."

The margrave replied, "I have never denied you anything."

[2152] Mighty Etzel also began to plead. Both of them got down on their knees in front of that man. The noble margrave was at his wit's end. The faithful warrior spoke with despair, [2153] "That I had to live so long to experience this! Everything granted me by God—honor, duty, and courtliness—is lost. Oh God in heaven, why has death not spared me this? [2154] Whatever I stop or start, I will have acted badly and in bad faith. But if I do nothing, then the whole world will curse me. May He who granted me life counsel me now."

[2155] The king and his wife continued to beseech him. The result would be the death of many men at Ruediger's hands, but he would die as well. Here you can hear how much suffering he caused. [2156] He knew that he would gain only injury and terrible grief. He would have gladly refused the king and the queen, and he feared the world's hatred if he killed any of the Burgundians.

---

151. The risk to Ruediger's soul is not a question of religious doctrine but rather makes the connection between soul and honor in a way that the contemporary nobility would have understood. To be forced to break one loyalty in order to keep another would have been for Ruediger the equivalent to losing faith with God. Ruediger is asked to betray his friends, and he knows that his decision to do so is being forced by Kriemhild and her fiendish plot. The Burgundians made a different choice when asked to give up Hagen.

[2157] The bold man then said to the king, "Almighty king, take everything back that I have from you, all the lands and their towns. I will keep nothing. I want to walk into exile on my own."*

[2158] King Etzel replied, "Who would help me then? I give all of it to you outright, land and people, so that you, Ruediger, will avenge me against my enemies. You will be a mighty king alongside Etzel."

[2159] But Ruediger responded, "How can I do that? I invited them into my house, gave them to drink and eat, and bestowed gifts on them. How can I cause their deaths? [2160] People might think I'm a coward, but I gave my support to those nobles and their men. And I'm pained by the kinship that I entered into with them. [2161] I gave my daughter to Giselher. She could not have found a better match in all the world, with regard to courtesy and honor, loyalty and wealth. Never have I seen a king so young yet so virtuous."

[2162] But then Kriemhild spoke, "Noble Ruediger, take pity on our pain, mine and the king's. And consider that never before did a host have such destructive guests."

[2163] The margrave replied to the noble woman, "Today Ruediger will have to pay for what you and my lord have done for me. I will have to pay with my life. It can wait no longer. [2164] I know that today my towns and lands will be freed by someone's hands. I put my wife and my child in your merciful hands, along with all those suffering in Bechelarn."

[2165] "May God reward you, Ruediger," said the king. He and the queen were both cheered. "Your people will be safe under our protection. I trust in my own fortune and believe that you will live."

[2166] He was about to risk both his soul and his life. Etzel's wife began to cry. He said, "I have to keep the oath I made to you, but I don't want to fight my friends."

[2167] He was seen walking away from the king in great sorrow. His own warriors crowded around him. He said, "All of my men, arm yourselves! I have to fight the Burgundians."

[2168] They quickly ordered their weapons and armor brought to them, helmets and shields, everything was carried to them by their squires. The proud foreigners would soon receive the bad news. [2169] Ruediger and five hundred men were swiftly armed. He was supported by another twelve champions, who wanted to earn honor and glory in battle. They didn't know that death was very near. [2170] Ruediger could be seen fully armed, and Ruediger's men carried their sharp swords openly and in their other hand their broad, gleaming shields. The fiddler saw this and was deeply troubled.

[2171] Young Giselher saw his father-in-law coming toward him wearing his helmet. How was he to know that he meant him harm? The noble king was delighted to see him.

[2172] "I am lucky to have such family," said Giselher, "which we have gained along the way here. My wife will be of benefit to us right here. I am happy, truthfully, that we were married."

[2173] "I don't know why you take such comfort," said the minstrel. "Where have you seen so many men wearing helmets and carrying swords who were intent on peace? Ruediger wants to earn his towns and lands at our expense."

[2174] Before the fiddler had finished speaking, noble Ruediger appeared in front of the hall. He set his sturdy shield on the ground before him. He had to deny his friends his support and welcome.

[2175] The noble margrave shouted into the hall, "You bold Nibelungen, defend yourselves! You should have had my favor, now I bring destruction. We were friends, but now I renounce my loyalty."

[2176] Hearing this, the besieged men were shocked. No one was happy that their friend wanted to fight them. They had already experienced plenty of hardship from their enemies.

[2177] "May God in heaven prevent," said Gunther, "you from renouncing your support and the loyalty that we were counting on. I have faith in you that you won't go through with it."

[2178] "There is no way it can be avoided," said the bold man. "I must fight you because I took an oath. Now defend yourselves, bold heroes, if you value your lives! King Etzel's wife will have it no other way."

[2179] "Your rejection of the peace comes too late," said the mighty king. "May God reward you, noble Ruediger, for the loyalty and love that you have shown us, if only you would end this peacefully. [2180] I and my clan would forever be grateful for all that you have given us, if you let us live. Think, noble Ruediger, of your noble gifts when you brought us here to Etzel's lands in good faith."

[2181] "I would wish for you," said Ruediger, "that I could overwhelm you with gifts, given from the heart, as I had hoped. I would not be reproached for that kind of behavior."

[2182] "Never mind, noble Ruediger," said Gernot. "Never before did a host offer his guests a warmer welcome than you did us. This will be to your benefit, if we come out of this alive."

[2183] "May it be God's will," said Ruediger, "noble Gernot, that you would be on the Rhine and I would die with honor. Since I have to fight you, nothing worse was ever done by heroes against friends."

[2184] "May God reward you, Lord Ruediger," answered Gernot, "for this wonderful gift. Your death pains me, with you will be lost a most chivalrous spirit. Here I carry the sword that you, great hero, gave me. [2185] It has never let me down in all this strife. Many knights have perished by its edges. It is bright and hard, noble and strong. I don't think that a warrior will ever give a richer gift. [2186] And if you will not abandon your attack on us, and if you kill one of the few friends I still have here, then I will kill you with your own sword. I will then pity you, Ruediger, and your highborn wife."

[2187] "May it be God's will, Lord Gernot, that everything will come to pass as you wish it, and that your friends will live. My wife and my daughter should trust in you."

[2188] Giselher of Burgundy, beautiful Ute's child, spoke next, "Why are you doing this, Ruediger? Everyone who came with me is your friend. You are making the wrong decision. You want to make your young daughter a widow too soon. [2189] If you and your knights fight against me, then you will have repaid me poorly for trusting you more than any other man. That is why I took your daughter as my bride."

[2190] "Think back on your loyalty, noble and mighty king, if God lets you leave this place alive," said Ruediger. "Don't let the young woman suffer on my account. Stay true to yourself and be good to her."

[2191] "I will gladly do that," said young Giselher, "but if my nearest relatives, who are here, die at your hands, then the family ties that now exist between me and you and your daughter will be cut."

[2192] "May God help us all," said the bold man. They picked up their shields and prepared to charge at the foreigners in Kriemhild's hall.

Suddenly Hagen shouted down from the staircase, [2193] "Wait a minute, noble Ruediger," said Hagen. "We want to negotiate further, I and my lords. We are in dire straits. What good will our deaths do Etzel?"

[2194] "I am in grave danger," said Hagen. "The shield that Lady Gotelind gave me has been hacked to pieces by the Huns. I brought it to Etzel's lands, but not to fight. [2195] If God in heaven would allow me to carry a good shield like the one you have in your hand, noble Ruediger, then I would have no need for chainmail in combat."

[2196] "I would gladly give you my shield, if I could do so without Kriemhild watching. Here, take it anyway, Hagen, and carry it well. It would be good if you could take it home with you to Burgundy."

[2197] Since he was so willing to give his shield to him, many wept openly until their eyes were red. It was the last gift that Ruediger of Bechelarn ever gave to another hero. [2198] As tough and strong minded as Hagen was, the gift that the hero made so close to the end made him feel compassion, and he was saddened, as were many other noble knights.

[2199] "May God reward you in heaven, noble Ruediger. There will never again be the likes of you, giving foreign warriors such splendid gifts. May God grant that your chivalry live on. [2200] This situation pains me," continued Hagen. "We've had enough problems already and should cry to God that we are now supposed to fight against friends."

The margrave answered, "I am truly sorry."

[2201] "May God reward you for this gift, noble Ruediger. However these mighty warriors may act toward you, my hand will not be raised against you in battle, even if you kill all the Burgundians."

[2202] Brave Ruediger bowed to him in respect. There were tears on both sides that no one could end this suffering. It was a great tragedy. When Ruediger died, so did the father of many virtues.

[2203] Volker, the minstrel, then spoke from inside the hall, "Since my comrade Hagen has declared a truce, then you will have the same from me. You have earned it, since you brought us into this land. [2204] Highborn margrave, you are to be my emissary. The margravine gave me these red-golden arm bands, so that I might wear them here at the festival. You can see them here for yourself, as my witness."

[2205] "May God in heaven grant," said Ruediger, "that the margravine could give you even more. I will gladly deliver the message to my wife, should I see her alive again. You can be certain of that."

[2206] After he had pledged him this, Ruediger lifted up his shield and became enraged. He could wait no longer and charged at the foreigners like a true fighter. The mighty margrave dealt out powerful blows. [2207] Volker and Hagen stood out of the way, just as the two warriors had promised him, but he met bold defenders at the ramparts, and Ruediger became involved in a perilous battle. [2208] Gunther and Gernot let him into the hall with murderous intent on vengeance. They were heroes, but Giselher withdrew. He was deeply conflicted and did not want to die, so he avoided Ruediger.

[2209] The margrave's men rushed against the enemy and followed their lord as warriors should, wielding their swords openly in their hands. Many helmets and solid shields were shattered. [2210] The exhausted men returned the heavy blows against those from Bechelarn. Their swords struck deep and clean through the chainmail into their bodies. They accomplished great feats of arms in that battle. [2211] The entire noble household was now inside the hall, and Volker and Hagen leaped in to join them. They gave quarter to no one except for that one man. Their work caused the blood to flow from beneath helmets. [2212] How terribly the swords reverberated there in the hall. Many shield rims burst apart under the blows, and jewels, hacked to pieces, rained down into the blood. They fought so ferociously that the likes will never be seen again.

[2213] The Lord of Bechelarn fought from one end of the hall to the other. He knew how to fight bravely. Ruediger showed everyone that he was a real warrior, bold and worthy of praise. [2214] There stood Gunther and Gernot, and they both killed many a hero in that battle. Giselher and Dancwart weren't sorry about that. They brought many others to the end of their days. [2215] Ruediger showed that he was strong, bold, and well armed. How many heroes he slew! A Burgundian [Gernot] saw all this and became furious. Noble Ruediger's death was near.

[2216] Gernot the strong called out to the hero. He said to the margrave, "Noble Ruediger, you aren't leaving any of my men alive. This pains me greatly, and I can't bear to watch it anymore. [2217] Your gift sword may come back to haunt you, now that you have taken so many of my friends from me. Turn to face me, noble and bold man. I will earn your gift as best I can."

[2218] Before the margrave could reach him, gleaming metal rings were colored darkly. The two men, thirsty for honor, fell upon each other. Each sought to protect himself against the gravest wounds. [2219] Their swords were so sharp that no defense was adequate. Ruediger gave Gernot such a blow to his rock hard helmet that blood began to flow out. The bold and brave knight paid him back on the spot. [2220] He raised Ruediger's gift high above his head, and despite his mortal wound landed a blow right through his shield to his helmet. This killed beautiful Gotclind's husband. [2221] Such a great gift was never so poorly repaid. Gernot and Ruediger both fell to the ground, each killed in battle by the other. Hagen now became enraged as he saw the great loss.

[2222] The hero of Troneck said, "This is an evil turn of events. We have suffered a great loss in both of them. Their people and their lands will never be able to recover from it. Ruediger's heroes will have to pay the price for this."*

[2223] "Oh my brother, who is dead. I am visited by one disaster after another. And Ruediger's death will haunt me forever. The loss and great pain is equal on both sides."[152]

[2224] When Lord Giselher saw his father-in-law dead, those still inside the hall were made to suffer. Death soon found his companions, and not a single man from Bechelarn survived. [2225] Then Gunther and Giselher, and Hagen, Dancwart, and Volker, brave warriors all, walked up to where they found both men lying. The heroes wept openly on the spot.

[2226] "Death is a thief," said young Giselher. "Stop your crying and let's get some fresh air so that our chainmail might cool off. We are all weary from combat. I think that God in heaven won't give us much longer to live."

[2227] Some of the warriors could be seen sitting down, others leaning against the wall, where they were able to get some rest. Ruediger's heroes were lying dead. The clamor had stopped, and the silence lasted so long that Etzel became angry.

---

152. Assuming that it is Giselher who speaks in the preceding strophe, it is still curious that Giselher seeks to avenge his father-in-law's death rather than his brother's. He continues to fight those from Bechelarn, but it is clear that everyone ends up losing in one sense or another.

[2228] "What kind of service is this?" said the king's wife. "It doesn't seem steady enough to make Ruediger's enemies feel his wrath. He wants to escort them back to Burgundy. [2229] What good did it do, King Etzel, that we gave him whatever he wanted? This hero has failed in his duty. The one who was to avenge us now wants reconciliation."

Volker, that great warrior, answered her, [2230] "Unfortunately, that's not true, noble queen. If I dared call a noblewoman a liar, then you would be guilty of an evil lie against Ruediger. He and his warriors failed in reconciliation. [2231] He did exactly what the king ordered him to do, and as a result he and his household lie here dead. Look around you, Kriemhild. See if there is anyone left to command. Ruediger, the hero, served you unto death. [2232] If you don't believe it, then see for yourself."

They showed her so that she would be upset. They carried out the hero's mangled body for the king to see. Etzel's warriors had never before been so distraught. [2233] As they were carrying out the dead margrave, no writer could have written down or told how the women and men expressed their heartfelt pain. [2234] Etzel's pain was so great that he roared like a lion as he cried out. His wife did the same. Their mourning for Ruediger was extreme.

38. Dietrich's Men Are Killed

[2235] The great lament could be heard all around, as the palace and its towers echoed with the cries. One of Dietrich of Bern's men heard it as well, and he ran quickly to deliver the distressing news.

[2236] He said to the nobleman, "Listen, my Lord Dietrich. I've been through a lot, but I've never before heard such lamentation as I've heard just now. I think that King Etzel himself must have been wounded. [2237] How else could they all be acting this way? The king or Kriemhild, one of them must be dead, killed by the bold foreigners on account of their hatred. Many great warriors are weeping uncontrollably."

[2238] The hero of Bern responded, "My dear comrades, let's not jump to conclusions. Whatever the foreign warriors have done, they did out of necessity. I offered them my peace. Make sure you honor it."

[2239] Bold Wolfhart then spoke, "I will go there and find out what happened, and I will then return to report, my lord, what I have learned about this grieving."

[2240] Lord Dietrich then said, "Wherever enmity is found, difficult questions will only offend warriors even more. Wolfhart, I don't want you asking them any questions."

[2241] He ordered Helfrich to go there quickly and seek out Etzel's men or the foreigners themselves to find out what had happened. No one had ever seen people mourning to such an extreme.

[2242] The envoy asked, "What happened here?"

One of those present answered, "Every bit of joy that we had here in Hunnish lands has been destroyed. Ruediger lies here, killed by the Burgundians. [2243] Of those who entered the hall with him, none came out alive."

Helfrich couldn't have been more moved. Never before had he so unwillingly given his report. The envoy returned to Dietrich with tears in his eyes.

[2244] "What do you have to tell us?" asked Dietrich. "Helfrich, why are you crying so?"

The noble warrior answered, "I have good reason to mourn. The Burgundians have killed the great Ruediger."

[2245] The hero of Bern spoke, "God can't want such a thing! That would be terrible vengeance and a devilish mockery. What did Ruediger do to deserve this? I know that he was a friend of the foreigners."

[2246] Wolfhart answered him, "And if they did do it, then they should all have to pay with their lives. If we let them get away with it, we will be dishonored. Brave Ruediger provided well for us."

[2247] The Lord of the Amelungen ordered them to find out more. Despondent, he went to sit in a window niche. He told Hildebrand to go to the foreigners to find out from them what had happened.

[2248] Master Hildebrand, that battle-hardened fighter, carried neither shield nor sword. He wanted to approach the foreigners with courtesy, but he was criticized for it by his nephew.

[2249] Fierce Wolfhart said, "If you go there unarmed, they'll ridicule you, and you'll have to return in disgrace. If you go well armed, they'll think twice."

[2250] The man of experience heeded the voice of inexperience. Before he knew what was happening, all of Dietrich's men had likewise armed themselves and held up their unsheathed swords. The hero was displeased and wished he could have prevented it. [2251] He asked them where they were going.

"We want to go with you. Maybe then Hagen of Troneck won't mock you the way he usually does." When he heard that, he allowed them to come with him.

[2252] Bold Volker saw the warriors from Bern, Dietrich's men, fully armed. They had strapped on their swords and had their shields in their hands. He reported this to his lords from Burgundy.

[2253] The fiddler said, "I can see Dietrich's men approaching as adversaries, armed and wearing their helmets. They want to fight. I think things have taken a turn for the worse."

[2254] Hildebrand arrived around the same time. He set his shield down at his feet and asked Gunther's men, "What did Ruediger ever do to you, brave heroes? [2255] My Lord Dietrich sent me here. If one of you killed the noble margrave, as we have heard, then we would not be able to forgive such a grave wrong."

[2256] Hagen of Troneck responded, "The story is true. For your sake, I wish that the messenger had deceived you. And I wish that Ruediger were still alive, for whom men and women will always weep."

[2257] When they heard that he really was dead, the warriors grieved for him, motivated by their loyalty. Dietrich's men could be seen with tears streaming down their beards and chins. They had been sorely wronged.

[2258] Duke Siegestab of Bern said, "The security that Ruediger gave us after our difficulty is now at an end. The happiness of all foreigners has died along with Ruediger."[153]

[2259] Wolfwin, a hero from Amelungen, spoke, "If I were standing at my own father's grave, I could not be more saddened than by this man's death. Who can now safeguard the noble margrave's wife?"

[2260] Wolfhart said angrily, "Who will lead these warriors into battle, as the margrave did so often? Noble Ruediger, how could we have lost you like this?"

[2261] Wolfbrand, Helfrich, and Helmnot and all their friends mourned his death.

Hildebrand was all choked up but went on with difficulty, "Now, warriors, do what my lord requires. [2262] Bring Ruediger's body out of the hall to us. With him our happiness has fallen into grief, so let us now serve him for the great loyalty he showed us and many others. [2263] We are outcasts and foreigners, as Ruediger was. Why are you still making us wait? Let us carry him off with us, so that we can repay the man after his death, though we would rather have done it while he was still alive."

[2264] King Gunther responded, "That is the best support that a friend can provide for his friend in death. I call that true loyalty. You are right to repay him in this way, he did you many a good deed."

[2265] "How much longer are we supposed to beg," asked Wolfhart, "since you killed our best supporter and took him from us? Let us carry him away from here so that we may bury him."

---

153. Siegestab seems to be alluding to the common bond between foreigners and exiles at Etzel's court as well as to the support received from Ruediger when Dietrich and his men from Amelungen first came to Etzel's court as exiles.

[2266] Volker answered him, "No one is going to give him to you. Go get him yourself inside the hall, where he lies mortally wounded in his own blood. This is how you can serve Ruediger."[154]

[2267] Bold Wolfhart spoke, "God knows, sir minstrel, you don't have to add insult to the injury you've already done us. I don't dare do more in front of my lord, or you'd be sorry. He won't allow us to fight here, which is why I have to restrain myself."

[2268] The fiddler said, "That's being a bit too afraid, if one is willing to avoid doing everything that is forbidden. That's not what I call a true hero's spirit." Hagen was enjoying his compatriot's speech.

[2269] "Be careful what you wish for," said Wolfhart. "I'll rearrange your strings for you so you won't forget it, if you get back to the Rhine, that is. Honor won't allow me to take any more of your arrogance."

[2270] The fiddler replied, "If you disturb my strings so that they're out of tune, then I'll smudge your shiny helmet a bit, whether I go back to Burgundy or not."

[2271] Wolfhart wanted to strike out at him, but his uncle, Hildebrand, would not allow it and held him fast. "It seems to me that your childish wrath is getting the better of you. You would have lost my lord's favor forever."

[2272] "Let the lion off his leash, master! He's raving mad. If I get my hands on him," said Volker, the brave warrior, "and even if he had defeated all the world by himself, I would beat him so that he wouldn't live to tell about it."

[2273] The men from Bern were infuriated. Wolfhart, a brave and skilled warrior, raised his shield. Like a wild lion he charged, and his comrades quickly fell in line behind him. [2274] He ran to the hall with great bounds, but old Hildebrand caught up with him in front of the stairs. He didn't want to let him be the first one inside. They found what they were looking for with the foreigners. [2275] Master Hildebrand lunged at Hagen, and the swords in both their hands rang out. They had worked themselves into a frenzy, which was plain to see by how their two swords whipped up a fiery wind. [2276] In the melee of combat, they were separated by the onrushing strength of those from Bern. Hildebrand quickly turned away from Hagen. Mighty Wolfhart charged at bold Volker. [2277] He struck the fiddler on his solid helmet, and the blade cut all the way through the joints. The bold minstrel returned the favor and hit Wolfhart so hard that sparks flew. [2278] They ignited fires in each other's chainmail. They loathed each other, but Wolfwin of Bern separated them. Only a hero could have accomplished that.

---

154. This statement seems to contradict the previous removal of Ruediger's body for Kriemhild to see (str. 2232), but the point is that the Burgundians still have possession of the body and refuse to hand him over.

[2279] Gunther gladly faced the famous heroes of Amelungen, and Lord Giselher turned gleaming helmets red and wet with blood. [2280] Dancwart, Hagen's brother, was a ruthless man. All that he had accomplished previously against Etzel's warriors was nothing in comparison. Bold Aldrian's son now fought like someone possessed. [2281] Ritschard and Gerbart, Helfrich and Wichart had never spared themselves in previous battles, and they gave Gunther's men a taste of that now. Wolfbrand could be seen fighting magnificently. [2282] Old Hildebrand fought like a madman. Many brave men were struck down into the blood by Wolfhart's sword. These bold and brave heroes took revenge on Ruediger's behalf. [2283] Lord Siegestab's courage guided him in the fight, and Dietrich's sister's son smashed many an enemy's helmet. He could not have fought any harder.

[2284] Volker became enraged when he saw that bold Siegestab was turning iron chainmail into streams of blood. He threw himself at him, and Siegestab quickly [2285] lost his life to the fiddler, who gave him a taste of his talent, and he soon lay dead, struck down by his sword.

Hildebrand took vengeance as his bravery demanded. [2286] "My dear lord," said Master Hildebrand, "who now lies dead at the hands of Volker.[155] It's time for the fiddler to meet his end."

Bold Hildebrand could not have been more unyielding. [2287] He struck Volker the bold minstrel so hard that pieces of his shield and his helmet flew off in all directions in the hall. This proved to be the end of Volker.

[2288] Dietrich's men then engaged in the fight, bearing down and causing rings of chainmail to go flying as the tips of their swords soared through the air. Hot streams of blood came flowing out of helmets.

[2289] Hagen of Troneck saw that Volker was dead. This was for him the greatest loss of family or men at those festivities. Hagen set about to avenge his death.

[2290] "Old Hildebrand won't have much time to relish his victory. The best companion and comrade that I ever had lies dead at the hands of that hero." He raised his shield and rushed in swinging.

[2291] Bold Helfrich killed Dancwart. Gunther and Giselher were anguished to see him fall in battle. He made many pay for his own death. [2292] At the same time, Wolfhart was moving from one end of the hall to the other, raining down blows on Gunther's men. He had already made three round trips through the hall. Many a warrior fell at his hands.

[2293] Lord Giselher called out to Wolfhart, "Ahhh, that I ever gained such a harsh enemy. Come back this way, bold knight. I want to end it now, we can't go on like this."

---

155. Siegestab is Dietrich's nephew, and as a member of the ruling house, he is Hildebrand's lord as well.

[2294] Wolfhart turned back to face Giselher in battle. Both of them caused grievous wounds. Wolfhart ran at the king with such force that blood splashed up over his head. [2295] Beautiful Ute's son greeted Wolfhart, the bold hero, with hard and strong blows, but as strong as he was he couldn't save himself. There had never before been a young king so bold. [2296] He struck Wolfhart through his sturdy chainmail so that blood streamed from the wound. He wounded Dietrich's man to the death. Only one hero could accomplish such a thing.

[2297] Bold Wolfhart, feeling that he had been wounded, let his shield fall. He raised his sturdy sword even higher with both hands. The hero then struck Giselher through his helmet and armor. [2298] Each one handed the other a bitter death. All of Dietrich's men had been killed. Old Hildebrand saw Wolfhart die, and that must have been, I think, the greatest loss of his life.

[2299] Gunther's men were all dead, as were Dietrich's. Hildebrand went to the spot where Wolfhart had fallen into the blood and wrapped his arms around the bold and brave hero. [2300] He wanted to carry him out of the hall, but he was much too heavy, and so he had to leave him there. The dying man, lying in the blood, opened his eyes and saw that his uncle was trying to help him.

[2301] The fated man said, "My dear uncle, you can't help me anymore. Watch out for Hagen, that's my advice. His heart is filled with bitterness. [2302] And if my family wants to mourn me after my death, then tell the dearest and the noblest of them not to cry for me. It is not necessary. I die here like a king, struck down by a king's hand. [2303] I have also made them pay dearly for my life, and the ladies have every reason to bewail their brave knights. If anyone asks you, you can tell them straightaway that at least a hundred lie dead by my hand."

[2304] Hagen also thought about the minstrel, killed by bold Hildebrand. He said there to that man, "You will pay for my losses. Here in this hall you have taken many warriors from us."

[2305] He struck at Hildebrand so that one could hear Balmung ring out, the sword he took from Siegfried when he killed him. The old man [Hildebrand] still knew how to defend himself, he was certainly courageous. [2306] Dietrich's hero wielded a broad sword that could cut deep. He struck Hagen with it, but was unable to wound Gunther's man. In turn, Hagen hit him hard on his well-made chainmail. [2307] As soon as old Hildebrand felt the wound, he feared he would suffer even more at Hagen's hand. Dietrich's man threw his shield over his back and, gravely wounded, fled.

[2308] Not one of the heroes was left alive, with the exception of Gunther and Hagen. Old Hildebrand retreated, covered with blood. He brought Dietrich painful news. [2309] He saw him sitting sadly alone. The nobleman was to endure even more pain. He saw Hildebrand in his blood-red armor and asked, out of concern, what had happened.

[2310] "Now tell me, Master Hildebrand, why are you wet with blood? Who did this to you? It seems to me that you've been fighting with the guests in the hall. I ordered you not to do so, you should have obeyed me."

[2311] He answered his lord, "It was Hagen. He wounded me inside the hall as I was trying to remove myself. I was hardly able to escape from that devil with my life."

[2312] The Lord of Bern said, "You got what you deserved. You heard me as I offered the warriors friendship, and still you broke the peace that I guaranteed them. You should pay with your life, if it weren't such a great dishonor for me."

[2313] "My Lord Dietrich, curb your anger some. My comrades and I have suffered enough. We wanted to carry Ruediger out of the hall, but King Gunther's men would not allow it."

[2314] "Oh what a disaster! Ruediger is dead. This is the greatest pain of all. Noble Gotelind is my cousin. Pity all those left alone there in Bechelarn. [2315] His death brings to mind loyalty and past suffering." He began to weep, as was appropriate for such a hero. "Ah, I have lost a loyal comrade. I will never get over the death of King Etzel's vassal. [2316] Can you tell me, Master Hildebrand, who the warrior was who killed him?"

He replied, "Mighty Gernot accomplished that with all his strength. That hero in turn was killed by Ruediger's hand."

[2317] He said to Hildebrand, "Tell my men to arm themselves quickly. I will join them, and have them bring my bright armor. I will go myself to inquire of the Burgundians."

[2318] Master Hildebrand asked, "Who will accompany you? Those of yours who are still alive are standing in front of you. I am alone. All the rest are dead."

This news roused him to his feet, as well it should. [2319] He had never before suffered such agony.

He said, "And if all my men are dead, then God has forsaken me, unfortunate Dietrich. I was once a great king, powerful and prosperous. [2320] How could it happen," asked Dietrich, "that all of these famous heroes are dead, killed by those who were already weary of battle and had endured so much? My own ill fortune has brought them death. [2321] Since I have been so cursed, tell me, are any of the foreigners still alive?"

Master Hildebrand replied, "God knows, no one but Hagen and the mighty King Gunther."

[2322] "Oh, dear Wolfhart, if I have lost you, then I must regret the day that I was born. Siegestab and Wolfwin and Wolfbrand, too. Who will help me get back to the land of the Amelungen? [2323] Bold Helfrich is slain,

Gerbart and Wichart, how can I recover from their loss? This is the demise of all my joy. If only it were possible to die from sorrow."

39. Dietrich Captures Gunther and Hagen

[2324] Lord Dietrich then went to fetch his own armor, and Master Hildebrand helped him as armorer. The powerful man cried out so loudly that the entire house shook. [2325] He regained his heroic fighting spirit. The courageous hero was filled with grim determination as he was being armed. He took up a sturdy shield, and then he and Master Hildebrand quickly departed.

[2326] Hagen of Troneck said, "I see Lord Dietrich coming. He wants to attack us after the great losses that he's suffered. Today we'll see who is the best. [2327] Lord Dietrich of Bern may feel as strong and terrible as he wants, but if he wants to avenge himself for what has happened," said Hagen, "then I'm ready to defend myself."

[2328] Dietrich and Hildebrand heard this speech. Dietrich stepped up to where the other two heroes were standing outside of the hall, leaning up against the wall. Dietrich set down his shield.

[2329] Dietrich, filled with pain, spoke, "Mighty King Gunther, why have you acted so toward me, a foreigner here? What did I do to you? I stand here alone, bereft of all support. [2330] It wasn't enough of a tragedy for you to rob us of that hero Ruediger. You have deprived me of all my men. I never harmed you like this. [2331] Think of yourself and your own suffering, the death of your family and friends, and your hardships. Doesn't it weigh on the minds of you brave men? Oh, how Ruediger's death grieves me! [2332] A man has never in this world suffered more anguish. You gave little thought to my pain, or to your own. Whatever I had for friends, they have all been killed by you. I will never be able to grieve for my family properly."

[2333] "We are not as guilty as all that," said Hagen. "Your warriors entered into this hall fully armed and in great numbers. It seems to me that you have not been apprised of all the facts."

[2334] "What am I to believe? Hildebrand told me himself that my knights from Amelungen asked to have Ruediger's body surrendered from the hall, but all you could do was mock the bold heroes from above."

[2335] The king of the Rhine responded, "They said that they wanted to carry Ruediger out. I commanded that they be refused, to scorn Etzel, not your own men. And then Wolfhart started to goad us."

[2336] The hero of Bern said, "And so it had to be. Gunther, noble king, for the sake of your sense of justice, right the wrongs that you have inflicted on me, and compensate me, bold knight, in such a way that I can consent. [2337] Give yourself up to me as a hostage, you and your retainer, and I will prevent as best I can that any of the Huns harm you. You will find I offer only loyalty and good intentions."

[2338] "May God in heaven prevent," retorted Hagen, "that two warriors surrender while they are still standing in front of you, fully armed and able to move about freely among their enemies."

[2339] "You should not refuse," said Dietrich. "Gunther and Hagen, you both have injured me so gravely, in heart and soul, you know that it is only right that you compensate me. [2340] I give you my word and surety that I will ride home with you to your lands. I will give you an honorable escort, or I will die trying. And I expect you to act so that I may forget this great pain."

[2341] "Stop with these demands!" exclaimed Hagen. "People should not say that two bold men surrendered themselves to you, when I don't see anyone standing next to you except Hildebrand."

[2342] Master Hildebrand spoke up, "God knows, Lord Hagen, that if someone offers you peace, there may soon enough come a time when you will want to accept my lord's bargain."

[2343] "I would sooner accept such a proposal," replied Hagen, "than shamefully run away from a hall, Master Hildebrand, as you did. I would have thought that you had more guts in the face of the enemy."

[2344] Hildebrand answered him, "How can you insult me like that? Who was it who sat on his shield at the Waskenstein, as Walther of Spain killed so many of his friends?[156] Take a good look at yourself first."

[2345] Lord Dietrich then interrupted, "It is not fitting for heroes to insult each other like old women. I forbid you, Hildebrand, to say anything else. I am a warrior in exile, and I am grieving. [2346] Let us hear, mighty Hagen," said Dietrich, "what both of you brave warriors said when you saw me coming at you fully armed. You said that you wanted to fight me single-handedly."

[2347] "No one is denying that," replied Hagen. "I'm willing to give it a go with strong strokes, unless, that is, Nibelung's sword should fail me. I am angered that both of us should be made hostages here."

[2348] When Dietrich heard how unwavering Hagen was, that brave man quickly raised his shield. Hagen in return immediately leaped down at him from the top of the staircase. Nibelung's trustworthy sword gave out a loud ring as it hit Dietrich. [2349] At that point Dietrich knew that the bold man was filled with an iron will. The Lord of Bern began to defend himself against the grievous strokes. He could easily tell it was Hagen, that famous fighter.

---

156. This is a reference to the events of the *Waltharius* story. Hagen had declined to fight against his friend Walther and was accused by Gunther of cowardice. Hildebrand now renews the charge as a rebuttal to his own retreat from the fight with Hagen. The Waskenstein is a rock formation located in the Vosges Mountains of France.

[2350] He dreaded Balmung, an amazingly strong weapon. Dietrich was able to deliver a clever counterstroke now and again until he finally vanquished Hagen. He gave him a wound that was both deep and long.

[2351] Lord Dietrich thought, "You are exhausted from all this fighting. I will gain little honor if I kill you now. I want to see if I can overwhelm you instead and take you captive."

This was a risky decision. [2352] He threw down his shield—he was enormously strong—and wrapped his arms around Hagen of Troneck and so overpowered the bold man. Noble Gunther was dismayed.

[2353] Dietrich bound Hagen and led him to where he found the noble queen. He handed over to her the greatest warrior who ever carried a sword. She was pleased indeed after all her suffering.

[2354] Etzel's wife bowed before Dietrich in joy. "May you always be blessed, in body and soul. You have recompensed me for all my suffering. I am at your service until death takes me."

[2355] Lord Dietrich spoke, "You should let him live, noble queen. If it is still possible, he will compensate you for all he has done to you. It is not his fault that you see him in chains here before you."

[2356] She commanded that Hagen be led to the dungeon, where he was locked up out of sight. Gunther, the noble king, began to shout, "Where is the hero of Bern? He has done me wrong."

[2357] Lord Dietrich went to meet him. Gunther's bravery was praiseworthy. He could wait no longer and ran down from the hall, where their swords clashed loudly. [2358] As renowned as Lord Dietrich was, Gunther was filled with anger and rage, and his anguish had made them mortal enemies. People still say that it was a miracle that Dietrich survived. [2359] Their courage and their strength were equally great. The palace and towers echoed with the blows that they brought down on their stout helmets. King Gunther was filled with might and strength. [2360] The Lord of Bern overpowered him, though, as he had Hagen. One could see blood streaming through the hero's chainmail, cut by the sharp sword that Dietrich carried. Despite his exhaustion, Gunther defended himself magnificently. [2361] The king was tied up by Dietrich, although kings should not have to suffer such restraints. He thought that if he left them unbound, the king and his vassal, they would kill anyone who crossed their path. [2362] Dietrich of Bern took him into his custody and led him to Kriemhild. His suffering put an end to her own.

She said, "Welcome, Gunther, from Burgundian lands."

[2363] He replied, "I should bow to you, my dear sister, if only your greeting were more gracious. I know that you, queen, must be angry, if you give me and Hagen such a half-hearted greeting."

[2364] The hero of Bern said, "Noble wife of a king, never before have such noble knights become hostages as these that I have presented to you, almighty lady. You should let these foreigners live, for my sake."

[2365] She said that she would do so gladly.[157] Lord Dietrich left the praiseworthy heroes with tears in his eyes, but Etzel's wife then took horrible revenge. She killed both of these famous warriors. [2366] She separated them out of callousness so that neither would see the other again, that is until later, when she carried her brother's head for Hagen to see. Kriemhild's revenge fell hard on them both.

[2367] The queen went to see Hagen. Filled with enmity, she spoke with the hero, "If you will give me back what you once took from me, then you can return home to Burgundy alive."

[2368] Hagen, unwavering, replied, "You're wasting your breath, noble queen. I swore an oath that I would never reveal the treasure's location as long as any one of my lords was still living. I will not give it up to anyone."*

[2369] "I will put an end to all this," said the noble woman. She commanded that her brother be executed. He was decapitated, and she carried his head by the hair for Hagen to see. He was filled with grief.

[2370] When the wretched man saw his lord's head, the warrior defied Kriemhild. "You put an end to it as you saw fit, and it has also ended for you as I thought it would. [2371] The noble king of Burgundy is now dead, as is young Giselher and also Gernot. No one except God and I know where the treasure is buried, and it will remain forever hidden from you, you fiend."

[2372] She said, "This is poor compensation indeed from you. But I will keep Siegfried's sword. My dearly beloved carried it the last time I saw him. You are the cause of all my heartache."

[2373] She pulled the sword out of its scabbard, there was no way he could prevent it. She intended to kill the hero, and she lifted his head and hacked it off with the sword. King Etzel was witness to this, and it pained him greatly.

[2374] "No!" cried the king. "How is it that the greatest warrior of all lies here, killed by the hand of a woman? He was the greatest who ever fought in battle or carried a shield. As much as I hated him, it still pains me."

[2375] Old Hildebrand spoke, "She has gained nothing by daring to slay him. Regardless of what may happen to me, and he almost killed me himself, I will avenge the bold man of Troneck's death."

[2376] Hildebrand rushed at Kriemhild with rage, swung his sword, and struck the queen with a great blow. She was terrified of Hildebrand, but her screams could not help her.

---

157. Kriemhild's word at this point is worthless, and her lie to Dietrich only makes the final killing even more deceitful.

[2377] All those fated to die were now dead. The noble woman had been cut to pieces. Dietrich and Etzel wept as their hearts mourned the loss of family and men. [2378] Great honor was dead.[158] People had only pain and sorrow left to them. The king's festival concluded in misery, as happiness always turns to sorrow in the end. [2379] I can't tell you what happened after that. I only know that knights and ladies, and their squires, too, wept for the sake of their departed loved ones. And so the story ends. This is the downfall of the Nibelungen.[159]*

---

158. This is a declaration of not only the end of the battle but the end of an era. All the heroes of the age are dead (except for Hildebrand and Dietrich), but more than that, honor as a way of life has ended perhaps as it must, caught in a web of allegiances and loyalties that caused first the Burgundians to decline giving over Hagen, Ruediger to choose one oath over familial ties with the Burgundians, and finally Dietrich to avenge the needless deaths of his own men.
159. The last line can also be read more directly as a title: "Here the story ends: it is [called] "The Downfall of the Nibelungen."

The *Klage*[1]

[1] **T**his is the beginning of a tale that might be worth telling and would be well told if it didn't make people cry.[2] Whoever understands it correctly is compelled to shed tears over it and is miserable. **I**f only I had the skill [10] to make everyone who encounters this story love it. It has been told since olden times, and it is true. If it displeases someone, he should reserve judgment and listen to more of the tale. **A** poet had this old story written down in a book, [20] which is why today we still know how the Burgundians long ago lived their lives in glory and honor.[3]

Dancrat was the name of the king who left those extensive lands to these brave and noble heroes and to his wife Ute, who ruled with him. [30] They had everything in abundance that kings ever wanted or needed. **A**nd it is true that they had a beautiful sister. Her marriage to her husband was later to

---

1. The text has been divided into major narrative segments by translators and editors, but only manuscript C, among the major manuscripts, divides the text into "chapters" with headings and large, pen-flourished initials. I have chosen to include the C manuscript chapter divisions and headings, five in total, even though the text in C is often considerably different than the edition's B manuscript text. The first chapter in manuscript C is simply called: "The Adventure (or Story) of the *Klage*," which could also be taken as a title for the entire work. Verses are numbered according to Heinzle's (2015) edition, and I indicate manuscript B's format by representing large initials as capital letters in bold type.
2. The word from which the story has its title, *klage*, is among the most difficult to translate in this text. The range of meaning is broad, and the English word "lament" expresses only one fairly narrow aspect of this range, since the word *lament* is itself somewhat out of use at the time of this writing. The concept of *klage*, and its verb form, *klagen*, involves public displays of sorrow and grief, demonstrated through tears, cries, screams, self-flagellation, and other outward signs of an inner state of sadness and distress. It is connected to public mourning rituals, but it can also be as benign as in the opening of this text: a complaint about a story that brings sadness, not joy; a story that is meant to moralize, but not entertain, and has as its task the completion of a narrative in the *Nibelungenlied* that ends without an ending, or more precisely, an ending without a satisfactory didactic conclusion.
3. In contrast to the anachronistic, and younger, "first" strophe of the *Nibelungenlied* in manuscripts A and C, the *Klage* poet begins his text with a reference to the book, not the oral and aural presentation of the story as in the *Nibelungenlied*. The book is the guarantor of authenticity and longevity, not the poet or listener. The fact that the poet claims to have had the text written down is a sign that the transition from orality to literacy was already well underway, and the poet addresses a readership as well as an audience of listeners. The tale's veracity is guaranteed by its age and tradition, but its permanence is guaranteed in its written form.

be the reason why many great warriors would die. He would die as well on account of his overconfidence.[4]

[40] Later she took another husband, a great man from the land of the Huns, and lived with him in great splendor after her grief. The master of this story directed that it be written down how mighty this king was.[5] The story is well known that he had twelve kings serving him at all times. [50] I have this on the best authority. He was highly regarded by all. Never before had anyone, Christian or heathen, lived so magnificently, and those who knew this rode to his lands to serve him. His name was Etzel.

His father's name was Botelung. He had left Etzel a great empire upon his death, which he rules to the present day.[6] [60] The story tells us that Etzel had a wife who was the most virtuous woman alive. Her name was Helche, and her passing was a great loss for him. Almighty death robbed him of his happiness. Later his relatives would advise him to take Lady Kriemhild, [70] who was noble and generous.

You have already heard tell how she ruled in the land of the Huns as noble Helche had once done, but it pained her constantly that she was a foreigner there and far from home. She lived in constant sorrow, her heart broken and bereft of all happiness. [80] Her next of kin Had deprived her of her dear husband. It came to pass that Ute's child was served and feared by all the Hunnish clans as they had once served Lady Helche, and she had more ladies in waiting than she had had at home. [90] There were many brave champions in her great army, and she saw chivalrous acts performed every day. None of this could help, though, and she cried all the time.

After she had consolidated her power, she secretly [100] plotted to avenge Siegfried, her dear husband, whose death had been caused by her brother Gunther, along with Hagen and the king's wife [Brunhild]. It was Hagen who murdered him. It should have been impossible for Siegfried to be killed

---

4. Siegfried's overconfidence, or arrogance (*übermuot*), was mentioned in the *Nibelungenlied* as a character flaw, especially by Kriemhild (str. 896,3), but it is presented here in the manuscript B version of the *Klage* as the direct cause of his death. Other manuscripts, however, are intent on laying the blame for Siegfried's death elsewhere. Manuscript C reads: "the *übermuot* of other people" and manuscript D reads: "the *übermuot* of other warriors," both clear references to Hagen and Gunther.

5. The text refers both to the master (*meister*) as well as the poet (*tihtaere*) of the text. They may be one and the same person, or they may represent different aspects of the process of writing and rewriting a book ostensibly based in a preliterate tradition. The master of the story (*rede*) was intent on recording (*tihten*) Etzel's greatness, whereas the poet ordered the book to be written down (*scrîben*).

6. This strange anachronism is directly contradicted by the additional text at the end of manuscripts B and C concerning Etzel's demise. The line here seems to reflect a tradition that emphasizes the never-ending glory of Etzel and his kingdom as well as the extension of history into the present.

by another hero's hand, since he had defeated countless lands with his great strength. [110] This broke her heart, and she forswore any kind of joy or happiness.

Regardless of how many kings mighty Kriemhild had at her beck and call, and there were always at least ten or more, she couldn't have cared less. [120] Siegmund's son's devotion to her made her think constantly about Sieglinde, his mother, and how she [Kriemhild] had lived with him in joy and happiness. Neither family could have prevented her from personally avenging her loss many times over if she had been a man, [130] of this I am sure. But she could not because she was a woman.[7]

The poor woman thought of nothing else. This would have dire consequences for those responsible for her loss. She had the right to avenge herself. **N**o one should fault her for that. [140] If someone who was faithful had to regret that faithfulness, then he would soon think twice about acting out of loyalty. Faithfulness serves to make men esteemed and honors beautiful women as well. Their upbringing and their heart [150] oblige them to avoid acting dishonorably.

This was true for Lady Kriemhild as well, as no one ever had reason to criticize her behavior. Anyone who can fairly judge this story would have to proclaim her innocence, because the noble and highborn woman acted out of faithfulness when she took revenge for her great suffering.

You have often heard it said [160] that Etzel invited mighty lords to his kingdom to attend a great festival. He wanted to demonstrate his power and authority with his army of heroes. Lady Kriemhild was clever enough to make sure that all of those she wanted to see came along. [170] I have no idea when that happened or how many there were, or how they traveled to the land to which mighty **E**tzel had invited them.[8]

The rulers from the Rhine arrived with great splendor. This would lead to a great loss of men and kin. [180] Kriemhild was by no means disappointed that they had come to the Huns in such grandeur, in fact she was overjoyed. **N**o one had ever seen such chivalrous and brave warriors as those brought by Gunther [190] and his brothers Giselher and Gernot, but they left Kriemhild's hoard of gold on the Rhine. Cursed be the moment that they first heard

---

7. This is the first argument put forth in Kriemhild's defense. Honor and loyalty demanded that Siegfried's death be avenged. A man could have exacted revenge by challenging the guilty party to combat or in court, but since none of her male relatives took on that responsibility, it was left to Kriemhild to do so in a way that relied on deception rather than strength. The argument defends Kriemhild on the basis of her loyalty as the motivation that led her to avenge herself in the only way she could.

8. The feigned ignorance of the poet at this juncture is curious, and he seems to assume that his readership's knowledge of the *Nibelungenlied* does not rest solely on the written version preceding his own text.

of that treasure. I think it was this old sin for which they paid, and nothing else.[9]

The praiseworthy and mighty ruler joyfully went out to greet them [200] and welcomed them to his kingdom. He offered his service to them as a friend, a pledge that Kriemhild, the noble queen, prevented him from fulfilling. **T**hat she ever saw such heroes should be deplored before God. Many a mother's child suffered as a result. [210] Etzel's household was happy to see them and thought that its honor had been increased, though later it was to be extinguished. Their final days were quickly approaching, and it was a great tragedy [220] that they should die at the hands of those whom they welcomed so gladly.

Regardless of how much Etzel, that powerful king, wanted to serve them, and they in turn by rights were to serve him, it all had to end badly because of an old debt. [230] Hagen, who was arrogant and imposing, had squandered all of Kriemhild's trust in him and had left her with no alternative but to avenge everything that had been done to her. As a result everyone who carried a weapon there would die. Before that one man, Hagen, was killed, forty thousand other men had to die. As much as Kriemhild wanted to separate him from the others, [240] she could not.[10]

Unable to do otherwise, she let things take their course. That resulted from her troubled mind.[11] Death became the friend of those doomed to die,

---

9. This commentary by the poet would seem to indicate that the Burgundian rulers, along with Hagen, had to pay for the sin of stealing the Nibelungen treasure, which of course could only have been achieved by first killing Siegfried. Greed is therefore Gunther and Hagen's "original sin," which led to murder and the eventual destruction of the Burgundian ruling house. Verse 227 refers to an "old debt" (*alten schulden*) that prevented the Burgundians from supporting Etzel as they should have for his hospitality. The debt may refer back to the "old sin" just mentioned in v. 196, or it may refer more generally to the debt owed Kriemhild, both in terms of a real reconciliation as well as payment of damages for the loss of her husband, let alone compensation for the loss of her treasure (cf. *NL-C* 1785).

10. This is the second argument for Kriemhild, one that was mentioned in the *Nibelungenlied*, especially in the C version, namely that she wanted vengeance only on Hagen (*NL-B* 1717; 1763; 1771; *NL-C* 1755–57). Kriemhild tried to separate Hagen from the others but was unable to carry out her plan because her brothers would not give him up as a hostage. It is debatable to what extent she actually tried to exact revenge on Hagen alone, given that she remained unreconciled with Gunther and Gernot. Of course, an argument can be made that Giselher was innocent, but that he, too, had to die once the conflagration of full-scale warfare took hold. This is made explicit in vv. 480–81.

11. This is a critical and difficult passage to translate. The third argument for Kriemhild is that she had a "troubled mind" (*krankem sinne*), and was therefore less culpable. The meaning of this phrase could range from "she had difficulty coming up with a plan" to "she was out of her mind." McConnell translates: "she lacked good sense" (1994, 15). *Sinne* usually denotes some aspect of rationality: reason, knowledge, intellect, or thought, including the idea of forethought or intentional planning. There seems in any case to be some misogynistic connection to the fact that she is a woman, and therefore less capable in matters of the

although they would rather have lived on in happiness. By that time, [250] the plan that Kriemhild had devised had already done so much damage that they [the Burgundians] could not leave. Etzel was to endure the greatest loss that any king can suffer short of death, and it was all caused by his wife.

She imagined that it would all end very differently. [260] She really only wanted one man to be killed. Her pain and anger would have completely vanished, and no one else would have been harmed. But the lords whom Hagen accompanied would not allow him to be killed, [270] and so all of them died together in battle, locals and foreigners, lowborn and highborn, Christians and heathens, the good and the bad, lords and servants. They all got caught up in the battle, those from near and far, [280] as soon as they saw their friends lying in front of them, dead. It didn't have to be that way; it could have easily been prevented. If Etzel had been told the truth from the beginning, he could easily have avoided all that terrible suffering, but the Burgundians were too arrogant to stop. [290] Kriemhild, however, cunningly made sure that Etzel was kept in the dark. That's why he lost everything and never recovered afterwards.

It was decreed that all this be written down, how many of them died, and how life became insufferable for all of them. [300] The Huns had to follow their hearts and their spleen.[12] They learned to hate the proud Franks from the Rhine and hoped for famous King **E**tzel's thanks, as if he had wanted it all. Instead it was abhorrent to the king. They [the Burgundians] were all prepared to die, [310] regardless of how well their host treated them. Those who sat next to the Burgundians and walked with them in friendship and who had welcomed them so well before would all lie dead beside them. This was a tragedy to end all tragedies.

It is a marvel of the ages that so many heroes were killed on account of a woman's wrath. [320] These hand-picked warriors, who were always battle-ready, had been brought to this land by Lord Dietrich and bold Hildebrand. All six hundred of them died. No matter how magnificently those on both sides had acquitted themselves in previous battles, [330] it did them little good here. Lord Bloedelin lost three thousand of his best men there. He started it all with evil intent on account of the pain of a woman [Kriemhild].

---

mind. Most examples of this usage in other texts point to an inability to discern the correct or appropriate answer or truth, especially in matters of religious doctrine. This inability can stem from emotional distress or a lack of knowledge. Clearly the phrase was problematic, given that mss. A, C, and D substitute *krank* with *Kriemhilt*, so that C/D reads: "Kriemhild began her vengeance according to her thoughts (*nâch ir sinne*)." Ms. A reads *von chrimhilt sinne*, which makes little sense.

12. The original has the gall bladder (*galle*) as the organ traditionally associated with the choleric humor, linked to bitterness, irritability, and anger, but in translation spleen best conveys this idea today.

He lost his life and all his honor out of a sense of loyalty. He acted to gain the respect of a woman who was promised to him as a wife, [340] but instead he was the first to pay the price. The Burgundians defended themselves so well that they earned honor and praise.

Duke Hermann, a nobleman from Poland, and Sigeher of Wallachia were eager to avenge noble Kriemhild's suffering. [350] They had brought two thousand proud knights with them to the festival, all of whom were later slaughtered by the forces of the noble foreigners. Highborn Walber brought twelve hundred of his men from Turkey by way of Greece. **A**ll of those who had traveled through Greece were lost, [360] regardless of how much of Kriemhild's gold and Etzel's payment they had taken. They served them with burning devotion, but their children wept for them. They had hoped to gain honor, but instead won only death. They were crushed by the great tragedy. [370] Those who had sought out mighty Etzel for protection served at great peril.

I want to tell you about three men who were so bold that nowhere in the world could you find anyone like famous Irnfried, Hawart, and Irinc.[13] I heard it said [380] that all three had been exiled on account of some great transgression. There were numerous attempts to try to have them pardoned by the Roman emperor, but they lived as exiles for the rest of their lives. Etzel's generosity made sure that they would do his bidding at any time, [390] and they were prepared and willing to avenge beautiful Kriemhild's suffering when the time came.

It was recorded, as I heard it told, where they had come from. Irnfried, who was known far and wide, left Thuringia, where he had once been lord, when the emperor banished him. Hawart, that powerful hero, [400] was the ruler of Denmark. Irinc, a famous fighter, was born in Lorraine and was a powerful and bold man. Hawart was able to make him his vassal with extravagant gifts. This is what the source tells us. They had selected thirty-three hundred men to come with them into that land. [410] Volker's hand killed many of them in battle, a deed that will be recounted for all time.

That famous hero, the clever fiddler, killed mighty Irnfried in a glorious struggle. The hero from Troneck killed Irinc, that bold and celebrated man from Lorraine. [420] He had always thought himself the boldest of men, but the one he wanted to defeat made him pay the ultimate price. That was

---

13. Irnfried and Irinc are known in stories that describe the fall of the Thuringian kingdom, a historical event that took place between 531 and 534. Irnfried is the king of the Thuringians, Irinc is Hawart's vassal. Irinc seems to be the more popular of the two, however, as evidenced in the *Nibelungenlied*, in which his battle with Hagen takes up an entire chapter, and his special mention in the *Klage*, vv. 1080–1130. There does not, however, seem to be any clear narrative tradition that adequately explains the events alluded to here, i.e., crimes that led to banishment, attempts at reconciliation, and a lifetime of exile.

Hagen, who among the noble foreigners survived until the very end of that disaster. Dancwart killed Hawart, whose bravery had never been wanting in battle. [430] I'm surprised that death dared to take him on, since it is said that he accomplished such deeds that it would have been a miracle had twelve bold men been able to accomplish the same.

From wherever they all came, in whatever lands they had been found, [440] all of them were destined to die at the hands of the Burgundians. Gernot himself killed so many men that the story of his bravery was told in thirty kingdoms. He also killed Ruediger, that magnificent margrave, in single combat. [450] People saw how mighty Ruediger in turn valiantly killed Gernot, the strong. On both sides they lost kin and vassals. Ruediger brought five hundred skilled knights with him. None of them survived very long after the first charge into battle. [460] They had always been successful fighting for mighty Etzel, but the Burgundians defeated them with such great force that the steel bands of their shields flew apart under the crush of their swords. Those whom they had hoped to defeat defended themselves well. Mighty Giselher [470] was loath to see the steaming stream of blood flowing from Ruediger's wounds.

Regardless of the great losses the Burgundians incurred during their expedition to the Hunnish court, the greatest catastrophe of all was that no one could prevent Giselher's death. [480] He was completely innocent of Siegfried's death in thought and deed. They also mourned for Gernot, whom they saw lying dead at the hands of Ruediger. The hero from Burgundy, who had lived all his days in honor up until that hour, lay there pitifully. [490] God wanted to release him from his guilt.[14]

Gunther was unable to regain his sister's forgiveness. After all, he had counseled that Siegfried, her first husband, should be killed. For that reason her hatred of him only grew over time. Both injury and indignity were rife, [500] and what made it even worse was the fact that her only child was killed as well. This could not go without a response from those who were obliged to avenge it and who wanted to serve mighty Etzel. This all came to grief.

Who would have believed that Lady Kriemhild herself would be killed? [510] All this suffering and pain was caused by what she said, but she had to die along with those who wanted to live. Regrettably those who took revenge yet still wanted to control their own fate could not live longer. Not one of them would survive.

Whatever calamities had occurred up to that time, [520] when old Hildebrand killed the highborn lady out of malice and anger, and even before King

---

14. The question of Gernot's guilt is never made explicit. We are left to assume it has to do with the "original sin" of v. 196, i.e., greed and the theft of the treasure, or that it might refer more generally to Gernot's role as one of the conspirators against Siegfried.

Etzel saw what had happened, the people rose up in agony. As a consequence, grief was left to rule from the high seat. Many women were completely bereft of happiness. [530] Young and old alike lost all joy. Etzel, that great king, stood there alone in his great sorrow. Whatever was going to happen was done, since no one else who bore arms had survived. They were all lying there dead, fallen into the blood. [540] Those who had hoped to live in happiness were devastated. Their sadness was sent to them by God, and they could do nothing else, day and night, except weep and lament.[15]

Cursed be the moment the whole tragedy started and Kriemhild first set eyes on noble Siegfried. [550] As a result many a beautiful woman was robbed of love. Whether they were heathens or Christians, this one woman's scheming caused such grief that men and women alike believe the story that she is burning in hell for her sins, [560] and that she had so acted against God's mercy that God, our Lord, rejected her soul. Anyone who wants to prove that would have to go to hell. I would certainly prefer not being sent to hell to find out.

The master of this book said it once before: [570] "Faithlessness offends the faithful."[16] She died because of faithfulness, and so she will live eternally in heaven in God's love. God has promised us all the same: whoever dies out of faithfulness has earned a place in heaven.[17] It is true that he sins before God who judges another out of hatred.[18] [580] How can we know how God will judge? No one can consider himself so good and free from sin that he will have no need of God's mercy at the Last Judgment, when we will all receive our just reward.[19]

---

15. It is difficult to know if this means that the people have been cursed by God or are being punished as a whole for some sin. Their sadness (*swaere*) is given them by God, but the sense may be that all things come from God, joy and sadness alike, and that the inevitable demise of all those in the battle is an outcome ultimately guided by God.

16. This most likely refers back to vv. 140–45, where it was said that the faithful should not have to regret their own faithfulness.

17. This statement reflects a general belief that faithfulness, obedience, and endurance will be rewarded by God in heaven with eternal life. To die out of loyalty would reflect this kind of obedience, ultimately reflected in Jesus' crucifixion and death. Two New Testament references that would support this view are James 1:12, "Blessed is the man who remains steadfast under trial, for when he has stood the test he will receive the crown of life, which God has promised to those who love him," and 2 Tim. 4:7–8, "I have fought the good fight, I have finished the race, I have kept the faith. Henceforth there is laid up for me the crown of righteousness, which the Lord, the righteous judge, will award to me on that Day, and not only to me but also to all who have loved his appearing."

18. This is most likely a reference to Matt. 7:1–2, "Do not judge, or you too will be judged. For in the same way you judge others, you will be judged, and with the measure you use, it will be measured to you."

19. The C version (str. C573–602) elaborates on this section by once again stressing the great love between Kriemhild and Siegfried, and that Kriemhild's revenge out of loyalty was

2. How Lord Dietrich Had the Dead Carried Away[20]

The hall had collapsed on all the warriors who had entered it to do battle. [590] The ruler of the land passed his time in pain and grief, and his great fame and honor had been brought low. Sighs gave expression to the sorrow that was buried in the noble's heart. While once he had been held in high esteem, sunny days now turned to darkness. He had lost all happiness. [600] I think that the sun refused to shine for him, and the happiness that he should have enjoyed was completely gone. He only saw the streams of blood running from grievous wounds that had in an instant robbed him of his joy. [610] He saw nothing that gave him pleasure. Death had stolen what joy he had.

He wrung his hands and beat his head so violently as no king has done since or before. It was incredible to see his pain and suffering. [620] One thing could be said of Etzel: truly no man has since mourned to such an extreme. He howled out in pain. The nobleman's voice, like a bison's horn, sounded out his grief so loudly [630] that the towers and the palace shook. Where there had been little joy, there was now none at all. He had lost his mind, and so he was unable to recognize at any given moment if he was acting shamefully.[21]

Many of those left behind helped him express his grief. [640] If you want to hear something amazing, consider this lack of self-control. Any lament heard in the world was but a shadow in comparison. Never before had so many noble mothers' children mourned as were there weeping together with Etzel. Many young women wrung their hands until they cracked. [650] Nothing else was spoken but "oh" and "ah." As loudly as the king screamed, the women all joined him in a chorus of screams. Even today it is still customary when someone is grieving that others hide their own happiness in his presence. And so joy was abandoned. The common people's lament grew to be boundless. [660] Young women in their grief loudly beat their hands until they had broken bones.

When they heard what had happened, the people from the countryside came rushing tearfully to see for themselves and to lament. Some came to plunder and others to avenge their loved ones, [670] but there was no need for slashing and striking. Their friends and enemies alike were already dead without their intervention. The people were told to remove the bodies of the dead as quickly as possible. First they cleared a path to the hall, removing all

---

justified. This is clearly meant to soften any of the speculation that Kriemhild could have been condemned to hell for her acts.

20. This heading, as well as the next three, is taken from manuscript C.

21. As with Kriemhild, the text excuses some of Etzel's inappropriate behavior by pointing out his altered mental state. His mind (*sin*) has changed or been changed (*verwandelt*), and he is therefore not fully culpable for his dishonorable and unchivalrous behavior.

of those they found outside [680] where Volker and Hagen had killed them. They were ordered to carry them away from the building far enough so that people had access to the hall. Death had taken away all their happiness. If anyone [690] who survived had family among the dead, he now wished that he, too, could be among them. Many blood-red coats of mail were removed from the casualties. Smashed helmets were taken off as well. Their entire armor was soaked in blood, and many magnificent shields were totally destroyed.

[700] There were so many mighty and worthy dead carried away that people, hearing about it, wondered if anyone in all the land could still be happy. The great heroes no longer cared what anyone said.[22] Young women were tearing their hair out. [710] Wives went around wailing, their clothing bloodied from the wounds. The commoner and the nobleman all lay there together, the rain of blood had soaked them through and through. Any woman who [720] failed to weep over their wounds lacked a womanly heart.

Hildebrand, that brave hero, heard the household servants crying and wailing loudly. One of beautiful Ute's children lay in front of the hall. [730] Tears ran down from clear eyes, this is true, on account of those wounds. It was the queen, whom Hildebrand had killed in his mad rage, as she had killed Hagen of Burgundy. People are still talking about how it happened that Hagen, [740] who had accomplished such feats of strength, was killed by a woman. People still earnestly believe that it's not true. But it is true that Lord Dietrich had subdued and bound that famous hero. The king's wife then personally finished him off with a sword stroke. [750] She, too, then needlessly lost her life at the hands of Hildebrand.[23] It was completely appropriate that people lamented the queen's death. Knights and squires alike had every right to do so. Everyone in Etzel's lands who heard about it was filled with pain and sorrow.

Lord Dietrich came upon Kriemhild's corpse [760] with grief. He told the people there for God's sake to stop their crying. As much as they assured him they would, they could not. What they had seen with their own eyes was so horrific that no one [770] could be joyful. Lord Dietrich said, "I've seen a lot in my day, dear highborn lady, and I never heard tell of a more beautiful woman. Oh, that death would take you so soon. Your scheming took all of my dearest relations, but still I am compelled to grieve for both you and me with sorrow. [780] Truly, I do this with such great sadness that I cannot blame

---

22. The meaning being that they don't care because they are dead. While not exactly humor, this touch of irony adds a bit of variety to a fairly tedious passage.

23. The poet editorializes by stating that she died needlessly (*âne nôt*), although we are left to speculate why or what the consequences of leaving her alive would have been. She may have been killed without cause because she was a (noble) woman, or she might have received a just punishment through a judicial proceeding.

you for your loyalty.²⁴ You never refused anything that I asked of you. Now is the time and place that I should repay you, lady. [790] I derive no joy from the fact that I am only able to do this after your passing." The brave man then grabbed hold of her and ordered everyone there to carry away her corpse.

Before she was placed on the bier, the nobleman had carried her head to join its body. Hildebrand, who killed her with his own hands, could be heard mourning. [800] Etzel the Hun then appeared, filled with sorrow and pain, as was fitting for him. No one could help but grieve with him out of sorrow. He cursed his great ruin. He had inherited a great treasure trove of misfortune [810] and clutched at the breast of his worthy wife, a woman who had never uttered a false word in her life.²⁵ He kissed her pale hands and grieved with great longing. Only now did Dietrich tell the king the whole story.

"**O**h, my suffering," said Etzel, the highborn. [820] "How is it that a poor man such as I have lost both my child and my wife? Not to mention the many brave souls from my own kin as well as the joy of my life, my brothers-in-law, who acted honorably as long as they lived. How is it that I have been given such cares and such great pain? [830] If I had only recognized the great loyalty in her, I would have abandoned with her all my lands before losing her. Never was a more faithful woman born of a mother. Oh, you great noblemen, Gunther and your brothers, and my great warriors, my brother and my kin, [840] who were all so terribly ensnared by death! How can I ever honor all the brave champions who came to my festival from lands far and wide, along with them all my men, whatever their names, Christian and heathen alike, who increased my honor always?"

[850] After this lament he collapsed, as if asleep. Dietrich of Bern took him to task for this. He said, "You're not acting as a wise man should. If it isn't helping, then stop doing it. That's my advice.²⁶ **D**on't delay any longer," said the brave warrior. [860] "Take your little son to be with his mother."²⁷

---

24. Dietrich deplores Kriemhild's plan or its execution (*rât*), but he does not blame her for her loyalty (*triuwe*), both to him and presumably also to Siegfried. Curiously, there is never any explicit reference to the loyalty she would have owed her second husband, Etzel.
25. This praise of Kriemhild seems a bit exaggerated. While she could be excused for many things, the claim that she always told the truth (*unvalschiu wort*) can only be explained by the poet's continuous attempts to paint her in the most positive light possible. It is true that Etzel praises her loyalty in the next section, but this in rather general terms and not specific to his own relationship with her. Etzel seems intent on not assigning blame to anyone.
26. Dietrich is the only one at the moment who upholds the masculine virtues of chivalry, which would demand a more stoic response by Etzel, who is painted throughout the *Klage* as weak and incapable of making the decisions necessary for a ruler. Dietrich's advice could be paraphrased by a saying attributed to Will Rogers: "If you find yourself in a hole, stop digging."
27. McConnell, 1994, and Heinzle, 2015, both note that the manuscripts diverge here, with manuscript B standing alone with its reading of "your" little son, while most others read

His servants went inside to where they found Ortlieb, who was lying in the blood, headless. Oh, what great honor Etzel lost with his death! Never again will a king suffer such a great loss. [870] The sovereign also thought of Bloedelin's death. He had his corpse brought to where the other two lay. Even though they were heathens, they were still worthy of pity. People all around wailed and screamed, and the noblewomen beat their breasts. [880] Many beautiful women had lost their love and gained great pain.[28]

They did as he commanded. When they brought Bloedelin to where the king could see him, the son of Botelung said, "Oh, my dear brother, your lands and mine are now deserted. [890] There are no campaigns in the kingdoms. You have not done well by me, my dear brother. How could I imagine that you would anger my guests, the best of warriors, so much that they would kill you, famed hero? [900] I have to grieve for those same heroes, because I had invited them by sending emissaries to their lands. Those who came in good faith and wanted to be faithful should have been left alive, they should have been spared. What were they to do, those who had always defended themselves, [910] when they were given no choice but to fight? They didn't tell me on account of their arrogant pride. I could have easily prevented what happened here. And you, too, famed hero, should have left them alone. What of it if the noblewoman maintained some old hatred for them? [920] You should not have risked honor and life for that. I knew all the stories about what Hagen had done to her. As much as I loved her, I would never have killed him. And if he had stayed here as a guest for a thousand days, I would never have raised my sword against him. [930] Brother, your foolishness betrayed you.[29]

"Curses," said the good king, "that I was ever born! I have lost all hope from them [the Burgundians] and from my own kin. Gunther and his men would have supported me willingly in any way that I asked. [940] Whatever a king might desire of brave warriors, I would have received from them. But alas it never came to that. Oh, that no one told me the truth about the enmity that existed between them and their sister, Kriemhild. The loss and my shame are both so great that, [950] as much as I once wanted to live, I now have no desire to live even one more day. The rod of God has struck me down. Now

---

"my." I have followed both of these editors/translators in preferring that Dietrich continue his instructions to Etzel. The "he" in v. 883 could be either Dietrich or Etzel.

28. This line repeats one of the leading themes of the entire *Nibelungenlied*, that of love and pain (*liebe* and *leit*) and their persistent symbiosis.

29. Bloedelin's failing is caused by his youth, inexperience, or by the resulting series of bad decisions, all of this expressed in the original *tumplicher muot*.

they all lie powerless, those whom his power has laid low.³⁰ I was always sure that I would not need to [960] nor want to fear him.

I curse my gods now that the Almighty has shown his great anger. Where now is the great honor that Mahumet and Machazen had preserved so long?³¹ As far as my horse would carry me, everything was under my sway in those days. [970] He who gave me life and in divine wisdom let the day dawn over Jews and Christians alike protected me with his power as if I were his vassal. Now my grief inspires me, if he would have mercy on me, to consider converting again, if he would help me do so. [980] But now I fear he will not, because I betrayed him once before. My gods caused me to deny his great divinity and reject Christianity. It is without a doubt true that I was a Christian for five years, but they succeeded in getting me to renounce my faith, and I served them as before. [990] Even if I now wanted to embrace a Christian life and the truth, that could never be. I so shamelessly worked against him that he no longer wants me. A thousand kings would have difficulty dealing with my fate. I well knew that he had power over the greatest heights [1000] and the lowest depths, of whatever he wanted. I have no hope left of ever coming before him whom I should serve. This pain has robbed me of all joy and enthusiasm. Nothing would please me more than to lie here dead like the others."

The king groaned, as well he should. He wailed all louder. [1010] This pained Dietrich, Lord of Bern, who could not stand to listen anymore. He and Master Hildebrand went to the king, and when he saw Etzel, he spoke as if things were only half as bad.

"Damn it if anyone hears it told in this land [1020] that you are standing here wringing your hands like a weak woman who neglects her bearing and herself on account of her friends. We are unaccustomed to seeing you behave in this unmanly way. You should instead, noble and brave king, care for poor Dietrich as a friend."³²

---

30. These lines definitely have a biblical ring to them. The rod is the symbol of God's anger and retribution. "I will visit their iniquities with the rod and their transgressions with stripes" (Ps. 89:32). The Assyrian king, conquering Judah, is "the rod of God's anger" (Isa. 10:5). Suffering Job cries out, "Let him take his rod away from me" (Job 9:34). Etzel's fearful outburst seems best reflected in Isaiah, Chapters 11 and 13: "And He will strike the earth with the rod of His mouth, and with the breath of His lips He will slay the wicked" (Isa. 11:4); "I will punish the world for its evil, the wicked for their sins. I will put an end to the arrogance of the haughty and will humble the pride of the ruthless" (Isa. 13:11).
31. As Heinzle, 2015, and others have noted, it was a common belief in the West in the Middle Ages that Muhammad was worshipped by Muslims as one god among many. To make the point, the poet adds another alliterating god, possibly taken from Maozim in Dan. 11:38, 39. Etzel blames his fate on his own apostasy and God's vengeance, precipitated by the king's lack of a vassal's faithfulness to God as his lord.
32. Dietrich's intent is to remind Etzel of his responsibilities to his vassals.

He replied, "How can I help? [1030] I have been robbed of everything I ever had in the world. All I have left is my life and my rattled nerves. God's hatred has cruelly brought me down. I was powerful and mighty in my lands, but now I stand here like a pitiful pauper [1040] who never owned a thing."

The man from Bern said, "Lord King, leave your complaint and show whether or not you will help Dietrich in his need. Everyone is dead who would have helped restore my honor.[33] [1050] I deeply regret the loss of my comrades. You, King, can easily recover from the loss of your men. You can still find plenty of men who will support you. My situation is unfortunately quite different, as you can see for yourself. They lie here butchered, fallen into the blood, [1060] those who risked their lives and livelihood for my sake. Death lay in wait for them and cruelly took them from me."

The king spoke, "I will say this. I have heard and seen, heard tell that death, common enough, never before had such power as in this great devastation."[34]

[1070] The king then commanded that the bodies of his child and his wife and his dead brother be taken away on biers. Everyone who witnessed it was distraught. Many more bodies still lay near the hall, those whose doomsday had come and taken their lives. [1080] The king came upon Irinc's body, whom Hagen had shot through with resolve and a determined hand as he was running away in fear. Even though Hawart's vassal had fought well against brave Hagen and even wounded him, [1090] the bold man from Troneck managed to kill him. Mighty Etzel and the Lord of Bern together mourned for him. His terrible wounds were horrible to behold. Old Hildebrand joined in the mourning [1100] so that everyone could plainly hear it.

The women were there to lend their support in the lament, and the bold Dane was mourned by rights. No man had ever gained beautiful women's favors in foreign lands as he had. He should also be given credit for fighting so magnificently and dying so bravely, something witnessed by many warriors. [1110] They didn't want to let him attack Hagen,[35] and if he had avoided this heroic action, he would have survived.

The king spoke, "It was meant to be. If I had been told everything, then I could have prevented all of this pain and my own suffering. Lord, what did I

---

33. Dietrich is probably including the restoration of his rule and rights to his own lands in his concept of honor. Since Dietrich is an exile at Etzel's court, the ability to overcome his exile rested solely with the military force that has now been destroyed.

34. Manuscript C adds another fourteen verses (C1084–97) after v. B1069. They have Etzel turn the focus to the many heroes and warriors from near and far who made the ultimate sacrifice.

35. Heinzle (2015) is certainly correct (note to vv. 1110–11, pp. 1548–49) that the original, *gelouben*, is used here with the meaning "to allow," as shown in Grimm's *Woerterbuch*, under *glauben* (Section V. A. 1), and not "to believe," as McConnell, 1994, and others would have it.

do to Gunther and his kin? [1120] Now they have killed all of my men and relatives. And they, too, have lost their lives and their honor." The king cried for Irinc's bravery, along with that of his men.

The sovereign of the land ordered that Irinc and thirty of his men, [1130] who were found dead next to him, be taken away. After they were carried off on biers as he had commanded, the mighty king found still more warriors, including Gunther, that powerful king, who was lying there pitifully where he had been decapitated. They wept over his body.

When King Etzel saw him, [1140] filled with pain he said, "Oh, my dear brother-in-law, if only I could send you back to the Rhine alive and well. If only my own hands could have fought for you when yours were unable. I would always be glad if it could be so."

Lord Dietrich spoke, "My king, it was because of him [1150] that I fought so hard for your good will and respect. I could not spare that hero; I had no choice. After they had killed all of our men, self-satisfied Hagen taunted me from the hall above, to my humiliation. [1160] After that I simply couldn't let them go. When my forces had been destroyed along with your men, Lord, I pleaded with Gunther to make peace, but bold Hagen refused the peace. He said, what would be the point since both [1170] Giselher and Gernot were already dead, and my old Hildebrand [*had killed Volker of Burgundy. Hagen complained greatly that Hildebrand*]³⁶ had escaped after he had wounded him here outside the hall, striking blows [1180] against that bold fighter through his solid chainmail.

"Then I asked Gunther to recognize my losses for his own honor's sake. I told him that I would risk my life to guarantee his safety, that he should be your hostage, King, and mine as well, and that I would bring him safely back to the Rhine. [1190] He was determined to leave no one alive, and that might have happened, if he hadn't been so exhausted. That hero knocked me down three times, believe me, so that I could hardly regain my composure. I was saved by my skill and my rested hand, [1200] and I was able to capture and tie up that wounded nobleman. I immediately handed him over to Kriemhild, my lady. How could I know that she would have that hero executed? I would never knowingly have handed him over to die. His sister's rage made things all the worse for him. [1210] Here now lies that highborn man."

The king spoke through his tears, "Oh, that it ever came to pass that I welcomed him and his men. If I had been told earlier, they could have all lived. There were never greater heroes on the face of the earth. I don't think there will ever be such bold champions again. [1220] This is why all my lands have

---

36. This section (vv. 1172–75) is missing from manuscript B, a simple case of eyeskip (parablepsis), with the scribe skipping over the lines because of the double occurrence of Hildebrand's name in close succession. The text has been amended based on manuscript A's reading.

descended into pain and horror. There are many alone at home in their own lands who would want to welcome them back with joy. Now I can't let my enemies go unmourned."

Master Hildebrand then spoke, "Lord, please stop your weeping [1230] and order the nobleman to be carried away."

Lord Dietrich said, "I believe that the likes of this exceptional nobleman was never before born nor will be hence. I regret his loss very much."

Botelung's son responded, "Unhappily what they had to do was to my detriment, [1240] but they gained nothing from it either, after they had been attacked by my warriors. Now I grieve the deaths on both sides. I have every right to mourn my warriors and theirs as well. I had so many heroes here, but they failed to warn me."

Master Hildebrand said, [1250] "You can see lying there the devil who started it all. That it was not resolved peacefully is Hagen's fault. They [the Burgundians] could have easily regained my lady's favor. My king, if we had known the whole story, we would have certainly prevented your suffering. [1260] Bloedelin wanted to avenge my lady's injury, which should never have happened, and it sowed the seeds of calamity. Who would have believed that so many bold men would die here on account of Siegfried's death, and that this terrible catastrophe would unfold right here at your court? [1270] I can't explain it in any other way except that these remarkable heroes had long before earned God's dreadful anger. Their time had come, and so things could not stand as they were, even for one more day. They had to suffer God's judgment for their excessive pride.[37] This is why so many brave heroes lie here now. [1280] They had proven themselves in many hard battles, but they all died here and have only themselves to blame."

The mighty king said, still gracious in his grief, "Have Hagen carried to his lord, Gunther, and to his own kin. Oh, that I am still alive. May God have mercy on me [1290] and not let me, a poor man, live on in such pain. That death should take me," said the king, "is my greatest wish."

When people spotted Hagen, they ran up to him and cursed him terribly. Their joy and honor had been destroyed by him, [1300] and in their anger the people blamed it all on him. He would not have lost their sympathy if the queen had not sent Bloedelin to kill Hagen's brother. Then none of this would have happened. The champion defended himself, [1310] and so all of those from Burgundy had to involve themselves in the battle, where great

---

37. Hildebrand's explanation seems to place the blame squarely on the Burgundians' ("they") and especially Hagen's pride and arrogance (*übermuot*), and cannot be generalized to all heroes on both sides. The fact that God's anger was earned long ago can only lead us to the conclusion that this is connected to the "old sin" previously mentioned (vv. 196, 227) and that *übermuot* is equated with the sin of *superbia* in this and probably most other such passages. God's judgment, long held in abeyance, was now due and had to be exacted there in that carnage.

wounds were inflicted. This is how the devil instigated it all. They could find no one who would help them, and so they all had to die.[38]

In the meantime [1320] the king and the two men, loudly wailing along the way, came to where Lord Dietrich found many of his dear warriors lying dead. He saw someone lying along the wall outside the hall. His chainmail had been soaked through with blood.

The brave hero [Dietrich] asked, "Hildebrand, who is this?"

[1330] He answered him without malice. "Lord, that is Volker. He alone did us the greatest harm in these lands and earned his pay in a way that could never gain my favor. He gave my coat of mail such a blow [1340] that I thought I must surely die. The hero fought alone against me after I attacked him. There never was a hero more bold with a 'fiddle.' If Helfrich hadn't cut a path out for me, I tell you this, Volker would have killed me."

"Ahhh!" cried the mighty king. [1350] "His upbringing and manners were praiseworthy, and he always acted like a man. It will forever pain me that he had to die before his time."

Etzel asked where he was born.

Master Hildebrand replied, "He came from the land along the Rhine, as did Gunther. [1360] The daring hero was born in Alzey. His exceptional courage perished all too soon."

Lord Dietrich wept over the champion. His faithful character caused him to cry for that brave hero.

"Why are you weeping?" asked Hildebrand. "Volker caused us such great harm here [1370] that we will never be able to repair it. Single-handedly he must have killed at least twelve of your own men. I thank God that he did not survive. When I was fighting him, he defended himself so fiercely that it sounded like thunder, but finally I was able to injure him. [1380] These gaping wounds were caused by my own hand. That he died through me while in exile is something that I regret, because I, too, am a foreigner. His overly proud bearing harms us still to this day. He struggled for honor, all or nothing. Because he knew how to play a fiddle, [1390] people always called him a minstrel. I can assure you that he came from a freeborn family, and he was

---

38. This section has confounded most commentators, as it seems to undermine the case that has up to this point been made to deflect blame from Kriemhild and heap it on Hagen. It should therefore not be surprising that manuscript C treats this part quite differently, and it is obvious that the various redactors were unsure of what to do with this argument. Kriemhild is blamed for sending Bloedelin to attack Dancwart, Hagen's brother. Hagen is exonerated in that he was only trying to defend himself, and the Burgundians as a whole are cast as the hapless foreigners who had no support at Etzel's court. The culprit for everything that went wrong now seems to be the devil himself. Manuscript C (C1365–84) puts this argument into direct speech, spoken by an unnamed member of the gathering crowd. Hagen is squarely in the crosshairs and himself named the devil (*vâland*). That he ever came to Etzel's lands was the work of the "evil devil's hatred."

dedicated to serving beautiful women.[39] Many a noble fighter now lies here, maimed by him. Never before had a fiddler's hand achieved such feats [1400] as did this fearless man in this battle. This robs my heart of any joy."

The king had him carried away to where the others were being mourned. What proud and brave heroes were being pulled out of the blood where they were found! [1410] Crazed with pain, the man from Bern went to look at his losses. The first one he came upon was Hagen's brother, Dancwart of Burgundy. He had smashed many coats of mail in the hall. They said that Hagen of Troneck was incredibly brutal, [1420] but Dancwart, that magnificent fighter, killed more men in the hall than four Hagens.

"I am sorry for him," said Dietrich. "His character was faultless. If he had been a king, that famous hero could not have acted more magnificently."

"You can stop praising him," said Hildebrand. [1430] "When you see how his hand served you in his final days, then you will be less pleased with his bravery. I really don't know if any one of them did us more damage than he did."

The king then commanded that the marshal from the Rhine be carried to the others. [1440] Those who saw the hero broke down and wept. They began their screaming and terrible shrieking anew. Men and women shouted, "He killed Bloedelin!"

The king heard all the shouting. The yelling and weeping broke his troubled heart. [1450] Now you will hear tell of a marvelous thing.

3. How Etzel and Dietrich Mourned Their Men

He walked into the hall where the great calamity had taken place and saw a man lying there. His beautiful chainmail gleamed brightly out of the blood. His sturdy helmet had been smashed clean through. Dancwart had done this all by himself. [1460] He was one of Dietrich's men by the name of Wolfbrand. The noble man and champion from Bern recognized him, and the sight reminded him of all his pain. He was then rid of all the joy that his heart had ever held. The hero began to weep in pain over his suffering, [1470] and the mighty king joined him.

Etzel spoke on behalf of Dietrich, "Oh, that I ever saw this hero lying here dead. He had bravely survived many tough battles. Whoever stood shoulder to shoulder with him was strengthened."

They couldn't help themselves and had to weep uncontrollably. [1480] Never again, I think, will there be such a terrible and loud grieving as there

---

39. Volker is praised as the ideal *minnesinger*, with nobility and musical ability placed in the service of beautiful women.

was for Wolfbrand. **N**ext to that hero they found mighty Siegestab, the Duke of Bern, lying there wretchedly. The jewels of his armor shone like stars. [1490] "Who was it who killed you?" asked Lord Dietrich. "Hero, your death torments me, you dear, brave warrior. My father and your mother, they were children of the same father. How terrible are your wounds, noble and mighty fighter. My honor rested on your great shoulders."

[1500] "Volker killed him," replied Master Hildebrand, "which is why I killed Volker. I was standing next to both of them, but there was no way I could intervene except at the very end."

"Curse this, my exile!" cried the man from Bern. "If only I had been killed, then God would have been merciful. [1510] What friends I have lost, poor man that I am. May God have mercy."

He ordered that Siegestab's shield be removed from his arm. Dietrich and Hildebrand shed their tears for him, and Etzel's happiness was shattered along with theirs. They had only their terrible sorrow left to them. [1520] Joy was gone.

Then he recognized Wolfwin by the gleam of the helmet he was wearing. It had been bright but was now wet with blood. The brave warrior had fallen dead against the wall.

Master Hildebrand spoke, "Lord, this is my nephew [1530] and your burgrave, son of bold Nere. I have never seen a hero so battered in all my life. Look at how the blood flows from his wounds. This warrior could certainly never be accused of cowardice. In this battle he fought like a true champion. [1540] He was killed by the mighty king, young Giselher, lord of the Nibelungen.[40] He also killed Nitger. After he had laid both of them low, and had done us much harm, the noble and mighty man leapt up against Gerbart. The heroes did not spare the sharp weapons in their hands. [1550] The bands of their helmets lit up in a red firestorm of sparks. Terrible Giselher destroyed these heroes, all three of them. Next to them lies bold Wicnant, whom Gunther, the Lord of Burgundy, killed. All of your men together could not help [1560] him escape his death. He also killed Sigeher, a famous hero, along with bold Wichart. Both of them did their best in battle. Their misery must haunt us always."

Lord Dietrich sighed deeply in his pain. [1570] Etzel, that mighty king, groaned loudly. His powerful cry so shook the air that it seemed as if the building above the mighty king might collapse.

After they had finished grieving over those they had found there, they looked around and saw that the hall [1580] was surrounded by a wall of corpses. Dietrich commanded that all of them be carried away from there.

---

40. This is one of only two references in the *Klage* to the Nibelungen. In this case, Giselher is in short succession identified with both the Nibelungen and the Burgundians (v. 1786).

Their pain was so abject and their lament so great that no one could describe it. Outdoors the women were crying, and many young women stood around in great sadness [1590] at that pitiful sight.

Then something very extraordinary happened. There were not enough men to remove the armor from those who were found dead. See here, couldn't they have avoided having beautiful girls and women strip the dead? [1600] The master [of this tale] says that this is not a lie. In their heartfelt pain and with woeful complaint, the women cut the straps they could not loosen. When the king saw that they were cutting them out of their armor, he wept in a way that exceeded all that had come before. [1610] His suffering overwhelmed him.

He saw many men who had come on account of the tragic events only to find their kinsmen dead. The king reproached them harshly. "Do you want to gain honor by having women care for the dead while men, who should be doing it, stand around?"

[1620] He ordered them to remove the warriors' armor. The ruler made the people suffer. They had to pay with harsh service against their will, but they did not know how to get them out of their armor. The king was beside himself [1630] and quickly left them to go see Dietrich.

Lord Dietrich was agitated when he saw people lying all around him like so many stones. The man from Bern did not have to carry this burden alone, as the king was also appalled at his great losses. Blood flowed out everywhere through the gutters. [1640] Wherever they went, all they found were the dead. The hall was reddened with the blood of the massacred. Those who were still alive became ill from their grieving. There had never been a day with so much wailing. More than eight hundred of them had already been carried out. [1650] A new lament went out. It was from Master Hildebrand, who had found Wolfhart.

When he found his nephew, he said to his lord, "See here, noble Dietrich, how death has reaped its harvest. I could never have imagined that such an inexperienced man [1660] like Giselher, that champion, could slay such a famous warrior. Now both of them lie here, the king and my nephew. May God hear our complaint that the two of them ever faced each other in battle."

Lord Dietrich looked at his vassal. How deeply he was hurt. He saw Wolfhart lying in the blood, [1670] his beard reddened. The brave hero was reminded of all his suffering and loss, and both of them wept terribly, while Etzel supported them openly in this. Wringing his hands, [1680] the mighty king stood next to Dietrich in his sorrow.

Wolfhart, the champion, had held his sword so tightly in battle that Dietrich and Hildebrand could not remove it from the raging hero's death grip. They had to use pliers to tear it [1690] from his long fingers. After they had wrested the weapon from him, Dietrich said, "Strong sword, who will wield you now? Never again will you deliver such blows in the company of powerful kings as when Wolfhart expertly wielded you. [1700] I curse the day I was born! Now that my support is gone, where shall I, an exile, go?"

Wolfhart, his teeth clenched, was still lying in the blood in front of the warriors. They had the brave hero lifted up out of the ashes. His lord ordered him to be washed and freed from his armor. [1710] With his loss went all sense of hope. He stood over the worthy warrior, and his death filled him with pain. He recalled what great service that man had rendered him and began to speak of it.

"Oh," said Lord Dietrich, "I am pained that you, hero, will never again bring me [1720] such honor in battle as you did so often in the past. God had little regard for me by not letting you live. Wherever the fight was toughest, you were always at my side. Now I can never again rely on your presence. Etzel, the mighty king, owes many victories to you. [1730] Regrettably now it has come to this. Your support is denied us. You have turned pale from the wounds that Giselher inflicted. If at this moment I knew from whom I should seek vengeance, how gladly would I serve you, virtuous man, as you so often served me. But that is not possible. [1740] All my consolation lies here at an end. My long exile will never end. Cursed be the day that I left Bern. You gladly went along with me, my clan and my men. Whatever I set out to accomplish, you helped me. [1750] Now I stand here completely alone."

Master Hildebrand then spoke, "Noble hero, why don't you stop your grieving? If it would help us at all, I would forever lament this great warrior. He was my sister's son. Lord, please stop. Turn your heart away from grief. [1760] It does no good to lament."

The warrior was then carried away. The people from the country watched over him for a long time and gently caressed the hero who had passed. The hero was touched by many pale hands. Everyone who knew him, whether man or woman, [1770] wrung their hands and wept for him. If someone can gain honor by being mourned in death, then he truly gained much honor there. Along with him were lost his many strong sword strokes. But even if one grieved for a thousand years, at some point it would be forgotten.[41]

[1780] **T**he ruler of the land sat down in the blood under the door. The brave hero had wept so much that no one could console him. Shortly thereafter they found the noble champion, Giselher of Burgundy, at the spot where he had killed Wolfhart. Many of those whom he had also slain still lay all around him. [1790] Lord Dietrich and Hildebrand began to lament their enemy.

---

41. The meaning of this passage is difficult to assess, as it either undermines the notion of epic narrative as *memoria*, or it is meant to emphasize that the passage of time eventually destroys all things, including honor. The second might be preferable with its apocalyptic undertones, emphasizing the notion that all things of this world are destined to perish.

They said, "Oh, you have left your land without an heir, and you can no longer give away your gold as you once did. You were so constant in honor that whatever you did to provide the world with joy and pleasure was never too much. [1800] Great deeds led you to death. Your hands brought us such great losses here. Never before had such an inexperienced hero avenged himself so grimly. Your renowned bravery took thirty or more men from Bern from me. If only it had happened [1810] as that bold warrior and singer Volker had advised him. Then this young and mighty king would have become the margravine's husband. They had decided this when they were with Ruediger in Bechelarn. He had vowed to take her as his wife and to live a long, happy life together. She had also vowed to take that warrior as her husband. [1820] Now their hope and my joy have been destroyed. I would never again be banished by kings if that mighty warrior were still alive. The margravine Gotelind is my cousin and my heir. Now her beautiful daughter is sadly widowed all too soon. [1830] I don't know what else to do except to ask God to end it all."

With strained hands they lifted up the famous hero. He was much too heavy and so fell back down onto the field of battle. The hall reverberated anew with the wailing of women and men. He was finally carried away to where Kriemhild was. [1840] The squires from Burgundy were all brought together as well. This was done in the consolation that they were all Christians, and that their angels knew exactly where their souls should go. If wailing from heartfelt sorrow had been heard before, [1850] now Christians and heathens alike wept unashamedly.

Next they found Gernot, disfigured with a massive wound. His fatal wound was below his chest and a good foot long. Although the warrior knew well how to carry his shield, Ruediger's hand had wounded him so gravely [1860] that the famous hero could not survive it. And so he had to die, since he had been challenged to combat by that great hero, Ruediger of Bechelarn. He in turn had slain Ruediger, whose loss could never be sufficiently lamented [1870] to the end of days. Old Hildebrand saw in Gernot's hand the gift that Ruediger had given him. Had the hero not done that, what would have happened then? No one could have been bolder than Lord Gernot, and the sword, wet and red with blood, could still be seen in his hand. [1880] Master Hildebrand tested the sword's edges. There were no nicks or flaws to be found. Ruediger knew how to give most generously. His whole life he had strived for honor, and he was mourned all the more for it.

The mighty king said [1890] to Lord Dietrich, "If this hero had lived, then everything I own would have been well passed on to my son. He was supposed to go live in Burgundian lands, where they always excelled at all things. My son would have done likewise, and I would have left all my lands to him. He would have been so wealthy and powerful [1900] that everyone could have put their faith in that warrior. Now all Gernot's clan is dead, the best that he ever had. Oh, that I can't undo your wounds and your death, virtuous Gernot. This I will regret my whole life long. Kriemhild could have easily separated Hagen from the other three. [1910] But a woman's mind knows only what's right in front of her. Instead they listen to their foolish hearts and think that they know more than someone who knows how to achieve honor. We have my dear wife as an example. She wanted to be clever, but even a man with little sense [1920] could have achieved more."[42]

[1921] **Gernot**, though burdened with guilt, had turned his mind away from all dishonor.[43] The great king ordered that he be carried away. That man was well built and tall, and [1930] the door through which they had been carrying the dead proved to be too narrow. Whereas before that brave and famous man had been quick enough, he was now just dead weight. Once they had gotten him through the door, women seeking recognition came to gaze at him. It would have been better for them, [1940] I have to say what I think, to have done so while he was alive. God did not want to grant them the pleasure that they should see him while he was still alive, and so he was deeply mourned by many women. There was nothing left but weeping and grieving. [1950] The young and the old grieved together, as did fools and wise men. They grieved together so that the very stones in the walls might have broken apart. The bold man was carried farther away from there.

A short time later they found Ruediger. [1960] Never before had a hero been so mourned in all the world. All of the happiness in the world was in truth lost along with him. A single family had never lost as much honor as when the margrave died. But we want to leave this sorrow and tell you what Dietrich said [1970] when he and Master Hildebrand found the mighty margrave lying on top of his shield.

The Lord of Bern said, "I could just as well have died twelve years ago. You have left me in my misfortune, so that I would have been better off back then buried instead.[44] On whom can I rely now? The best of my family, [1980]

---

42. Despite the poet's attempts to exonerate Kriemhild, the misogynistic rationale in his argumentation is hard to overhear. Kriemhild as a woman is by default less culpable because women lack the ability to think rationally (*lützel wîbes sin*), that is, in a linear fashion, like bringing a plan to fruition. The poet argues that any man could have managed to keep Hagen separate from the three Burgundian kings (he doesn't say how), but that women lack both the ability to develop a complex plan and, in listening to their foolish hearts (*tumben herzen rât*) then think themselves more clever again by half.

43. McConnell's note 61, 1994, (93) explains that Gernot's "guilt" is related to his "responsibility" for killing Ruediger, thereby avenging the deaths of his own men. The guilt of the dead man has already been established, however, both in the *Nibelungenlied* as well as the *Klage*. He was one of the conspirators in Siegfried's death and the theft of the Nibelungen treasure.

44. Dietrich recounts in this section parts of an episode that occurred "twelve years ago," known from other so-called Dietrich epics. In an attempt to regain his lands, Dietrich had returned from exile to fight his enemies in the battle of Ravenna. It was a victorious battle, but

my joy and my happiness have left with you. There never was a more faithful warrior and, I think, there will never be such a one on earth again. You were for me the perfect role model. When I had to flee my lands on account of my enemies, I found true loyalty with you alone, Ruediger. [1990] Etzel, the mighty king, was so furious with me that no one could promise me that he would let me live. I rode back to meet my enemies with your assurances. You, Ruediger, vowed that Etzel, the mighty king, would have to hang you [2000] before you allowed me to be taken prisoner. You were able to gain Etzel's mercy so that he forgave me for my grave fault, and you did this as an act of faithfulness. You also covered for me when others saw me in your company. I was close to Etzel, oh hero, only under your protection, [2010] until good Lady Helche, that noble queen, noticed that you were protecting me in my misfortune. The lady's virtue commanded her to make every effort to find a way to get me back in his good graces, along with you, virtuous man. [2020] You did everything in your power that mighty Etzel might generously take me back into the fold. And during all this you never once refused me your loyalty and protection. Whatever I and my men were lacking in exile, your generosity more than compensated for it. [2030] Oh, he who made your greeting a thing of the past has taken all my treasure. Your death is particularly hard for me in this foreign land. God would have done well to let you live." Dietrich unashamedly screamed so loud in his anguish [2040] that mighty King Etzel was terrified, as well he should be.

The great noble ruler then spoke, "I have every reason to mourn Ruediger as you do. His loyalty carried me ever higher, as the wind does a feather. There never was a man so utterly lacking in disloyalty. [2050] I don't think that a king ever lost a man so bold. Ever since I came to know him, he never once gave me bad advice when he was part of my council. Whatever that hero advised me to do, I carried it out immediately. That is now all in the past, and my heart is burdened with a heavy weight. [2060] If he were still alive, he would be generous to a fault and not worry about giving away as a single man what a thousand kings might call their own. Oh, if only we could die before it is our time, then I would lie here dead where I see so many great warriors lifeless before me. [2070] They all lie there like prey that had been hunted by lions. Now those who hold a grudge against me can easily threaten me. To them I have lost my bite."

Lord Dietrich spoke, "Noble king, since he served you so well, think of my dear cousin [Gotelind] and of Ruediger's child, [2080] who have brought you much honor and praise in your court."

---

his brother and Etzel's two sons were killed. Etzel was understandably enraged over the loss of his sons, but Ruediger intervened on Dietrich's behalf and eventually reconciled the two.

Botelung's son said, "It is only fitting for me to do so, even if you had not asked, Dietrich. They can always count on me as if I were their father."

He asked Hildebrand [2090] to lift the great hero up out of the blood. Hildebrand himself had been wounded by dreadful Hagen's hand. When the man bent down, his own wound began to bleed, and this pained the famous hero. Ruediger, much praised, was simply too heavy for him, and he carried him with difficulty. When he had reached the door, [2100] the hero could not carry him all the way through for lack of strength. Any man today would still fail at such a task.

The king looked at the warrior, whose strength was at an end. He was ghostly pale and sank down to where Ruediger lay. The noble man from Bern [2110] was taken aback. It was painful for him, too. They called for water to restore Hildebrand's strength, and King Etzel knelt down to him in the blood and poured water over him. Hildebrand was ashamed, his head lying in the king's hands, covered with sweat. [2120] The one whom he had served for so many years was now serving him, as it should be. To win his favor, Hildebrand had ridden fiercely into battle, and it would have been a shame if Etzel had abandoned him now. Hildebrand asked that the door to the hall be widened. Outside there was a great clamor [2130] when people heard what was happening.

They didn't hesitate a minute longer and carried out Ruediger, the father of many virtues. There was no one more faithful, from childhood to his final days. The people could no longer keep silent, and the entire household [2140] began to wail, each one in his own way. All of them made a great noise, both poor and rich, totally bereft of joy, so that the earth under their feet might have swallowed them up. Girls, women, and men wept for Ruediger with heartfelt pain, so that towers and halls [2150] and all the walls echoed with the noise. Their eyes brought forth the stream of tears that issued from their hearts. Many of the beautiful women were completely out of control: they tore the clothing from their bodies. Many a noble maiden tore at her hair. [2160] The tragedy had gained control over them. Faces were stained with blood, and pale hands beat at breasts. Old and young wailed so loudly that nothing like it will ever be heard again. [2170] It was as if screeching cranes had suddenly flown over the land. Etzel's and Dietrich's pain was increased by the grim reality of the loss.

They had the best men that were still found there immediately borne away. Seventeen hundred Christians were separated out from the heathens.[45] [2180]

---

45. Although of relatively little consequence, the manuscripts differ in their description of this act, with manuscript B separating Christians "from" (*von*) the heathens, while A and C read "and" (*unde*), i.e., that the best of Christian and heathen nobility was separated out from the others. The second reading makes more sense given the preceding two lines, and *von* could easily be a misreading of *vn*, an abbreviation for *vnd*, according to Heinzle's note, 2015, (1571).

Friend and foe alike were placed together on the bier. The lament that had taken place before was nothing in comparison to what many noble young women did now. The splendid household, in sorrow and joyless, the kin of mighty kings, processed [2190] with sixty-eight maidens whom Lady Helche had raised herself. Their happiness had been built on a rainbow.[46] Who would have thought that they could fall so low? They had been robbed of all solace.

I will tell you the names of some of them that I found written down in the story. [2200] There was Helche's niece, elegant Lady Herrat. Dietrich's heart broke even more. Still more noblewomen processed. King Nitger's child, the lovely Sieglinde, came to see the suffering along with Lady Gold-run, a king's daughter. [2210] He was named Liudeger and ruled in France, and Helche had affectionately raised his child. Along with these young women came Hildeburg and Herlind, daughters of two powerful nobles. Hildeburg, who was without fault, was born in Normandy. Herlind was from Greece. [2220] Many of the women had fallen ill from their grieving. Right after them came the Duchess Adelind, bold Sintram's daughter. That hero was known by all and lived near Austrian lands. There is a castle on the border with Hungary that is still called Pitten.[47] The girl [2230] I am speaking of grew up there.

We don't know all of them who were brought up by Helche, and then later by Kriemhild, in the land of the Huns. They had been sent in honor of Etzel and Helche. There was no nobleman anywhere who, knowing of Helche's virtues, did not gladly send his daughter to her. [2240] At least eighty daughters of counts and barons came there to the uproar. All of the widows had come whose husbands and family members were lying there dead. There commenced the greatest weeping and despair that had ever been witnessed in the world. Etzel's lands were completely void of all happiness.

The horrible news caused the people from the countryside to rise up [2250] with an anguished strength. They came streaming from all around and at all times of the day. They immediately searched for their loved ones on the field of battle, in front of the main building and in the hall, just like looking through stalls at the market. Death had sown his seed far out into the countryside. [2260] As each person found his own where he had fallen, many of them could be seen carrying their loved ones out of the blood. Then good women began their weeping again as if they had never even begun.

Their faithfulness was apparent in their sorrow. People saw how women, young and old alike, [2270] tore elegant dresses from their bodies. They

---

46. The image of the rainbow is here meant to convey the impermanence and insubstantiality of earthly joy. Building on a rainbow is a bit like building on sand in that it provides an unstable foundation for permanent happiness, given a rainbow's short existence.

47. Pitten today lies about twelve kilometers south of Wiener Neustadt in Austria. It's about thirty kilometers from the current Austrian/Hungarian border.

didn't want the gold to complement their pain. As disagreeable as corpses are to people, you could see the dead being kissed and caressed despite their mortal wounds.

4. How the King Sent Their Horses and Weapons Home

The palace, [2280] which had been full of the dead, was emptied. No one could be consoled, neither the highest nor the lowest born. However people had grieved before, or told of grieving, or could still grieve, here boundless grief came together all at once. Lord Dietrich heard beautiful Herrat's voice. [2290] He had suffered much, but he took pity on her. She and many other young women had to do as he commanded. He was able to relieve them a bit from their agony, and so he ordered that they be led away. Lord Dietrich and Lord Hildebrand were shouldered with great and burdensome responsibilities. They immediately had the three mighty kings laid into coffins. [2300] May God reward Dietrich that he showed his devotion by having the noble and the mighty lords separated. It was the right thing to do.

The king quickly went to where he found his wife and his son on the biers, but the pain was so great that he fell unconscious. [2310] His grief had brought him to the point where blood flowed from his ears and his mouth. The great hero grieved so severely that it was a miracle that he didn't die of grief. But who could have stopped their grieving? All those who gazed at the horror had to weep along with him. [2320] Knights and ladies pleaded with the mighty king in their tearful sorrow that he not lose his life in this way but take heart. That would benefit them and him. They were able to console the king in this way.

A coffin was made for them that was large and strong and in which they were to be laid. [2330] They had a precious and costly silken material, worked in gold and from faraway heathen lands, in which they wrapped his son and his wife. They were both laid to rest with royal honors. For their salvation, they prayed that God might care for their souls. [2340] The same was done for Bloedelin, warrior and son of the great Botelung. What else could Lord Dietrich do than what his loyalty commanded? He ordered that whatever men could be found who could sing a Mass should be brought together quickly, and so he was able to bring the Christians their priests, and the heathens their own. [2350] They quickly carried brave Ruediger with great honors to his grave. Many crosses could be seen carried by priests. All those who wore a stole prayed to God in heaven and Saint Michael [2360] to have mercy on their souls.[48] Those who were nobility they delivered without delay into the earth. The kings were worthily interred in several caskets. Hagen, the strong, and his comrade in arms Volker, and Dancwart, the mighty warrior, were all three [2370] laid to rest next to their lords. Hawart, the strong, the king of Denmark, Irinc, and Irnfried, these three were buried with great ceremony. [2380] Those who had come to the festival from other lands were also given kind consideration. Both natives and foreigners were quickly left to begin their eternal sleep.

The people did not rest. It took until the third day before all the nobility had been buried, and their weariness would increase before they had finished burying all the rest. They had to receive what was their right as well. Etzel and Dietrich [2390] conferred and agreed that there would be no end if the foreigners were all to be buried individually. They were to have one grave, so deep and wide that it could be completed in a reasonable time. The king ordered that all the people from the country [2400] should work together and dig a pit seven spear shafts wide and just as deep. I think that never again will a grave be dug with such sorrow. The squires were carried off, the household from the Rhine, whom Gunther and his men had brought with them into the land. [2410] They found nine thousand there, those who had been the first to suffer death. The people were compelled by their pain to wring their hands for their suffering in foreign lands.

Even more dead were found there. In sorrow and in pain they were buried, as I have often told you. After they had all been buried, [2420] those who left the graves could be heard wailing and screaming more than ever before. It was a bitter leave-taking from Christians and heathens. They grieved so vehemently that one could talk about it [2430] until Judgment Day. Since cheerfulness was completely inappropriate, no one paid attention to anyone else who was still alive.

Etzel was seen behaving in a most unbecoming manner. When he could find no brave heroes on either side of him, he said to Dietrich, the Lord of Bern, [2440] "I wish that I still had many of those I must now be without. My misfortune has cheated me of all happiness."

Dietrich replied, "You should cease your incessant lament. Not everyone is buried who has yet to serve you. Lord King, you may still confer your lands

---

48. There are two important aspects of the Archangel Michael that are in play in this scene. He was associated with the care and weighing of souls, and as the commander of the armies that fought against Satan in heaven, played a significant role as a warrior saint. Michael was the patron saint of the Holy Roman Empire and was revered by several military orders. In his other role, Michael was considered the angel of death, and as such carried the souls of the deceased to heaven. Often depicted holding scales, he was thought to weigh souls and determine their ultimate fate.

on heroes. [2450] God can still mercifully compensate you for your loss. You still have the two of us, myself and Hildebrand, with you in these lands."

"What good is all that?" he asked. "I could never be happy again, even if I lived a thousand years. Who could make me feel any differently or show me how? [2460] Those who would have gladly done so are sadly now all dead. What good is my red gold or other wealth? Power and worldly fame are lost to me. My men are dead, and so are my son and my wife. What good is life, scepter, or crown, [2470] such as I had by rights all my life? I will never wear them again. Joy, honor, and a worthy life, these I will give up. I will lay down all my worldly responsibilities since they no longer matter. I couldn't care less when death takes me."

They wanted to comfort him, [2480] but it was all in vain since he had lost too much. Misfortune had taken over his life. The greatest portion of his ill fortune had overtaken him now that everything had been stolen from him, the best of everything that he had ever enjoyed. The king began to weep, as he had done from the beginning. [2490] Even Dietrich's confidence was lowered a bit. The weary hero sank down into a window niche.

Hildebrand then said to Lord Dietrich, "Lord, what are you still waiting for? Let me give you my advice," said the champion. "Given that the entire country has been devastated, what are we doing here? [2500] What Queen Helche gave you, noble Dietrich, it seems to me advisable that we take that and leave this land. Your daring and my fighting ability, these both should protect my Lady Herrat, as we have sworn to do. We should not forget our loyalty on account of our losses. [2510] However low our own happiness may have sunk, we should always be men who know how to remain constant and faithful."

"I will gladly do as you advise," said Dietrich. "How can I recover from these sorrows with honor, given the ruin I have suffered? Oh, what terrible news must make its way back to [2520] where these warriors came from to this festival. Ah, what good swords lie without a master in this hall, countless shirts of mail and helmets. We don't know who should have them now, since those who wore them once are now all dead. I will forever complain to God that I [2530] had to leave so many worthy men behind here, dead."

"We should," said Hildebrand, "have the brave warriors' armor cleansed of blood and the valuable and unbroken weapons put away. If Etzel regains his wits, it may still be of use to him and bring him great advantage."

When Etzel heard that, [2540] he thought it was good counsel and delayed no longer. According to the advice from both of them, he had the equipment stored, and the best swords they could find he also had put away.

Lord Dietrich said, "I would like to tell you, noble and mighty king, if you want to act admirably after your great loss, [2550] then we both advise you, I and Master Hildebrand, that you should send back to those left behind in each land (don't let anyone change your mind), whatever originally came from the lands that left their dead here. You will gain honor for this. The young ones will be more useful to you than the equipment [2560] that death has made masterless here."

Botelung's son replied, "That is obviously the right thing to do, and I gladly follow your counsel."

The first to be summoned were Ruediger's squires. They saw the tears flowing from their eyes. There were only seven who came before Etzel outside the hall.

[2570] The mighty king said, "Send whatever message you think best, Lord Dietrich, to the great margravine in Bechelarn."

Everyone there was disheartened, but the brave hero acted nonetheless. Ruediger's sword, his armor, and his horse, wherever they could be found, were to be delivered straightaway. [2580] How could any woman be more distressed than his wife when she was told the story of what happened?

Master Hildebrand said, "Who will be the messenger to take this news to Burgundy, since all of the knights and squires have perished?"

[2590] "The king is obligated to send his own emissary to the Rhine" [said Dietrich.]

"That should be Swemmel," said the king without hesitation. "He is well acquainted with the way there."

Twelve men were gathered along with the fiddler who would bring back the weapons and armor that the famous heroes had carried in battle. [2600] The envoys should tell the story, there on the Rhine, of everything that had happened. The nobles agreed that the messengers should delay no longer. They were sent to the wives in their homeland with the news and with the equipment that the fallen had once worn. [2610] Their friends and family felt the pain as much as it was felt by those who had mourned before. They could well curse the day on which the festivities had sent so many brave heroes to their deaths. Anyone who was told the news was left completely bereft of joy.

Along with the others who were to go to the Rhine, [2620] Swemmel appeared before Etzel, the king, who said, "You must not hesitate to tell Brunhild, the powerful, exactly how everything happened, and how my lands are filled with sorrow, and that guests never before brought their host so much suffering. [2630] But the two of them, Brunhild and Ute, do not have to pay for this," said the king. He continued, "You should also not fail to tell them of my innocence, these two worthies on the Rhine, and that neither I nor my people deserved such a tragedy, because I gladly offered them everything in friendship. [2640] In return they offered only enmity. What I have lost has been their loss as well."

The fiddler then spoke, "I have never before delivered such terrible news. The joy and honor of the lands are now completely gone. Those who once were able to live in happiness and splendor, [2650] who wore their crown with joy, will receive my embassy with anger. I am worried about how I can present this news and not lose my life."

The king replied, "You will be accompanied by men from Bechelarn." [2660] They were soon ready to depart.

Lord Dietrich spoke, "I must also send an equally unhappy message. I would gladly give my life to avoid it. That I should have to break the noble Brunhild's heart is something that gives me no pleasure. You should not," said Dietrich, [2670] "say anything of this news along the way. Don't let people know about this calamity when you depart. They would only trouble you all the more. Say nothing to anyone about Ruediger's death. There will be plenty of pain for a long time once they have been properly told, [2680] and they will be forced in their anguish to weep for many days. Those who once were so good to me, please assure them of my service, and that I remain always beholden to Gotelind and to the margravine's daughter, my splendid niece. If they want to know when Ruediger is coming home, [2690] tell them that you heard him say that the king will not allow him to leave. He has to stay until the guests have returned with their contingent to the Rhine, where he must escort them. This is my intent: I plan to visit the margravine along with Ruediger. [2700] You should also tell Dietlinde[49] that if this is not possible, then I will visit my niece soon enough in any case."[50]

The emissaries' hearts were filled with many dark thoughts, and the Lord of Bern dismissed the ambassadors with a heavy heart.

5. How the Weapons Were Sent Home

They left behind, [2710] of this you can be assured, mournful relatives, past joy, along with friends and family for whom death was near. Some of them who were still alive struggled with death on blood-drenched biers. The others had by now been buried, [2720] which filled their hearts with sorrow. They also took their leave of the margrave.[51] They led his horse along the road, all the while crying and wailing loudly without restraint. Wherever they rode through the land, they were asked what the matter was, but no one received an answer. They often had the urge to tell their story, [2730] but

---

49. This is the only reference to Ruediger's daughter's name. It is not known if the name was taken from some other source or invented here.

50. Dietrich's instructions seem to try to achieve two things: give the messengers some sort of cover story that will protect them from Gotelind's wrath, and delay the delivery of any bad news until he has a chance to travel to Bechelarn in person. That such a deception will hardly work becomes clear enough in time.

51. Ruediger has been buried and his body will not be delivered back to his home.

the Lord of Bern had forbidden any squire to speak of it. They were right to leave it unsaid. No one was the wiser until Ruediger's men rode into Austria, where children ran up to the minstrel's entourage, as was their custom. They thought [2740] that it was the king or mighty Ruediger. The people together asked the minstrel, "Where have you left the king?"

The fiddler then told them that the king was still in his lands with many other champions. Those who wanted to, believed it. [2750] There were so many others along the way who wanted to ask questions that the bridges and paths were packed. Coming from the land of the Huns, they arrived in the town of Vienna. They were invited to take lodging with a courtly lady who resided there, the wealthy duchess Isalde, a beautiful young woman. [2760] It was impossible to keep a secret from her, and she discovered it from the messengers. She was so moved by sorrow and sadness that blood sprang from her heart out of her mouth. Oh, how terrible it was for her to hear the messengers' news. It became widely known from the young woman's lament. [2770] Everywhere in the town people began to make a great noise, poor and rich alike. Those who had just arrived and had witnessed the previous grieving said that this was just the same. The masses came to offer their support in the lament. [2780] The emissaries could not prevent the news from reaching all the leading citizens and merchants, and the prosperous town was filled with sorrow.[52]

The emissaries quickly left the town of Vienna. They could now hardly comply with Dietrich's orders, [2790] since they encountered many men along the road who wanted to share their sorrow with them, and so they journeyed on to Traismauer in their anguish. Neither knight nor peasant was told the news until the fiddler had arrived at Bechelarn. [2800] Ruediger's squires entered the land not as they had previously or according to custom. They were greatly troubled that they had to keep secret what they would have gladly divulged.

Lady Gotelind was well acquainted with the road up the Danube. [2810] The emissaries rode into her lands along the same path where she had often seen her husband joyfully depart. Along with the margravine, many beautiful young women had gathered along the parapets. They saw the messengers riding toward the castle with great exertion, and as expected they saw a cloud of dust rise up [2820] in Ruediger's lands.

Many young women said, "Praise to you, Lord God. Just look, Lady Margravine! We can see people riding back from the festival. Our lord is returning!"

---

52. This sojourn in Vienna, and the details provided, seem to be intended to emphasize the town's wealth and importance. By 1200, Vienna was indeed a powerful and prosperous town, having just been enriched by a part of the ransom paid for Richard the Lionheart to Leopold V, Duke of Austria, which he used to build the town's walls, among other things.

Their protector and consolation remained far away with the Huns, [2830] by Gernot's hand. Only seven men who came from this land returned, leaving the margrave and bringing his equipment. Lady Gotelind had now heard about the arrival. She went to see her daughter, and both thought [2840] that they would receive love without pain,[53] as they had so often done before with the sight of their loved one. But they received only heartbreak and long-lasting suffering.

The squires were in the habit, when they rode to Bechelarn, of making a joyous noise along the way. Now things were completely different. [2850] Each one of them was slouched down on his horse, and their grief was so great that they could not sing as they had often done before. Ruediger's horse, Boimunt, was led by one of the squires, and it kept looking back. They were used to this behavior. Whenever it couldn't see its master, [2860] it would often break free from its reins and run back down the road. Now he who had once ridden him and often fought on his back, as a nobleman should, was dead. His daughter noticed the way the squires were behaving and took a deep breath.

Ruediger's child said, [2870] "My dear mother, Gotelind, never before has such a thing happened, that I see so few of my father's messengers riding here. Before when they arrived, we could clearly hear that they were in a joyful mood. If only the festival for my lady had been a success. [2880] But I don't think it was."

The elder margravine replied, "If God wills it, then they shall all remain unharmed, except that I had a terrible dream. I saw your father Ruediger last night, and he had gone completely gray. The men he had with him were all covered in snow. [2890] A rain was tormenting them and they were drenched. My daughter, you may believe this: my head was completely bald, I had lost all my hair! He asked me to go into a dark room, and there he was, standing inside. He closed the door. [2900] We could never leave, although I didn't want to be there." So spoke the margravine.[54]

Ruediger's daughter said, "Dear mother, some dreams are pleasant, others are harsh. In my dream I saw my father's horse bucking and jumping, and his silver chainmail coverlet was making all sorts of noise. [2910] My dear

---

53. This line (v. 2840) again reminds the reader that *liebe âne leide*, love without pain, is an illusion.

54. This haunting dream contains several elements that are difficult to interpret. There is the aging of both Ruediger and Gotelind, he turning grey, she losing her hair. There is the coldness in snow and rain, and finally there is the dark room from which there is no escape. These elements are often found in medieval exile literature, where exile is commonly described as a cold, dark place. The sense of "otherness," of solitary existence, is heightened in the closed, dark room. All of these point to death and are meant to foretell Ruediger's demise in a foreign land, where he is fated to remain in the cold, dark ground, forever an exile.

mother, listen to this: it drank some water and then sank out of sight on the spot."[55]

They said no more to each other, and instead walked away together. The messengers had come so near, as I said before, that everybody could see them. They rode directly to their stables. [2920] The squires were not behaving according to their old ways, but according to courtly tradition the knights rode out to meet them and welcomed Etzel's fiddler. Illustrious heroes greeted the emissaries from the land of the Huns, and afterwards they immediately greeted their lord's men. [2930] They heard them answer with short, sharp words. Whatever had once made them high spirited was now gone. They had nothing good to report about the festival. The squires could be seen taking the harnesses off of the horses.

Gotelind immediately noticed how the squires were acting. [2940] Nothing had made her so sad in years. She said, "I would give anything in the world to find out what has happened to them."

The most senior among them said, "Etzel, the mighty king, assures you of his fidelity, his favor, and great esteem, along with his constancy and goodwill. [2950] He is always ready to support you with word and deed. Know this to be true. My lord [Ruediger] also bids me to tell you that no matter how far he is from you, he is near to you in his faithfulness. You should know that he favors you above all other women, and remains so inclined to his dying day. [2960] He does not know if he will be able to come home any time soon. The king relies on him for everything. He is leading a military campaign for him, a matter that had been discussed for a long time. My lord has departed for this conflict."

She said, "May God and all heavenly hosts protect him. Be he on land or sea, wherever he travels, may Christ watch over him [2970] to honor his supremacy. May Etzel's enemies not take my husband from me."

The daughter asked, "Tell me, dear emissary, why is my father Ruediger behaving so? I am very unhappy," said the girl, "because I was always the first [2980] to be given a message when he sent someone to his lands. He was never so angry that I didn't receive a message from him. I have every reason to be sad."

The girl began to cry. She looked at her mother, and both of them began to weep. I think that they suspected the worst in their hearts. [2990] Terrible pain loomed before them.

---

55. Dietlinde's dream is about Boimunt, Ruediger's horse. It seems to be riderless and disappears into a watering hole or some body of water. There is no consensus on the interpretation of this dream, and in some ways it differs from other dreams in the *Nibelungenlied*, where death is usually foretold by violence. Here, the sinking of the horse probably represents doom or destruction, as in Ps. 69:14, "Rescue me from the mire, do not let me sink; deliver me from those who hate me, from the deep waters."

The messenger spoke, "Please don't cry. I have more news to convey to you, which Lord Dietrich has kindly sent to this land. The champion told us with respect that we should assure you in all sincerity of his support. [3000] He sends to you, noble margravine, his love and good wishes, faithfulness, and commitment. You have no need to question whether anyone in your family was ever more sympathetic to you. He orders me to let you know— this, my lady, I am bound to tell you—that he wants to come see you in Bechelarn in twelve days."

[3010] "May God will that it be so," said the margravine. "That would make me glad from the bottom of my heart."

The fair young woman then said, "Tell us more about how mighty Kriemhild welcomed her brothers and their men. And what was her greeting for Hagen? [3020] How did she act toward that hero or toward Gunther? Was she still very angry at both of them? Or did they make up?"

The messenger said, "The queen greeted them in friendship and welcomed them lovingly. She acted in every way as if she were inclined toward them. [3030] Etzel, the famous king, received the nobles in such a way that showed he was glad of their coming, he and all his men. I didn't see anyone there who carried any sort of grudge against them."

She said, "Tell me why King Giselher, that young nobleman, did not give you a message for me? [3040] I have to ask. Since he had no message for me, I'm afraid that I may never see him again, for whatever reason. The mighty king told me that he wanted to marry me."

"Dear lady, please don't say that. We left him in the best of health. They will return soon, rest assured, noble margravine, [3050] when they go back to the Rhine. Don't worry yourself about that. The king looks forward to seeing you. When he returns to his lands, he wants right away to take you with him, lady, to the Rhine. There you will be his queen."

To continue to tell such lies, given their despair, hurt one of them in particular to such an extent [3060] that he could no longer stand the injury and the pain in his heart. His eyes filled with tears, even though he would have gladly concealed it. Others then broke out in tears as well. The great margravine saw them all crying.

Her daughter said right away, "Oh, my dearest mother, [3070] I think that we have lost all joy and happiness. Sadly, my Lady Kriemhild's welcome of her family was insincere. It has turned out worst for us, and we have every reason to cry now. They and my father are surely dead."

Just as she said this, one of those present could not repress a cry of pain. [3080] He thought he could prevent it by keeping his mouth closed, but no heart could keep something like that still. The cry burst forth from his bloody mouth. When the good-hearted squire cried out so loudly against his will, everyone else was so upset that they started to weep, too.

[3090] The mighty margravine said, "Oh, poor woman am I that I was ever born! I have lost all the joys I thought I ever had. In my pain I am completely separated from them. You emissaries, by your faith, don't let me suffer so without knowing what happened. [3100] Tell me exactly how you left my husband."

So the lying had to come to an end. Swemmel, the famed fiddler, then said, "Lady, we wanted to keep from you what had to be told, but no one could conceal it. You will never again see Margrave Ruediger [3110] alive."

They heard her cry out loudly. "Sir, who killed him?"

He said, "That was Lord Gernot. They killed each other."

The mother and the daughter screamed. I don't know that anyone ever cried more for a loved one. Those who were there or who came [3120] because of the noise all wailed as one. The pain felt at the hero's death was not greater before at the Hunnish court.

The great sorrow caused the margravine and her noble daughter to bleed at the mouth.[56] They both lost consciousness, and any sense of appropriate behavior vanished. [3130] All of the people had by now learned the truth. Whatever they had heard before, this news now turned all joy to grief. Gotelind's heartbreak was so great that people splashed her with water and dabbed her eyes. They could not tell if she was still alive. [3140] Women and men alike wept, as did everyone who was there in the town of Bechelarn. She was carried away from the others. Both of the margravines were in great distress as they lay there unconscious. Mighty Gotelind could be heard crying hysterically for her husband.

[3150] Their daughter said pitifully, "Oh, never before did a girl bear such pain. What will become of my Lady Honor in the kingdom, now that those who bore honor have so mercilessly fallen? Who will raise her up again when her strength fails? [3160] My dear father Ruediger was master in this regard. Lady Honor will never again be borne up with such earnestness as during his life.[57] Death is so vulgar that it allows no one to find refuge with family when he tries to escape. [3170] The Lord of Bern would certainly have saved my father if anyone could have avoided death."

The fiddler answered, "The entire story is something you already suspected. Everyone from the land of the Amelungen is dead. Your uncle, Dietrich, survived with much difficulty. [3180] And if that mighty king, Etzel, had been allowed to join the battle, we would have lost him, too."

---

56. The idea that the heart could be so damaged by heartache and sorrow that someone would spit up blood is a common one during the Middle Ages. It is certainly common in the *Klage*: cf. vv. 2310–13; 2762–65; 3084–85; 3662–65.

57. The personification of virtues is commonplace, but the depiction of honor (*êre*) as Lady Honor (*vrou Êre*) occurs here for the first time in medieval German literature.

She said, "Now tell me, Sir Swemmel, how is it that my father fought against Gernot, since we gave them so many red-gold bands and found them to be so friendly? [3190] It was not good for either one that someone tore them apart, if all they wanted was to be loyal."

He said, "Most eminent maid, that was none other than the queen herself. Men and women far and wide have had to pay for that. From the beginning of time until the end of days [3200] there will never again be a more terrible plot. It did her little good since she herself was to die as a result. She was the cause of the enduring catastrophe that has beset the kingdom of the Huns. They are all dead, all those who should have given us joy. But you, lady, can still experience many happy days, [3210] for as much joy as you had in those who were killed with the Huns, you will end your lament, because God is the father of orphans. Lady, I counsel you in all honesty and by my faith, compose yourself and moderate your mourning. The king says that [3220] he will support you for all the days that God leaves him, as did Ruediger, the mighty margrave."

Their grief was given full expression in their sighs and cries. The whole story, everything that happened, came to light. The squires wanted to be sure that Ruediger's arms and armor that had been sent home were properly stored. [3230] Whoever wanted to look saw the bloody sparkle, but where once the rings had been whole, now they were cracked and broken. In this armor the consolation of Ruediger's wife and many others was destroyed.

Now a very strange problem occurred. No one had offered the guests any water or wine to drink. [3240] "How much longer do we want to stay here?" asked the fiddler. "The noble margravine is in such a state of despair that she can't think to greet us properly."

The people were all behaving in the same way throughout the castle. The main residence shook from the noise, as did the foundation beneath. [3250] They could also hear the people down in the town of Bechelarn acting out as the tragedy forced them. The margravine still managed to do her duty in her grief, even though it's a miracle that she lived to see the end of the day. With her own hands she tore off her gown from her body. [3260] There was never such a great lament as one could find there. The news caused the hearts of others elsewhere to let loose a stream of tears.

The lady sadly commanded that Etzel's emissaries be given friendly lodging in the town. The mighty margravine was completely at her wits' end, [3270] and she recognized neither friend nor stranger. The emissaries wanted to leave Gotelind's lands for the Rhine. The young margravine was still able to think somewhat coherently. She asked that they convey friendship and love to the noble and munificent Brunhild. She also commanded that Lady Ute be told [3280] that Giselher, the good, and she were engaged, and how tragically it all had ended. It could not have been worse for her. She also sent word that Gernot had killed her father.

The emissaries asked for permission to leave. Swemmel rode off on his way, [3290] up into Bavaria, which was the direction he was heading. Between the Danube and the Inn Rivers there still lies an old town called Passau, which was the seat of a mighty bishop. His fame, his honor, and his court were well known far and wide, and his name was Pilgrim. The whole story was made known to him. [3300] The proud Burgundians were his sister's children, and he soon found out exactly what happened to those heroes in the land of the Huns.[58]

The messengers crossed the Inn River. People ran out ahead of them to announce to the court that the devout bishop should welcome his nephews, [3310] but they were not close by as he thought. He was never to see them again.

He said to his knights, "You should all go out and welcome my kin. All the officers of the court who wish me well should receive my sister's sons [3320] and those who are with them. Be sure that nothing is lacking."

He would gladly have provided night lodgings for his guests, but he didn't know that their lives had come to an end in the Hunnish lands. If even only one of them had come. This at least would have consoled him somewhat. They told him immediately that all of them had been killed. [3330] This news gave him no joy. It seemed to him inconceivable, but he reconsidered and knew he had to believe it. He ordered that the messengers be provided with accommodations.

He said with great grief, "The joy I thought to have in my family members now lies slain with the Huns. [3340] I will always be saddened by that as long as I live, to my dying days. I knew all along that this festival was cursed. Etzel should never have ordered it, the cause of an agonizing death for so many praiseworthy men." He said, "Oh heavenly Son of God, why have you done this to me?"

[3350] Swemmel, the fiddler, went to him, and after their greeting Pilgrim asked him what had happened. He told him everything precisely as it had occurred, since he was an eyewitness.

---

58. Bishop Pilgrim plays a prominent role in the *Nibelungenlied* and the *Klage*, both as a participant in the events, being Queen Ute's brother and therefore uncle to Gunther, Gernot, Giselher, and Kriemhild, as well as the authority behind the preservation of the story in writing. His namesake was bishop of Passau from 971–91. This historical person became somewhat of a cult figure in the 1180s, drawing pilgrims to Passau right around the time of our text's composition. The actual bishop of Passau at this time, Wolfger, certainly would have had an interest in promoting the prominence of one of his predecessors, as well as the prominence of his town in the events of the *Nibelungenlied*.

The bishop broke down and cried. There was a great uproar throughout the entire court. [3360] Priests were unable to pray their hours on account of their grief, and lay people and priests alike wept openly. Later Bishop Pilgrim, the good, told them to end their grieving.

"I have no doubt that, if I could get them back with weeping and laments, [3370] I would never cease. My sister's children, who were so grievously killed in Etzel's lands along with many other loyal warriors, I can never stop mourning for them. If only they had come back alive."

He called for monks and priests from all around. [3380] The noble ordered that the priests sing masses for the departed according to the Christian liturgy. The bells from the churches could be heard throughout the town, as the bishop had ordered. There was a great crowd of people at the service, where the bishop himself said Mass in honor of God in heaven, [3390] to increase the salvation of Christians and to aid the souls of the dead. The bishop suffered greatly in his grief.

After the service had been completed, the messengers wanted to be on their way.

"Wait a bit longer," a chaplain said to him. "You should appear before my lord, who told me to say this to you. [3400] I think he wants you to convey something to Lady Ute, his sister on the Rhine, concerning her great grief."

The fiddler then appeared before the good bishop, who said, "Since Etzel's court was destroyed in this tragedy, then Kriemhild, my niece, received [3410] her brother and his warriors most horribly indeed. She would have done better to spare Giselher and Gernot. If those who had murdered Siegfried had paid, then she would have been blameless, after all, it was Hagen who killed him. Because of him we now have more than enough time to mourn for our friends. [3420] Cursed be that his mother ever bore him! We have to complain to God that he caused such long-lasting sorrow and such a horrible tale and all this pain throughout the world.[59]

"Swemmel, tell my sister not to grieve. They would have died at home as well. [3430] The red gold of the Nibelungen, if they hadn't taken that they could have easily traveled to their sister with her blessing. On account of their own transgressions and their excessive pride, we lost all of these brave warriors in Etzel's kingdom. And tell the queen [3440] that I can think of nothing better to advise her, since I have always wanted what was best for

---

59. Bishop Pilgrim, whose authority can hardly be questioned, weighs in on the question of guilt and places it squarely on Hagen's shoulders. He exonerates Giselher and Gernot, and although he criticizes his niece's reception of her brothers and her inability to separate the guilty ones, only Hagen is singled out as Siegfried's murderer. The next section does return to the old sin (*schuld*), however, that is the theft of the treasure and the brothers' own arrogance and pride (*übermuot*). So while Hagen is to blame for the murder, it is ultimately pride and the resulting theft that precipitated the cascade of events.

her, than that she should grieve within reason. We have to let them go, those who are taken from us every day by death. It is his custom to separate us with pain from what we love. That's all there is. And tell Gunther's men [3450] that they should remember how the king always upheld their honor day after day, and that they should demonstrate their loyalty and take into their care his small child, now his heir, and raise him up into manhood. This will bring them eternal honor.

"**S**wemmel, give me your hand as a pledge [3460] that when you ride through this land again, I ask you as a friend, that you will come to visit me. This all must not be forgotten. I will have it written down, the battles and the great downfall, and how they died, how it all started and happened and how it all ended. Everything you saw, in fact, [3470] you can tell me then. I also want to talk with all their relatives, women and men, whoever can say something about it. For this purpose I will send my messengers to the land of the Huns. There I will find out the whole story, because it would be a sin if it were not preserved. [3480] It is the greatest epic in world history."[60]

Swemmel quickly replied, "Whatever you want me to do, lord, I am at your service."

The messengers promptly departed. The bishop commanded his men to escort them along the road as far as they could be supplied with food and security. [3490] Whoever encountered them in Bavaria did them no harm, this was so on account of their lord. Instead they were presented with gifts. Swemmel and his companions continued on with the news through Swabia and on to the Rhine. As Swemmel traveled through Bavaria, he spread the news along the way. [3500] How could he not tell of the painful tragedy, and how they all died there at the festival?

The story was then also communicated to Lord Else. He said, "I should feel sorry for them, but I can't. I will forever protest to God that they crossed the Rhine. [3510] My brother was killed here on account of their expedition, something I did not deserve, as they themselves would have to admit. Now I have had my revenge. As the old saying goes, whoever is avenged by the wolf is well avenged, and no further vengeance is needed," said the mighty margrave.[61]

[3520] Some others said, "May God in heaven be praised, that Hagen finally fought his last fight. He could never get enough of battle. He is now in a place where his arrogance can no longer harm us."

---

60. This depiction of Pilgrim's interest in preserving history is extraordinary, in that it details his considerations of gathering eyewitness testimony and accounts, having the story written down from beginning to end, with an emphasis on determining the motivation of the main characters and events.

61. The origin of this saying is difficult to determine, but the meaning seems clear and fairly universal: if a wolf, or some other actor, intervenes unwittingly in an unrelated matter and eliminates the offending party, then the spirit, if not the letter, of the law has been fulfilled.

Let's say no more about that. When the emissaries had crossed the Rhine and arrived at Worms, [3530] they were carefully scrutinized. They were recognized in part by their clothing, which was curiously wrought according to the Hunnish style. The town's people wondered at this strange sight and where they came from or how they had come by Gunther's fine horse. [3540] People were somewhat uneasy even before they actually heard the news. Those who had been sent from afar arrived at the court. The household readily recognized their horses and equipment. Without delay it was reported to the court [3550] that the noblemen's armor and horses had arrived. Brunhild, the powerful, was overjoyed.

She said amiably, "I will richly reward whoever tells me exactly where the messengers have left the nobles along the way."

After this, the emissaries dismounted [3560] in front of the palace. The people rushed there to find out where King Gunther, the mighty noble, was.

The fiddler answered somewhat cautiously, "I can't tell the story to everyone. [3570] I need to keep quiet except where it is properly told. If you bring me there, you do well, where I can by rights recount the news. There I will not conceal the truth."

One of Gunther's men quickly went to the queen and asked if she wanted the messengers to appear before her. [3580] "Of those we welcomed earlier, we do not know a single one of them. But they bring our lords' equipment to our lands. Swemmel is with them, Etzel's minstrel."

She said, "Tell them to come here. I want to hear when the lords are due to arrive."

Swemmel, [3590] accompanied by his traveling companions, went before the queen with a heavy heart. When she saw them come before her, the lady said happily, "Sirs, you are welcome! I would gladly like to hear from you where you have left my husband. I am happy to part with a reward for telling me. [3600] My heart is full of cares, and if you can take some of them from me, it will be to your advantage and to my happiness. Do it quickly, and I will gladly give you my treasure. I can't help but wonder, though, how it is that he didn't send any of his men whom I would have recognized. He never did that to me before. [3610] That worries me a great deal."

The fiddler then said, "If you will allow me to speak, mighty queen, then I will come right out with the news that I have. First off I want security from you that it will not be detrimental to me."

She said, "You can be free from fear that anyone here will harm you. [3620] No one here has the right to do a messenger any harm." She continued, "I fear that the apple of my eye is now all too far from me." She could not help herself and started crying even before she heard the news.

The fiddler spoke, "That most high-minded man from the kingdom of the Huns wishes you all that is dear and precious. [3630] Lord Dietrich also offers you his service. We heard it most clearly that your sorrow is both worrisome and distressing to them. The devout Bishop Pilgrim also sends you his assurance of support, and he commanded that you be told that every sorrow should be mourned within reason. [3640] He is prepared to do everything for you both with deeds and words that will bring you success and honor in this world. I also heard directly from him that he asks all of the king's men who want to remain loyal to protect you and your son. Your husband is dead. [3650] Giselher and Gernot will not wear a crown here. All three of them have been slain. Hagen and Volker and Dancwart, that great warrior, remain with them, dead, in the land of the Huns, where they thought they would find happiness. Not a single member of their company survived."

[3660] The greatest noise arose since what had happened with the Huns. Never before had the heart's blood shot out of someone's mouth from such great pain as it did from hers. Neither of the grieving margravines in Bechelarn had wept so much [3670] that Brunhild, the powerful, could not equal them now. There were no more questions, no one said a word to the messengers. Swemmel only saw them all wringing their hands and altogether lamenting their agony and their pain. It was not just King Gunther's wife [3680] who abused herself. There were many more who grieved.

Ute, that most modest woman, was in her retreat in Lorsch, where she knelt praying and reading all day from her psalter in a large church that she herself had endowed. When she found out what had been reported in Worms, [3690] she was overwhelmed with despair. The news about her dearly beloved children was horrifying. Never before had such a loud cry been heard from a woman. She wanted to see Brunhild as quickly as possible, and she was immediately brought to her. [3700] The entire population was in an uproar. Nothing compared to their screams. The poor and rich alike were told what the lament was all about.

Women and children were soon weeping in the large town of Worms, [3710] helping Brunhild express her pain. Many noblewomen as well as the wives of burghers were so downcast that not a single joyful person could be found. Many hands cracked as they ripped out their beautiful hair. What else can I say, except that their weeping [3720] did not cease until three days had passed. The most prominent and the lowliest could not be consoled.

The local lords then arrived, great heroes in large numbers, the vassals of the three noble sovereigns. The wise ones grieved more calmly, the inexperienced ones excessively. The honorable men of all the land were seated next to the throne. [3730] There it became clear what they had to mourn. The best among them did not want to forget their duty. They calmed mighty Brunhild's distress and were able wisely to free many a woman from her pain. Nonetheless, Brunhild's confidence was gone, [3740] and she thought little of any of the counsel that she received.

Sindolt, the king's cupbearer, soon arrived. He had often demonstrated his faithfulness, as he did again now. He said to the queen, "Lady, moderate your lament. No one can wish away another's death. [3750] And even if your suffering continued without end, it would not bring them back to life.[62] As powerful as it may be, grief must have an end. You are not left completely alone; you may well still wear the crown yourself. Lady, in a few days' time your son will wear the crown by your side. The child will compensate you and all of us for this great sorrow. [3760] You can still find here many pleasant things. We will serve you and your heirs with the same fervor as we did mighty Gunther."

She said, "May Christ, who has power over all things, reward you, that your reason and counsel have made my heart lighter. And if I should survive this, [3770] then it will be on account of your advice."

Only now were the envoys called to provide answers and tell the story of all that had happened. The young king was also brought in. Swemmel stood in front of those gathered there and began to tell them the story. "Because Siegfried was murdered long ago, this is the reason they are all now dead."

[3780] Many of them responded, "My father lies there now without cause."

[Swemmel continued,] "The warrior Hagen killed him to injure his wife. They all were killed for that and her revenge. I never heard of a hatred so harmful as that which the lady sustained. I don't have the ability to explain it to you.

[3790] "Etzel's brother was killed. That was my Lord Bloedelin, who was the first among them. Dancwart killed him in the hall where the hero and the squires were attacked. They all had to fight, young and old alike, [3800] because the Huns had forced their way into their quarters, which were fairly out of the way. Not one of the squires survived, whether older or younger, only Dancwart did, and he quickly ran out of the hall. The bold and famous hero made his way to the court in spite of them and told his lords what had happened, as they were sitting [3810] and dining at the feast. Hagen then killed the ruler's son in front of his eyes. He collapsed in front of the table, and Hagen's hand was covered with his blood.

"With that, your three kings leaped into the fray. There was no stopping it then, and a great noise arose from the clash of swords. [3820] The heroes were seen recklessly pressing into the fray. They all met their death, some there or somewhere else. Nowhere before had such a great battle been fought. As long as they still lived, Volker of Alzey dealt out great pain with willing hands. [3830] That hero horribly avenged your family's injury. There were

---

62. Sindolt recommends a consolation strategy that Bishop Pilgrim and Dietrich had applied before, that is that lament, no matter how heartfelt or lengthy, will not bring someone back to life. Along with this very rational approach, Brunhild is asked to moderate her grieving, which is to say that she should maintain her courtly and noble composure, thinking instead about her son and the future of the dynasty.

real wonders performed there. There was no one who wanted to gain honor who didn't get what he was looking for. They had to fight for their king and queen. During the most critical part of the battle, [3840] Lord Dietrich and his men were on the sidelines, because the ruler of Bern was distressed by the suffering on both sides.

"Ruediger, that famous hero, also did not participate in the enmity. This he did on Giselher's account, because he had given him his daughter in marriage, but that did him little good later on. [3850] Because they had lost so many friends and the damage done was so great, everyone had to get involved in the fight. The armies were fighting everywhere on account of that disaster. Etzel asked and then ordered that his son be avenged. The queen pleaded with Ruediger until he, too, faced the mighty warriors in combat. [3860] He and his men died in battle. He and Lord Gernot killed each other. Next, the bold men of Bern became enraged. These famous heroes said that they wanted to avenge Ruediger, even though Lord Dietrich had strictly forbidden his men to become involved. [3870] Wolfhart was so infuriated that he wouldn't let it go until they had attacked your forces. Before Lord Dietrich could take notice, there was no one left alive from the land of the Amelungen who could threaten them except for old Hildebrand. There was no one left alive from your side either, [3880] except King Gunther and Hagen of Troneck.

"Hildebrand had to make his report after being wounded by Hagen, something he barely survived. After all this had transpired, Lord Dietrich was shocked at the extent of his losses in family and men. [3890] The hero, filled with pain and sorrow, then immediately went with Master Hildebrand to where he found the two fighters. That great warrior would still have saved both of them, but they did not want to live with the pain of losing the others. There was nothing left to do for Lord Dietrich but to avenge himself. [3900] Gunther, the mighty king, fought against him like a true warrior, as tired as he was. The man from Bern overcame him with sword strokes and took that famous hero captive. Right away Hagen, his vassal, took up the fight. This was confirmed later.[63] They would never have let him live [3910] if they had been rested, but they had already been fighting for two long summer days and could go on no longer. Everything I'm telling you is the truth. They [the Burgundians] destroyed the nobles and their great warriors there, forty thousand and more, with their courage. They put an end to anyone who ever wore a helmet, the best warriors

---

63. In the *Nibelungenlied*, Hagen is the first to be attacked and captured by Dietrich. This may simply be a contradiction in the *Klage*, or the poet may want to correct "the record," something he emphasizes with his statement that these facts as stated were later confirmed, presumably by other eyewitnesses.

[3920] who had come from many lands to King Etzel. They could have withstood the Huns if it hadn't been for the Christians [the Amelungen, Dietrich's men], who left them no choice, as I told you before. They had to kill each other. They would give no quarter, which is why they all fell [3930] except for those two men, but Hagen and Gunther were unable to continue the fight.

"Dietrich overcame them both and handed them over to the queen with great reluctance. She ordered that they both be led away and then took horrible revenge on them. She had both of those praiseworthy fighters put to death. [3940] For that Master Hildebrand in turn killed that noble woman. No one else was doomed to die, although some people wished that they could join the others in death. And so I left those who sent me back there in that misery."

Brunhild's people immediately raised a great cry of lament, [3950] prompted by their immense sorrow. They were well aware of their loss and misfortune. Ute, the great and powerful, later wretchedly mourned unto death for those heroes, her children. No one could think of any way to console her grief. After seven days the lady died of grief. [3960] The queen was barely able to survive the same anguish, and she lay unconscious until they revived her with water. The people's laments increased throughout the whole land. Kriemhild's injury had been harshly avenged. When mighty Brunhild could speak again, [3970] she thought about the fact that she had brought all this pain, which she now had to suffer, on herself. She now suffered as much pain as had formerly been Kriemhild's.

The lady spoke miserably, "Oh, that I ever saw noble Kriemhild. When the woman who craved honor angered me with her words, [3980] that great hero Siegfried, her husband, lost his life. Now I have to suffer as a result. Her loss of happiness has come back home to me."[64]

Who could still be happy there? Noble Ute was buried in her abbey at Lorsch. She who once wore a crown before heroes had her heart broken by the pain. [3990] Girls and women alike were distraught, and beauties drenched their clothes with tears. All of Gunther's lands were beset with sorrow. Then the greatest and wealthiest nobles came to the court. [4000] The assembly advised the lady and her child as best it could, mindful of the honor of Burgundy. They wanted the queen to moderate her grieving, and they didn't want to remain without a ruler. The people there advised

---

64. This is as close to a statement of regret that we get, and it is clearly meant by the poet to be a final vindication of Kriemhild, which is to say that Kriemhild was right to feel angered by Brunhild, and her ultimate revenge was that Brunhild now felt the same loss that she had suffered.

that the child be made a knight, and this relieved some of her extreme mourning.

[4010] "We want him to wear the crown so that we are no longer without a king."

They made sure that the child was well prepared. The royal household chose one hundred squires who were girded with swords that same day. Rumolt had also arrived, as he had heard the news at home in his own land. [4020] He was hurt out of loyalty that his beloved lord came to such harm for not following his counsel. We have often heard that he was beholden to them, and he sorely grieved for the proud and famous heroes.[65]

He said, "Lord God almighty, curse that I was ever born. [4030] I have lost my lords because of Hagen's arrogance, which often brings great harm. When, out of great disloyalty, he took Kriemhild's husband from her and stole her fortune, I could see from her unhappiness that they would be killed for it someday, however she managed it. [4040] Hagen repeatedly caused her harm and insult for no reason and in spite of her innocence. He should not have done these things, to be honest, because it went far beyond his position. This is why I don't want to blame her. What did Siegfried, her husband, do to him? He was killed without reason. [4050] I heard the whole story later. What of it, if both of the highborn ladies made each other angry in their foolishness? It should have been resolved, and he should have been left alive. But after that became impossible and she became queen in the land of the Huns, then it would have been best to leave the journey there undone.

[4060] "If my lord had done as I loyally advised him when he left this land, then he would not have died. Along with him died the very best champions that kings in any land had ever won or could ever win. They all died with him there. [4070] Those who live in this land will never be able to recover, whether man, woman, or child, rich or poor. May God have mercy, since my counsel was unable to alter events. For this reason the land is now without joy and much of its honor. But our grieving is not going to help us. [4080] Make it so that our young prince wears the crown."

All of them gave the same advice. No one told us, but we have learned it since, that such a great festival had never before been set up so magnificently in such a short time. [4090] Worms, a large town, was filled with guests. They did their very best with great devotion. They could see the

---

65. Rumolt is also redeemed in the *Klage*, and as he returns he is allowed to shed any hint of cowardice that might have arisen from his ill-fated counsel in the *Nibelungenlied*. Rumolt's *rât* is therefore no longer the humorous episode that seemed to espouse "wine, women, and song," but the sadly prophetic advice that is in the end proven correct. Rumolt emphasizes Hagen's crimes of disloyalty and pride, which now in hindsight seem clearly at the root of what is listed as a series of events in a causal chain that could not be broken.

mighty young king wearing his crown, and all of them received their fief-doms from the boy. The court and the nobility gained back some of their happiness.

[4100] **S**wemmel then asked for leave to return home. He reported every-thing to the one who had sent him to the Burgundians. He returned to the land of the Huns, where he saw Etzel and Lord Dietrich. They all asked how the return journey had gone. [4110] He told them all he could about what he had seen and heard.[66] Etzel was never to be happy again. Dietrich of Bern also wanted to return to his own land. Lady Herrat and Hildebrand were glad about that. When the king found out that they didn't want to stay, [4120] this caused even more pain than he had suffered before. He reminded both Hildebrand and Dietrich of their loyalty.

"Are you going to leave me now that I've lost my army? How will I be able to manage all alone?"

The Lord of Bern replied, "How could you ask that I should stay without support and without my people? [4130] It is right that a man should be in the company of his own. You can see perfectly well what my situation is. I and my bride should not live in exile any longer."

As much as Etzel pleaded and begged, they could not be persuaded, and so he had to stay behind without them. They quickly prepared to leave [4140] and left behind them many widows and orphans. Etzel lost his mind from this enormous loss just as they were getting ready to leave him.

As we were told, Lady Herrat took along what Queen Helche had given her. Much of it had to stay behind, though, since it was not possible to carry it all. [4150] They took with them at the time what she wanted, a value of eighty thousand marks. Lady Herrat then said goodbye. The ladies there could only cry and lament. From the treasury they took a valuable saddle, with which Lady Helche had often gone out riding in style. [4160] The saddle blanket was stitched with the best gold thread that anyone owned in the world. I can't describe in any detail how marvelous it really was. It was heavy with gold and precious gems. A king's wife never rode on a better saddle. [4170] The precious saddle cloth hung all the way down to the grass. When she was ready for the journey to her satisfaction, she kissed each of the ladies there. There was not one among them who did not weep as profusely as when Helche, the great, was taken from them by death. [4180] There had

---

66. In this short section, the compression of time seems extreme. Swemmel returns and is quickly asked about his trip, and the action seems to continue exactly where it had stopped when he left on what was a fairly long journey. Dietrich and Hildebrand are standing ready to leave, just as they were in vv. 2497–2514. This can only be explained in that the end of the text is very near, and any semblance of narrative cohesion seems of little importance at this point.

never been a more sorrowful parting by ladies at the court than that. That was plain to see.

As they took their leave of the sovereign, the king fell to the ground as if dead, even before they had left the court. The sorrow caused him such pain that he lost his senses and was so distraught that he lay there unconscious. [4190] If he lived on after that, he had no real sense of it. His heart had been so penetrated by regret and sorrow that the pain prevented him from uttering a single word. He was neither here nor there, neither dead nor alive. He drifted in a dreamlike state after that, I don't know for how long. [4200] As great and powerful as he once was, it had come to the point that people left him alone and paid him no heed. What happened to his mind after Lord Dietrich left, no one has told us.

Once they had gotten under way, the great hero ordered Hildebrand, the gray, [4210] to escort his lady to Bechelarn, where his relatives lived.[67] Their company consisted only of the highborn maiden and the two men, along with a pack horse that carried Lady Herrat's wardrobe. Lord Dietrich rode through the lands with great sorrow. [4220] They hurried on, filled with sorrow and cares. These foreigners arrived at the castle of Bechelarn on the seventh day. The people heard the news that the Lord of Bern had arrived, and they were glad. They told Dietlinde, [4230] Ruediger's daughter, who was still in great distress. Her mother had died three days before. She was unable to come to terms with her solitary and secretive suffering for her beloved husband. The virtuous woman died of this great pain.

The two young women were introduced to each other. [4240] Each one of them had thoughts of joy and pain. They exchanged kisses in a courtly greeting, and Lady Herrat then embraced Dietlinde.

She said, "Things will work out alright for you as long as my fiancé Lord Dietrich is alive. Be of good cheer."

She replied, "All my cheer [4250] is now buried with my father and mother. I don't think a young woman ever lost more family and friends."

Lord Dietrich found her to be very distraught. He consoled the praiseworthy young woman, as family should do. "Niece, be of good cheer and ease your grieving. [4260] I am truly sorry about both of them, your father and your mother. I will mourn them until my death. Should I ever be able to overcome my misfortune and return to my homeland, I give you my hand as a pledge that I will do my best to protect you from sorrow and pain."

[4270] This promise she received from the man from Bern. The famous hero said, "Should I live a while longer, I will find a husband for you who will live with you in your lands."

---

67. Dietrich is Gotelind's cousin, as he is the son of Gotelind's uncle.

He immediately gave the young woman over to the guardianship of her father's vassals, and then they departed. There was no laughter. [4280] As the margravine saw Herrat riding off, she began to tremble all over, because the weight of responsibility and honor had now been placed on her alone. She was later cared for as her honor required it, however, and no one was inclined to do her any harm. [4290] The young woman waited there in faith and constancy for the Lord of Bern to fulfill his promise. She waited in joyful anticipation.[68]

[4323] *What happened to Etzel and the truth about how he lived after Lord Dietrich left him, I can't tell you, nor can anyone else. Some say that he was killed, others say no. [4330] I can't discern between what is true and what is a lie, because there is much uncertainty. I can't help but wonder if he disappeared or just vanished into thin air, or was buried alive or raised up into heaven, or jumped out of his own skin [4340] or crawled into a cave somewhere, or how he met his end or what took him in, or if he went to hell or if the devil consumed him, or if he disappeared in some other fashion, no one yet has found the truth. [4350] The poet who wrote this story for us tells us that he would not have left it out and would have gladly recorded it, so that people knew [what happened to him, if only the information had come to him or if he had heard it from someone, anywhere in the world. This is why no one yet knows where King Etzel ended up [4360] or how he met his end.]*

[4295] **B**ishop Pilgrim of Passau ordered that this story be written down out of love for his nephews. Everything that happened was written in Latin [4300] so that it would be considered the truth by anyone who came upon it later.[69] From the beginning to how it all ended, including the death of the brave squires and how they all perished, all this he had written down. He made sure nothing was left out. The fiddler had since given him [4310]

---

68. The following section in italics is found at the very end of the B manuscript, after the line, "This poem is called the *Klage*" (v. B4322), where it seems out of place. It is placed here according to the more logical positioning of manuscript C, i.e., before the section beginning "Bishop Pilgrim of Passau ordered . . ." (v. B4295). Verses 4354–60 ("what happened to him . . .") are recovered from the C and "a" manuscripts, since the B manuscript has lost this text at the very end where the page was trimmed too aggressively.

69. Although there is no known Latin version of either the *Nibelungenlied* or the *Klage*, it is possible that such a text existed, as shown by the Latin version of the *Waltharius* story. As Heinzle points out (2015, 1606), a similar claim for the authenticity of a Latin version is made in *Herzog Ernst*. The point that the poet makes here, though, is less about an actual version but rather about emphasizing that the story is true, and an original version in Latin would clearly place it in the tradition of historiography rather than epic. The vernacular version(s) would then have taken its rightful place as secondary but still accurate, based as it was on a Latin, or literate, original. The transition from oral history to book culture is in evidence in this passage.

a full account of what transpired and how it happened, because he had heard and seen it himself, he and many others. His scribe [chancellor], Master Konrad, set out to record the story.[70] It has since often been put into verse in German. Old and young alike know the story well. [4320] I will say no more about their joy or their suffering. This poem is called "The *Klage*."[71]

70. There is no historical record or evidence of who this Konrad might have been, although several clerics of that name are recorded in Passau around 1200 at Bishop Wolfger's court. The title of master would indicate that Konrad, if he was in fact a real person, might have been an officer of the bishop's court, perhaps chancellor.
71. Although still uncommon in medieval texts, we have here a clear indication within the text of the title. The poem (*liet*) thereby follows in the footsteps of the *Nibelungenlied* and its endings, the manuscript C, or *liet* version, ending with str. 2440,4 "daz ist der nibelunge liet" (this is the poem/epic of the Nibelungen), while the B, or *nôt*, version ends str. 2379,4 "diz ist der nibelunge nôt" (this is the downfall/ruin of the Nibelungen).

Manuscript Additions and Variants

The following selections represent significant variations and additions to the standard B manuscript text, where an alternate reading is considered significant if it provides the reader with additional information that could appreciably affect the understanding of the "standard" text. A few selections are from manuscript A, but the vast majority are from the C manuscript, a version written by a redactor whose main purpose was to smooth away inconsistencies and illogical aspects of the B narrative. While doing so, he added a considerable number of strophes (ninety-six included here), especially in the second part of the epic, that either represent information possibly gleaned from other sources (including oral sources), or were composed by the redactor himself. It can be argued that the redactor's purpose generally is to excuse Kriemhild from guilt while demonizing Hagen. The inclusion of these strophes in a translation such as this is unorthodox, but it represents an attempt to stress the nonstandard nature of the text, along with its complex manuscript tradition. There is no single *Nibelungenlied*. The C manuscript and those manuscripts related to it were, in fact, among the most copied and read versions of the epic. It is hoped that these additions to the text will allow the reader to appreciate the variety that existed in a medieval text such as this.

Variants or additions are indicated in the main text with an asterisk. Strophe numbers in this addendum are indicated in square brackets, with the B version numbers first for ease of reference, followed by either the variant or addition from A or C. The A or C strophe numbers are also in square brackets, with numbers preceded by the letter of the source manuscript. Additional strophes are indicated with a "+" symbol following the B strophe number, followed by the A or C strophe number. If a B strophe has been largely replaced with another, then the "=" symbol is used to indicate replacement. Where an individual line within a strophe has been significantly altered, the relevant B text is first given in italics, with the alternative reading following in plain text. Deletions of strophes, not uncommon especially in C, are not recorded. Finally, most entries are followed by a short commentary that seeks to provide some context to the alternate readings from the perspective of the "standard" translation. These are, of course, strictly the translator's views, and the reader is encouraged to question the meaning of these alternatives and their significance for the narrative as a whole.

P. 3 [21] + [C21] Even before this hero grew to manhood he had already achieved incredible feats that were to become the subject of songs and tales. But these will have to wait until later.

> The C redactor gives a nod to the songs and tales, the *singen unde sagen* that celebrated the traditional hero Siegfried. The oral tradition is therefore duly acknowledged, even if it is pushed to the side for the purposes of this "new," written narrative.

Pp. 5–6 [43] + [C43] Once he started to bear arms, all had great respect for him. He never missed an opportunity to prove himself in combat and win praise, and his powers gained him fame across the world and for all time.

> Here is an interjection that explains a gap in the timeline during which Siegfried gained fame as a hero, alone in a world unlimited in time and space, that is, a mythical world, before his journey to the Burgundian court.

P. 10 [93] + [C94] He left the treasure undivided, and as a result the companions of the two kings attacked him. But with the help of their father's sword, which was named Balmung, the brave warrior seized the treasure and the lands of the Nibelungen as well.

> This rearranges the B version by adding this strophe and deleting B95. The C redactor makes clear that the defeat of the kings grants Siegfried possession of both the treasure and the lands and their people.

P. 11 [105,4] . . . *in appreciation for the extraordinarily friendly welcome.* [C105,4] He and his men demonstrated their fine manners in the way they carried themselves.

> The B version emphasizes the greeting by the Burgundians, the C version emphasizes the *zuhteklîche*, or courtly behavior of the guests.

P. 11 [114,4] *Hagen and Gernot were quick to object.* [C114,4] Gernot was the only one to speak up and object.

P. 12 [118,4] *Twelve of your kind wouldn't stand a chance against me.* [C118,4] Someone like you has no right to challenge me to a fight.

> Rather than focus on Siegfried's strength, the C redactor places the emphasis on Siegfried's royal standing and Ortwin's inferior nobility.

P. 12 [124,3] . . . *we would gain no honor and you no advantage.* [C124,3] . . . we would gain no honor if we chose to do so.

P. 13 [131] + [C132] At court, elegant ladies wanted to know who that proud stranger was. "He's incredibly handsome and has expensive taste in clothes." The answer came from all sides: "That's the king of Netherland!"

> The C redactor stresses both Siegfried's courtliness as well as his noble lineage, making him an equal, in the eyes of the ladies, of the kings at the Burgundian court.

P. 13 [137,4] *He, too, suffered great hardships on account of her love* [von ir minne]. [C138,4] He suffered great hardships on account of courtly love [*durch hôhe minne*].

> The subtle change from "her love" to "high love" in C, or what was by 1200 recognized as the convention of courtly love, makes Siegfried even more an ideal knight in the eyes of a fashion-conscious contemporary reader.

P. 19 [213,4] . . . *as missiles and sharp spears flew overhead.* [C214,4] The two heroes were fighting for their honor.

> The redactor finds an opportunity to emphasize that the heroes are fighting for honor (*êre*), a line one would expect to find in any courtly romance of the period.

P. 24 [272] + [C274] He said: "I ask all of you, family and friends, for counsel. How may we conduct these festivities properly, so that we will not be criticized in the future? It is said that any lasting praise must ultimately be based on deeds."

> This addition includes the axiom that honor and reputation are based on, and must be constantly renewed by, action, not words.

P. 26 [292,2] . . . *he was blushing* . . . [C294,2] . . . *she* was blushing . . .

> The C redactor, by changing a single word, has returned to the conventional image of the blushing female.

P. 28 [325] + [C328] "I would like your counsel on where I might find the wife best suited for me and my kingdom, in nobility and beauty. I will share my lands with her, and you will know when I have found her."

> The C redactor moves the decision to find a wife into a more political realm with the traditional gathering of counsel. The B version makes Gunther's decision seem practically autonomous. This also ends the chapter with a more definitive decision to seek a royal mate rather than just a beautiful woman.

P. 29 [328] + [C332] One day the king and his men were sitting around, debating back and forth which woman would make the best match for their lord and for the land.

> This is, in C, a continuation of the typical counsel theme introduced at the end of the previous chapter.

P. 29 [330] + [C335] King Gunther answered, "The woman hasn't been born, no matter how powerful and strong, that I couldn't best in battle with my own strength." "Don't say that," said Siegfried. "You have no idea what power she possesses. [C336] And if there were four of you, her grim fury would be too much for you. You should give up your plan, that is my sincere counsel. Unless you have a death wish, don't torture yourself over her love."

> The redactor emphasizes the danger in the upcoming bride quest and may be hinting at Gunther's real strength as contrasted with his boasting.

P. 29 [335] + [C342] I have heard it said about strange dwarves who live in caves that they have something marvelous they wear that protects them. They call it a cloak of concealment. Whoever wears it around his body is protected [C343] from blows and slashes. When he has it around him, he is invisible. He himself can hear and see whatever he wants, but no one can see him. The story also tells us that he will become stronger.

> The C redactor is intent on providing more information to introduce the cloak of invisibility, and these details move the encounter unmistakably into the realm of the fantastic.

P. 31 [353,4] *Kriemhild would later become his wife.* [C361,4] He was to gain her as a wife through his arduous service [*dienst*].

> C adds the aspect of service to Siegfried's amorous quest, again bringing his accomplishments in line with the contemporary courtly ideal.

P. 33 [382,4] *No one except Siegfried knew where they were.* [C390,4] Even Hagen of Troneck had never seen it before. (End of Chapter 6 in C, which starts Chapter 7 with str. 383; C391.)

> The C transition to a new chapter is more logical here, with the arrival (388; C390) in Iceland the end of one, and Gunther's reaction to what he sees the beginning of the next chapter. Manuscript B's start of Chapter 7 (389) is much more *in media res*.

P. 33 [383] + [C392] To tell the truth I've never seen in all my days such well-built castles as I see before us now. Whoever built them, he must be very powerful.

> The redactor's addition may intend to emphasize Gunther's satisfaction at having met a worthy opponent, but he attributes any display of power to a male ruler, not a woman.

P. 33 [386,4] *He will then be able to achieve all of his goals.* [C395,4] We will then be successful in imposing our will on her.

> At this critical juncture, the C redactor may very well want to shift the emphasis from Gunther alone to the collective "we." Siegfried's instructions to the other three to follow his lead in deceiving Brunhild's court into believing that he is Gunther's man places them all at risk, but is deemed necessary in Siegfried's plan to ensure a successful outcome.

Pp. 33–34 [396,3] *Beautiful women were looking through windows.* [C405,3] The lovely women looking out of the windows witnessed the scene.

> What can be assumed in B is made explicit in C. The redactor is emphatic that the women are actually looking at the scene in which Siegfried humbles himself as Gunther's servant, since the witness of the act makes it a fact, a reality.

P. 38 [442] + [C452] You should know that he was worried and frightened. All of his arms and armor were delivered to him, and so the mighty king was well armed. Hagen almost lost his mind from worry.

> The C addition seems intended to emphasize Gunther's, and Hagen's, concern about success in the contests. This can both give the reader an increased sense of the high stakes, and slim chances, in the competition, as well as Gunther's timidity as compared to Siegfried's cleverness.

P. 39 [447] + [C458] "Whether they're armed or not is all the same to me," said the queen. "I have not feared the strength of anyone I have met so far, and I'm confident that I can beat him in single combat."

> Here Brunhild seems especially intent on putting Hagen in his place.

P. 41 [469,4] *Dancwart and Hagen were happy enough for that.* [C480,4] They were all saved from harm by Siegfried's strength.

> The C redactor wants to leave the reader in no doubt as to who is in fact the victor of the bridal quest.

P. 42 [484,3–4] *[in a land] at least a hundred raster [about two hundred miles] away. The people there were called Nibelungen, where he kept his great treasure.* [C495,3–4] It was called Nibelungen, and these were his subjects. Lands and castles, everything was under his rule.

This passage demonstrates the interchangeable uses of the term *Nibelungen*, both for the people as well as the land.

P. 44 [506] + [C518] Someone with little experience might easily say, "That has to be a lie. How could so many knights be equipped all at the same time? Where did they eat? And where did all the equipment come from? It's just not possible, even if thirty different lands were at their disposal." [C519] But as you have already heard, Siegfried was wealthy beyond compare. The kingdom and treasure of the Nibelungen were at his disposal. From this he supplied his warriors with more than they needed, because whatever was taken from the treasure hardly diminished it.

This is a curious addition by the C redactor, who apparently found it important to heighten the tale's marvelous aspects by insisting on their truth, a kind of insistence that would seem unnecessary, given what the reader already knows about the otherworldly nature of Nibelungenland. But of course, the redactor points out the veracity of the story only to emphasize its exaggeration.

P. 44 [512] + [C526] ([C526] = [513]) The queen commanded that gold and silver, horses and garments, which her father had given her after his death, should be distributed among the foreigners and friends, all honorable men. [C527] She also told the noble knights from the Rhine that they should take some or all of her treasure and transport it to Burgundy. Hagen answered her, filled with satisfaction.

The C manuscript has Hagen as the keeper of the keys rather than manuscript B's Dancwart. There may be little difference, although the C redactor may want to emphasize that Hagen has already taken control as the overly generous distributor of foreign treasures, as he does later with Kriemhild's share of the Nibelungen treasure.

P. 45 [523,4] *They then prepared themselves for the journey and rode down to the shore.* [C531,4] . . . until Gunther will be able to rule the land himself. + [C532] Then she chose a thousand brave men from her followers who would accompany her on the journey to the Rhine, along with the thousand men from Nibelungenland. They prepared themselves for the journey and rode down to the shore.

This strophe is present in all manuscripts except AB, and the Bartsch/de Boor edition includes it as strophe 524, without any indication that it is not part of the base text but is "borrowed" from *C (*liet* version). See Heinzle's edition, note on p. 1169f.

P. 50 [592,4] *No one could see anything of them that was not as nature intended.* [C597,4] People said it was no lie that they both deserved the prize for most beautiful in any land.

The B manuscript emphasizes that neither woman's beauty is enhanced by makeup, or any other unnatural means, whereas C states that the two are equal in their beauty.

P. 52 [611] + [C616] She had no idea what was going to happen. Then Dancrat's son [Gunther] spoke to those of his family. "Support me so that my sister will take Siegfried as her husband." All of them answered of one accord. "It would be an honor for her to take him."

The C redactor wants to emphasize that Brunhild had no knowledge of the betrothal of Kriemhild to Siegfried. It was this lack of knowledge, and one might presume inability to intervene, that later leads to Brunhild's disgrace. The marriage of her soon-to-be sister-in-law was a matter that, although legally the purview of her elder brothers and male kin, as demonstrated by the C redactor's approval of Gunther's male counselors, would have rightly been of great concern to the new queen.

P. 53 [626,3–4] *Kriemhild and Brunhild encountered each other on the steps outside the hall. There was as yet no hatred between the two.* [C631,3–4] I assume that the two women parted courteously and in friendship.

The C redactor allows himself an authorial comment here, feigning ignorance as to whether the two women were actually on good terms at this early state of their relationship or not, perhaps hinting at some underlying motivation for their later estrangement.

P. 53 [629,4] *He would not have wanted a thousand other women in her place.* [C634,4] She was truly deserving on account of her many virtues.

Without having to change the rhyme scheme, the C redactor chooses to emphasize Kriemhild's *tugend*, or virtues, as the source of her and Siegfried's happiness, and that Kriemhild had in fact "earned" Siegfried's love as a result of her superior character, not just beauty.

P. 54 [639,4] *If he had ever had any strength, there was no sign of it now.* [C644,4] The king had very little to be happy about.

> The C redactor allows himself a healthy dose of sarcasm at Gunther's expense.

P. 55 [651] + [C657] "Just take a look at how swollen my hands are. She squeezed them so hard as if I were just a child. The blood came out from under my fingernails. I didn't think that I was going to survive."

> Again, C adds a strophe that seems intended to undermine Gunther's manliness.

P. 57 [674] + [C680] Even though she was on top of him with her whole weight, his anger and his great strength allowed him to force himself up again. He was in dire straits. They threw each other around the room with gusto. [C681] King Gunther was also frightened and did his best to avoid their fighting back and forth. They wrestled so intensely that it was a miracle that either one remained alive. [C682] The king was concerned for both of them, but most of all he was worried about Siegfried, because it seemed that Brunhild was close to killing him. Gunther wanted to come to his aid, but he couldn't risk it. [C683] The struggle between the two went on for a long time, but Siegfried was finally able to force the lady back to the bed. As much as she resisted, she finally had to give in. The king imagined all sorts of things in his anxious state of mind.

> The C redactor seems to take delight in adding considerable detail to the bedroom battle, giving hints that heighten the suspicion that Siegfried had forced himself on Brunhild sexually.

P. 59 [700,4] *Count Eckewart joined Siegfried's followers.* [C707,4] Count Eckewart left with his lady.

> C's version is more logical, as will become evident later, that Eckewart joined Kriemhild's service, not Siegfried's. Some other manuscripts agree with C.

P. 61 [721,1,3] *He was served by all the warriors of Nibelungen along with the treasure that had belonged to the two kings.* [C728,3] In addition he ruled over his father's birthright. He was a great warrior.

> C leaves out explicit mention of the Nibelungen army and treasure.

P. 61 [725,2–3] *She was irritated that they had not come to visit and that she had received no fealty from Siegfried's lands.* [C732,3] That she had seen no taxes paid from Siegfried's lands . . .

The concept of paying taxes (*zins*) is more specific in C than the general term *dienst* and is therefore clear in the expectation of formal fealty. This terminology is echoed in an additional strophe in manuscript C (C821) a bit later.

P. 62 [730,3–4] *I remember how we sat together when we were first married. Siegfried can consider himself honored to be married to her.* [C737,3–4] And how she welcomed me when I first came to this land. No one had ever been received in such a way in all the world.

> The C redactor avoids the mention at this point of Siegfried's supposed inferior standing, ostensibly raised as it is in manuscript B by the marriage with Kriemhild.

P. 64 [757] = [C764] They were given lodging and made comfortable. The lord [Siegfried] spoke graciously to his guests, "Don't worry about the mission you were given by our kin. We will soon give you an answer."

P. 65 [774,4] *If only we could get that treasure to Burgundy!* [C780,4] If only we could divide it up here in Burgundy!

> This is the first mention of an attempt, or at least a desire, to gain control of the mythical treasure of the Nibelungen for Burgundy. It seems appropriate that Hagen is the instigator, but it's difficult to know how to take his exclamation, preceded as it is by the shout of *hei*, making it somewhat more a kind of statement of wonder rather than a secretive plot. The same sentence in manuscript C is a bit more conspiratorial, as Hagen speaks of its division among the ruling house of Burgundy. The C redactor generally tends to paint Hagen as more conspiratorial in any case.

P. 65 [776] = [C782] Ortwin and Sindolt, the two bold warriors, were kept busy. During that time they had to act as cupbearer and seneschal and were in charge of setting up all the furniture for dining. Their staffs helped them in the effort, and Gunther thanked them for that.

> Manuscript C follows the more logical, and consistent, naming from the beginning of the epic of Ortwin as seneschal (*truhsaeze*) and Sindolt as cupbearer (*schenke*), whereas manuscript B inserts Hunolt, who was the chamberlain (*kameraere*). The differences are fairly insignificant, except as an example of where C tries to be more consistent.

P. 65 [777] + [C784] The women were also hard at work preparing their wardrobes. They adorned them with precious gems set in gold that gave off a brilliant light, meant to impress everyone.

P. 68 [813] + [C821] The queen thought to herself, "I can't stay silent any longer. Whatever I have to do, Kriemhild has to tell me why her husband, who is our vassal, has withheld taxes for so long. This is the question I have to ask." [C822] And so she bided her time, guided by the devil's counsel. She ended the joy and festivities with pain and suffering. What was buried deep in her heart had to come to light. People in many lands were to hear about her suffering.

> These two strophes end the chapter in C with a glimpse into Brunhild's psyche and motivation. They provide a bridge to the fateful scene in the next chapter in which the two queens compete against each other as to who has the greatest husband. The redactor also introduces the devil into the mix, a counselor who is sure to make things turn tragic, and is most often the instigator who can be counted on to accentuate the sin of pride, or *superbia*.

P. 72 [854,4] *Oh King, I will be forever grateful to you for that.* [A797,4] . . . I will never sleep with you again.

> This significant variation in the A manuscript (C corresponds to the B reading in this instance) may well come from a different source. Heinzle, 2015, (p. 1227f.) speculates that the analogous threat in the Norse *Völsunga saga* might point to a common oral tradition that Brunhild typically used a denial of sex as leverage.

P. 74 [875,4] *I'll find out more about him from his wife.* [C883,4] His wife will tell me where he is vulnerable.

> The C redactor makes Hagen's murderous intent crystal clear.

P. 74 [880,4] *The king became enraged when he heard this message.* [C888,4] Gunther became enraged, as if this were really news to him.

> The redactor allows himself a sarcastic commentary at Gunther's expense, typical for him.

P. 76 [905] + [C913] His lord asked him what he had found out. "If you can get the campaign turned around, then we'll go hunting. I know now exactly how to defeat him. Will you be able to make that happen?" The king replied, "Yes, I will."

> The C version is intent on making it clear that the plot, and the backup plan of the hunting expedition, are all Hagen's idea, but committed under Gunther's authority.

P. 77 [915] + [C923] Each one of them was informed as the traitors prepared to kill Siegfried. Giselher and Gernot chose not to go along on the hunt, but I don't know what kind of animosity prevented them from warning him. They had to pay for it in the end.

> The C redactor is more intent on problematizing the disloyalty and treachery that Hagen and Gunther demonstrate, but is less sure that Giselher and Gernot should be so easily let off the hook. Gernot is one of the plotters, Giselher has counseled against it, but neither one, although not active participants, can bring himself to warn Siegfried and thereby foil the murderers, to whom they must also demonstrate a familial and legally binding loyalty.

P. 81 [964] + [C973] The bold but fated man was not able to imagine that he could be so betrayed. He was in all ways virtuous and free from deceitfulness. His death was later to be avenged on those who were not even involved.

> The C redactor continues to use every opportunity to stress Hagen's guilt and Siegfried's innocence. Hagen's guilt is disloyalty (*untriuwe*), while Siegfried is full of virtue (*tugend*) and free from wrongdoing (*valsches*).

P. 83 [995] + [C1005] "There was never a more treacherous murder done," he said to the king, "than this. I preserved your life and honor through many dangers. I have had to pay a high price for all the good I did for you."

> The redactor adds considerably to this key scene, perhaps incorporating additional material, both oral and written.

P. 83 [997] + [C1008] He was hunched over in agony and spoke through his pain, "You may still regret this murder. Believe me when I say that you have only doomed yourselves."

P. 83 [1001] + [C1013] I will tell you the truth about the spring where Siegfried was murdered. At the edge of the Odenwald is a village called Odenheim. The spring still flows there, of that I am sure.

> The town of Odenheim still exists and is located about twenty-five kilometers south of Heidelberg. A spring outside of town has been designated as one of three Siegfried springs and displays an inscription *Siegfried Brunnen* that would seem to correspond to the C redactor's addition.

Pp. 88–89 [1072] + [C1082] Kriemhild lay unconscious throughout the day and night until the next morning. She was unable to comprehend anything anybody said. King Siegmund suffered in the same way. [C1083] He was brought back to consciousness only with great effort. He had been completely weakened by his suffering, which was not surprising. His men said to him, "Lord, you must head home, we can't stay here another minute."

The C redactor continues to add strophes at the end of a chapter, both to smooth the transition to the next chapter as well as to add motivation and logic to the narrative.

P. 91 [1105,4] . . . *great courage.* [C1116,4] . . . great strength and loyalty.

The term used in manuscript B (*ellen*) implies that Kriemhild's courage is more appropriate for a warrior, that is, a man, than for a woman, and indeed the *Klage* supports this view, stating that she was left to avenge her husband like a man only because none of her male relatives would assume that responsibility. Manuscript C's divergence in this important passage is interesting, and the redactor, although linked to the *Klage*, emphasizes once again Kriemhild's loyalty (*triuwe*) to Siegfried as the motivation for her vengeance.

P. 92 [1112] + [C1124] She said, "I will have to receive him then, since you won't have it any other way, but he has committed a great sin. The king caused me much heartache, without any fault on my part. My lips will mouth reconciliation, but my heart will never forgive him." [C1125] "This will make it better," said her relatives there. "Maybe he can even make her happy again. He can certainly make restitution," said Gernot. The pitiful woman replied, "You see, I'm doing everything that you ask."

P. 92 [1114] = [C1127] Since she was willing to reconcile with him, Gunther approached her courteously. He did it out of love for the treasure. This was the reason that that treasonous man had counseled in favor of the reconciliation.

The C redactor is very clear in pointing to the treasure as Gunther's motivation for seeking a reconciliation with Kriemhild. He therefore shares Hagen's guilt in every way. It is not entirely clear if the "treasonous man" is Gunther or Hagen, but it makes more sense that the reference is to Hagen who did in fact advise the king to seek a resolution. Manuscript B remains silent on this point.

P. 93 [1124] + [C1138] After Gernot and young Giselher had taken possession of the treasure, they became masters of lands and towns and many warriors, who all had to serve them out of fear of their might.

It is unclear whether Gernot or Giselher actually have in their possession the golden rod, which apparently bestowed great power. The object is not mentioned again, nor does it seem to play any real role in upcoming events. The additional strophe does serve to implicate further the two younger brothers in the plot to acquire the treasure.

Pp. 93–94 [1134,3] . . . *That would be the right thing to do.* [C1148,3] . . . so that no one else can ever have it.

> The B manuscript's text for the second half of line 1134,3 is a later insertion into a space left empty by the original scribe. Perhaps the source was faulty. Other manuscripts concur with the reading in C.

P. 94 [1136] + [C1151] The nobles swore oaths that, as long as they lived, they would not reveal or part with any of the treasure, unless in joint council they agreed it would be a good thing. They were to lose the treasure because of their greed.

P. 94 [1137,4] *He was hoping someday to make use of it.* [C1152,4] He intended to have it all to himself. That day never came. + [C1153] He was unable to gain control of the treasure, as it still often happens to the disloyal today. He had hoped to possess it for himself during his lifetime, but he was never able to use it nor give it to anyone else.

> The C redactor is more moralizing at this point and draws the lesson that wealth has always eluded those who gain it through disloyalty or treason. The idea that Hagen alone could have possessed the treasure seems, on the other hand, spurious, given the fact that Hagen always acted out of a sense of loyalty to the house of Burgundy.

P. 94 [1138,4] *Giselher alone wanted to remain loyal to her.* [C1154,4] The nobles pretended that they had turned against Hagen.

> The redactor refuses to let even Giselher off the hook.

P. 94 [1142] + [C1158] After Dancrat's death, Queen Ute had founded an affluent monastery with her own means. It was furnished with valuable properties, which it has even today. The Lorsch monastery is still highly regarded. [C1159] Kriemhild later contributed significantly to the abbey for the sake of Siegfried's soul as well as all souls. She gave gold and precious gems with great generosity. We have never heard of a more faithful wife. [C1160] Lady Kriemhild had reconciled with Gunther, but she had still lost the great treasure on his authority, and this increased her grief a thousandfold. The noble woman wanted to depart from there. [C1161] Lady Ute had a manor house in Lorsch near her abbey, and it was stately indeed. The widow had retired there away from her children, and the noble lady is still buried there in a stone tomb. [C1162] The queen said, "My dear daughter, since you can't stay here [in Worms], you should come live with me at my estate in Lorsch, where you can quit your crying." Kriemhild answered her, "Who would then watch over my husband?" [C1163] "You should leave him here in Worms," said Lady Ute. "May God in heaven prevent that," said that blameless woman. "My dear mother, I would never do that, he must come away from here with me." [C1164] Overcome by pain and grief, she ordered that he be exhumed. His revered remains were then immediately reburied with great honors in the church in Lorsch. The hero lies buried there still in a long sarcophagus. [C1165] Yet Kriemhild had to stay [in Worms], as it was meant to be, just when she was supposed to leave with her mother. Messages that came from afar to the Rhine prevented that.

> The C redactor's lengthy addition possibly represents another version of the ending of the first part of the story, but it is also intended to set Kriemhild up as a woman about to embark on the cloistered *vita contemplativa*, a common choice for a noble widow, but pulled back to the *vita activa* by events beyond her control. She is thereby forced to take matters into her own hands and become active in a way that goes well beyond her traditional role as a woman, wife, widow, and even former queen. The C redactor is also clearly reacting to and promoting a local tradition at the abbey of Lorsch that connected it with the burial of the legendary clan of the story as well as the final resting place of the hero Siegfried.

P. 97 [1174] + [C1198] Wherever the troops rode, they were left alone by thieves. They were well served on their journey, as was appropriate. Knights and squires were well outfitted. This is how the powerful margrave went forth from Bechelarn.

P. 106 [1288,3–4] *They arranged for daily lodgings all the way to the Danube. Gunther only rode out a short way from the town.* [C1311,4] They arranged the lady's daily lodgings. Volker was her marshal, whose responsibility was to secure lodging. [1288] + [C1312] After the farewells, many tears were shed even before they had left the town and arrived at the fields below. Others rode out with them without needing to be asked. Gunther only rode out a short way from the town.

> The C version replaces 1288,4 with a new line, only to reinsert the line from B in the added strophe C1312,4. The additional information highlights Volker as marshal, or commander of the troops.

P. 107 [1289] + [C1314] The emissaries were in a hurry, and they were anxious about the journey on account of the honor and the large reward they would receive. When they had arrived in the land with the news, King

Etzel heard the gladdest tidings of his life. [C1315] For this wonderful news, the king ordered that the emissaries be given such great gifts that they could live carefree for the rest of their lives. The king's cares and sorrow had been replaced with happiness.

> These additional strophes may be a reaction to the abrupt beginning of the next chapter, which wants to move quickly away from the messengers. The C redactor wants to give the messengers their due before dismissing them.

P. 107 [1295] = [C1321] Once they had crossed the Danube into Bavaria, the news spread that Kriemhild the queen was traveling to the Huns. This delighted her uncle, who was a bishop by the name of Pilgrim.

> The C version attempts with this rewrite of str. 1295 to introduce Pilgrim somewhat more smoothly into the narrative.

P. 107 [1297] + [C1324] They were housed in Plattling. People could be seen riding from all over to greet them. They were gladly provided with whatever they wanted. They accepted it all respectfully, and the same was to repeat itself later on.

> C provides more detail, including the town of Plattling, which was located at the western edge of Passau's sphere of influence, on the border with the bishopric of Regensburg.

P. 114 [1393,1] *That could happen, if I could get him to come here to this land.* [C1420,1] She wished that her mother was with her in the Hunnish lands.

> The C redactor includes Kriemhild's mother in this reverie, that is, the two people in the world that Kriemhild could still trust: her mother and her youngest brother.

P. 116 [1412,4] *King Etzel replied, "At the next summer solstice."* [C1439,4] The queen was relieved when she heard this. + [C1440] The mighty king replied, "The festival that you will announce at the Rhine, so that you know for sure, I want to celebrate at the next summer solstice. Those who love us in good faith will not fail to make the journey."

P. 119 [1450,3–1470,3; 1496,2–1591,3; 1617,1–1642,3] = [*C1478,3–*C1503,3; *C1529,2–*C1631,3; *C1657,1–*C1682,3] A total of six leaves have been lost in this section from manuscript C. A leaf (one page front and back) is missing between 56v and 57r. Another four leaves are lost between 57v and 58r, and one more between 58v and 59r. The resulting loss of text (all or parts of 155 strophes) is restored for *C with the use of the related manuscript "a" (Cologny-Geneva, Bibliotheca Bodmeriana, Cod. Bodm. 117; fifteenth century).

P. 120 [1468] + [*C1497] "If you had nothing else to sustain you, I would always provide you with cuts of meat cooked in oil, as much as you like. That is Rumolt's advice, since the Huns are so dangerous. [*C1498] I know that my Lady Kriemhild will never forgive you, and you and Hagen deserve nothing else. This is why you should stay here, or you will be sorry. You will come to learn that what I have told you is the truth."

P. 121 [1470] + [*C1501] "Truly," said Rumolt, "I may well be the only one who does not cross the Rhine for Etzel's festival. Why should I risk everything I have here? As long as I can, I want to stay safe and alive." [*C1502] "I agree with that," said Ortwin, the warrior. "I will take care of business here at home with you." Many others said that they would not go. "May God give you, my lords, safe passage to the Huns." [*C1503] The king became angry when he saw that they wanted to enjoy the comforts of home. "This is no reason to quit, we must make the journey. The wise are ever wary."

> The considerable additions of the C manuscript bear some scrutiny. Rumolt assumes the role of oracle with his uncanny forewarning of danger. He tries to entice the king and his brothers to stay with the amenities at his disposal, which are food, wine, and entertainment. He is making an appeal to the Gunther of Part One, the king who is most concerned with the state of his court and its reputation for civil hospitality. The Gunther of Part Two, however, is a risk-taker who leads from the front. Gunther's proverbial response that the wise are ever wary is an affirmation that the Burgundian court of splendor and lavish entertainment is a thing of the past.

P. 125 [1519] + [*C1553] Before they left, the king held a council with his highest advisers. He made sure to leave lands and towns in good hands, so that those under his rule were to be watched over by numerous specially chosen knights.

P. 125 [1520] + [*C1555] One could hear much crying and wailing. Queen Brunhild carried her child in her arms to the king. "Why do you want to orphan both of us? You should stay for our sake," said the inconsolable lady. [*C1556] "For my sake, dear lady, do not cry. You should stay here at home without fear and in good spirits. We will return soon, with gladness and in good health." And so they took their leave from their friends and relatives.

> The insertion of Brunhild and her son (Siegfried) by the C redactor is striking. The narrative thereby gains a sense of the dynastic element and acts as an effective foreshadowing of the Burgundian annihilation.

Pp. 125–26 [1523] + [*C1559] In those days the faith was still weak, but they took along a chaplain, who said Mass for them. He returned alive because he was just able to escape. The others all left their lives with the Huns.

> The C redactor acknowledges that the *Nibelungenlied* is not a particularly religious text by pointing out that the Christian Church at the purported time of these events was weak, although we don't get that sense at all in the scenes in Passau that include Bishop Pilgrim and his considerable authority.

P. 129 [1573] + [*C1609] The ship was long, well built, wide and large, which was to the advantage of many a knight in that throng. It could carry at least four hundred across at once. Many others had to help with the rowing that day.

P. 130 [1584] + [*C1621] When the chaplain saw the ship hacked to pieces, he called to Hagen across the water, "You traitorous murderer! What did I ever do to you that you would try to drown an innocent man?" [*C1622] Hagen answered him, "Be quiet! By my faith, I'm just sorry that you were able to save yourself, and that's no lie." The poor chaplain said, "I will forever praise God for that. [*C1623] I'm not afraid of you anymore, you can be certain of that. You are now riding to the Huns, and I'm headed back to the Rhine. May God prevent you from ever returning to the Rhine: this is my solemn prayer. You almost killed me!" [*C1624] Then King Gunther spoke to his chaplain, "You will be fully compensated for what Hagen did to you in his anger if I return to the Rhine alive, you can rest assured of that. [*C1625] Go back home now, that is the way it has to be. I send my dear wife and my other family members greetings, as it is appropriate. Tell them that we are all still well."

> The C redactor ends Chapter 25 with this lengthy addition that is clearly meant to place Hagen in a bad light, part of his continuing campaign to shift blame away from Kriemhild. It also puts Hagen in direct opposition to the Church, potentially bringing the wrath of God down on the Burgundians through the chaplain's curse, even though Hagen's actions could be explained away as a last-ditch attempt to cheat fate.

P. 138 [1697,4] . . . *but he refused her offer.* [C1736,4] The hero was gladly willing to accept.

> The C redactor tries to clarify a somewhat clumsy narrative by turning a negative into a positive reply. The B version has Hagen refusing the specific gift that Gotelind offers him in order to make a controversial request that she give him Nudung's shield. According to the *Thidrekssaga*, Nudung was Gotelind's brother, who had been killed by Witege. The C redactor has Hagen accepting Gotelind's offer of a gift in general, then making a specific request for Nudung's shield.

P. 140 [1717] + [C1755] When the queen heard the news, her sorrow was somewhat diminished. Many men from her own land had come to visit her. King Etzel would later suffer much as a result. [C1756] She thought secretly, "It can still be done. The one who robbed me of all my joy, if I can manage it, will come to harm at this festival. That is my solemn resolve. [C1757] Regardless of what happens later, at this festival I will make sure that my vengeance hits that villain hard. He is the one who stole my happiness, and I will be repaid."

> The C redactor adds another lengthy addendum to the end of a chapter, this one designed to emphasize that Kriemhild's revenge is still focused on one individual, Hagen, and on him alone.

P. 142 [1744] + [C1785] [Kriemhild:] "I'm not saying that I want to have more gold. I have so much still to give away that I don't need your gifts. But I suffered a murder and two larcenies, and as a dispossessed woman I deserve compensation."

> The C redactor tries to mitigate the charge that Kriemhild was mainly motivated by wealth. Here the emphasis is on justice and a fair compensation for her husband's murder as opposed to repossession of her husband's treasure.

P. 148 [1817] + [C1859] Mighty Etzel had spared no expense and effort when it came to building his residence. The palace and towers, heated rooms without number, and a great hall, all were enclosed within an enormous castle. [C1860] He had ordered that it be built to great proportions in length, height, and width, because he always had so many warriors as guests. Along with his own household, he hosted twelve powerful kings and many more worthy warriors [C1861] than any other king ever had, at least that's what I heard. He lived in great splendor. The great lord was surrounded by the noise and crowds of his family, vassals, and many brave warriors. Of all this he was very proud.

> The C redactor now follows his routine of adding strophes to round out virtually every chapter toward the end of the epic, even if the information seems somewhat superfluous, it adds detail nonetheless.

P. 149 [1837] + [C1882] Before Kriemhild had sent the knights out, she told them, "When you find them, then for God's sake remember to kill only one man, disloyal Hagen. You are to let the others live."

> As in the *Klage*, the C redactor is intent on making it clear that this first attack was meant to kill or capture Hagen only. The fact that the plan went awry was due to circumstances beyond Kriemhild's control.

It is clear that the Huns are as much if not more intimidated by Volker than Hagen. The message is clear that together, these two heroes present an awesome force that is bound by unshakeable loyalty (*triuwe*).

P. 152 [1879] + [C1924] She thought to herself, as it almost came to pass, "If one of them were to be injured, then I could imagine that a fight would begin. I would be avenged against my enemies, I could be sure of that."

P. 154 [1898] + [C1943] Much to Etzel's regret, he saw many of his men fully armed who, out of hatred for the foreigners, were excitedly rushing after the lords as they were going to their tables. They wanted to avenge their next of kin, if given an opportunity. [C1944] "If you would rather eat with your armor on than not," said the host, "then this is extremely discourteous. But whoever harms even a hair on my guests will be killed, let that be a warning to all you Huns."

> This addition seeks to put Etzel in a good light as the constant broker of peace and order. In the *Klage* he claims ignorance as to the state of hostilities, but this seems somewhat implausible given all the evidence.

P. 154 [1900] + [C1947] She said, "Hagen has done me great harm. He murdered Siegfried, my dear husband. If someone could separate him from the others, he would receive my gold. But if anyone else were to be injured, then I would be truly sorry." [C1948] Master Hildebrand spoke, "How would it be possible to kill him in their presence? I could show you, if someone tried to attack here, how easily a fight would break out that would leave rich and poor alike as casualties."

> Following up on C1756–57 and C1882, these strophes have Kriemhild trying to avenge herself on Hagen alone.

P. 155 [1911] + [C1960] Let me tell you how she went to her table. Mighty kings were seen carrying her crown before her, while many other highborn nobles and praiseworthy warriors preceded her in a most courtly manner. [C1961] The host had his guests shown to their seats, the highest ranking and the finest with him in the hall. He had different dishes served to the Christians and the heathens, but everyone was served lavishly, as the wise king had ordered. [C1962] The rest of the households ate in their lodgings. They had been assigned chamberlains who were to look attentively to their needs. Their accommodation and their joy were later to be weighed against grief.

P. 155 [1912] = [C1963] Once the nobles had all been seated and had started eating, Etzel's son was brought into the hall to join them. The mighty king won only great grief afterwards.

The C redactor needs to intervene here by replacing str. 1912 in order to remove the blame from Kriemhild for her own son's death. The notion that she would use the boy as bait for Hagen's anger is horrific, and Kriemhild can only be held less culpable if she is first exonerated in her son's murder.

P. 156 [1920] + [C1972] Many of those who heard this and were hostile toward him wanted to attack him. The king wanted to do the same but was deterred by his concern for his own honor. Otherwise Hagen would have been in real danger. But later Hagen did even worse by killing his son in front of his own eyes.

> To end the chapter, the C redactor explains why Etzel does not respond to Hagen's insult. The answer: Etzel's concern for his own honor. This seems curious, in that one might expect a response, whether violent or not, in defense of honor. However, the need to maintain peace at his festival is Etzel's primary concern, and his honor, that is his reputation, is based on the stability and joy of his own court.

P. 158 [1951] + [C2004] It was precisely at the same moment when Dancwart came through the door that Ortlieb was being carried from one table to another among the highborn nobles. The terrible news was to be the boy's undoing.

End of Chapter 32 in C.

P. 159 [1961,3] ... *in the king's lap.* [C2014,3] ... in Kriemhild's lap.

> The difference here, with the boy's head landing in his mother's lap in C, perhaps increases the horror of the moment even more, and could help explain, or even excuse, Kriemhild's actions from this point forward. Manuscript B is alone in its reading, however, so the possibility remains that B is simply based on a scribal error.

P. 162 [2002] + [C2056] The mighty fighters, the Lord of Bern and Ruediger, retired to their lodgings. They wanted nothing to do with the fighting and ordered their own troops to leave them [the Burgundians] in peace. [C2057] But if they [the Burgundians] had known what hardships the two still would cause, they would surely not have left the building so easily. These bold warriors instead would have inflicted significant casualties.

> The C version clarifies the absence of the two main leaders in Etzel's service in the following melee and also portends the growing conflagration.

P. 164 [2026,4] = [C2080,4] "They should be anxious to earn these castles and this red gold." [2026] + [C2081] Mighty Etzel was overcome by pain and sorrow, and he bitterly lamented the death of his kin and vassals. Many warriors from many different lands stood there, lamenting the king's great loss along with him. [2027] = [C2082] Bold Volker began to mock them. "I see lots of strong warriors sniveling here. They provide weak support for their lord in his great need, but they've been shamefully eating his bread for quite some time now." [2027] + [C2083] The best among them said to themselves, "He's telling the truth." But none of them were as distraught as Irinc, the hero from Denmark, which was to become obvious in short order.

> The C redactor seems again intent on concluding a chapter with a more anticipatory bridge to the main events in the following chapter, here with the introduction of Irinc of Denmark.

P. 168 [2086] + [C2143] She had not wanted this horrible battle. She had really only wanted to manage things so that Hagen alone would die. But it was the vile devil who made sure that everyone suffered.

> While Hagen has accused Kriemhild of being the devil himself, the C redactor brings the devil into play as the instigator of the slaughter, or more precisely of the failure of Kriemhild's plan to isolate Hagen. This will be reemphasized in the *Klage*. Kriemhild makes a final offer to hand over Hagen so that the others might be spared (str. 2104). The refusal to hand over Hagen is the pivotal question for the Burgundian rulers, and their honor demands that they all die rather than sacrifice one of their own. This loyalty is what defines friends (*vriunt*), and Giselher declares that he remains loyal to his brothers, his extended family (*mâge*), his clan (*sippe*), and his men, all of them considered to be "friends." This loyalty is demonstrated in the readiness to defend themselves as knights (*ritterlîcher wer*, again in str. 2128).

Pp. 170–71 [2120] + [C2178] It was to the foreigners' great advantage that the hall had a solid vaulted ceiling. As a result more of them survived the danger, and they only suffered from the fire near the windows. This is how the courageous warriors saved themselves.

> The C redactor wants his readers to know that he is thinking along with them, and his additions often offer explanations that serve to demystify rather than to amaze. The fact that the ceiling was stone rather than wood may logically have saved many of those inside.

P. 174 [2157] + [C2216] "Giving up all property, I will clear out from your lands and take only my wife and my daughter with me. I would rather refuse your red gold than die in dishonor and disloyalty."

> Severing the ties of fealty would allow Ruediger to withdraw rather than fight for Etzel and Kriemhild against his own family, now that Giselher is his son-in-law.

P. 178 [2222] + [C2281] Mercy could not be granted to anyone. Many who had not yet been wounded were now knocked down. They might have survived if not for the huge crush from above, so that they drowned in the blood although otherwise unharmed.

P. 189 [2368] + [C2428] He was sure that she would not let him live. Could there have ever been a greater betrayal? He was afraid that, after she had killed him, she would let her brother go home.

> This is one last swipe taken at Hagen by the C redactor. Even as Hagen honors his oath, he is blamed for betraying Gunther, fearing that the king might betray their oath and give up the treasure while letting Hagen die. There is nothing in the B version to support this, and the addition in C seems to be on very shaky ground, but may reflect other sources.

P. 190 [2379] = [C2439] I can't tell you what happened afterwards, except that Christians and heathens alike wept, women and squires and many a pretty girl. They suffered great anguish for their friends. [2379] + [C2440] I will tell you no more of this great catastrophe, or what the Huns did to arrange their affairs. Let us leave the dead lying where they were killed. And so the story ends, the epic of the Nibelungen.

> The two different endings, of course, give the versions their titles, that is the *nôt*, or downfall version (*AB) and the *liet*, or epic version (*C). It is interesting to note how various English translations have rendered this final line and "title" of the story taken from the B, or *nôt*, manuscript: "such was the Nibelungs' Last Stand" (Hatto); "that is the Nibelungs' doom" (Edwards); "that was the fate of the Nibelungs" (Mowatt); "this is the fall of the Nibelungs" (Ryder); "this was the Nibelungs' downfall" (Lichtenstein); "with the fate that fell on the Nibelungs" (Raffel); "this is the Nibelungers' fall" (Lettsom).

Place-Names in the *Nibelungenlied* and *Klage*

Entries marked with (K) are found only in the *Klage*, those with (N) only in the *Nibelungenlied*. Entries not so marked occur in both texts.

Alzey, town about thirty kilometers northwest of Worms; birthplace and home of Volker.

Amelungen lands, ancestral lands of Dietrich of Bern (Verona) in northern Italy; named for the Amal or Amali clan, forerunners of the Ostrogoths.

Arabia (*Arabî*), unspecified lands renowned for gold and silk materials. (N)

Arras, town in northwestern France; part of Flanders until the end of the twelfth century; famous for its costly cloths. (N)

Austria (*Ôsterland, Ôsterrîche*), the eastern marches (*marcha orientalis*); the land on either side of the Danube from Mautern in the west to Hainburg in the east. Historically Austria became an independent duchy in 1156 and incorporated the duchy of Styria in 1192.

Azagouc, fictitious land or town in the East known for silk materials. In Wolfram's *Parzival*, it was situated in North Africa and ruled by King Isenhart. Gahmuret, Parzival's father, took control of Azagouc after defeating Isenhart. (N)

Bavaria (*Beierlant*), an ancient duchy ruled by the Welfs under Henry the Lion from 1156 to 1180; following his ban, awarded to Otto, a member of the Wittelsbach family, in 1180. In the *Nibelungenlied*, Bavaria was ruled by the counts Gelfrat and Else. Bavarians seem to have a reputation for lawlessness and brigandage in the *Nibelungenlied*.

Bechelarn (Pöchlarn, Austria), the home and castle of Ruediger and Gotelind; on the Danube about thirty-five kilometers southwest of Melk.

Bern (Verona, Italy), since 489 a residence in northern Italy of Theoderic the Great, the historical Dietrich of Bern. In the *Nibelungenlied* and *Klage*, Dietrich's capital is assumed to be Bern, and his family is from Bern.

Burgundy, a kingdom on the middle Rhine with its capital at Worms, ruled by Gunther and his brothers. Originally occupied by the Ostrogothic tribe of the Burgundians in the fourth century, this ancient kingdom was consolidated by King Gundahar in 413. The Burgundians were defeated by the Roman general Aetius in 437 and resettled to the west.

Danube (*Tuonouwe*), a major European river and thoroughfare from west to east. Crossing the Danube becomes a major undertaking for the Burgundian army at a ferry landing near Mehring. Kriemhild had crossed earlier at Vergen. In the twelfth century, a bridge across the Danube already existed in Regensburg (1146), although this crossing point is not mentioned in the *Nibelungenlied.*

Denmark (*Tenelant, Tenemark*), homeland of King Liudegast, brother to King Liudeger of Saxony. The two declare war on the Burgundians but are defeated by Siegfried and Gernot. Hawart and his vassal Irinc, both at Etzel's court, are also from Denmark.

East Franconia (*Ôstervranken*), that part of the duchy of Franconia that lies between the Main and Danube Rivers. The Burgundians pass through it on their way east. (N)

Eferding (*Everdingen*), an Austrian town on the Danube, about twenty-five kilometers west of Linz. Kriemhild passes through the town on her way to Etzel. (N)

Elbe, central European river, mentioned only as the eastern border of European influence. (N)

Enns (*Ense*, river and town), southern tributary of the Danube, enters at the town of Enns. The river formed the western boundary of Ruediger's influence, as he and Gotelind greet Kriemhild here on her journey east through his territory; granted town privileges in 1212. (N)

Etzelnburg, Etzel's residence; thought to be either at Esztergom (Gran) or Óbuda (Old Buda). Emperor Frederick Barbarossa passed through Gran on crusade in 1189. (N)

France (*Vrancrîche*), mentioned only once in the *Klage* as a brief reference to a King Liudeger of France, whose daughter Goldrun was in Helche's entourage. (K)

Gran (Esztergom, Hungary), possibly the location of Etzel's capital, Etzelnburg. Gran is the German name used in the *Nibelungenlied*, etymologically related to the river Hron. (N)

Greece/Greek (*Kriechen/Krieche*), a contingent of warriors from Greece serves Etzel. In the *Klage*, it is the homeland of Herlind, a lady in Helche's court.

Hainburg (*Heimburc*), a town on the Danube at the eastern end of the Austrian marches, near Hungary, about fifteen kilometers west of present-day Bratislava. Kriemhild and Etzel spend a night there on the way to Vienna. (N)

Hessen, mentioned only as a land through which Siegfried and the Burgundian army ride on their way to fight the Danes and Saxons. (N)

Hungary (*Unger, Unger lant, Unger mark*), Etzel's kingdom, land of the Huns. In the *Nibelungenlied*, the Huns are portrayed as eastern, non-Christian people, and while they are noted for their own dress and battle formations, their behavior seems to correspond to the courtly culture of the West. The historical Hunnish empire quickly declined after Attila's death in 453. The Huns have nothing to do with the origins of modern-day Hungarians, or Magyar, who settled in the Carpathian Basin in 895.

Iceland (*Îslant*), the home territory of Brunhild; not necessarily synonymous with the present-day country or island. A twelve-day sea journey from Worms, this far-off land represents an "other" world where courtly norms do not necessarily hold sway, and where magic (Brunhild's strength in connection with her virginity) is a factor for heroes to contend with. (N)

India, a land known for its precious gems. (N)

Inn (*In*), a river that flows into the Danube at Passau. A wooden bridge crossed the river there since 1143.

Isenstein, Brunhild's capital in Iceland. The town and her kingdom are left in the hands of regents when she leaves with Gunther for Worms. (N)

Kiev, Russian homeland of a group of warriors at Etzel's court. (N)

Libya, an exotic land known for its fine silks. (N)

Loche (Lochheim, Germany?), site on the Rhine where the Nibelungen treasure is sunk by Hagen. While this medieval town between Mainz and Worms may be meant, the text could also simply be referring to sinking the treasure into a "hole" (*Loch*). (N)

Lorraine (*Lutringe*), mentioned as the birthplace and homeland of the hero Irinc. In the *Nibelungenlied*, Irinc is from Denmark, the homeland of his lord, Hawart. (K)

Lorsch, a small town about fifteen kilometers east of Worms, site of an important Benedictine monastery (founded 764). Queen Ute builds a church and hermitage there for her retreat after her husband's death. According to the C manuscript, Kriemhild joins her mother there after Siegfried's death and reinters his body in the abbey.

Main (*Meun*), tributary of the Rhine from the east, entering near Mainz. The river was a major feature for travel through eastern Franconia. (N)

Mautern (*Mûtâren*), town on the Danube; stop for Kriemhild after Melk. Her uncle Bishop Pilgrim accompanies her this far on her journey. (N)

Mehring (Großmehring, Germany), town where Hagen and the Burgundian army cross the Danube. (N)

Melk (*Medelicke*), an Austrian town on the Danube; home to Astolt. Kriemhild passes through after her stay in Bechelarn. (N)

Metz, town in Lorraine; home of Ortwin, an officer at the Burgundian court. (N)

Miesenburg (Moson, Hungary; German: Wieselburg), a town on the Danube about thirty kilometers south of Bratislava. Kriemhild boards a ship here to complete her journey to Etzel's capital. (N)

Morocco (*Marroch*), along with Libya, known for its fine silken materials. (N)

Netherland (*Niderlant*), homeland of Siegfried; ruled by his father and mother; later by him and Kriemhild; its capital is Xanten, a town on the lower Rhine. Although the Middle High German name is plural, the form here is singular to avoid confusion with the modern country of the Netherlands, with which it has very little in common. (N)

Nibelungen land, the territory in the north that was the homeland of the Nibelungen clan, ruled by the brothers Nibelung and Schilbung; also the home of a fantastic treasure hoard, guarded by the dwarf Alberich. Siegfried becomes king of the land and commander of its troops when he kills the brothers. He, and later his widow, have control of the treasure, which is then taken from Kriemhild by Hagen.

Nineveh (*Ninnivê*), a source of expensive silk; originally an ancient Assyrian city of Upper Mesopotamia, located on the outskirts of modern-day Mosul. (N)

Normandy, homeland of Hildeburg, a lady in Helche's household. (K)

Norwegian march (*Norwaege*), the fairly unspecific location of Nibelung's castle, meant to indicate its position in the far north. Siegfried and Kriemhild are residing there when invited to the festival at Worms. (N)

Odenheim, a town in Germany mentioned in manuscript C, along with the Odenwald, that is purportedly the site of the spring where Siegfried is killed. It lies about twenty-five kilometers south of Heidelberg and commemorates the site outside of town with a stone inscription. (N)

Passau (*Pazzouwe*), ancient town on the confluence of the Inn and Danube Rivers; seat of a bishopric and in the *Nibelungenlied* Pilgrim, its bishop; portrayed as a powerful religious center, with many churches, monasteries, and an extensive territory. It is thought to have played an important role in the production of both the *Nibelungenlied* and the *Klage*, given the prominence of its bishop in both stories and the detail of the surrounding vicinity in the texts.

Pitten (*Püten*), site of Sintram's castle on the Hungarian border. (K)

Plattling (*Pledelingen*), mentioned only in the C version, a small Bavarian town located where the Isar River enters the Danube, and where Kriemhild meets her uncle Pilgrim on her way east.

Poland (*Poelân*), homeland of Duke Hermann, a vassal of Etzel. (K)

Rhine (*Rîn*), a major European river and scene of much of the action in the first part of the *Nibelungenlied*. The Burgundian capital Worms lies on the banks of the Rhine, and Xanten, the main town in Netherland, is on the Rhine as well. Various delegations and armies travel it north and south. The Burgundians are often titled "from the Rhine."

Rhone (*Roten*), river mentioned along with the Rhine, Elbe, and Mediterranean as boundaries of European kingdoms. (N)

Rome, the emperor of Rome is mentioned only once in reference to the exile of Irnfried, Hawart, and Irinc. This probably refers to the emperor of the Holy Roman Empire who was crowned in Rome as opposed to the Roman emperors of classical antiquity. (K)

Russia (*Riuzen*), homeland of a group of warriors in Etzel's service. (N)

Saxony (*Sahsen lant*), northern German homeland of King Liudeger, who declares war on the Burgundians. He and his brother are defeated when Siegfried and Gernot invade Saxony in a preemptive campaign. Historically, Saxony was an ancient duchy controlled by the Welfs during most of the twelfth century until Henry the Lion was stripped of his lands in 1180. (N)

Schwalbfeld (*Swalvelt*), an area between East Franconia and the Danube, situated between Würzburg and Donauwörth, probably named for the Schwalb River. (N)

Spain (*Spânje*), homeland of Walther, a hero who spent part of his youth as Etzel's hostage. (N)

Spessart (*Spehtshart*), a large tract of forest to the east of Frankfurt, mentioned by Hagen once to Siegfried as the location to which he had mistakenly sent the wine for their hunt, an obvious lie. (N)

Speyer (*Spîre*), the bishop of Speyer is among the party that says farewell to the ill-fated Burgundian expedition to Hunnish lands. Speyer was an important town in the Middle Ages, with one of the largest cathedrals of the time (completed in 1106), the burial site of eight German emperors and kings. (N)

Swabia (*Swâben*), since 496 an ancient Frankish duchy representing the territory of Alemannia; mentioned as a thoroughfare for travel from west to east.

Thuringia (*Düringen lant*), a medieval landgraviate (border land); German homeland of Irnfried and his men, in exile at Etzel's court.

Traisen, a tributary of the Danube, it seems to form the westernmost boundary of Etzel's empire. (N)

Traismauer (*Treisenmûre*), town on the river Traisen, belonging to the bishopric of Salzburg around 1200; a stop for both Kriemhild, and in the *Klage*, Swemmel, on his way west with the news from Etzel's castle. It is confused with the town of Zeiselmauer in several manuscripts (A, B, D).

Traun (*Trûne*), a tributary of the Danube, entering near Linz, Austria. Kriemhild crosses the river before her arrival in Enns. (N)

Troneck (*Tronege*), Hagen's birthplace and homeland, geographically undetermined. There is a modern Dhronecken, spelled Troneck in the Middle Ages, on the

Dhron River about 130 kilometers west of Worms, but its association with Hagen is purely speculative.

Turkey, homeland of Walber, a vassal of Etzel. (K)

Tulln (*Tulne*), a town on the Danube about thirty kilometers northwest of Vienna. Etzel meets Kriemhild here before leaving for Vienna the next day. (N)

Vergen (Pförring, Germany), a small town on the Danube on the medieval border to Bavaria, about fifty kilometers southwest of Regensburg. The name means ferry landing in Middle High German, and so it could refer to several spots along the river. It seems to mark the eastern boundary of the Burgundians' sphere of influence, as this is the farthest point to which Gernot and Giselher accompany their sister Kriemhild on her journey to Etzel's lands. (N)

Vienna (*Wiene*), originally a Celtic, then Roman settlement (*Vindobona*), a large town on the Danube and part of Etzel's empire in the *Nibelungenlied*. Kriemhild and Etzel are married in Vienna, followed by a seventeen-day festival. Vienna benefited from the large ransom that Leopold V received for capturing Richard the Lionheart, who was found to be in Vienna shortly before Christmas, 1192. Around 1200, the town was the capital of Leopold VI's Austrian duchy and march.

Wallachia (*Walâche*), an area southeast of Hungary and Moldavia, homeland of Count Ramunc, a vassal of Etzel. The *Klage* mentions a Sigeher of Wallachia.

Waskenstein (Wasigenstein, France), a rock formation in the northern Vosges Mountains in northeastern France, very close to the modern French-German border. It does not play a role in the *Nibelungenlied* except as a reference to events in the epic story of Walther of Aquitaine. (N)

Waskenwald, the Vosges Mountains in Alsace, opposite the Black Forest on the upper Rhine, site of the hunt during which Siegfried is killed. (N)

Worms (*Wormez*), town on the middle Rhine; capital of the kingdom of Burgundy; seat of King Gunther. Although historically never the capital of a kingdom, Worms was captured by the Burgundians in 413.

Xanten (*Santen*), town on the lower Rhine; capital of Netherland; seat of King Siegmund and Queen Sieglinde; later Siegfried and Kriemhild ruled there.

Zazamanc, along with Azagouc, fictitious land known for costly silk materials. In Wolfram's *Parzival*, it is situated in North Africa and ruled by Queen Belacane, its capital is called Patelamunt. Gahmuret, Parzival's father, takes control of Zazamanc after marrying Belacane. (N)

Zeiselmauer (*Zeizenmûre*), a small town on the Danube near Vienna mentioned as a stopover for Kriemhild, although most manuscripts have Traismauer (see above) instead. (N)

Personal Names in the *Nibelungenlied* and *Klage*

Entries marked with (K) are found only in the *Klage*, those with (N) only in the *Nibelungenlied*. Entries not so marked occur in both texts.

Adelind, daughter of Sintram, a lord of the Austrian marches; lady in Helche's household. (K)

Alberich, a dwarf in Nibelungen land; treasurer of the Nibelungen hoard. (N)

Aldrian, father of Hagen and Dancwart; formerly Etzel's vassal. (N)

Amelrich, brother of Gelfrat's ferryman, forced to leave his lands on account of a feud. Hagen poses as Amelrich to gain the ferryman's assistance. (N)

Astolt, Lord of Melk. (N)

Balmung, Siegfried's renowned sword, taken from the kings of Nibelungen; later owned by Hagen. (N)

Bloedelin, Etzel's brother. Inspired by Kriemhild's promise of treasure, lands, and a bride, he leads the first attack against the Burgundian squires and is killed by Dancwart.

Boimunt, Ruediger's horse, returned to Bechelarn by Swemmel and Ruediger's squires. (K)

Botelung, former king of the Huns; father of Etzel and Bloedelin.

Brunhild, queen of Iceland; resident in Isenstein; wife of King Gunther. In Nordic mythology, she was a Valkyrie and daughter of Odin. In the *Nibelungenlied*, she is a warrior queen who must first be defeated in contests of strength by her future husband. Her great strength is linked to her virginity. Her feud with Kriemhild sets the plot to kill Siegfried in motion.

Dancrat, former king of Burgundy; husband of Queen Ute; father to Gunther, Gernot, Giselher, and Kriemhild.

Dancwart, son of Aldrian, younger brother of Hagen; marshal of the Burgundian court. A great hero, Dancwart fights in the war against the Saxons, accompanies Gunther and Siegfried to Iceland, kills Gelfrat in the rearguard action in Bavaria, and then at Etzel's court kills Bloedelin. He is later killed by Helfrich.

Dietlinde, Ruediger and Gotelind's daughter, betrothed to Giselher (named only in the *Klage*).

Dietrich, Lord of Bern (Verona); leader of the Amelungen; betrothed to Herrat; historically linked to Theoderic the Great (454–526). Most popular of all Germanic heroes, he lives in exile at Etzel's court, waiting for the opportunity to reclaim his lands. One of the few survivors of the final battles in the *Nibelungenlied*, he plays a major role in the *Klage* where he directs the burial of the dead.

Eckewart, Burgundian margrave; Kriemhild's chamberlain. He volunteers to accompany and serve Kriemhild at Siegfried's and then Etzel's court. He is found sleeping by Hagen while guarding the border. (N)

Else, margrave in the Bavarian marches; Gelfrat's brother. He is attacked by Hagen and Dancwart in a rearguard action but manages to escape while his brother is killed.

Etzel, king of the Huns; husband of Helche and then Kriemhild; father to Ortlieb; historically linked to Attila (c. 406–53). Etzel's court is a gathering place for great heroes and exiles. He is not involved directly in the fighting at his court and so survives. His fate is unknown, but the *Klage* states that his ability to rule vanishes along with his mental faculties, and so his kingdom declines.

Gelfrat, lord in Bavaria; Else's brother. He attacks the Burgundian army to avenge the ferryman's death and is killed by Dancwart. (N)

Gerbart, one of Dietrich's men; killed in the final battle by Giselher.

Gere, margrave, duke, and high-ranking vassal at the Burgundian court. He leads the delegation to Nibelungenland to invite Siegfried and Kriemhild to attend a festival in Worms. Later he accompanies Kriemhild to Etzel's court. (N)

Gernot, brother of Gunther, Giselher, and Kriemhild. He leads the campaign against the Saxons. Although not directly involved in executing the plot to kill Siegfried, he had foreknowledge and conspired with the murderers. He kills Ruediger with a sword that Ruediger had given him as a gift. He is in turn killed by Ruediger.

Gibeche, a Hunnish king at Etzel's court. In Norse tradition, he was Gunther's father. (N)

Giselher, youngest brother of Gunther, Gernot, and Kriemhild (therefore his epithet *kint*); later betrothed to Ruediger's daughter, Dietlinde. He is killed by Wolfhart, one of Dietrich's men, whom he also kills.

Goldrun, daughter of Liudeger, a king in France; lady in Queen Helche's household. (K)

Gotelind, margravine; wife of Ruediger; cousin of Dietrich; sister of Nudung. In the *Klage*, she dies of grief after hearing of Ruediger's death.

Gunther, ruler of Burgundy and oldest brother of Gernot, Giselher, and Kriemhild. He marries Brunhild, queen of Iceland, after scheming with Siegfried to cheat at the contests of strength. A weak figure in the first part of the *Nibelungenlied*,

Gunther shows himself to be a leader and heroic warrior in Part Two. In the end, he is executed by his sister Kriemhild for his part in the murder plot against Siegfried. He has been linked historically to King Gundahar, a Burgundian defeated by the Roman general Aetius and a force of Hunnish auxiliaries in 437.

Gunther, Siegfried and Kriemhild's son, named after Kriemhild's brother. He is raised by his grandparents in Netherland and so disappears from the story. (N)

Hadeburg, one of the water nymphs that speaks with Hagen. She lies about the outcome of the expedition to Etzel's court. (N)

Hagen, Lord of Troneck; eldest son of Aldrian; Dancwart's brother; kinsman and vassal to the Burgundian kings; Siegfried's killer. In childhood a hostage at Etzel's court, Hagen was widely traveled and had knowledge of far-flung lands and heroes. He is characterized as proud and arrogant, but a great fighter. He survives the final battle only to be executed by Kriemhild with Siegfried's sword.

Hawart, king of Denmark; in exile at Etzel's court; killed by Hagen.

Helche, queen of the Huns; first wife of Etzel. Her death leads Etzel to search for another wife in Kriemhild.

Helfrich, one of Dietrich's men; kills Dancwart in battle and later killed by an unknown warrior.

Helmnot, one of Dietrich's men; also figures in some of the Dietrich epics. (N)

Herlind, lady of Helche's, and presumably Kriemhild's, household; originally from Greece. (K)

Hermann, Duke of Poland; Etzel's vassal. (K)

Herrat, daughter of Nentwin; Helche's niece and former head of her household; then lady to Kriemhild; betrothed to Dietrich.

Hildebrand, close adviser and master-at-arms (*meister*) to Dietrich; one of the survivors of the slaughter at the Hunnish court. He kills Kriemhild, exacting revenge for her execution of Gunther and Hagen. In the *Klage*, he continues to serve Dietrich as counselor.

Hildeburg, lady from Normandy; former member of Helche's household. (K)

Hildegund, a Burgundian or Frankish princess; betrothed to Walther of Spain; once a hostage at Etzel's court; not a character in the *Nibelungenlied*. (N)

Hornboge, warrior at Etzel's court. (N)

Hunolt, chamberlain to the Burgundian court. (N)

Irinc, margrave in Denmark; originally from Lorraine; vassal of Hawart; killed by Hagen in a monumental battle.

Irnfried, landgrave of Thuringia; exile at Etzel's court; killed by Volker.

Isalde, duchess in Vienna. She is the first outside of Hunnish lands to learn of the disaster at Etzel's court. (K)

Konrad (*Kuonrât*), scribe or chancellor (*schrîber, meister*) of Bishop Pilgrim of Passau. He is responsible for writing or overseeing the production of the *Klage*, according to the poet, and may be identical with the Master in *Klage* verses 44 and 569. (K)

Kriemhild, sister to Gunther, Gernot, and Giselher of Burgundy; wife of Siegfried of Netherland; later wife to King Etzel. She feuds with Queen Brunhild at the Burgundian court and, after Siegfried's murder, is convinced to remain at the court instead of taking her rightful place as queen of Netherland. She later marries Etzel even though he is not Christian, and at his court plots to avenge her husband Siegfried's death. In the final battle, her son Ortlieb is killed by Hagen, and she in turn executes Hagen and her eldest brother Gunther. She is killed by Hildebrand.

Liudegast, king of Denmark; brother and ally to Liudeger of Saxony. He is captured by Siegfried and taken hostage, eventually to be released without a ransom. (N)

Liudeger, king of Saxony; brother to Liudegast of Denmark. (N)

Liudeger, king in France; Goldrun's father. (K)

Machazen, supposedly a pagan god of Muslims; name possibly taken from Maozim in the Book of Daniel. (K)

Mahumet, presumably represents Muhammad, the Holy Prophet; depicted in most European medieval stories as a god worshipped in Islam. (K)

Michael, saint; archangel; patron of knights; attendant and weigher of souls. (K)

Nentwin, father of Herrat, Dietrich's bride. (N)

Nere, father of Wolfwin, one of Dietrich's men. (K)

Nibelung, coruler of the Nibelungen clan, along with his brother Schilbung, both sons of King Nibelung. The two brothers are killed by Siegfried, who takes possession of the Nibelungen treasure and their lands. (N)

Nitger, a king; vassal of Dietrich; killed by Giselher. (K)

Nudung, Gotelind's brother (or possibly son); killed by Witege in another epic. His shield is given to Hagen, and his widow and lands are offered by Kriemhild to Bloedelin as a prize for killing Hagen. (N)

Ortlieb, Etzel and Kriemhild's only son. He is killed by Hagen while still a child at a banquet at Etzel's court.

Ortwin, Lord of Metz; seneschal (steward) to the Burgundian court; nephew of Dancwart and Hagen. According to the C manuscript redaction, Ortwin stays at home in Burgundy rather than travel to Etzel's court. (N)

Pecheneg (*Petschenaere*), a contingent of warriors at Etzel's court; described as wild and skilled at shooting birds with arrows. (N)

Pilgrim, bishop of Passau; brother of Queen Ute; uncle to Gunther, Gernot, Giselher, and Kriemhild. In the *Klage*, he is credited with preserving and memorializing the story of the downfall of the Burgundian royal house by collecting the stories of witnesses and directing that a book be written in Latin. May refer to a historical Bishop Pilgrim of Passau (bishop from 971 to 991, venerated in the late twelfth century), and may serve as a proxy for Bishop Wolfger of Erla, bishop of Passau from 1191 to 1204.

Ramunc, Duke of Wallachia; Etzel's vassal. (N)

Rhine Franks (*Rînvranken*), an appellation for the Burgundians found only once in the *Klage*. (K)

Ritschard, one of Dietrich's men. (N)

Ruediger, margrave and lord of Bechelarn; vassal of Etzel; husband of Gotelind. He leads the mission to ask for Kriemhild's hand on Etzel's behalf and vows to support Kriemhild. Renowned for his generosity (*milte*), he supports the Burgundians in their expedition to Etzel's court, but is forced to attack them in order to stay true to his oath to protect Kriemhild. He is killed by Gernot while killing him in turn.

Rumolt, officer and kitchen master of the Burgundian court; most famous for advising against the expedition to Etzel's court (so-called Rumolt's *rât* or counsel). He is made regent in Worms during the rulers' absence.

Schilbung, coruler of the Nibelungen clan, along with his brother Nibelung, both sons of King Nibelung. (N)

Schrutan, one of Etzel's men. (N)

Siegestab, Duke of Bern (Verona); Dietrich's nephew; killed by Volker. He plays a role in other Dietrich epics.

Siegfried, Germanic hero; king of Netherland and the Nibelungen; husband of Kriemhild; killed by Hagen. Renowned for his great strength and conquests, he is made invulnerable by bathing in dragon's blood (except for a spot between his shoulder blades). He controls the legendary Nibelungen treasure, including the cloak of invisibility. He helps Gunther win Brunhild as his wife, and in return gains Gunther's sister's hand in marriage. At first exonerated after the feud between Kriemhild and Brunhild, he is killed by Hagen and later avenged by Kriemhild; buried and later removed by Kriemhild to Lorsch.

Siegfried, son of Gunther and Brunhild; made a knight and crowned king of the Burgundians at the end of the *Klage*.

Sieglinde, mother of Siegfried; wife of Siegmund; queen of Netherland. She dies around the same time that Siegfried and Kriemhild's son Gunther is born. Kriemhild assumes her role as queen.

Sieglinde, one of the mermaids who speaks with Hagen. She tells him the truth about the ill-fated expedition to the Hunnish court. (N)

Sieglinde, daughter of King Nitger; lady in Helche's household. (K)

Siegmund, father of Siegfried; husband of Sieglinde; king of Netherland. Unable to convince Kriemhild to come with him, he returns to his kingdom alone after the death of his son.

Sigeher, nobleman from Wallachia at Etzel's court. (K)

Sindolt, nobleman in Burgundy; cupbearer to the king. This office was originally responsible for cellars and the buttery. He remains in Worms during the court's journey to Etzel.

Sintram, a lord who lives in a castle close to the Hungarian border in Pitten. (K)

Swemmel, minstrel and ambassador at Etzel's court; he carries the invitation to the summer solstice festival to Worms, and in the *Klage* is responsible for bringing back news of the annihilation of the Burgundian ruling house and its army.

Ute, queen of Burgundy; mother of Gunther, Gernot, Giselher, and Kriemhild; wife of Dancrat; sister of Bishop Pilgrim of Passau. She later founds and retires to a monastery in Lorsch, where she dies of grief and is buried upon hearing the news of her children's demise.

Volker, minstrel and warrior; Lord of Alzey; vassal of the Burgundian kings; killed by Hildebrand. The epitome of a *minnesinger*, or courtly singer-songwriter, he performs for Ruediger and Gotelind in Bechelarn and promises to sing Gotelind's praises at Etzel's court. He is known as "the fiddler" (*videlaere*), although his fiddle and bow are often metaphors for his sword play.

Walber, a Turkish lord at Etzel's court. (K)

Walther, a lord from Aquitaine or Spain; formerly a hostage at Etzel's court along with Hagen. He is the hero of the epics *Waltharius* and *Waldere*. He does not play a role in the *Nibelungenlied*, except when Hagen is reminded by Hildebrand that Hagen once refused to attack him in support of Gunther, his lord. (N)

Waske, Irinc's sword. (N)

Werbel, one of Etzel's minstrels; accompanies Swemmel as an envoy to Worms. Hagen chops off his hand at Etzel's banquet. (N)

Wichart, one of Dietrich's men; killed in the final battle. (N)

Wicnant, one of Dietrich's men. (K)

Witege, hero of the Dietrich epics; killer of Nudung. (N)

Wolfbrand, one of Dietrich's men; killed in the final battle.

Wolfhart, Hildebrand's nephew; vassal of Dietrich; killed by Giselher, whom he kills in return. He has a reputation as a hothead.

Wolfwin, one of Dietrich's men; an Amelungen of Bern; son of Nere.

Manuscripts Containing the *Nibelungenlied* and *Klage*

Unlike other lists of manuscripts, this inventory is not organized by manuscript abbreviation, age, current location, or paper versus parchment. Rather, it arranges manuscripts according to one of the two main branches of manuscript transmission, known as the *liet* and the *nôt* groups, or to a third group that is a combination or hybrid of these two. This allows for a quick appreciation of those manuscripts, both complete and fragmentary, that represent one of these branches, their ages, as well as the distribution of manuscripts that include the *Klage*. An initial glance will confirm that all nine extant and complete manuscripts containing the *Nibelungenlied* also contain the *Klage*, while the fragments, by their very nature, may or may not show signs of both works in a single manuscript.

Following convention, the letter abbreviations of the manuscripts are capitalized for the parchment manuscripts of the thirteenth and fourteenth centuries, while the lowercase letters designate parchment or paper manuscripts from the fourteenth to the sixteenth centuries. For further convenience, the corresponding numbers to the online *Handschriftencensus*, which lists manuscripts alphabetically by current location, are provided in square brackets.

The *nôt* Group

Complete manuscripts:
- A, Munich, Staatsbibliothek, Cgm 34 (with the *Klage*). Fourth quarter, thirteenth century, around 1280. [25]
- B, St. Gall, Stiftsbibliothek, Cod. 857 (with the *Klage*). Second third, thirteenth century, around 1260. [30]

Fragmentary manuscripts:
- g, Heidelberg, Universitätsbibliothek, Cpg 844 (copy of ms. L; *NL*, str. 133r–149v). Fifteenth century, paper. [13]
- L, (a) Cracow, Biblioteka Jagiellońska, Berol. Mgq 635 (*NL*, str. 906–1592). Mid-fourteenth century. [17]

  (b) Mainz, Martinus-Bibliothek, fragment from Ink. 712 (*NL*, str. 109–64; 191–245).

  (c) Mainz, Martinus-Bibliothek, Fragm. germ. 1 (*NL*, str. 1–109; 178–91).

  (d) Mainz, Gutenberg Museum, StB-Ink. 1634 (*NL*, str. 1760–1832).
- M, Linz, Landesmuseum, Ms. 122. Around 1300. [21]

The *liet* Group

Complete manuscripts:

    a, Cologny-Genf, Bibliotheca Bodmeriana, Cod. Bodm. 117 (with the *Klage*). Second quarter, fifteenth century, paper. Does not include first five chapters, although no pages are lost. [10]

    C, Karlsruhe, Landesbibliothek, Cod. Donaueschingen 63 (with the *Klage*). Second quarter, thirteenth century, around 1240. [14]

Fragmentary manuscripts:

    E, Berlin, Staatsbibliothek, Fragm. 44. Second third, thirteenth century. Scribe also wrote part of ms. B. [4]

  (F), Alba Julia, Romania, Batthyaneum, Cod. R III 70, lost since 1898. Second half, thirteenth century. [1]

    R, Nürnberg, Germanisches Nationalmuseum, Hs. 22066. Around 1300. [27]

    U, (a) Nürnberg, Germanisches Nationalmuseum, Hs. 42567 (*NL*). First half, fourteenth century, around 1330. [28]

        (b) Bressanone, Provincial Library of South Tyrol Capuchins, no sign (*Klage*).

    X, Vienna, Nationalbibliothek, Cod. 14281. End of thirteenth century. [34]

    Z, Klagenfurt, Universitätsbibliothek, Perg.-Hs. 46. Second or third quarter, thirteenth century. [16]

Hybrid Group

Complete manuscripts:

    b, Berlin, Staatsbibliothek, Mgf 855 (with the *Klage*). 1436–42, paper. Only manuscript with illustrations. [8]

    D, Munich, Staatsbibliothek, Cgm 31 (with the *Klage*). First half, fourteenth century. [24]

    d, Vienna, Nationalbibliothek, Cod. Series nova 2663 (possible copy of ms. O; with the *Klage*). 1504–16. [36]

  (H), formerly Munich, lost. Copy by Bernhard Joseph Docen in Berlin, Staatsbibliothek, Mgq 825a. Thirteenth or fourteenth century. [37]

    h, Berlin, Staatsbibliothek, Mgf 681 (likely copy of ms. J; with the *Klage*). 1450–55, paper. [7]

    J, Berlin, Staatsbibliothek, Mgf 474 (with the *Klage*). Around 1300. [5]

Fragmentary manuscripts:

    K, (a) Berlin, Staatsbibliothek, Mgf 587 (*NL*, str. 1774–1836; 2317–76). Around 1300. [6]

        (b) Berlin, Staatsbibliothek, Mgf 814 (*NL*, str. 1414–1534).

    (c) Dülmen, Herzog von Croy'sche Verwaltung, Hausarchiv Nr. 54 (*NL*, str. 2268–2307).

    (d) Koblenz, Landeshauptarchiv, Best. 701 Nr. 759,60 (the *Klage*).

    (e) Berlin, Staatsbibliothek, Mgf 923 Nr. 13 (not *NL*).

l, Basel, Universitätsbibliothek, Cod. N I 1 Nr. 99a. Mid-fourteenth century, paper. [3]

N, (a) Würzburg, Universitätsbibliothek, Deutsche Fragmente 2 (*NL*, str. 1443; 1475; 1602–45; 1891; 1902; 1912; 1921). Early fourteenth century. [26]

    (b) Nürnberg, Germanisches Nationalmuseum, Hs. 2841a (the *Klage*).

    (c) Nürnberg, Germanisches Nationalmuseum, Hs. 4365a (*NL*, str. 1437–42; 1444–74; 1476–80; 1886–90; 1892–1901; 1903–11; 1913–20; 1922–26; 2085–2125; 2205–44).

O, Cracow, Biblioteka Jagiellońska, Berol. Mgq 792. Fourth quarter, fourteenth century. [19]

Q, (a) Freiburg i. Br., Universitätsbibliothek, Hs. 511 (*NL*, str. 969–1057). First half, fourteenth century. [12]

    (b) Rosenheim, Stadtarchiv, HS-g 1 (*NL*, str. 617–796; 1165–1499).

    (c) Munich, Staatsarchiv, Fragm.-Slg. A II 1 (*NL*, str. 1859–2151).

S, (a) Prague, National Library, Cod. XXIV.C.2. (*NL*, str. 1–246). Second quarter, thirteenth century. [29]

    (b) Prague, National Library, Cod. I E a 1 (*NL*, str. 914–82).

    (c) Prague, National Library, Cod. I E a 2 (the *Klage*).

V, Vorau, Stiftsbibliothek, fragment from Cod. 138. Early fourteenth century. [32]

W, Melk, Stiftsbibliothek, Fragm. Germ. 6. Fourth quarter, thirteenth century. [23]

Y, Trento, City Library, Ms. 3035. Fourteenth century. [31]

Not Assigned

Complete manuscripts:

    k, Vienna, Nationalbibliothek, Cod. 15478. (Lienhart Scheubel's *Heldenbuch*, an adaptation of the *NL*.) Around 1480–90, paper. [35]

    n, Darmstadt, Universitäts- und Landesbibliothek, Hs. 4257. (Shortened adaptation of the *NL*.) Around 1450, paper. [9]

Fragmentary manuscripts:

    (c), Vienna, Hofbibliothek, Cod. Q4793, lost. Formerly belonged to Wolfgang Lazius (1514–65). [33]

i, Cracow, Biblioteka Jagiellońska, Berol. Mgq 669. First half, fifteenth century, paper. [18]

m, Darmstadt, Universitäts- und Landesbibliothek, Hs. 3249. (*Darmstädter Aventürenverzeichnis*, from an adaptation of the *NL.*) Second half, fourteenth century. [11]

Manuscripts Containing Only the *Klage*

Fragmentary manuscripts:

G, Karlsruhe, Landesbibliothek, Cod. Donaueschingen 64. Around 1300. [15]

P, Cracow, Biblioteka Jagiellońska, Berol. Mgq 1895 Nr. 8. First half, fourteenth century. [20]

AA, Amberg, Staatsarchiv, Hss.-Fragm. 74. Fourteenth century. [2]

Selected Bibliography

Major Editions (listed by date, with annotation of *Leithandschrift*):

Der Nibelunge Noth, mit der Klage. Edited by Karl Lachmann. Berlin: Reimer, 1826. 2nd ed., 1841. [ms. A]

Das Nibelungenlied. Edited by Karl Bartsch. Deutsche Classiker des Mittelalters 3. Leipzig: Brockhaus, 1866. [ms. B]

Diu Klage: Mit den Lesarten sämtlicher Handschriften. Edited by Karl Bartsch. Leipzig: Brockhaus, 1875.

Das Nibelungenlied: Nach der Ausgabe von Karl Bartsch. Edited by Helmut de Boor. Leipzig: Brockhaus, 1940. 13th ed. Wiesbaden: Brockhaus, 1956. [ms. B]

Das Nibelungenlied. A Complete Transcription in Modern German Type of the Text of Manuscript C from the Fürstenberg Court Library Donaueschingen. Ed. Heinz Engels. With an Essay on the Manuscript and Its Provenance by Erna Huber and an Introduction in English. New York, Washington, London: Frederick A. Praeger, *Publishers*, 1969. [Copyright 1968 Verlag Müller und Schindler, Stuttgart.]

Das Nibelungenlied: Mittelhochdeutscher Text und Übertragung. Edited and translated by Helmut Brackert. 2 vols. Frankfurt: Fischer Verlag, 1970/71. [ms. B]

Das Nibelungenlied: Paralleldruck der Handschriften A, B und C nebst Lesarten der übrigen Handschriften. Edited by Michael S. Batts. Tübingen: Niemeyer Verlag, 1971. [mss. A, B, C]

Das Nibelungenlied: Kritisch herausgegeben und übertragen. Edited by Ulrich Pretzel. Stuttgart: Hirzel Verlag, 1973. [ms. A]

Das Nibelungenlied nach der Handschrift C. Edited by Ursula Hennig. Altdeutsche Textbibliothek 83. Tübingen: Niemeyer Verlag, 1977, 2011. [ms. C]

Diu Klage, mittelhochdeutsch-neuhochdeutsch. Einleitung, Übersetzung, Kommentar und Anmerkungen. Ed. Albrecht Classen. Göppinger Arbeiten zur Germanistik, Bd. 647. Göppingen: Kümmerle, 1997.

Die Nibelungenklage: Synoptische Ausgabe aller vier Fassungen. Edited by Joachim Bumke. Berlin: De Gruyter, 1999.

Das Nibelungenlied: Nach der Handschrift C der Badischen Landesbibliothek Karlsruhe. Edited and translated by Ursula Schulze. Darmstadt: Wissenschaftliche Buchgesellschaft, 2005. [ms. C]

Das Nibelungenlied: Mittelhochdeutsch/Neuhochdeutsch. Edited by Ursula Schulze and translated by Siegfried Grosse. Universalbibliothek 644. Stuttgart: Reclam, 1997, 2010. [ms. B]

Das Nibelungenlied und Die Klage: Nach der Handschrift 857 der Stiftsbibliothek St. Gallen. Edited and translated by Joachim Heinzle. Bibliothek des Mittelalters 12. Berlin: Deutscher Klassiker Verlag, 2013, 2015. [ms. B]

Translations into English (listed by date):

The Nibelungen Lied; or Lay of the Last Nibelungers. Translated by Jonathan Birch. Berlin: A. Duncker, 1848.

The Fall of the Nibelungers: Otherwise the Book of Kriemhild, a Translation of the Nibelunge Not, or Nibelungenlied. Translated by William N. Lettsom. London: Williams and Norgate, 1850.

The Nibelungen Lied: Lay of the Nibelung. Translated by Alfred G. Foster-Barham. London: Macmillan, 1887.

The Fall of the Nibelungs. Translated by Margaret Armour. Everyman's Library 312. London: Dent, 1897.

The Lay of the Nibelungs. Translated by Alice Horton. London: G. Bell, 1898.

The Nibelungenlied. Translated by George H. Needler. New York: H. Holt, 1904.

The Nibelungenlied. Translated by Daniel B. Shumway. Boston: Houghton Mifflin, 1909.

The Nibelungenlied: Translated with an Introduction and Notes. Translated by D. G. Mowatt. Everyman's Library 312. London: Dent, 1962.

The Song of the Nibelungs: A Verse Translation from the Middle High German Nibelungenlied. Translated by Frank G. Ryder. Detroit, MI: Wayne State University Press, 1962.

The Nibelungenlied. Translated by Helen M. Mustard. In *Medieval Epics: Beowulf; The Song of Roland; The Nibelungenlied; The Poem of the Cid.* Translated by William Alfred, W. S. Merwin, and Helen M. Mustard. New York: Random House, 1963, 1998.

The Nibelungenlied: A New Translation. Translated by A. T. Hatto. Baltimore: Penguin Books, 1965.

The Nibelungenlied. Translated by Robert Lichtenstein. Lewiston, NY: Mellen, 1991.

The Lament of the Nibelungen (Div Klage). Translated by Winder McConnell. Columbia, SC: Camden House, 1994.

Das Nibelungenlied: Song of the Nibelungs. Translated by Burton Raffel. New Haven, CT: Yale University Press, 2006.

The Nibelungenlied: The Lay of the Nibelungs. Translated by Cyril Edwards. Oxford: Oxford University Press, 2010.

Secondary Literature in English (listed alphabetically, including a few of the more important references in German):

Andersson, Theodore M. *The Legend of Brynhild.* Ithaca, NY: Cornell University Press, 1980.

———. *A Preface to the Nibelungenlied.* Stanford, CA: Stanford University Press, 1987.

———. "Why Does Siegfried Die?" In *Germanic Studies in Honor of Otto Springer*, edited by Stephen J. Kapolowitt, 29–39. Pittsburgh, PA: K&S, 1978.

Bäuml, Franz, and Eva-Maria Fallone. *A Concordance to the Nibelungenlied.* Leeds: Maney, 1976.

Becker, Hugo. *The Nibelungenlied: A Literary Analysis.* Toronto: University of Toronto Press, 1971.

Bostock, J. K. "The Message of the *Nibelungenlied.*" *Modern Language Review* 55 (1960): 200–212.

Ehrismann, Otfrid, ed. *Nibelungenlied: Epoche – Werk – Wirkung.* 2nd ed. Munich: C. H. Beck, 2002.

Fenik, Bernard. *Homer and the Nibelungenlied: Comparative Studies in Epic Style.* Cambridge, MA: Harvard University Press, 1986.

Flood, John. "The Severed Heads: On the Deaths of Gunther and Hagen." In *German Narrative Literature of the Twelfth and Thirteenth Centuries: Studies Presented to Roy Wisbey on His Sixty-Fifth Birthday,* edited by Volker Honemann, Martin H. Jones, Adrian Stevens, and David Wells, 173–91. Tübingen: Niemeyer, 1994.

Frakes, Jerold. "Kriemhild's Three Dreams: A Structural Interpretation." *Zeitschrift für deutsches Altertum* 113 (1984): 173–87.

Gentry, Francis G. Triuwe *and* Vriunt *in the Nibelungenlied.* Amsterdam: Rodopi, 1975.

Gentry, Francis G., Winder McConnell, Ulrich Müller, and Werner Wunderlich, eds. *The Nibelungen Tradition: An Encyclopedia.* New York: Routledge, 2002.

Gillespie, G. T. "*Die Klage* as a Commentary on *Das Nibelungenlied.*" In *Probleme mittelhochdeutscher Erzählfomen: Marburger Colloquium, 1969,* edited by Peter F. Ganz and Werner Schröder, 153–77. Berlin: Erich Schmidt, 1972.

Hatto, A. T. "The Secular Foe and the *Nibelungenlied.*" In *German Narrative Literature of the Twelfth and Thirteenth Centuries: Studies Presented to Roy Wisbey on His Sixty-Fifth Birthday,* edited by Volker Honemann, Martin H. Jones, Adrian Stevens, and David Wells, 157–71. Tübingen: Niemeyer, 1994.

Haymes, Edward. *The Nibelungenlied: History and Interpretation.* Urbana: University of Illinois Press, 1986.

Haymes, Edward, and Susann T. Samples. *Heroic Legends of the North: An Introduction to the Nibelung and Dietrich Cycles.* New York: Garland, 1996.

Heinzle, Joachim. "The Manuscripts of the *Nibelungenlied.*" In *A Companion to the Nibelungenlied,* edited by Winder McConnell, 105–26. Columbia, SC: Camden House, 1998.

Heinzle, Joachim, Klaus Klein, and Ute Obhof, eds. *Die Nibelungen: Sage – Epos – Mythos.* Wiesbaden: Reichert Verlag, 2003.

Jaeger, C. Stephen. "The Nibelungen Poet and the Clerical Rebellion against Courtesy." In *Spectrum Medii Aevi: Essays in Early German Literature in Honor of George Fenwick Jones,* edited by William C. McDonald, 177–205. Göppingen: Kümmerle, 1983.

Kragl, Florian, ed. *Nibelungenlied und Nibelungensage: Kommentierte Bibliographie 1945–2010.* Berlin: Akademie Verlag, 2012.

Krogman, Willy, and Ulrich Pretzel. *Bibliographie zum Nibelungenlied und zur Klage.* 4th ed. Bibliographien zur deutschen Literatur des Mittelalters 1. Berlin: Erich Schmidt, 1966.

Mahlendorf, Ursula, and Frank Tobin. "Legality and Formality in the *Nibelungenlied.*" *Monatshefte* 66 (1974): 225–38.

McConnell, Winder. "Marriage in the *Nibelungenlied* and *Kudrun.*" In *Spectrum Medii Aevi: Essays in Early German Literature in Honor of George Fenwick Jones,* edited by William C. McDonald, 299–317. Göppingen: Kümmerle, 1983.

———. *The Nibelungenlied*. Boston: Twayne, 1984.

———. "The Problem of Continuity in the *Klage*." *Neophilologus* 70 (1986): 248–55.

———, ed. *A Companion to the Nibelungenlied*. Columbia, SC: Camden House, 1998.

Mowatt, D. G., and Hugh D. Sacker. *The Nibelungenlied: An Interpretative Commentary*. Toronto: University of Toronto Press, 1967.

Müller, Jan-Dirk. *Rules for the Endgame: The World of the Nibelungenlied*. Translated by William Whobrey. Baltimore: Johns Hopkins University Press, 2007.

Mueller, Werner. *The Nibelungenlied Today: Its Substance, Essence, and Significance*. Chapel Hill: University of North Carolina Press, 1962.

Reichert, Hermann, ed. *Konkordanz zum Nibelungenlied nach der St. Galler Handschrift*. 2 vols. Vienna: Fassbaender, 2007.

Rings, Lana. "Kriemhilt's Face Work: A Sociolinguistical Analysis of Social Behavior in the *Nibelungenlied*." *Semiotica* 65 (1987): 317–25.

Salmon, Paul. "Sivrit's Oath of Innocence." *Modern Language Review* 71 (1976): 315–26.

Scholler, Harald. *A Word Index to the Nibelungenklage*. Ann Arbor: University of Michigan Press, 1966.

Starkey, Kathryn. "Brunhild's Smile: Emotion and the Politics of Gender in the Nibelungenlied." In *Codierungen von Emotionen im Mittelalter/Emotions and Sensibilities in the Middle Ages*, edited by C. Stephen Jaeger and Ingrid Kasten, 159–73. Berlin: De Gruyter, 2003.

———. "Performative Emotion and the Politics of Gender in the *Nibelungenlied*." In *Women and Medieval Epic: Gender, Genre, and the Limits of Epic Masculinity*, edited by Sara Poor and Jana Schulman, 253–72. New York: Palgrave, 2007.

Thomas, Neil, ed. *The Nibelungenlied and the Third Reich: Celtic and Germanic Themes in European Literature*. Lewiston, NY: Mellen, 1994.

Thorp, Mary. *The Study of the Nibelungenlied: Being the History of the Study of the Epic and Legend from 1755 to 1937*. Oxford: Clarendon, 1941.

Wailes, Stephen. "The *Nibelungenlied* as Heroic Epic." In *Heroic Epic and Saga: An Introduction to the World's Great Folk Epics*, edited by Felix J. Oinas, 120–43. Bloomington: Indiana University Press, 1978.

Willson, Bernard. "*Ordo* and *Inordinatio* in the *Nibelungenlied*." *Paul und Braunes Beiträge zur Geschichte der deutschen Sprache und Literatur* 85 (1963): 83–101; 325–51.

Wunderlich, Werner, and Ulrich Müller. "Waz sider da geschach." *American-German Studies on the Nibelungenlied: Text and Reception, with Bibliography, 1980-1990/91*. Göppingen: Kümmerle, 1992.

Wynn, Marianne. "Hagen's Defiance of Kriemhilt." In *Mediaeval German Studies Presented to Frederick Norman*, 104–14. London: Institute of Germanic Studies, 1965.

A note about online resources:

The three main manuscripts (A, B, C) are available online, but rather than give URLs here that may change in the future, any search will easily find digitized versions at the sites of the Bavarian State Library, St. Gall Abbey Library, and the Baden State Library.